"A personal travel guide into the beautiful and bewildering landscape of Christian faith and its complex relationship to psychology, with a thoughtful and careful buildup of the worldview and philosophical underpinnings of the various approaches."

—**R.J. Filius**
Health Psychologist and Psychotherapist

"Writing in an engaging personal style, Dr. David Entwistle provides an up-to-date, thoughtful, carefully researched overview of a huge array of scholarly literature relevant to the psychology/Christianity integration. He manages to strike just the right balance, providing a 'big picture' perspective on the field while carefully attending to its many nuances."

—**Julie Exline**
Professor, Department of Psychological Sciences, Case Western Reserve University

Praise for the second edition:

"Integrative Approaches to Psychology and Christianity belongs on the bookshelves of students, clinicians, and researchers alike. In this book Entwistle provides readers with a conceptual roadmap for exploring, examining, and understanding Christian integrative approaches —while serving as a knowledgeable mentor along the way—offering in-depth analyses, theoretical insights, and practical applications."

—**Jamie D. Aten, PhD**
Dr. Arthur P. Rech and Mrs. Jean May Rech
Associate Professor of Psychology, Wheaton College
co-editor of Spirituality and the Therapeutic Process

"This book is a great resource for teaching the integration of psychology and Christianity. It is difficult to find a resource that articulates the main philosophical and theological ideas underlying good integration in one book. David Entwistle provides a thorough treatment of integration that is both understandable and readable. I strongly endorse this book for any educator tasked with teaching courses regarding the integration of psychology and Christianity."

—**Dominick D. Hankle, PhD**
Assistant Professor of Psychology, Regent University

"Entwistle's book should be required reading for all students studying the integration of psychology and theology! With questions aimed at addressing one's personal journey in the integration process, the book provides both a comprehensive review of the current integration research and application exercises for the growth of the individual student.

In the new edition, Entwistle takes another important step in formulating the integration of psychology and Christianity by addressing personal views of integration through the eyes of top psychological researchers in this field! This addition highlights diversity and personalization in the study of integration for key scholars hailing from variant Christian traditions."

—**April L. Cunion, PsyD, LCP**
Department Chair and Assistant Professor of Psychology
Regent School of Undergraduate Studies

Integrative Approaches
to Psychology and Christianity

*. . . to think christianly is a very different thing
from thinking secularly about Christian matters.*
—Harry Blamires

*The knowledge of man is as the waters,
some descending from above,
and some springing from beneath;
the one informed by the light of nature,
the other inspired by divine revelation.*
—Francis Bacon

Integrative Approaches to Psychology and Christianity

An Introduction to Worldview Issues,
Philosophical Foundations,
and Models of Integration

THIRD EDITION

David N. Entwistle

CASCADE *Books* · Eugene, Oregon

INTEGRATIVE APPROACHES TO PSYCHOLOGY AND CHRISTIANITY
An Introduction to Worldview Issues, Philosophical Foundations, and Models of Integration, Third Edition

Cascade Books
An Imprint of Wipf and Stock Publishers
199 W. 8th Ave., Suite 3
Eugene, OR 97401

www.wipfandstock.com

ISBN 13: 978-1-4982-2348-5

Cataloging-in-Publication data:

Entwistle, David N. (David Nelson)
    Integrative approaches to psychology and Christianity : an introduction to worldview issues, philosophical foundations, and models of integration / David N. Entwistle.

    3rd ed.

    xiv + 368 p. ; 25 cm. —Includes bibliographical references and indexes.

    ISBN 13: 978-1-4982-2348-5

    1. Psychology and religion. 2. Christianity—Psychology. 3. Christian philosophy. 4. Knowledge, Theory of. 5. Cosmology. I. Title.

BR110 E58 2015

Manufactured in the U.S.A.

Scripture quotations are taken from the following translations:

The Bible in Basic English. (BBE). Cambridge: University Press in association with Evans Brothers, 1965, © 1949.

The Holy Bible Translated from the Latin Vulgate, Douay-Rheims Version. (1899). Baltimore: John Murphy.

The Holy Bible, New International Version®, NIV®. Copyright © 1973, 1978, 1984 by Biblica, Inc.™ Used by permission of Zondervan. All rights reserved worldwide.

The New American Standard Bible®, Copyright © 1960, 1962, 1963, 1968, 1971, 1972, 1973, 1975, 1977, 1995 by The Lockman Foundation. Used by permission.

The New Century Version®. Copyright © 2005 by Thomas Nelson, Inc. Used by permission. All rights reserved.

The Twentieth Century New Testament: A Translation into Modern English Made from the Original Greek, Westcott & Hort's Text. (20ᵗʰ Cent.). 1904. New York: Revell.

To my family: my wife, Debbie, our daughters, Kristen and Lauren, and our son, Cameron. They have taught me that integration is not just about academics and ideas but also about how we live our lives before our God and with each other. For their grace and love, I am grateful beyond words.

Contents

Preface

Vicesimus Knox ended an eighteenth-century sermon with the benediction, "Let us go forth to our various employments, resolved to walk worthy of our Christian vocation." My father modeled this benediction as a surgeon in the United States and as a missionary doctor in Africa. He cared about his patients' physical and spiritual well-being because that was his calling. He understood that every sphere of life embodies an invitation to worship and service.

My early church experiences, on the other hand, sometimes included appeals from well-meaning church leaders to enter "full-time Christian ministry." In their fragmented view, most people served God part time in church while working full time at "secular" jobs where faith was largely seen as irrelevant. My academic experiences from middle school through high school reinforced the idea that God did not have much to do with what I studied. Such experiences made it hard for me to heed Knox's benediction.

In college, I encountered people who were committed to the idea that Christ is sovereign over all of life. Christian liberal-arts education rejects the pervasive tendency to compartmentalize life into sacred and secular domains. Although this sacramental view of life made sense to me, I found that many people keep faith carefully segregated from the rest of their lives. Some professors made token attempts to integrate faith and learning by saying a prayer before class, and proceeded to give lectures that were devoid of deep reflection on how Christianity might have anything to do with the topics we studied. I also began to encounter the perspectives of people who thought that religious beliefs were inherently unhealthy and of others who suggested that religious belief was okay as long as its influence never strayed beyond the parking lot of a church. More personally, I discovered in myself and in others the hypocrisy that exists between what we profess and how we actually live. Sadly, it became obvious to me that most of us live very fragmented, compartmentalized lives.

I have become convinced, though, that we can strive to make intentional and productive links between Christian faith and all aspects of life. This book is born out of a desire to help Christians who are interested in the study or application of psychology "to walk worthy of our Christian vocation."

Psychology is a discipline with rich historical and philosophical roots. It is a broad field that studies biological, intra-psychic, and interpersonal phenomena across the life span. As a Christian, I am convinced that Christian faith and Christian theology are very relevant to this discipline. But I have also been frustrated by overly simplistic efforts to define or react to "Christian psychology." This book is an attempt to bring about a more adequate and sophisticated answer to the question of how Christian faith intersects with the field of psychology. Specifically, I have attempted to create a book that frames the issue of the integration of psychology and Christianity with adequate attention to worldview issues, philosophical underpinnings, and models of integration.

The third edition of this book is due in large part to the welcome reception that the first two editions received, and to the encouragement of my editor at Wipf and Stock, K. C. Hanson. K. C. has been a gracious editor and a good conversation partner who pointed me to several resources on a variety of issues. I have received welcome support and beneficial critique over the years, and many of the changes that I have incorporated into the third edition are due to the suggestions offered by insightful readers, including my students at Malone University. The basic premise of this book has remained fundamentally unchanged throughout these three editions, but I have attempted to clarify and improve the text as well as to expand on several topics and correct some errors along the way.

One substantial change in the third edition is the inclusion of a sixth model for relating psychology and Christianity. In the first edition of this book, I introduced the analogy that various ways of relating psychology and Christianity are somewhat like five different ways that nations can relate to each other. An approach that did not neatly fit into the existing models has been gaining momentum for several years. This approach, which goes by the name *Christian psychology*, is not entirely new, but it has acquired a significant following. *Christian psychology* shares elements of both the *Colonialist* and the *Allies* models, but it is sufficiently distinct that I have classified it as a sixth model, which I call, *Rebuilders*.

A Note to Professors and Students

When I wrote the first edition of this book, I anticipated that it would be used in courses at Christian colleges and graduate schools. I have tried to keep each edition current and to improve pedagogical aids to promote comprehension and discussion. Some of the material in the current edition has been expanded, such as significant additions to the sections on intellectual virtues, forming a Christian worldview, and tradition saturated integration. Additionally, some of the material has been rearranged to create better flow. I am grateful that so many professors have found this book to be useful as a text, and that so many students continue to use it as they form their own approaches to relating Christian faith and psychology.

The new edition incorporates a number of changes which are designed to help students interact with the contents of the book. One of the most noticeable changes is the addition of text boxes that emphasize important concepts or provide opportunities for reflection. There is now a website where course materials and suggested assignments are available for professors. The materials are protected by copyright, but professors are free to modify, photocopy, or post any of the material electronically. The address for the textbook website is: http://wipfandstock.com/integrative-approaches-to-psychology-and-christianity-third-edition.html.

My hope continues to be that this book will help us to reclaim a holistic view of God's sovereignty, and that it will promote an integrative framework that is both psychologically and theologically sound. Beyond this, my simple prayer is that it will lead its readers to worship God as they consider the works of His hands and recognize their place within His world.

Acknowledgments

As the third edition of this book goes into print, I continue to recognize that I am deeply indebted to many people for forming my life and my thinking. My parents provided a home with a rich Christian heritage and a love of learning. Across these three editions I watched them face increasing age, declining health, and death, but their impact on my life continues. My colleagues across many disciplines at Malone University compose a supportive and vibrant community of scholars, teachers, and friends. Students at Malone and elsewhere have welcomed me into their classrooms and their lives, privileges that I do not take lightly. Clients and research participants have granted me the unique honor of sharing their struggles and hopes. Pamm Ohlinger and I co-taught a Sunday school class many years ago that helped to create the basis for chapter 4 of this book.

Several people have been instrumental in conversation and in reviewing all or parts of this manuscript including Dr. Stephen K. Moroney, Dr. Matthew Phelps, Dr. Ebenézer de Oliveira, Dr. Shawn Floyd, Dr. Bryan Hollon, Dr. Peter Koritansky, and Dr. Robert Suggs (all of whom sojourned along with me at Malone University at some point in time). Academics from other institutions also provided valuable feedback, including Dr. Brian Eck, Dr. Dennis Hiebert, Dr. John McNeil, Dr. Daryl Stevenson, Dr. Harvey Payne, Dr. Craig Steven Titus, STD, PhD, and Fr. Donald Miller, OFM, PhD. My daughter, Kristen Entwistle, provided valuable feedback and proofreading. I also want to thank Dr. K. C. Hanson, Ian Creeger, and the staff at Cascade Books for making this a much better book through their talents and efforts. While any book of this scope is bound to have errors and omissions, their critique has helped me to think through some critical issues and to correct some of my mistakes along the way; any errors or omissions that remain are my own responsibility.

Finally, I am grateful to Malone University for supporting a sabbatical that afforded me the opportunity to read, reflect, and write which culminated in the first edition of this book, and for the support and encouragement of the Malone academic community that

continues to challenge me and to shape
my life and my thinking.

In Christi Glorium
David N. Entwistle
Malone University

Introduction: The Fork in the Road

When you come to a fork in the road, take it.

–Yogi Berra

Yogi Berra, that wonderful icon of American baseball who gave us such memorable phrases as "It's déjà vu all over again" and "It ain't over 'til it's over," might have captured the thrust of this book best when he said, "When you come to a fork in the road, take it." Berra was giving Joe Garagiola directions to his home in Montclaire, New Jersey.[1] According to one version of the story, the final fork in the road was an intersection onto another road that would lead to Berra's home no matter which way you turned, because the road looped back to his house in both directions. In a similar way, one might say that if you are trying to understand human nature, you will come to a fork in the road where psychology goes off in one direction and Christian theology diverges in another direction. In some ways, they clearly go in different directions, but that does not mean that the two are opposed to each other. Rather, the two disciplines diverge at one point,

only to converge again, providing different approaches to understanding and studying human behavior. Because they come from different directions, with different assumptions, methodologies, and goals, they provide unique perspectives that together have the potential to provide a more complete picture than either of them would provide in isolation.

Approaching something from divergent directions can sometimes lead to startling discoveries. I was reminded of this when I visited my daughter at a Christian college in New England. During my visit, I took several hikes on a wooded trail that circled one of the lakes on the campus. My first hike was on a moonless autumn night. The light from the campus buildings shimmered on the lake, but I could barely see the trail in front of me. I once saw something move near my feet. Startled, I paused, squinting in the darkness to discover a small frog jumping across the trail. I heard little but the sounds of my footsteps and the splash of a fish jumping in the lake.

---

1. Berra, *The Yogi book.*

The next morning I retraced my path counterclockwise around the lake in the early light of dawn. The differences were immediately apparent. I could hear the whirr of the morning traffic on the highway near the campus as I embarked on my hike, but the sounds of city life faded behind a hillock of dense woods, replaced by the sounds of many species of birds. Brown leaves, mostly beech and oak, covered the ground; the trees above were mostly bare other than the green needles of the conifers. I stopped to see a small tree, half felled by a beaver, shavings of wood surrounding its base. I heard the sounds of my footsteps and an occasional splash of a fish catching its breakfast. The beauty of God's creation filled me with peace and became an impetus to meditation, worship, and prayer.

Having arrived at the far end of the lake, I decided to head back, so I turned around, now heading clockwise around the lake. The sun, which had been behind me and to my left, was now in front of me and to my right. Facing this direction, I could see the sunlight glinting over the length of the lake, the span of which I could now see, but which had previously been imperceptible from my former trajectory. As I came around a bend, I saw a beech tree with fungi stacked like a ladder climbing upward along its south side. I stopped to inspect the tree, finding that it was diseased and littered with woodpecker holes. I wondered how I had failed to notice this sight before. I walked a few feet past the tree and turned around. Everything was identical, yet vastly different. The tree, from this perspective, looked healthy and unscathed. Had I seen the tree only from this angle, I would have thought that it was a prime specimen that would grow and flourish for many more years. When I saw the tree from the other side, though, I knew that no matter how full its leaves, the tree was doomed to death and decay. In the darkness of the preceding night, I had walked by the tree without seeing it at all. Yet even in the light of day, what I saw depended on my vantage point.

I resumed my hike, thinking about how one's perspective shapes what one sees. Because the ground was wet and muddy, I spent most of my time looking down, hardly noticing the limbs towering above me. On three hikes around this lake I had seen vastly different things, and had failed to see many things altogether. What I saw was dependent on my perspective, but my assumptions and experiences also shaped my perception. Even sharing the same vantage point, different people would see different things. Some people would hike along the trail and commune with God, while others would never recognize the hand of God in the beauty of nature. My friend Jeff could have told me so much about the birdsongs that I could barely distinguish from one another. My brother-in-law could have pointed out flora and fauna that I walked past in relative ignorance. These thoughts ran through my mind as the sounds of the highway returned and I headed back toward the campus buildings. Walking along the soccer field between the library and the science building, I thought about how nature is seen by poets and botanists, theologians and industrialists. I laughed at the flock of geese settled on the soccer field, unbothered by academic debates.

In some ways, every academic field is like my walk around the lake. Educational inquiry can draw us into worship and prayer if we perceive God's involvement in our experience. Every branch of learning provides unique views of God's world and unveils glimpses of Mystery that lie beyond creation. Academic disciplines—and even various perspectives within each discipline—help us to see reality through the lenses of various assumptions and methodologies. The various points of view can also obscure rather than illuminate because all of them are affected by human limitations and error.

Psychology is one of several academic disciplines that attempt to understand human behavior. It has many subdisciplines and a variety of methodologies and perspectives that give us tools to explore various facets of what it means to be human. Christian theology is a branch of inquiry that—among other things—seeks to understand what it means to be human. As systems of thought, both psychology and Christian theology provide useful perspectives through which we can study and understand human behavior, and together they can give us a more complete and accurate picture of human nature and functioning than either perspective can provide alone. Yet we must hasten to add that what we see through theological and psychological viewpoints will be shaped by the assumptions that we make at the outset. Psychology, for the Christian, is infused with theological beliefs about our place in God's world.

> Christianity is much more than theology; it is an encounter with Christ that redeems and reorients human lives . . . it is less a system of thought than it is a commitment to follow God with heart and soul and mind that lays claim to all of life.

While one premise of this book is that we can gain a more complete view of human nature by drawing on both Christian theology and contemporary psychology, the matter is not quite as simple as acknowledging that both perspectives have merit. As we will discuss in greater detail, our theological and psychological perspectives can easily be skewed by many things, and we must seriously consider our own propensity to see the world and our place in it incorrectly. Furthermore, thinking about psychology as Christians is not primarily about bringing the *academic discipline of theology* into dialogue with the academic *discipline or clinical practice of psychology,* although this will be part of the integrative task. Christianity is much more than theology; it is an encounter with Christ that redeems and reorients human lives and brings about "the kingdom of God," the redemption of all of creation. Christianity is less a system of thought than it is a commitment to follow God with heart and soul and mind that lays claim on all of life. This being the case, Christianity will orient our understanding of what it means to be human and how we can participate with God's work in the world.

Christian theology will provide some specific beliefs about God's sovereignty and about human nature that are foundational to a Christian view of human beings, including beliefs about some of the causes of human suffering and, conversely, things that promote human flourishing. This means that a Christian approach to psychology begins with certain assumptions. It also means that integration will be more than an intellectual project. While the integration of psychology and Christianity will entail an academic component as we consider the disciplines of psychology and Christian theology, it will also require the formation of Christian character, guided by a Christian sense of purpose, as we live out the call to be redemptive agents in the world.

Other disciplines, of course, provide additional perspectives on human nature as they approach their own destinations—philosophy and sociology, for example, must reflect on human nature and functioning en route to their own unique areas of concern. These diverse perspectives are a lot like circling around the tree that I encountered while hiking along the lake: different vantage points yield different insights, and any one perspective will illustrate some truths and obscure others. Yet there is one tree, and exploring the tree from different angles can help us come to a more complete

understanding, even—and perhaps especially—when our observations appear to be inconsistent with one another.

Much of what I have described above, and what we will explore in these pages, reflects the influence of the Reformed tradition in which integration is a scholarly enterprise of building a unified Christian worldview. It is important to note, however, that Christian theology cannot be separated from Christianity as a way of life; it is not just our minds that are being redeemed by Christ. Christian redemption entails the formation and transformation of character so that we may be more Christ-like (this is often seen in Wesleyan approaches to integration). Furthermore, Christian redemption takes place in Christian communities where we are shaped through relationships with others to pursue peace and justice as agents of Christ's redemptive love (this is a primary focus of Anabaptist and Mennonite approaches to integration). While much of my focus in this book will be on integrative scholarship from a Reformed perspective, it is important to note that each of these approaches to integration has unique emphases that complement each other.

A primary aim of this book is to help readers understand the issues that shape integrative scholarship. In the final analysis, though, integration that remains only a scholarly project might exercise the mind, but it wouldn't make much of a difference in the lives of individuals and communities. This being the case, another aim of this book is to help readers think about how integration can be applied and lived out in individual and corporate life.

As the title of this book suggests, several approaches have been used to define the relationship of psychology and Christianity. One purpose of this book is to ground the discussion about this relationship in the context of worldview and philosophical issues that are prerequisite to scholarly integration, but which are rarely discussed in books on integration. A second, related goal is to help readers become aware of the presuppositional backdrops that each of us brings to these issues, and to help readers critically evaluate the assumptions that they bring to this discussion. The third purpose of this book is to survey and evaluate models for relating Christianity and psychology. A fourth goal builds on the previous three: assisting readers to be intentional and reflective about how to relate Christianity and psychology. While readers will be encouraged to engage in scholarly reflection on integration, they will also be challenged to think about how integration should be lived out in personal and professional spheres.

In writing this book I realized that overtly and covertly my own opinions would inevitably exert their influence. I have thus opted to choose advocacy rather than neutrality in certain areas, and I trust that my views will provide grist for the mill, whether or not readers happen to agree with the opinions I express.

It is, of course, only fair to expect me to put my own commitments and presuppositions on the table. I approach the study of this topic as an evangelical Christian and as a person trained in clinical psychology. I am passionate about the importance of quality hermeneutics and exegesis. At the same time, I am committed to the rigors of the scientific method and to evaluating the philosophical underpinnings that lie beneath my discipline. I have been a practicing psychotherapist and an academician who has taught at the undergraduate and graduate levels. My research interests involve coping with chronic illness, among other topics. Clearly, the shape and direction of my arguments in this book reflect my own beliefs and history, even as I call for you, the reader, to critically evaluate the various approaches to the encounter between psychology and Christianity.

While writing this book, I sought to be guided by the admonition of the Apostle Paul to give praise and thanks to God in all things (Col 3:17). Integration is about seeking truth, recognizing God's sovereignty over all that we do, and proclaiming our praise and gratitude as we discover the wonders of His creation and His character. So, as you read this book, my prayer is that it will engage your mind and draw you closer to your Creator.

1

The Question of Necessity: Athens and Jerusalem

What indeed has Athens to do with Jerusalem?
—Tertullian

Buried deep in the inner recesses of the Sunday newspaper was a headline that caught my eye sufficiently for me to read beyond the title. A group of worshipers had gathered to praise God on a crisp Friday night at Spirit Filled Church of Our Lord Jesus in Columbus, Ohio. As the service wore on, the worshipers began to feel lightheaded and nauseated, and they began to pray for each other. Relatives became concerned when the worshipers failed to return home, and they relayed their concerns to the police. Paramedics entered the church at 1:30 Saturday morning to find the worshipers overcome with carbon monoxide poisoning from a malfunctioning heating unit. This exposure led to the hospitalization of eighteen of their number.[1]

As I reflected on the article, I thought about how the recorded events might be interpreted by different people. Was the carbon-monoxide poisoning the work of the devil? Were the worshipers unable to see science because they were blinded by faith? What about the prayers of the worshipers? Were the prayers a waste of time, spoken to a nonexistent God when their time would have been better spent opening the windows to get some fresh air? Were their prayers for healing right hearted but wrongheaded? Did God answer their prayers through the concern of relatives and the arrival of the paramedics? In a way, the article could serve as a metaphysical Rorschach test, the perception of the reader revealing more about his or her own beliefs than about the literal ink on the paper.

The events that occurred in the carbon-monoxide-filled church led me to think about the complex interface that exists between psychology and Christianity. A social psychologist could spend years investigating the psychological and sociological factors underlying religious belief (or unbelief) and commitment (or lack of commitment). Physiological psychologists could describe the neurological effects of carbon monoxide poisoning,

---

1. Worshipers overcome, A-5.

7

and perform brain-imaging studies of people while they are praying.[2] Researchers could study the efficacy of prayer for physical or psychological recovery. Clinical psychologists could look at the protective factors that accrue from positive religious involvement, and the detrimental effects of religious fanaticism. Developmental psychologists could study faith development, moral development, child-rearing practices, and a host of other intriguing phenomena among religiously committed individuals. All these studies might be interesting, yet none of them would prove or disprove the veracity of religious experience. They would, however, help us understand how the life of the church (individual and corporate life and doctrine) is expressed through psychological, sociological, and even biological media. This being the case, a thoughtful dialogue between theology and other disciplines is likely to enrich our understanding of human personhood and of the life of the church.

There are many events that raise both theological and psychological questions, and such events serve as useful springboards to investigate links between Christian theology and other disciplines.[3]

During the past century, the relationship of faith and science has been a topic of intense debate. A related dispute has involved encounters between religion and psychology.[4] The recent history of these two issues will be explored in the next two chapters, but it is important for us to note at this juncture that although these questions have modern overtones, they reflect ancient undercurrents. As Tertullian asked rhetorically eighteen hundred years ago, "What indeed has Athens to do with Jerusalem? What concord is there between the Academy and the Church? . . . With our faith, we desire no further belief."[5] Tertullian thought that Christians of his day had to make a choice between seeking knowledge through human reason (Athens) and faith (Jerusalem). Tertullian's answer was that human reason and biblical truth are essentially irreconcilable.[6] A modern Ter-

---

2. Some researchers assert that brain-imaging studies that reveal areas of the brain that are more active during intense religious practices such as meditation explain away the supposed spiritual origins of these experiences. Such studies clearly reveal that spiritual experiences are biological experiences, but they tell us little about the origin or meaning of these experiences. See Petersen, Mysterium tremendum.

3. A false dichotomy that removes the secu-

lar disciplines as objects of legitimate Christian concern and inquiry denies the sacramental view of reality celebrated by Christian orthodoxy. Ironically, individuals who espouse a sacred/secular split in an attempt to preserve theological supremacy actually minimize the scope of God's sovereignty. The antidote to such secularization is dialogue about contemporary issues based on a "Christian mind—a mind trained, informed, equipped to handle data of secular controversy within a framework of reference which is constructed of Christian presuppositions" (Blamires, The Christian mind, 16, and 42–43, respectively).

4. The words spirituality and religiosity are both topics of psychological interest, the former referring to private, individual beliefs and the latter to corporate, formal practices.

5. Tertullian, Against heretics 7, 246.

6. That there are points of incompatibility

tullian might frame this issue as a choice between science and religion. A modern fundamentalist in the lineage of Tertullian might claim that one must reject the "false doctrine" of psychology in order to find health and healing in Christ. Many of Tertullian's contemporaries failed to be convinced by Tertullian's argument to reject extrabiblical sources of knowledge. Many God-fearing people over the centuries have found that dialogue between Jerusalem and Athens is beneficial.

Harry Blamires, who was tutored by C. S. Lewis, provided a useful alternative to Tertullian's viewpoint. Blamires did not see Athens and Jerusalem as being in opposition to one another, but he did contrast two basic ways of thinking about the world, or what he called *secular thinking* and *Christian thinking*.[7] Blamires did not intend to suggest that Christian thinking is necessarily more accurate than secular thinking; Christians and non-Christians can draw correct or in-

correct conclusions. Blamires's point had more to do with the assumptions and implications undergirding Christian and secular thinking. In his view, our thinking is either bounded by purely temporal concerns, as is the case for secular thinking, or it is connected to the larger framework supplied by a Christian worldview. "To think secularly is to think within a frame of reference bounded by the limits of our life on earth: it is to keep one's calculations rooted in this-worldly criteria. To think christianly is to accept all things with the mind as related, directly or indirectly, to man's eternal destiny as the redeemed and chosen child of God."[8]

We should emphasize that both Christian thinking and secular thinking can be done well or done poorly. In fact, "bad" Christian thinking might be worse than "good" secular thinking in some respects. Allow me to illustrate this with an example. Imagine that you logged on to a social media site and found a post that said, "It's so sad that people will be more excited about the big sporting event tonight than they are about church. If you love God, repost this." After reading this, you begin to wonder if being more excited about a sporting event than church is, indeed, terrible. Sporting events are designed to be exciting, however trivial they are in the light of eternity. And isn't the purpose of church more about worship, spiritual formation, and a relationship with God and others rather than a vague emotional high? You then begin to see some problems with the idea that you

---

should be obvious: one cannot bow down to Christ and to pagan idols. Tertullian's reaction, however, was extreme, rejecting not just errant portions of Greco-Roman culture and philosophy, but seeing all human philosophy and learning as irreconcilable with biblical revelation.

7. Secular thinking or Christian thinking may be accurate or inaccurate, logical or illogical. "It is not part of our case to pretend that all secular thinking is bad and that all Christian thinking is good . . . To think secularly may be to think well or ill, logically or illogically, illuminatingly or platitudinously, fruitfully or to no purpose. Likewise to think Christianly may be to think well or ill, rationally or irrationally, knowledgeably or ignorantly, penetratingly or shallowly, lucidly or confusingly" (Blamires, *The Christian mind*, 47–48).

8. Ibid., 44.

can somehow judge a person's faith by his or her level of excitement. There are a lot of exemplars of faith who are commended for their love and their suffering, and excitement can easily be created in church settings without any necessary connection to a deep faith. Besides, shouldn't we come before God as we are, with our doubts, fears, anger, etc.? Then you begin to reflect on the role of "God-talk" in social media. Are posts like this effective evangelism or irritating? If you don't repost this, does it really mean that you don't love God—of course not! So, here we have two different types of "Christian thinking"—the social media post and your own reflections about it—which are qualitatively different from one another, the second being more thoughtful than the first.

> Christian thinking ought to be done in dialogue with secular thinking, building on and affirming what is good, and critiquing that with which we disagree.

Now, imagine that someone who is not a Christian posts a different message on social media. She reposts an article about human trafficking at major sporting events, and includes a link to a blog in which she deliberates carefully about the causes and consequences of prostitution. She raises questions about how we can bring justice and healing to those who have been harmed by others. Even though this "secular thinking" is

not consciously framed by any reference to a Christian worldview, it is clearly redemptive in some respect. At the opposite extreme, "secular thinking" that views people as means to an end and that encourages the exploitation of others for personal financial reward and sexual gratification are among the causes of sex trafficking. From these brief examples, we can easily see that both Christian thinking and secular thinking can be done well or done poorly. What distinguishes them is whether or not they are bounded only by temporal concerns or if they are framed by a broader outlook supplied by one's understanding (or misunderstanding!) of Christianity.

From these examples, we can also see how the best Christian thinking ought to be done in dialogue with secular thinking, building on and affirming what is good, and critiquing that with which we disagree. You might choose to affirm the woman's post about the complex problems of sex trafficking and join her in taking steps to do something about sex trafficking, for instance. Likewise, Christians need to dialogue with and critique each other, since Christian thinking, too, is not uniform. In both cases, though, we should dialogue with humility and respect.

In Blamires's view, "secular" thinking may be useful, but it is incomplete without the framework provided by a Christian worldview. Furthermore, since much of secular thinking is shaped by a worldview hostile to Christian assumptions, we need to be alert to areas of disagreement. Blamires helps us to see that we can learn from "secular" sources while framing our thinking with a Christian worldview and applying knowledge with Christian concern.

The tendency to buy into a dichotomy between the sacred and the secular is at the heart of seeing Jerusalem and Athens as mutually exclusive categories. Many Christians are caught in a trap in which the sacred and the secular are artificially severed. If we understand that all of what God created was good, then we must avoid creating an artificial separation between that which is sacred and that which is secular.[9] In this vein, A. W. Tozer called for us to recognize the sacramental nature of *all* of life. "[For the Christian] every act of . . . life is or can be as truly sacred as prayer or baptism or the Lord's Supper. To say this is . . . to lift every act up into a living kingdom and turn the whole life into a sacrament."[10]

A sacramental perspective provides a framework for how Christians think about and act in the world. Christ's admonition to love God with the entire being—heart, soul, strength, and mind—and to love neighbor as self (Matt 22:36–39), means that the ultimate purpose of life is expressed only when our actions express love of God and love for our fellow human beings. For this reason, Christian thinking must always ask how to love God and others in whatever we do. For the Christian, then, the question is not *whether or not* psychology (the "secular" study of human behavior) can be related to the Christian faith, but *how one should relate psychology to the Christian faith* and *how we can use this knowledge to love God and to love our neighbor.*

What Has Psychology to Do with Christianity?

Several years ago, a colleague asked me what made a *Christian* psychologist unique. Did I practice a different *kind* of therapy than she did? Was I explicitly religious whereas she sought deliberate neutrality? Perhaps more cynically, some people might wonder if the term *Christian psychology* is just thrown around as a marketing tool. These are all good questions, but each, I think, misses the mark of the crucial question: *What tangible difference does it make in one's life and practice to be a psychologist who is a devoted follower of Christ?* The way one answers this question reflects one's view of what has come to be popularly referred to as *integration.*[11] As we will see in the coming chapters, there have been intense debates about how to answer this question, on a continuum between those who see

---

9. We can, in normal parlance, refer to a "secular college" or a "secular writer" as a means of identifying the worldview that is embraced by an institution or an individual. On a philosophical and theological level, however, a Christian worldview recognizes that *everything is sacred*, that is, that it emanates from and ought to give praise to God. (I am grateful to Dr. Daryl Stevenson for highlighting this point.)

10. Tozer, *The pursuit of God*, 119–21.

---

11. The term *integration* has been subject to numerous definitions. See, for example, Faw, *Wilderness wanderings*. We will take up this issue in chapter 11 of the current volume.

psychology and Christianity as irreconcilable, on the one extreme, to a variety of perspectives on how they might usefully inform each other.

Every vocation is a calling in which to serve God and others with whatever abilities God has gifted us. What abilities and talents have you been given that might give shape to your vocational calling? If you are currently a student, how might your life be different if you view being a student as a vocation and a calling rather than as a means to an end?

A variety of objections can be raised about the integration of psychology and Christianity. Some people see Christianity only as a religious belief and psychology as a profession, with very little overlap between them. This view tends to compartmentalize life into purely religious and purely secular domains. For the Christian, all of life is sacramental, so it is somewhat erroneous to separate vocations into those that are "full-time ministries" and those that are "secular." The truth is that *every* vocation should be a calling into full-time Christian ministry in which we serve God and others with whatever abilities He has gifted us and in whatever positions we may find ourselves. Some people claim that psychology and Christianity overlap only in broad ethical or humane considerations.

In this view, being a "Christian psychologist" is much like being a "Christian dentist" or a "Christian plumber"; one term applies specifically to religious belief, the other to a profession, with relatively few connections between them. We must ask, though, if it is true that Christianity and psychology are so distinct that they seldom exert an impact on each other.

The first reason that we should reject this argument is that our thinking about any subject begins with a system of beliefs. For the Christian, Christianity provides a worldview from which to understand the nature of the world and the nature of humanity. There are often areas of harmony between Christian and secular perspectives. However, because many psychologists embrace assumptions about human nature that differ from Christian assumptions, there will be points where Christians should critique the deeply held assumptions that have shaped modern psychology. Christians may also propose alternative theories informed by Christian perspectives. By making our assumptions explicit, we can create a framework for dialogue. We can consider some of the deepest questions of human concern, yet without seeing empirical data or theoretical speculation as incidental. Psychology and theology can thus critique and inform each other with recognition of the unique vantage points from which their common subject is seen. This approach allows us to acknowledge the influence of our assumptions on our theorizing, and it allows us to be aware of the advantages and limitations of the psychological and theological disciplines as they each attempt to understand human nature and functioning.

Second, a Christian worldview should encourage us to apply our abilities towards humane and godly ends, while avoiding the misuse of our powers towards sinful ends. Unfortunately, if one is convinced of the depth of human depravity, then one must take into account that even when one seeks good, evil is crouching nearby. A Christian worldview allows us to recognize corporate and individual sins through which we might misconstrue or misuse psychology, theology, or any other branch of learning. A Christian worldview also reminds us that a central purpose of human life is to love and serve others.

Third, as Christians, we are called to do all things "as unto God," which means, at least, that we should do them with integrity, humility, and competence. This calling precludes the fragmentation that would be caused by compartmentalizing faith to a narrow set of doctrines and practices. Christian faith, rightly understood, cannot be cordoned off to a few hours on Sunday morning. Instead, it should permeate *all* of life, shaping our thoughts about our possessions, our livelihoods, our relationships, our thinking, and every facet of life. The calling to do all things "as unto God" demands that whatever we do—psychology included—should be done honestly, humbly, to the best of our ability, and as an act of stewardship and worship.

Further Objections

A second objection to integration is raised by people who think that psychology and Christianity are incompatible. We will deal extensively with this perspective in a later chapter, but it is illustrated in the following experience. I once met a pastor who was amused to find that I taught psychology at a Christian college. His eyes twinkled as he said, "I've heard it said that psychology is just sinful human beings sinfully thinking about sinful human beings." His comment seemed to imply the belief that he had just tumbled the house of cards on which my profession was built. While his argument may not completely undermine the attempt to understand human nature with human reason, it does, perhaps, raise an important caveat. If the tenets of Christian theology are correct, the effects of original sin permeate every aspect of human experience, including our thinking; error and self-deception have thus been added to the finitude of our creation as delimiters of human knowledge. This fact does not mean that our ability to know about the world and ourselves is obliterated, although it clearly puts constraints on the accuracy and certainty of knowledge claims. Human beings—sinful and limited though they are—have been able to understand enough about the world to create indoor plumbing, to bring a measure of healing to physically diseased or damaged bodies, to venture beyond the confines of our own planet, to harness the mysteries of atoms, and to unlock the secrets of cells. Yet our knowledge is imperfect and partial, and there is ample room for us to frame our knowledge claims tentatively and humbly (1 Cor 13:12).

> "Where the truth is, in so far as it is truth, there God is."
>
> —Cervantes

Human beings are inquisitive and self-reflective by nature. The psalmists often offered reflections on creation and on human beings as part of the creation. The books of Proverbs and Ecclesiastes include numerous insights about and reflections on the human condition. The people of God, it would seem, are called to exercise their inquisitive and self-reflective capacities in understanding God's world, exercising their creative capacities and care-taking roles in a godly manner. With the psalmists, we can hardly imagine going about these tasks without beginning with awe and ending with a benediction of praise: "O LORD, our Lord, whose glory is higher than the heavens, how noble is your name in all the earth!" (Ps 8:1, BBE).[12] As we explore the wonders of God's creation, we become inquisitive about the nature of our world, and we become builders of culture and relationship. Ideally these tasks begin in awe of our Creator, they result in a chorus of praise that deepens our relationship to Him, and they become means of serving God and tending to the needs of others.

It seems reasonable to conclude that we are still called to deliberate on the nature of God's world and our place within it. As we have already seen, psychology is one of many disciplines that attempt to understand human nature. What makes psychology distinct from philosophy or theology is that it uses some methodologies that are guided by the quest for empirical evidence. To be sure, psychology considers many questions for which empirical evidence is not available or even possible, at which time it essentially becomes a philosophical or a theological enterprise. So long as the methodologies or teachings of psychology do not fundamentally contradict a rightly understood Christian view of things, though, there is nothing to preclude one from being a Christian who studies behavior utilizing psychological theories and methods. Indeed, the rallying cry of integration is that *all truth is God's truth*, so that wherever and however truth is discovered, its author is God.

Christian Psychology: A Term in Search of a Definition

You may have noticed that terms such as *Christian psychology* and *Christian counseling* have been used sparingly in the preceding discussion. For the sake of convenience, I have sought only to demonstrate that one can claim the nouns *Christian* and *psychologist* as self-descriptive, and that doing so should make a tangible difference. The waters get murkier when one tries to use the term *Christian*

---

12. The psalm begins and ends with an identical phrase of awe and praise.

as an adjective to define and delimit *psychologist*, *psychology*, *counseling*, or other related terms. Allow me to illustrate this murkiness with several examples.

As a clinician, I have often had clients who begin their encounter with me by asking, "Are you a Christian psychologist?" How should one respond to such a seemingly straightforward question? In the process of answering this question, I have found that it is often helpful to inquire about what the client means by the term *Christian psychologist*. On one occasion, a person who had asked me this question on the phone responded as follows: "Well, if you're a Christian psychologist, it means that your services are free because this is a ministry." On another occasion someone said, "If you're a Christian psychologist, it means that you use the Bible to give me good advice." Sometimes clients who ask if I am a Christian psychologist just want to make sure that we share essential Christian beliefs, because they are afraid of being misunderstood or of their values being undermined.

As an academician, I have often experienced similar questions from students and parents. "Do you teach Christian psychology at this school?" Students often tell me that they want to become "Christian counselors." When I ask them what a Christian counselor is, they often have no idea beyond some vague notion that they want to help people and that faith should somehow be a part of doing so. Some students use the term to refer to pastoral counseling, and still others imply that Christian

counseling means that they will give "godly" rather than "worldly" counsel. Meanwhile, several academic institutions and even nonacademic programs offer degrees or "certifications" in *Christian counseling*. Some of these are reputable programs that provide competent training that meets educational requirements for professional licensure. Others are simply "certifications" provided for people who sign a form and pay a fee. There are many programs that fall between these extremes, including Internet-based courses or weekend seminars offered by church or parachurch organizations.

Integration involves identifying key Christian commitments that shape how we understand human beings, and it requires a firm grasp of the theories, methods, and findings of psychology.

Given the foregoing examples, it is evident that terms such as *Christian psychology* and *Christian counseling* are sorely in need of definition. If by the term *Christian psychologist* one means to propose that there is one explicitly consecrated form of psychology (as distinct from, say, behavioral psychology, psychoanalytic psychology, developmental psychology, or cognitive neuroscience), then I am inclined to find the idea unworkable. Psychology is a vast territory composed of many perspectives. Christianity, as well, is varied in its denominational expressions and diverse in the perspectives offered by a wide array of theological camps. The diversity of psychological theories and theological perspectives suggests that the result of integration will be a variety of psychological theories, informed by diverse theological positions, which, together, help us to understand the complexity of human nature and functioning.[13]

Rather than proposing that there is a unique form of Christian psychology, I argue that the integration of psychology and Christianity involves two key elements. First, integration is predicated on identifying key Christian commitments that shape how we understand human beings, their relationship to God and to others, and their potentials and their problems. These commitments form a framework from which we study psychology, engage in research, and apply psychotherapeutic interventions.

Second, integration requires that we have a firm grasp of the theories, methods, and findings of psychology. By bringing a Christian framework and insights into a constructive relationship with contemporary psychology, a variety of approaches to integration are possible. Central to any such approach though, is the commitment to draw on scripture, Christian theology, and contemporary psychological theory and research as we seek to understand human nature and to relieve human suffering.

Before leaving this topic, we must hasten to add that there is a relatively new approach to relating psychology and Christianity that has been named *Christian psychology* by its followers. Eric Johnson has been a driving force in establishing the Society for Christian Psychology, which "exists to promote the development of a distinctly Christian psychology (including theory, research, and practice) that is based on a Christian understanding of human nature."[14] The Society highlights the importance that core Christian beliefs, as reflected in Scripture and various church traditions, will orient and shape a Christian understanding of psychology. It recognizes that there will be a plurality of approaches to Christian psychology, because there is a rich diversity of understandings within the Christian tradition. It especially notes that Christian approaches will differ from other approaches in areas that are heavily dependent on worldviews

---

13. Robert Roberts proposed that we redefine *Christian psychology* as a "branch or type of psychology." In his proposal we should "retrieve the Christian psychology of the past," by identifying teachings from the Bible or other Christian sources that have "psychological" content or implications. While there is much to commend in Roberts's proposal, it seems to neglect *psychology as a science* and does not adequately tend to the data available from the broader discipline of psychology. The alternative that I am suggesting begins with a Christian worldview from which we engage the discipline of psychology. This approach allows us to make use of the psychological insights of the Christian tradition, but also allows us to engage modern research and to evaluate and apply its findings from a Christian vantage point. See Roberts, A Christian psychology view, 152–53. Among psychologists, Eric Johnson has been the strongest advocate of this view. See Johnson, *Foundations for soul care.*

14. Society for Christian Psychology, *About the society,* ¶1.

(e.g., personality and motivation) as opposed to those that are more mechanistic (e.g., neural transmission and memory formation).

In his 2007 book *Foundations for Soul Care: A Christian Psychology Proposal*, Johnson argues that "there are reasons to believe that the common, contemporary understanding of integration may be intrinsically flawed."[15] His desire is to develop "a distinctly Christian *version* of psychology."[16] Johnson provides an excellent critique of the extensive impact of modernism on contemporary thought. He argues that psychology should be built on a carefully constructed Christian worldview, making extensive use of Scripture and Christian tradition. Johnson's proposal to develop a unique Christian *version* of psychology, though, is quite ambitious (his initial proposal to define this approach runs to well over six hundred pages). The definition of *Christian psychology* offered by Johnson and the Society for Christian Psychology is intriguing and will likely be quite productive, though it is probably not what most people have in mind when they use the term *Christian psychology*, nor is it identical to that which will be used in this book. Because this new approach has become better established in recent years, the Christian psychology approach is now recognized in this book as a representative of a new model for relating psychology and Christianity, as will be seen in subsequent chapters.

Coming Full Circle: Is Integration Necessary?

Colleges founded by Christian groups were based on various models for understanding the relationship of Athens ("secular knowledge") and Jerusalem ("sacred knowledge"). Many of the earliest Christian schools followed the Bible college model, in which much more emphasis was put on religious instruction than on other forms of knowledge. Other Christian colleges followed a model in which students were exposed to all types of learning, often taught by professors who weren't necessarily Christians, while maintaining a core set of course requirements in Bible and theology. A third model, the Christian liberal-arts tradition, holds that it is beneficial to seek knowledge from multiple perspectives rather than exclusively from biblical studies, but that it is important to integrate faith, learning, and living throughout the curriculum. The integration of psychology and Christianity emerged largely, though not exclusively, from the Christian liberal-arts tradition.

The term *integration* suggests that it takes effort to find connections between psychology and theology because they have been *dis*-integrated, or torn asunder. Our lives and our experiences have been dis-integrated, and part of God's restorative grace is reintegrating that which has been artificially severed. In this context it may be helpful to think of integration as

---

15. Johnson, *Foundations for soul care*, 96.

16. Ibid., 9.

both a *noun* and a *verb*.[17] Integration is *a priori*, a thing that we discover when we are uncovering the fundamental unity that God created, however much it might currently appear to be *dis*-integrated. On the other hand, *integration* is also something we do as we create ways of thinking about, combining, and applying psychological and theological truths. If Christ lays claim to all of life, then the work of integration becomes not just feasible, but imperative, as we attempt to understand the essence of this unity.

Certainly other people disagree with the conclusions that such integration is possible, desirable, or necessary. To understand some of the reasons for this disagreement, we must look both at the historical relationship of Christianity and psychology (or between Christianity and science or culture on broader levels) and at the philosophical underpinnings for seeking knowledge. These will be the respective topics of the next several chapters, paving the way for a discussion of objectives for and models of integration. The contents of the next few chapters may be a bit challenging (particularly for undergraduate readers, as we take a detour through medieval Scholasticism!), but the importance of this material will become clear as we develop a historical understanding of the current state of affairs between psychology and Christianity.

---

17. I am indebted to Dr. Daryl Stevenson for bringing this distinction to my attention.

Questions for Reflection and Discussion

1. How might you explain the experiences of the worshipers at Spirit Filled Church of Our Lord Jesus from a psychological perspective? How might the theology of the church they attended help us understand their beliefs and behaviors? Do these factors explain away faith, or do they just help us understand its complexities? How might people interpret the experiences of the worshipers at Spirit Filled Church of Our Lord Jesus differently based on their own religious, nonreligious, or denominational affiliations?

2. From a theological point of view, how might someone explain phenomena such as religious conversions and experiences to which people attach spiritual significance? What spiritual and psychological factors are involved in such experiences?

3. The author noted that several subdisciplines of psychology (e.g., social, physiological, clinical, developmental) may be relevant to the experience of the worshipers at Spirit Filled Church of Our Lord Jesus. The vast majority of writing on the integration of psychology and Christian theology has focused only on clinical or counseling issues. Why do you suppose this is the case? Is it sufficient to integrate only the counseling aspects of psychology? Why or why not?

4. Recall Tertullian's statement: "What indeed has Athens to do with Jerusalem? What concord is there between the Academy and the Church?" Have your own experiences stressed Athens or Jerusalem? What is your view on the relationship of the academy (human philosophy or knowledge) and the church (Christian theology)? What factors in your own personal and religious background have led you to this view?

5. The author wrote that the crucial integrative question is, "*What tangible difference does it make in one's life and practice to be a psychologist who is a devoted follower of Christ?*" In what ways should being a follower of Christ make a tangible difference in how one approaches psychology?

6. The author quoted a pastor who defined psychology as "sinful human beings sinfully thinking about sinful human beings." How do you react to that statement? Does the statement contain truth? Does it abolish the validity of psychology? Does it place constraints on psychology? How might we profitably react to such a critique?

7. The final section of the chapter addressed the question, "Is integration *necessary*?" In what ways are Christianity and psychology (or the church and the academy) dis-integrated? Can they be reintegrated? Should they be? Why or why not? How might such integration be pursued?

8. What implications does the distinction between *integration as a noun* and *integration as a verb* have for how we think about integration?

9. The author discussed the difficulty of defining *Christian psychology*. Do you think that it is a useful term? What do you mean when you use the phrase *Christian psychology*? In your experience, how might people mean different things when they use this term?

2

Allies or Enemies?
Historical Views on Faith and Science

I do not think that it is necessarily the case that science and religion are natural opposites. In fact, I think that there is a very close connection between the two. Further, I think that science without religion is lame and, conversely, that religion without science is blind. Both are important and should work hand-in-hand.[1]

—Albert Einstein

Every morning we see the sun rise in the east. During the day we watch the sun traverse an arc across the sky before setting in the west. Intuitively, from our perspective, it seems as if the sun travels around the earth. The ancient Greeks and Romans pictured Apollo circling the earth in his chariot. Aristotle adopted Ptolemy's view that the earth was the center of the universe with the moon, the sun, and the planets revolving around it, while far above us were the heavens containing the fixed stars.

The Aristotelian (or Ptolemaic) model was reasonably useful for navigation and for predicting the seasons of the year. The Roman Catholic Church found the model useful for setting the dates of the liturgical calendar. It was also useful in teaching theology, since it represented the sun and stars as perfect spheres, uncontaminated by human sin. The earth, at the bottom of the universe, was imperfect, and only hell was further from heaven.[2]

In 1543 Nicholaus Copernicus published *De Revolutionibus Orbium Coelestium*, a resurrection and defense of Pythagoras's theory of a heliocentric solar system. By theorizing that the sun, not the earth, was the center of the universe, Copernicus could improve the accuracy of several astronomical predictions. The book, dedicated to Pope Paul III, was published shortly after Copernicus's

---

1. Bucky, *The private Albert Einstein*, 85. In fairness, it should be noted that Einstein did not believe in a personal God "who would reward or punish his subjects" or who "has the power of interfering with . . . natural laws" (85–86).

---

2. Axelrod, *Galileo's battle for the heavens.*

death. The book was discussed in academic circles as an interesting theory, but the Aristotelian model of the universe remained the sanctioned view of nearly all academics and of the Roman Catholic Church.

In 1612 the heliocentric theory was taken up yet again by Galileo Galilei who, aided by the improved telescope that he had designed, revealed empirical evidence that supported Copernicus's theory. Galileo discovered craters that blemished the surface of the moon, four of the moons that circled Jupiter, and imperfections on the surface of the sun. He also noticed that the phases of Venus corresponded to a heliocentric model but not to an Aristotelian model. He published his findings in several books that brought him much notoriety, but which also spurred controversy and jealousy.

Opposition to Galileo's teaching began academically (with objections raised by adherents of the rival Aristotelian theory) and spread to ecclesiastical objections, first voiced in a sermon by Thomasso Cassini, a Dominican friar. Theological objections were based on a handful of Scriptures that seemed to support an earth-centered universe. In 1616 Cassini became what might be called the lead prosecutor of Galileo in Rome, and Cardinal Bellarmine presided over an inquiry into Galileo's views. Galileo defended himself by saying that he affirmed the teaching of Scripture, but he quoted Cardinal Baronius's claim that "The Bible was written to show us how to go to heaven, not how the heavens go."[3]

As a result of the investigation of 1616, Galileo was barred from teaching the heliocentric theory as a contravention of church doctrine, and Copernicus's *De Revolutionibus Orbium Coelestium* was added to the *Index Librorum Prohibitorum* (the *Index of Banned Books*) until "corrections" could be added. Galileo apparently left the tribunal under the impression that the heliocentric view could be explored as a theory but could not be taught or held as true. In 1632 Galileo published *Dialogue Concerning the Two Chief World Systems* as a discussion between three men about the Aristotelian and Copernican systems. The book clearly laid out stronger evidence for the Copernican system. The Church's position was defended by a character named Simplicio, connoting the stupidity of the character and his views. Galileo ended the book with Simplicio winning the argument so that he could be seen as affirming the position of the church, but the ploy did not work. The church barred the printing and distribution of the book and summoned the recalcitrant Galileo to another tribunal in Rome.

The second trial of Galileo focused on whether he had promoted the teaching of the heliocentric view in direct contradiction of the first tribunal. Galileo claimed that his book was simply a theoretical discussion of the topic, but it was clear that he was trying to circumvent the Church's authority. The trial ended in

---

3. Rohr, *Science and religion.*

something of a plea bargain, which culminated in a condemnation on June 22, 1633. The inquisition of Galileo ended with the following verdict:

> We say, pronounce, sentence, and declare that you . . . Galileo, because of the things deduced in the trial and confessed by you as above, have rendered yourself according to this Holy Office vehemently suspect of heresy, namely of having held and believed a doctrine which is false and contrary to the divine and Holy Scripture: that the Sun is the center of the world and does not move from east to west, and that one may hold and defend as probable an opinion after it has been declared and defined contrary to Holy Scripture. Consequently, you have incurred all the censures and penalties imposed and promulgated by the sacred canons and all particular and general laws against such delinquents. We are willing to absolve you from them provided that first, with a sincere heart and unfeigned faith, in front of us you abjure, curse, and detest the above-mentioned errors and heresies, and every other error and heresy contrary to the Catholic and Apostolic Church in the manner and form we will prescribe to you. Furthermore, so that this serious and pernicious error and transgression of yours does not remain completely unpunished, and so that you will be more cautious in the future and as an example for others to abstain from similar crimes, we order that the book *Dialogue* by Galileo Galilei be prohibited by public edict. We condemn you to formal imprisonment in this Holy Office at our pleasure. As a salutary penance we impose on you to recite the seven penitential Psalms once a week for the next three years. And we reserve the authority to moderate, change, or condone wholly or in part the above-mentioned penalties and penances. This we say, pronounce, sentence, declare, order, and reserve by this or any other better manner or form that we reasonably can or shall think of.[4]

The seven cardinals trying his case signed the condemnation. Galileo knelt before them, his hands on the Gospels, and pleaded guilty, saying, "with a sincere heart and unfeigned faith I abjure, curse, and detest the above-mentioned errors and heresies."[5] The teaching of the heliocentric theory was prohibited, and Galileo was silenced.

The story of Galileo's forced recantation is far more complicated than this brief overview would make it appear. The confrontation had been spurred by academic and ecclesiastic power struggles. Within the academic community, Galileo's position ran counter to beliefs that had been held for centuries. If Galileo's views were embraced, they would undermine the views—and hence the prestige—of Galileo's academic rivals. Galileo also ran afoul of church politics. He was tried by the Roman Catholic Church at a

---

4. Finocchiaro, *The Galileo affair,* 291.

5. Ibid., 292. The story that Galileo defiantly though quietly muttered, "But it still moves," probably has no basis in historical fact.

time when it was eager to reestablish its authority in response to Protestant rebellion. Power struggles within the academic community and within the church were exacerbated by interpersonal conflicts caused largely by Galileo's arrogance and political miscalculations.[6] Nevertheless, the net result was that the Church had banished the evidence of empirical observation in favor of the canon of Church dogma.

Owing to examples like Galileo, the church (both universal and Catholic) is often portrayed as antiscientific, stuck in its narrow-minded ecclesiastical view of reality, in which any evidence that appears to be at odds with the prevailing view of Scripture is simply dismissed.[7] One must ask, though, if a few such notable stories accurately reflect the broader history of the relationship of the church and science. Since psychology emerged, at least in part, from science, and since theological reactions to science foreshadow later theological reactions to psychology, it is important for us to explore the history of Christianity and science.

The Roman Catholic Church and Science

Science, as we understand it today, is an outgrowth of the rapid changes that transformed Western society from 1600 to 1800. This is not to say that people prior to the seventeenth century were ignorant.[8] We have no cause to look on the residents of the last few millennia with intellectual disdain. Yet it must be noted that, prior to the seventeenth century, our progenitors did not have a well-formulated way of seeking knowledge through the application of a rigorous scientific method. Since the later part of the nineteenth century, Christianity has often been portrayed as an obstacle to the development of science. As we will see, it may be more accurate to speculate that Christianity contributed to the development of science. As modern science developed, however, it was accompanied by momentous cultural changes that became fertile ground for a worldview that challenged the position of the Church as the supreme mediator of knowledge.

From some of its earliest centuries, Roman Catholic theology borrowed heavily from philosophy and rational discourse, although ecclesiastical ends and sources were its main concerns. Most

---

6. The popular handling of the Galileo affair often includes gross misstatements of fact that seem designed to highlight tensions rather than to provide understanding. See Drees, *Religion, science, and naturalism.*

7. Browning referred to this phenomenon as "theological positivism," which he defined as the belief that "a theological perspective on human behavior is exhaustive and must therefore be intolerant of all other perspectives" (Browning. *The Protestant response to psychiatry,* 28–29). Obviously, such religious reductionism makes integration impossible, as does any form of reductionism from the scientific side.

---

8. Indeed, as C. S. Lewis dryly noted, "The whole modern estimate of primitive man is based upon that idolatry of artefacts which is a great corporate sin of our own civilisation. We forget that our prehistoric ancestors made all the most useful discoveries, except that of chloroform, which have ever been made" (Lewis, *Miracles,* 65).

theologians, like Augustine of Hippo (354–430), emphasized the priority of faith over reason, since faith comes from God via revelation, and philosophy from the reasoning of fallen human beings. Yet the two were not generally seen as irreconcilable, and overall philosophy was seen as useful to theology. Indeed, Anselm of Canterbury (1033–1109) conceptualized theology as faith seeking understanding (*fides quaerens intellectum*).

> "For I do not seek to understand in order to believe, but I believe in order to understand. For I believe even this: that unless I believe, I shall not understand."
>
> —Anselm of Canterbury

Throughout the Middle Ages, the Church was seen as the supreme source of knowledge, with philosophy being the handmaiden of theology. In the classical view, faith was not seen as opposed to the evidence of reason or observation; rather, the relationship of faith and reason was a collaborative one. Thomas Aquinas (1224–1274) expressed this relationship when he wrote:

> Sacred doctrine makes use even of human reason . . . to make clear other things that are put forward in this doctrine. Since therefore grace does not destroy nature but perfects it, natural reason should minister to faith as the natural bent of the will ministers to charity . . . Hence sacred doctrine makes use also of the authority of phi-

losophers in those questions in which they were able to know the truth by natural reason.[9]

Thus medieval Scholasticism saw no necessary contradiction between faith and reason, although the Church was seen as holding the preeminent authoritative position. This situation later culminated in the Copernicus and Galileo controversies.

The assertion of the Church's supremacy can be seen in Aquinas's claim that "[Theology] surpasses other speculative sciences . . . because other sciences derive their certitude from the natural light of human reason, which can err; whereas [theology] derives its certitude from the light of divine knowledge, which cannot be misled."[10]

This claim naturally led to the conclusion that theologians had the right and obligation to judge conclusions drawn from other approaches to knowledge, so that "whatsoever is found in other sciences contrary to any truth of this science must be condemned as false."[11] It was taken for granted that "orthodox" theological interpretation was correct, and that it held virtually the same authority as Scripture itself.[12] As we will

---

9. Thomas, *The summa theologica,* section Ia, I, 8, response 2.

10. Ibid., section Ia, I, 5.

11. Ibid., section Ia, I, 6, reply to obj. 2.

12. This would later be a point of contention in the Reformation; while Roman Catholics saw Church tradition as the authoritative interpretation of Scripture, the Reformers challenged some of its tradition with the cry, "*Sola Scriptura!*"

see in a later chapter, the failure to distinguish *the validity of theological interpretation* from *the authority of Scripture* is a
common error that persists today.

Theological scholarship flourished
under the influence of luminaries such as
Thomas Aquinas. However, the seeds of
later conflict were sown by placing theology above all other modes of intellectual pursuit, with little recognition of the
human capacity to err in putting theology together. The Church, charged with
saving souls, thought that it was important to protect the uneducated masses
from being misled by error or heresy that
might lead to eternal damnation. The
Roman Catholic Church was vigilant in
carrying out this task. If evidence from
philosophy or science was inconsistent
with theologically derived conclusions,
theology was considered to be the more
reliable road to truth, leading to the suppression of opposing views to protect the
reigning theological teachings. The consequence was that theology was insulated
from outside critique and was given preeminence over all other disciplines.

It would be easy to conclude that
Roman Catholicism in the medieval period valued extratheological means of inquiry while simultaneously insisting on
a repressive theological domination of
other academic disciplines. While this
conclusion may be partly valid, it would
neglect the important role that Christianity may have had in laying the groundwork for scientific understanding, which
is the topic of the next section.

Christianity and the Origins of Science

It is not uncommon to encounter claims
that religion and science are antithetical
to one another. A statement widely attributed to Richard Dawkins, for instance,
asserts, "I am against religion because it
teaches us to be satisfied with not understanding the world." Such sentiments can
be found in many antireligious diatribes,
but they are certainly not new. As long
ago as 1875, J. W. Draper had expressed
the belief of the antithetical nature of science and religion in his book *History of
the Conflict between Religion and Science*,
with the following salvo: "The history of
Science is not a mere record of isolated
discoveries; it is a narrative of the conflict
of two contending powers, the expansive
force of the human intellect on one side,
and the compression arising from tra-
ditionary faith and human interests on
the other."[13] It is worth asking, though,
whether science and religion are inevitably opposed to each other, as some would
have us think.

It is interesting to note that Draper capitalized the word *science*, elevat-
ing its status from the outset. His point
is clear: religious faith is an impediment
to science and progress.[14] This was a core

---

13. Quoted in Drees, *Religion, science, and
naturalism*, 54.

14. Draper and White are often cited as
examples of the "warfare" metaphor between
religion and science mainly because they provide stark examples of this viewpoint. However,
Sorenson noted that neither Draper nor White
was recognized as a scientific authority, nor

belief of the Enlightenment, in which ecclesiastical and scriptural authority were replaced by reason as the acceptable epistemic framework.

One can certainly point to numerous exchanges between members of the Catholic and scientific communities that were characterized by uncharitable and vitriolic hyperbole; but such tensions tell only part of the story. Despite the challenges brought to Christian theology by the rise of science, and the periodic antagonism that arose between the two during the Enlightenment, it is interesting to ask why scientific thought began to emerge in seventeenth-century Europe rather than in ancient China or the Roman Empire, or medieval Africa. Many ancient cultures produced libraries to catalog knowledge, and technologies to make life easier, but they failed to produce a truly scientific *method*. "Yet it was Christianized Europe and not these more advanced cultures that gave birth to modern science as a systematic, self-correcting discipline. The historian is bound to ask why this should be so."[15]

The philosopher and mathematician Alfred North Whitehead, responding to the growing antireligious sentiment held by some scientists and philosophers of his day, asserted that Christianity formed the philosophical landscape that allowed for the establishment of science.

The greatest contribution of medievalism to the formation of the scientific movement [was] . . . the inexpugnable belief that every detailed occurrence can be correlated with its antecedents in a perfectly definite manner, exemplifying definite principles. Without this belief the incredible labours of scientists would be without hope . . . How has this conviction been so vividly implanted on the European mind? When we compare this tone of thought in Europe with the attitude of other civilisations when left to themselves, there seems but one source for its origin. It must come from the medieval insistence on the rationality of God, conceived as with the personal energy of Jehovah and with the rationality of a Greek philosopher. Every detail was supervised and ordered: the search into nature could only result in the vindication of the faith in rationality.[16]

In other words, Whitehead argued that the worldview of medieval European Scholasticism, shaped as it was by Greek philosophy and the Christian understanding of a universe designed by a powerful and rational God, rather than being antithetical to science, as Draper insisted, had actually laid the groundwork for the emergence of science in seventeenth-century Europe. Indeed, if Draper's view is correct, how would one account for the fact that "most of the major figures in the early development of modern science were Christians[, including] Copernicus,

---

did either of them have a significant impact on scientific scholarship. See chap. 7 in Sorenson, *Minding spirituality*.

15. Pearcy & Thaxton, *The soul of science*, 21.

---

16. Whitehead, *Science and the modern world*, 13.

Galileo, Bacon, Kepler, and Newton?"[17] It would be absurd to think that Christianity alone created science (after all, sixteen hundred years separated Christ from the rise of modern science); but in Whitehead's view Christianity was a catalyst that produced a unique worldview. This worldview made it possible to pull together advances in mathematics, rational discourse, and a belief in the orderliness of nature that collectively made the rise of scientific thinking possible.[18]

Hooykaas furthered Whitehead's postulate, noting that, for science to come into being, a certain way of thinking about the world was necessary. In the animistic thinking of the ancients, demons and spirits controlled the workings of the world and the fates of the living. In Platonic thought, the world we inhabit is a mere shadow of the true world of forms, the immutable Ideas. For Aristotle the world was the center of a universe created, but not sustained, by a prime mover. In the biblical picture, however, we find a Creator who is distinct from, but involved with, the creation. In this view, the world is imparted with order, and human beings are created with the faculty of reason. Hooykaas argued that the worldview of Christianity was uniquely conducive to the development of science: "Contrary perhaps to what one would have expected, a more fully biblical world view has, since the sixteenth century, favoured the rise of modern science and of the world picture connected with it. The model of the world as an organism was replaced by that of the world as a mechanism."[19]

This mechanistic worldview, while not without its problems, allowed people to look at the world with an expectation of finding order that could be described with rational rules. Such a worldview is uniquely conducive, or even prerequisite, to the development of scientific thinking. In fact, Pearcy and Thaxton argue that rather than being an impediment to the rise of science, "Christianity was the backdrop to virtually all scientific discussion" in the formative stages of science.[20]

Given the evidence that Christianity helped pave the way for the development of science, and that framing the relationship of Christianity and science in terms of "warfare" is "simply inappropriate for

---

17. Gaede, *Where gods may dwell*, 42.

18. Many changes had to occur in order for the scientific revolution to take place, not the least of which were the destruction of the intuitively reasonable Aristotelian cosmology; overcoming an educational system that produced scholars but did not foster independent thinking or the application of a scientific method; the effects of economic and social constraints and changes; and so forth. Historians continue to argue over which factors were peripheral and which were essential to the rise of science, and many would disagree with the conclusion that Christianity in any way aided the development of science. In any event, it seems unwarranted to conclude that Christianity and science are necessarily antagonistic enterprises.

19. Hooykaas, *Religion and the rise of modern science*. Whitehead and Hookyaas acknowledge that other ancient cultures had made significant advances in numerous fields, but they did not develop a scientific *method*. For a volume that highlights the contributions of the ancients, see Neugebauer, *Exact sciences in Antiquity*.

20. Pearcy & Thaxton, *The soul of science*, xii.

the periods before 1850," one must ask why the warfare metaphor evolved in the first place.[21] Livingstone suggests that warfare vocabulary was "deliberately fostered by those antitheistic polemicists who had vested interests in using science to displace the church from the center of the social and cultural stage."[22] In other words, modernism's antagonism toward Christianity and its claim to be an authoritative mediator of truth and values was served well by framing Christianity as an opponent of scientific progress.

Did Christianity *cause* the rise of science? At best, one must admit that the Christian worldview was a contributing force to the rise of the scientific worldview that emerged in the seventeenth century, but it was only one such force.[23] As Davis concludes:

> The full historical picture is complex: science, philosophy, and theology are inextricably intertwined. To single out one factor as the sole cause is to misrepresent the actual situation . . . Voluntarist Theology [which sees natural science as an inevitable reflection of God's sovereignty] . . . was rather one factor, albeit a very important one, in giving modern science its strong empirical bent.[24]

A worldview from which God's handiwork could be studied as an ordered creation fashioned a favorable environment for the rise of empirical science, and it was just such a biblical perspective that was rediscovered by the late medievalists of the Roman Catholic Church.

Protestantism and Science

For all their protestations, Protestants owe a great deal to their Catholic progenitors. The Protestant view of the world largely mirrored that of their Catholic contemporaries. Still, Protestantism added something unique that propelled interest in the scientific approach to the world. Reviewing sociological research, Hooykaas concludes that Protestants were significantly overrepresented among the scientific community (proportional to their numbers in the general population), from the mid-1600s until recently. Alphonse de Candolle, in the late nineteenth century, reasoned that this overrepresentation was caused in part by the vow of celibacy taken by Catholic priests; while many Protestant clergy had children who

---

21. Livingstone, *Reflections on the encounter between science and faith*, 252.

22. Ibid., 253.

23. For some contemporary treatments of this subject from diverse viewpoints, see: Hannam, *Genesis of science*; Shapin, *The scientific revolution*; Gaukroger, *Emergence of scientific culture*.

24. Davis, *Christianity and early modern*

---

science, 89. Voluntarist theology departs from Aristotelian metaphysics in that while Aristotle believed that nature could not be other than what it is, orthodox Christianity sees nature as being the way it is because of God's volition: nature is what God made it to be and acts as He made it to act. Rather than assuming that reason alone can tell us how nature ought to behave, voluntarist theology recognized that observation and experimentation are means to perceive what God has created and the rules by which creation behaves. Voluntarist theology is thus an impetus to scientific interest and thinking.

became scientists, this was not the case for Catholic clergy.[25] While intriguing, de Candolle's hypothesis seems to miss the mark. Several Reformation forces may have encouraged an interest in science, including the Protestant work ethic and the increasing vocational opportunities available to the Protestant middle class. It may also be, however, that Protestants rediscovered the important truth that the entire world reflects the glory of God, and that the act of worship is to be found in studying both the book of God's Word, the Scriptures, and the book of God's works, the created realm.[26]

"How wrong it is to use God as a stop-gap for the incompleteness of our knowledge. If in fact the frontiers of knowledge are being pushed further and further back (and that is bound to be the case), then God is being pushed back with them, and is therefore continually in retreat. We are to find God in what we know, not in what we don't know."

—Dietrich Bonhoeffer, letter to Eberhard Bethge, 29 May, 1944.

---

25. See Drees, *Religion, science, and naturalism*, 77–78.

26. For an extensive discussion of the relationship of Protestantism and science, see chapter 5, Science and the Reformation, in Hooykaas, *Religion and the rise of modern science*. See also Livingstone, et al., *Evangelicals and science*.

The Protestant interest in studying God's Word and God's works can be seen in the founding of the first American universities. The first emblem of Harvard University was a coat of arms containing three open books, across which is written *vertias*, the Latin word for "truth." It was, in Ari Goldman's words, "just another, shorthand way of recognizing Jesus Christ, who was seen as the ultimate Truth."[27] Yet most of these early universities gradually shed their Christian heritage and commitments. Protestants from other traditions either spurned education outright or retrenched their forces into more narrowly ecclesiastical foci.[28] These trends came about, in no small part, due to the challenges of philosophical modernism and, especially, the rise of Darwin's theory about the origins of the human species.

Darwin, Science, and Christianity

The reactions of Catholicism and Protestantism to science since the late nineteenth century are diverse, but some trends can be seen. Clearly the most momentous event in this period was the publication of Charles Darwin's *On the Origin of Species* in 1859. We will begin by looking at the Roman Catholic encounter with evolutionary thinking,

---

27. Goldman, *The search for God at Harvard*, 67.

28. For a good summary, see Buss, *Educating toward a Christian worldview*.

and then proceed to explore Protestant encounters.

Darwin's theory about human origins, coupled with modernist scholarship that recast the biblical story of creation and fall in mythic, rather than literal, terms posed a problem for Roman Catholic theology. Without a literal Adam and Eve and a factual first sin passed on to posterity, the church's conception of original sin came into question, and with it, questions about Christology (why Christ came), ecclesiology (the purpose of the church), and soteriology (the nature of salvation). The theory of evolution was first rejected in 1860 by a Catholic synod in Cologne, and then again by the First Vatican Council in 1869–70.[29] The Roman Catholic Church continued to put constraints on scientific theories of origins, notably in its clash with Catholic theologian Pierre Teilhard de Chardin and in the 1950 papal encyclical *Humani Gereris*, which sought to establish a firm line between revealed truth and scientific conjecture. In the encyclical, Pope Pius XII cautioned that some "fictitious tenets of evolution which repudiate all that is absolute, firm and immutable" were dangerous and contrary to Catholic teaching.[30] His was a cautious view of how Roman Catholicism ought to engage evolution, wanting to maintain theological teachings about the origin of the soul but not wanting to forbid exploration of evolutionary scholarship.

Today, the Roman Catholic view is largely settled by affirming that God is the Creator behind everything that exists, but allowing that He may well have used evolution to form matter into its diverse forms. Joseph Cardinal Ratzinger (later Pope Benedict XVI), put it this way:

> My predecessors Pope Pius XII and Pope John Paul II noted that there is no opposition between faith's understanding of Creation and the evidence of the empirical science . . . In order to develop and evolve, the world must first be, and thus have come from nothing into being. It must be created, in other words, by the first Being who is such by essence.[31]

In 2014, while dedicating a bronze bust of Benedict XVI, Pope Francis echoed these sentiments.

> When we read in Genesis the account of Creation, we risk imagining that God was a magician, with such a magic wand as to be able to do everything. However, it was not like that. He created beings and left them to develop according to the internal laws that He gave each one, so that they would develop, and reach their fullness. He gave autonomy to the beings of the universe at the same time that He assured them of his continual presence, giving being to every reality. And thus creation went forward for centuries and centuries, millennia and millennia until it became what

---

29. See Wiley, *Original sin*, 120–25.

30. Pius XII, *Humani generis*, section 6.

31. Benedict XVI, *Address of Benedict XVI*, ¶ 3.

we know today, in fact because God is not a demiurge or a magician, but the Creator who gives being to all entities.[32]

Protestants largely reacted along one of two lines: to reinterpret Scripture to accommodate Darwin, or to castigate Darwin in defense of Christianity. The former tack was taken primarily by those denominations that might be called "liberal" or "neo-orthodox," while those of "fundamental" persuasion preferred the latter approach. Each camp handled apparent conflicts between faith and science differently, and their diverse responses reflected their differing views of Scripture as much as—or even more than—their beliefs about the relationship of science and faith.[33]

Liberal groups in the nineteenth century increasingly adopted a view of Scripture that focused on its moral and humane teachings and removed or minimized its authority concerning historical or scientific matters. "Within a liberal perspective . . . if genuine conflict between science and theology occurred, theology must give way, because the Bible had no special status or religious authority."[34] Neo-orthodoxy, likewise, used the method of higher criticism to build "a wall between theology and science," but with the aim of protecting faith by expunging it of elements that its adherents perceived as mythical rather than as literal or historical truth.[35]

Fundamentalism, unlike liberalism and neo-orthodoxy, maintained a literal interpretation of Scripture. It rejected Darwinism and higher criticism. Fundamentalists became suspicious of science, seeing it as having been hijacked to promote atheism and humanism. In reaction, fundamentalists tended to alter "their views on science to fit their religion."[36]

This general divide between conservative and liberal branches of Protestantism was accompanied by other shifts. The liberal wing of the church emphasized social concerns and accommodation to modernism, while the fundamentalist wing emphasized soteriological concerns and doctrinal defense. The former wanted to keep faith relevant by avoiding conflict with modern thought and sought to relieve the present ills of human suffering. The latter wanted to protect faith from modern thought and sought to bring spiritual revival to lands near and far. In a sense one could place social concerns and academic pursuits on one side, and missionaries and Bible schools on the other. This is, of course, an oversimplification, but it highlights a trend of social and intellectual engagement versus social and intellectual disengagement on the one hand,

---

32. Francis, Address at Inauguration of Bronze Bust of Benedict XVI, zenit.org.

33. For a good discussion of the topic of views of Scripture during the fundamentalist-modernist controversy and its implications in higher education, see Hart, *Evangelicals, biblical scholarship*.

34. Yandell, Protestant theology and natural science, 449.

---

35. Ibid., 459.

36. Hiebert, Modern physics and Christian faith, 443.

and a trend of soteriological and doctrinal relativism verses soteriological and doctrinal primacy on the other.

Evangelical Reactions

Evangelicalism has as its heritage the Protestant Reformation, Puritanism, and the revivalist movements in Great Britain and the United States. In the late 1800s, its primary expression was fundamentalism. Modern evangelicalism is a diverse phenomenon that largely emerged out of the fundamentalist reaction to Darwin and to theological liberalism.[37] In this emergence from fundamentalism, the situation for evangelical engagement with science has been somewhat divided. To Christians who were interested in the defense of the faith, the natural theology afforded by science was appealing. Natural theology focuses on what we can discern about God from the study of nature.

One example of natural theology can be seen in the following psalm: "The heavens declare the glory of God; / the skies proclaim the work of his hands. // Day after day they pour forth speech; / night after night they display knowledge. // There is no speech or language / where their voice is not heard" (Ps 19:1–3, NIV).

Likewise, the author of Romans asserted, "For since the creation of the world God's invisible qualities—his eternal power and divine nature—have been clearly seen, being understood from what has been made, so that men are without excuse" (Rom 1:20, NIV).

Protestants gravitated to science because of its potential to reveal glimpses of the Creator and His character. Science, then, became a venue of worship and praise. Moreover, science became a vocational calling that could produce tangible benefits to ease human suffering. The view of science as a sacred calling, however, was threatened by Darwinian theory.

Like fundamentalists, many evangelicals have been uncomfortable with the sociological and moral implications of Darwinism. Noll suggests that Darwin's influence on science resulted in something of a transition for evangelicals, gradually moving them from enthusiasm in the late 1800s to a cautious skepticism in the early 1900s.[38] Evangelicals had traditional-

---

37. Marsden pointed out that evangelicalism is a kaleidoscope of Christian traditions, ranging from separatist fundamentalists to black Pentecostals to Anabaptists to Southern Baptists. While its various denominations often work in isolation from each other, they share common traditions, histories, and theological commitment to the authority of Scripture, the historical unfolding of God's saving work as recorded in Scripture, salvation through personal faith in Jesus Christ, an emphasis on evangelism and missions, and individual sanctification. Increasingly, evangelicalism has become both a global phenomenon and an ecumenical one, so that some Christians from Catholic and mainline denominations describe themselves as evangelicals. See Marsden, *Evangelicalism and modern America*. For a brief overview of twentieth-century evangelicalism, see part 1, in Webber, *The younger evangelicals*.

---

38. "The relation of evangelicals to science . . . underwent a great shift between the Civil War and World War I. In antebellum America, evangelicals had been among the most ardent promoters of mainstream science (as doxological, Baconian, and realist), but developments in geology and biology . . . created a new situation

ly seen science as an ally in doing natural theology and were interested in the application of science to ease human suffering. With the advent of Darwinism, however, evangelicals began to see science as a threat to faith.[39] Darwinian theory called into question long-standing beliefs about the origins of human beings. It threatened to replace the view of nature as God's handiwork with a view of nature as a vast, impersonal, random process. Evangelicals also saw Darwinism as a movement that had adverse consequences for society, such as the collapse of morality that

might result if humans were understood as evolved animals rather than as directly created in the image of God.[40]

As evangelicalism emerged from fundamentalism in the early twentieth century, it has gone through three distinct phases in how it related to academic inquiry, to other church groups, and to social concerns. The earliest cycle of twentieth century evangelicalism spanned the years from 1925 to 1945. During this time, evangelicalism was primarily expressed through fundamentalism and can be characterized by the things it was opposed to; it was anti-intellectual, anti-ecumenical, and anti-social action.[41] During this phase, the primary reaction of evangelicalism to science was one of disengagement and rejection. The post–World War II era saw a split in which most evangelicals diverged from fundamentalism with a desire to engage and change the wider culture rather than to live in isolation from it. This led to a second phase of twentieth-century evangelicalism, which was pro-intellectual, pro-ecumenical, and pro-social action. The benefits of medical science, in particular, appealed to evangelical Christians, who saw it as a means of ministering to human needs and (especially when coupled with missions) as a means of spreading the gospel. However, many evangelicals feel uneasy

---

after the Civil War . . . They were troubled by possible atheism lurking in ateleological evolution, by agnostic conclusions promoted by popularizers of the new science, by the heartache in abandoning traditional interpretations of Scripture, and by efforts of scientific professionals to replace religious professionals as society's key arbiters of truth" (Noll, *Science, theology, and society*, 108).

39. A pivotal year for the fate of fundamentalism was 1925. In that year, John Scopes was tried and convicted for teaching evolution. The fundamentalist attack on Scopes, led by William Jennings Bryan, was successful in gaining Scopes's conviction, but the reporting of the event by H. L. Mencken led to a backlash against fundamentalism. A particularly wounding comment was made by Bryan, while serving as an expert witness on the reliability of the Scriptures, when he responded to Clarence Darrow's cross-examination by saying, "I do not think about things I don't think about." Darrow retorted, "Do you think about things you do think about?" to which Bryan replied, "Well, sometimes" (quoted in Marsden, *Fundamentalism and American culture*, 187). The result was that Bryan—and fundamentalists—were portrayed as ignorant, nonthinking fools. For an excellent account of the aftereffects of the Scopes trial, see Marsden, *Fundamentalism and American culture*, 184–95.

40. William Jennings Bryan claimed, "The evolutionary hypothesis is the only thing that has seriously menaced religion since the birth of Christ; and it menaces . . . civilization as well as religion." Quoted in Marsden, *Fundamentalism and American culture*, 4.

41. Webber, *The younger evangelicals*.

with other scientific disciplines due to lingering perceptions of conflict rooted in evolutionary theory. The debate over evolution, argued on rational, theological, scientific, and even legal grounds, has received renewed interest and has reinvigorated conflict through the *creation science* and *intelligent design* movements.[42]

"Almost 150 years after Charles Darwin published his groundbreaking work *On the Origin of Species by Means of Natural Selection*, Americans are still fighting over evolution. If anything, the controversy has grown in both size and intensity . . . Indeed, the teaching of evolution has become a part of the nation's culture wars [and] is likely to have a place in national debates on values for many years to come."

—Pew Research Center for Religion and Public Life.

Now that you have read about how different Christian groups reacted to Darwin, summarize common views held by various religious groups and the reasons for their reactions.

---

42. See Livingstone, Situating evangelical responses; and Numbers, Creating creationism.

A third cycle is now emerging as evangelicalism responds to postmodern thought and postmodern culture. As a result of postmodern influences, there is an increasing focus among evangelicals on how the biblical story intersects with the narrative of individual lives. It remains to be seen how this third cycle will develop, as evangelicalism addresses the postmodern situation. Additionally, evangelicalism will inevitably need to address the challenges that postmodernism has posed to rational and scientific thought.

The Contemporary Scene

Although some present-day scientists continue to be outspoken critics of religious belief, some contemporary scientists promote the idea that science and Christianity are compatible. One of the most prominent genetic researchers of our day is a committed Christian. Francis Collins, who was the director of the Human Genome Project and the director of the National Institutes of Health, was not raised in a religious home. As a graduate student in physical chemistry, Collins was comfortable with the belief that God did not exist; but when he pursued a medical degree, he found that neither his atheism nor science provided the answers to questions raised by his patients and their suffering.

Challenged by one of those patients, who asked, "What do you believe, doctor?," I began searching for answers. I had to admit that the science

I loved so much was powerless to answer questions such as "What is the meaning of life?" "Why am I here?" "Why does mathematics work, anyway?" "If the universe had a beginning, who created it?" "Why are the physical constants in the universe so finely tuned to allow the possibility of complex life forms?" "Why do humans have a moral sense?" "What happens after we die?"[43]

Collins's search for answers gradually led him to become a Christian. It also led him to struggle with some of the controversies that we have explored in this chapter.

> "Aren't evolution and faith in God incompatible?" "Can a scientist believe in miracles like the resurrection?" Actually, I find no conflict here, and neither apparently do the 40 percent of working scientists who claim to be believers . . . The God of the Bible is also the God of the genome. God can be found in the cathedral or in the laboratory. By investigating God's majestic and awesome creation, science can actually be a means of worship.[44]

Collins is at peace as a Christian and a scientist, seeing no necessary conflict between the two.

For most contemporary evangelical, mainline, and Roman Catholic Christians, faith and science are seen as complementary ways of knowing, but with the recognition that areas of tension will occur. Evolutionary theory continues to be one of those areas of tension, and Christians continue to diverge on whether to accommodate evolution to their theology, or to reject or modify evolutionary theory based on their theology. For the most part, though, the majority of Christians do not see science and Christianity as inherently incompatible. Striving for a more synthetic point of view, "orthodox theologians in the twentieth century . . . have seen the science-theology relationship in terms rather of bridges than of walls" that allow for a productive relationship between the two disciplines, without forcing either to submit to the primacy of the other.[45]

At the close of the twentieth century, Pope John Paul II expressed Roman Catholic teaching on the compatibility of science and faith in *Fides et ratio*, a 1998 papal encyclical. Speaking in reference to Thomas Aquinas, John Paul II wrote:

> Thomas had the great merit of giving pride of place to the harmony which exists between faith and reason. Both the light of reason and the light of faith come from God, he argued; hence there can be no contradiction between them. More radically, Thomas recognized that nature, philosophy's proper concern, could contribute to the understanding of divine Revelation. Faith therefore has no fear of reason, but seeks it out and has trust in it. Just as grace builds on

---

43. Collins, Why this scientist believes, ¶¶3–4.

44. Ibid., ¶¶8–11.

---

45. Yandell, Protestant theology and natural science, 461.

nature and brings it to fulfilment, so faith builds upon and perfects reason. Illumined by faith, reason is set free from the fragility and limitations deriving from the disobedience of sin and finds the strength required to rise to the knowledge of the Triune God.[46]

In the encyclical, John Paul II took the position that science and Christianity can coexist because their truths emanate from God. Underlying this openness, though, is a demarcation of the proper limits of theology and science. The pope reserved for the Church the role of mediating truth about human value and morality, while appreciating the role that science has in examining the mysteries of God's world.

> Finally, I cannot fail to address a word to *scientists*, whose research offers an ever greater knowledge of the universe as a whole and of the incredibly rich array of its component parts, animate and inanimate, with their complex atomic and molecular structures. So far has science come, especially in this century, that its achievements never cease to amaze us. In expressing my admiration and in offering encouragement to these brave pioneers of scientific research, to whom humanity owes so much of its current development, I would urge them to continue their efforts without ever abandoning the *sapiential* horizon within which scientific and technological achievements are wedded to the philosophical and ethical

values which are the distinctive and indelible mark of the human person. Scientists are well aware that "the search for truth, even when it concerns a finite reality of the world or of man, is never-ending, but always points beyond to something higher than the immediate object of study, to the questions which give access to Mystery."[47]

Thus Roman Catholicism has reaffirmed its Thomistic roots in a way that allows for a concord of faith and reason, the Church and science. The Catholic Church is certainly not alone in this regard, another notable example being that of the Dutch reformers, whose work was a major impetus to the Christian liberal arts tradition.

In what ways might Christianity have contributed to the development of a scientific outlook? In what ways might the Church be seen as having been an impediment to the development of a scientific outlook? How did different branches of the Church react to controversies between faith and science?

---

46. John Paul II, *Fides et ratio*, section 43, ¶¶1 and 2.

47. Ibid., section 106, ¶2. The section in quotations refers to another address by John Paul II.

Summary

Are Christianity and science allies or enemies? A historical survey would suggest that they have been both at various times over the past several centuries. In many ways the foundations of science were paved in part by a Christian worldview that allowed for the universe to be seen as an orderly place in which laws could describe the regularities found within it, based on the premise that the world was created by a powerful, rational, and personal Being. Nonetheless, conflicts have periodically arisen over the primacy of ways of knowing (ecclesiastical versus philosophical or empirical) and over findings or theories that have been objectionable to members of the church or members of the scientific community. The church has dealt with the tensions of this dialogue in various ways, ranging from theological accommodation of modernism in the liberal wing of the church to defensive disengagement in the more fundamentalist wing of the church, with some attempts at constructive dialogue in between. As we shall see in the next chapter, these various alternatives for dealing with faith and science are mirrored by the ways in which faith and psychology have been construed.

Questions for Reflection and Discussion

1. Imagine that you are Galileo. You have been asked to recant your belief in a heliocentric universe and to promise not to spread this teaching anymore or you will be excommunicated. What might you do? Why do you think Galileo recanted? Why do you think the Church was so threatened by Galileo's views?

2. In medieval Scholasticism, faith was typically seen as superior to other methods of attaining knowledge, since its source is divine revelation. Does this viewpoint still exist today? What presuppositions is this view based on? Are these presuppositions warranted?

3. Compare and contrast Draper's view of the relationship of faith and science to the view espoused by Whitehead and others. Which view comes closer to your own view? Are faith and science allies or enemies? Do you think the argument that Christianity laid the groundwork for science has merit?

4. The author noted that a recent dividing line in the relationship between science and Christian faith was the publication of Darwin's ideas. How have you seen the issue of evolution and faith dealt with in ecclesiastical and scholastic circles? The author noted trends in liberal versus fundamental reactions to Darwin. Can you see any of these trends in your own church background and experience? Is there a relationship between that issue and the way particular churches deal with other controversial matters in science or psychology?

5. According to Francis Collins, "God can be found in the cathedral or in the laboratory. By investigating God's majestic and awesome creation, science can actually be a means of worship." In what way could your studies lead you to a sense of awe and worship? Give a specific example of when you have experienced awe and how it led you to a sense of worship.

6. Reread the passages quoted from John Paul II's papal encyclical *Fides et ratio*. What do you find in his argument that you appreciate? Are there things that you disagree with or are hesitant about? Why?

7. *Fides et ratio* ends with a call for scientists to be aware that "the search for truth . . . always points beyond to something higher than the immediate object of study, to the questions which give access to Mystery." In what way can your studies—in literature, science, psychology, or other disciplines—lead you to see and appreciate the Mystery that lies beyond your immediate object of study? (Note: by capitalizing "Mystery," Pope John Paul II seemed to be suggesting that all of our studies can lead us to glimpse the Creator and stand in awe of Him.)

8. Christians have reasserted the concord between faith and science, but the rapprochement has often been one-sided. Consider the questions that are asked in the following quotation: "If science received much of its impetus from Christian assumptions, what will happen now that those assumptions have eroded—now that Christianity is no longer a public faith undergirding science . . . ? What will happen to science as the Christian motivation and intellectual scaffolding wither away? Contemporary science still lives off the accumulated capital of centuries of Christian faith. But how long will that capital last? And what will take its place?"[48]

9. Evangelicals were once at the forefront of social reform before largely abandoning social concerns and focusing almost exclusively on evangelism and missions. Read Luke 10:25-37. In what way do you see yourself and the church carrying out—or failing to carry out—these instructions? Why is the connection between orthodox belief and social action crucial to the gospel?

---

48. Pearcy & Thaxton, *The soul of science*, 42.

3

The Soul of Psychology and the Psyche of the Soul

Were one asked to characterize the life of religion in the broadest and most general terms possible, one might say that it consists of the belief that there is an unseen order, and that our supreme good lies in harmoniously adjusting ourselves thereto.[1]

—William James

"I'm tired of having to defend myself for majoring in psychology," Pam sighed. "Every time I come home from school my pastor asks me, 'Do you really think this is a good idea?' A lot of people in my church think there's something subversive about what I'm studying. Last week someone even asked me if I could really be a Christian and study psychology. It's almost like they think I'm making a pact with the devil."

"When I tell people at my church that I want to become a psychologist, most of them think that's great," responded Ray, bemused at Pam's experience. "I've never had anyone suggest that it could be a problem. In fact, I've often been encouraged to pursue my studies so I can use the talents God gave me to help people."

Ian frowned. "I'm interested in experimental psychology and I want to study memory construction in graduate school. My biggest problem is getting people in my church to understand that there's more to the field of psychology than counseling. But in all honesty, I don't see how my faith has much to do with what I'm studying."

The names and dialogues above are fictional, but they mirror the conversation of many Christian undergraduate psychology majors and graduate students in psychology programs. Like Pam, some students experience skepticism or hostility from other Christians in response to their choice of academic study and their professional goals. Others, like Ray receive affirmation for the same choices. Then there are those, like Ian, who struggle to explain that their interests do not fit the common assumption

---

1. James, *Varieties*, "Lecture 3," 61.

39

that psychology is only about counseling. Many students who take their faith seriously are often unsure how their academic interests relate to Christianity. Students like Ray, Pam, and Ian may all be committed Christians, but their churches epitomize very different reactions to psychology. The reactions of various branches of the church to psychology reflect the broader issue of the relationship of Christianity and science that we considered in the last chapter, but they also reflect a more specific issue, the overlapping interest of both theology and psychology in the nature and functioning of human beings.

As we saw in the last chapter, a Christian worldview that pictures the universe as an orderly creation that reflects God's glory and power is uniquely conducive to scientific inquiry. At the very least, people like Ian can recognize that when they study human behavior, they are studying God's creation. Beyond this, applied areas of psychology and Christianity share many insights and areas of concern. Christianity embodies a redemptive calling that includes ministering to the tangible needs of suffering people. Given the redemptive focus of a Christian worldview, one might expect that Christians would see psychology in a positive light. To some degree, this has been the case. In fact, just as Christianity may have laid the groundwork for the development of science, the culture of American Protestantism may have been an impetus to the development of American psychology.[2]

However, as we will see in this chapter, the ways that various branches of Christianity have engaged psychology have been quite diverse and intense.

One of the reasons that the interactions between psychology and Christianity are so intense is that they both make claims about what it means to be human, and about the avenues by which human ills can be cured. The closer one gets to considering psychotherapeutic and pastoral concerns, the greater the common ground and the greater the possibility for conflict. As Browning and Evison observe, "from the moment modern psychiatry emerged as a distinct profession, psychiatry and religion have overlapped and at times overtly competed. The reason for this is clear: both seek to heal forms of brokenness that stand on the ambiguous borderline between body and what is variously referred to as 'psyche' or 'spirit.'"[3]

In this chapter we will focus on the historical relationship of psychology and Christianity, and some of the points of overlap, cooperation, and tension that have emerged.

The Psychology before Psychology

As most introductory psychology textbooks will attest, psychology as a science began in 1879. Long before then, however, people thought about human behavior. Prior to the Enlightenment, psychology

---

2. Spilka, Religion and science.

3. Browning & Evison, Introduction, 3–4.

was a subfield of philosophy. Religion and medicine were also concerned with human nature. Insights about human character, whether rooted in philosophy, religion, medicine, or folk wisdom, often proved to be quite insightful, and many of these insights are still relevant today.

> Long before psychology emerged as a scientific discipline, questions about mind and behavior were considered by philosophy, religion, medicine, and folk wisdom. Although we now define psychology as a science, it is inevitably bound to questions that are metaphysical as well as empirical in nature.

When we turn our attention from human nature in general to the treatment of mental illness in particular, we find that the church was the prime vehicle for the care of the *soul* (psyche) in the Western world for most of the past two millennia. Gradually governments established asylums to house seriously mentally ill people, and the medical profession was given responsibility for their treatment. Often, asylums were quite inhumane, and treatments were typically ineffective.

Although there have been occasions when the church taught that demon possession or witchcraft was responsible for mental disturbances, these episodes are not representative of its larger teaching about or treatment of the mentally ill. Historically, the church has often been a force that advocated humane treatment and reform. St. Basil (329–380) established a monastery in Caesarea where mental patients received humane care, based on the notion that Christianity compels us to render care to others. Similar monasteries were founded by St. Jerome (343–420) in Bethlehem and St. Benedict (480–543) in Monte Cassino, and other monasteries cared for displaced people, many of whom were mentally ill. The Gheel Shrine in Belgium was founded in 1215 by devout Roman Catholics who implored St. Dymphna for "relief and consolation to all who suffer" from mental illness. To this day people with mental illnesses take pilgrimages to the shrine, and citizens of Gheel welcome them into their homes.[4]

Christians were often at the forefront of the movement to develop hospitals to care for mentally ill people. In 1410 a group of concerned citizens in Valencia, Spain, led by Father Juan Gilabert Jofré, a Mercedarian friar, opened the first mental asylum in Europe.[5] In the late Middle Ages, governments began to create asylums, but most of them were cruel, inhumane prisons where patients were shackled to the walls and floors. Some of the asylums, like St. Mary of Bethlehem,

---

4. Koenig, *Faith and mental health.*

5. Villasante & Dening, *The unfulfilled project.* However, it should be noted that humane asylums were probably founded in Muslim societies prior to this time; see Campbell, *Arabian medicine.*

began charging admission fees to people who could entertain themselves by watching the "lunatics" in their chains.

Humanitarian reforms were carried out by devout Christians such as Phillipe Pinel in France. Pinel, a Roman Catholic, had studied theology before settling on a career in medicine. The reforms that he instituted while he was the superintendent of the Salpêtrière and the Bicêtre asylums began a movement to provide humane care to the mentally ill throughout Europe. In England, William Tuke visited a fellow Quaker who later died in squalid conditions in York Asylum. Appalled by the conditions of the asylum, he appealed to his religious group to establish a mental hospital where the mentally ill could receive humane care. As a result of his appeal, he opened the York Retreat for the Humane Care of the Insane in 1796, where "restraint and abuse were replaced by kindness and tolerance."[6] This was the first private mental hospital in England, and new methods of treating the mentally ill were pioneered in a humane and caring environment.

In North America, Quakers founded Friends Hospital in Philadelphia in 1709. One of the buildings, completed in 1756, was specifically designed for the insane.[7] Several decades later Thomas Scattergood, another Quaker, visited the York Retreat and later traveled to America where he appealed to the Philadelphia Yearly Meeting to establish a similar facility "for such of our members as may be deprived the use of their reason."[8] In 1812 the Meeting appointed seven men to establish a self-sufficient asylum. Five years later, Friends Asylum opened its doors on a 58-acre farm where humane care was offered in buildings with ample windows, and where patients could walk freely among tree-lined paths and perform useful work on the farm. Friends Asylum was the first freestanding treatment facility for the mentally ill in the United States and became a model for other institutions.

Protestant religious revivals in the Netherlands in the mid-nineteenth century led many reform-minded individuals to conclude that the Dutch Reformed Church had become too liberal, and that it "had neglected its Christian duty of an active evangelical life and relief of social distress" in favor of a highly rationalistic compromise with Enlightenment thinking.[9] A series of separations ensued, during which some of the reformers established a private Christian asylum for the care of the insane in 1886 named Veldwijk. When Dutch immigrants came to the United States, many of them settled in Michigan. In 1910, a group of pastors and laypersons from the Reformed Church in America and the Christian Reformed Church in America established a mental health facility in Grand Rapids, known today as Pine Rest Christian Mental Health Services. In addition

---

6. Zilboorg & Henry, *History of medical psychology,* 572.

7. Van Atta, Roby, & Roby, *Friends hospital.*

8. Ibid., n.p.

9. Boschma, *The rise of mental health nursing,* 54.

to its inpatient facility in Grand Rapids, Pine Rest now operates twenty-two satellite offices throughout Michigan and Iowa, all of which exist to "express the healing ministry of Jesus Christ by providing behavioral health services with professional excellence, Christian integrity, and compassion."[10]

Christians from the Anabaptist tradition also have a pronounced, though less well-known, history of providing humane care for the mentally ill. The Mennonites established Bethania Hospital in Russia in 1910; Bethesda Hospital in Ontario, Canada, in 1932; and Hoffnungsheim in Paraguay in 1945, all for the care of the mentally ill. Following World War II, the Mennonite Central Committee formed a work group, which eventually became Mennonite Mental Health Services, which in turn established an association of eight Mennonite mental health facilities in the United States.[11]

Christian individuals, as well as Christian denominations, exerted a positive influence on the care of the mentally ill. Benjamin Rush, a Presbyterian, was a major figure in mental-health reform in the United States, as well as a medical doctor and signer of the Declaration of Independence.[12] He was an early advocate of moral treatment of the insane. In 1812 he published the first medical textbook on mental illness in the United States: *Medical Inquiries and Observations*

upon the Diseases of the Mind. Thomas Story Kirkbride, a Quaker, was a founding member (and later president) of the Association of Medical Superintendents of American Institutions for the Insane (which eventually became the American Psychiatric Association). He authored the Kirkbride Plan, which sought to create humane standards for treatment of the mentally ill and to design institutions that were aesthetically pleasing, in which care was provided in a comfortable environment.[13]

Not only has the church promoted humane care for people who suffer from mental illness, it has also created theological models to understand their suffering and pastoral interventions to minister to those who suffer. Across the past two millennia, pastoral concern for people who suffer from mental illness prompted the creation of a theological understanding of human nature and functioning, which in turn invested a counseling ministry to church leaders. "Pastoral theology began as an incidental discipline . . . Theological reflection on pastoral ministry appears to have developed in response to needs that emerged in the coming together of human concerns within the context of the development of Christianity amidst the wider social and political world setting of the early church."[14]

The insights of the desert fathers, of Gregory of Nazianzus, John Chrysostom, Cassian, Augustine, Thomas Aquinas, and many others still provide a rich

---

10. Pine Rest Christian Mental Health Services, Organizational history.

11. Neufeld, *If we can love*.

12. Butcher, et al., *Abnormal psychology*.

13. Tomes, *The art of asylum keeping*.

14. Purves, *Pastoral theology*, 5.

resource for pastoral care. "Clearly, the healing of souls (and what we now call counseling) was central to the mission of the church long before modern psychotherapy came on the scene."[15] The rich tradition of pastoral care is valuable, and much of it can be recovered and used in contemporary pastoral care.[16]

"Mental disease is no different [from] bodily disease, and Christianity demands of the humane and powerful to protect, and the skillful to relieve the one as well as the other."

—St. Vincent de Paul, 1581–1660

How might Christianity have been an impetus to reform movements in the care of the mentally ill?

In summary, long before modern psychology emerged in the mid-nineteenth century, profound insights into human behavior were made by philosophers, medical practitioners, and theologians, among others. Christianity, in particular, often promoted humane and

compassionate care for distressed people. However, as scientific psychology emerged, some beliefs about human nature that were rooted in philosophy, religion, and folk wisdom did not mesh well with modern psychological views. Tensions also arose because the responsibility of caring for troubled individuals gradually passed from the church to secular professionals, a situation that continues to have repercussions today. The reactions of various segments of the church to modern psychology has a complex history, and to understand these reactions we must begin by looking at the founding of psychology as a science, and the establishment of psychotherapy as a method of treatment.

From Leipzig to Vienna

Ask most people what they think of in response to the word *psychology* and the image of a patient on the couch with a cigar-smoking psychoanalyst nearby is probably not far out of mind. Modern psychology traces its origins, though, not to Sigmund Freud's Vienna, but to 1879 and the establishment of the Psychologisches Institut, Wilhelm Wundt's laboratory in Leipzig, Germany. The fledgling discipline apparently attracted little attention from the religious community. Wundt's laboratory simply studied psychological phenomena—such as visual perception, attentional processes, reaction times, and so forth—using scientific methods.

Wundt's approach was novel, even controversial, academically. From

---

15. Johnson & Jones, A history of Christians in psychology, 17.

16. Purves does an excellent job of demonstrating how to reclaim this rich tradition. Likewise, Roberts argues that much of this "Christian psychology" should be sought out and reclaimed by Christian psychology. See Purves, *Pastoral theology*; and Roberts, Christian psychology view.

Aristotle onward, psychology had been a metaphysical discipline.[17] Wundt, while not denying the importance of metaphysics, argued that questions about the nature and purpose of life could not be decisively answered by philosophy. Instead, he proposed, psychology should follow the paradigm of the natural sciences and utilize the experimental method to explore the workings of the mind. "As soon as the psyche is viewed as a natural phenomenon," he wrote, "and psychology as a natural science, the experimental methods must also be capable of full application to this science."[18] Thus Wundt established psychology as an experimental enterprise.[19]

As we saw in the previous chapter, much of Christendom saw science as a noble and godly calling. Johannes Müller, the physiologist who paved the way for experimental psychology, was a devout Roman Catholic.[20] Wundt himself was the son of a Lutheran pastor,[21] as was Gustav Fechner, the founder of psychophysics.[22] Several notable pioneers in the fledgling field of psychology likewise hailed from the families of ministers including Edward Thorndike,[23] whose father was a Methodist minister, and Ivan Pavlov, whose father was a Russian Orthodox priest.[24] Numerous other psychologists came from religious families.[25]

Little is known about the reception these early psychologists received from the religious community.[26] Most text-

----

17. As a metaphysical discipline, psychology had been the domain of philosophers, and was advanced on purely rational grounds and *a priori* assumptions. Wundt, influenced by German philosophical realists (who had been influenced by Locke, Hume, and Comte) sought to build the foundations of empirical psychology on observable phenomena alone, and largely rejected metaphysical speculation; "for the present there can be no question of setting up comprehensive metaphysical systems which, like those that have just gone down, must seem to the next generation phantastic illusions rather than works of science" (Wundt, Philosophy in Germany, 518).

18. Wundt, Contributions, 70.

19. Psychology functions as a science only so long as it uses the scientific method in application to its subject. As soon as it considers metaphysical questions, it returns to being a philosophical enterprise. Thus it stands on the border of science and philosophy, leaning one way or the other depending on the question at hand and the means by which the question is considered.

20. Misiak & Staudt, *Catholics in psychology*, 20.

21. Hunt, *The story of psychology*, 131.

22. Ibid., 123.

23. Ibid., 246.

24. Ibid., 248.

25. Note, though, that such an observation is correlational. While religiosity and later psychological pursuits may have co-occurred, the case may sometimes have been that faith supported those pursuits (William James may well fit this paradigm), that the two merely co-existed, or that the individual's psychological pursuits were in part a reaction *against* religious faith (as was perhaps the case for Sigmund Freud). In many cases the relationship may have been complex; for example, Carl Rogers's views are likely both rooted in selected values of his Protestant upbringing *and* a reaction against the authoritarianism of his mother's fundamentalism. It is also remarkable that so many of the pioneers of the clinical psychology movement were of Jewish ancestry. For an excellent summary of Judaism and psychology, see Kepnes, Jewish response.

26. The reactions of Roman Catholic schol-

books, if they deal with the subject at all, simply see religious thinking as something that had to be overcome in order for science to become established, although, as was demonstrated in the last chapter, that viewpoint is highly suspect. Nonetheless, the surviving echoes of whatever dialogue there was between this early psychology and the church are generally of a suspicious and oppositional nature.[27]

Wundt's approach, admirable as it was, ran into a cul-de-sac of methodological problems.[28] Meanwhile, debates

in France about the nature of hypnosis and Freud's pioneering work on hysteria in Vienna began to lay claim to an applied science of psychology.[29] It is at this point that religious voices, both for and against the fledgling field of psychology, still echo in the tones of modern conversation.

As psychology moved from psychophysics to psychopathology, it seemingly encroached on theology's domain, the soul. In what ways might the new secular science of psychology and psychotherapy appear to have been a threat to religious views of health and healing?

It is interesting to ask why the discourse began in earnest in France and Vienna rather than in Leipzig. Part of the answer may be that the work of Wundt and his colleagues was simply about *how* the mind worked; sensation, perception, reaction time, and attentional processes were the core concerns of Wundt's laboratory. These concerns seemed

---

ars are better preserved than the reactions of Protestant scholars, probably due to the more cohesive nature of Roman Catholicism and the fact that its adherents are both more numerous and situated in a more hierarchical system than are members of other denominations.

27. Misiak and Staudt noted that early opposition to experimental psychology by Catholic scholars was usually rooted more in a preference for the maintenance of the status quo of philosophical psychology than to outright religious objections. However, as early as 1891, Father Masionneuve saw psychology as the enemy of Christianity, and in 1894, Father Hughes stated that the new psychology was incompatible with Christian faith. These objections are noteworthy because they precede later objections to clinical psychology and are a direct assault on the legitimacy of studying psychological phenomena experimentally. Still other Catholic scholars came to appreciate and contribute to the new discipline of psychology.

28. As David Myers noted, psychology, in its struggle to define itself, began under Wundt as "the science of mental life," became "the scientific study of observable behavior" during the behaviorist revolt (1920–1960), and today reclaims both domains as "the science of behavior and mental processes" (Myers, *Psychology*, 5–6).

29. Reaction against Freud's ideas came from a variety of sources, including from rival psychological views, and philosophical and religious objections. Not to be discounted, though, was the general anti-Semitic fervor of the times. Self-described as a "godless Jew" (by which Freud meant that he was culturally Jewish but a practicing atheist), Freud was condemned for his atheistic views, and as a Jew, he suffered as a result of widespread anti-Semitic prejudice and discrimination.

inconsequential to theology; Wundt merely looked at how God had put the machinery of the mind together. However, when Charcot opened the door to the unconscious mind in treating patients, and Freud claimed to have elucidated its darkest secrets, the role of the church in healing the soul diminished, and the moral teachings of the church appeared to be threatened.[30] As psychology moved from psychophysics to psychopathology, it seemingly encroached on theology's domain, the soul.

The nature of moral concern within the religious community toward Freudian ideas was based partly on a misreading and misapplication of Freud's findings. Freud's belief that psychopathology was caused by anxiety-motivated repression was popularly misconstrued as a tacit recommendation to rid ourselves of our inhibitions and unleash our darker impulses.[31] Yet a fair reading

of Freud clearly indicates that he was attempting to *describe* what he observed in the free associations of his patients, rather than to *sanction* the contents as something to celebrate. Even so, the images that emerged were dark, frightening, and incestuous—in a word, sinful. The church was thus in the position of either having to deny that such evils ubiquitously lurk in the hearts of humankind, or to see psychoanalysis as a means of exposing and dealing with these evils. Yet even if psychoanalysis was embraced, there remained the very real danger that it would become the new religion of society, and confession would become the domain of its practitioners rather than of the clergy.

Christian Responses to Psychotherapy

The Christian response to science was not a monolithic one, and the same is true of its response to the rise of psychotherapy. In fact, to a large degree, the responses of the various elements of the church to science are mirrored by their respective responses to psychotherapy. Roman Catholics generally moved from their initial suspicion of psychology to engaging psychotherapy while putting constraints upon it. Liberal and neo-orthodox factions tended to embrace psychotherapy, while fundamentalist factions tended to

---

30. While the church has a long and rich history of pastoral care, it must be admitted that little healing came from these methods where serious psychopathology was involved. While rare, the occasional detours into exorcism further diminished regard for pastoral interventions. By the mid-nineteenth century, care for the mentally ill had largely passed to the government asylums and to families, who have always shouldered the bulk of such burdens. In later collaboration with the new psychotherapies, the pastoral-care tradition was reenergized under luminaries such as Anton Boisen, and expressed in programs like the Emmanuel movement. It continues to have significant influence today in Clinical Pastoral Education and seminary programs in pastoral care and pastoral counseling.

31. C. S. Lewis was aware of this misconception when he wrote that the common under-

standing of psychoanalysis left the impression that "the sense of Shame is a dangerous and mischievous thing" (Lewis, *The problem of pain*, 50).

see the new field as something to be defended against. The reaction of evangelicalism to psychology has been divided, with one faction favoring openness, and one mirroring fundamentalist rejection. Thus the intensity of the issue within evangelical circles has often been greater than that found within other segments of Christianity, as we shall see.[32]

Catholic Responses

Angelo Roncalli was born in Italy on November 25, 1881, to parents who were poor farmers and devout Catholics. The young Angelo chose to enter seminary and become a priest. His priesthood was interrupted by World War I, during which he served in the medical corps and later as a chaplain. He spent World War II as an archbishop in Istanbul, and later in France, seeking to heal the damage of war to people of various faiths.[33] Roncalli was theologically conservative yet thoroughly engaged in a modern world. When Pius XII died in 1958, Roncalli surfaced as a compromise candidate for pontiff and was elected by the College of Cardinals on October 28, 1958. Pope John XXIII,

as Angelo chose to be called, "knew the modern world, and was not afraid of it."[34] Early in his pontificate, John XXIII convened an ecumenical council, known today as the Second Vatican Council, or Vatican II, which ushered in momentous changes for Roman Catholics—most tangibly seen in the change from the Latin Mass to the presentation of Eucharist in the vernacular languages of the world.

Psychology emerged as a science and as a form of intervention in a pre–Vatican II world, in which Catholic doctrine was set in opposition to the philosophy of modernism. The Second Vatican Council sought to adapt the Church to a culture inhabited by people who had inherited a modernist world of technological and scientific advancement, but in which they lived in fear of nuclear war, religious conflict, and interpersonal alienation. The Church seemed to many to be out of step with the times. Having dealt with such issues personally, John XXIII desired for his Church to engage the modern world. John XXIII died of cancer in 1963 and did not live to see the results of what he initiated.

Vatican II produced sixteen official documents that profoundly shaped the way the Catholic Church today views itself and its relation to the world. One of its core documents was the *Pastoral Constitution on the Church in the Modern World*, known more commonly as *Gaudium et Spes* ("Joy and Hope"). *Gaudium et Spes* fundamentally altered Roman Catholicism by calling for ecumenical

---

32. Not surprisingly, the heat of the argument is often directly proportional to the passions one has about the issues under discussion. The other major factor in determining the intensity of arguments is the relational propinquity to the person with whom one is arguing—family arguments tend, after all, to be passionate and enduring.

33. For a detailed biography of Roncalli, from which this information was obtained, see Brusher, *Popes through the ages*.

---

34. Duffy, *Saints & sinners*, 355.

healing and social engagement. The changes inaugurated by Vatican II have had direct implications for the relationship of Catholicism and psychology.

Prior to Vatican II, the primary response of Catholicism to psychology—both experimental and clinical—was antagonistic in nature, with some notable exceptions.[35] Some Catholic thinkers were not opposed to biological insights into psychopathology, but most were strongly opposed to psychoanalysis, to the extent that its use was considered to be a mortal sin.[36] Even prior to Vatican II some Catholics were open to both clinical and experimental psychology, but the climate following Vatican II became much more conducive to such openness.[37] Yet this openness was not a blanket endorsement. Roman Catholic theologians were especially concerned to redress the negative portrayal of religion by many psychological theorists, to affirm the essential spiritual nature of humanity, to reassert the proper place of morality and sexuality, and to counter the determinism of scientific reductionism and psychoanalysis with an appreciation of the human capacity for self-determination.[38] This approach constituted a constructive foundation whereby Catholicism could make use of the insights of psychology while using theology to reorient its direction and rectify its shortcomings.

The use of psychology, construed within a Catholic framework, can be directly seen in the following quotation from *Gaudium et Spes*.

> Although the Church has contributed much to the development of culture, experience shows that, for circumstantial reasons, it is sometimes difficult to harmonize culture with Christian teaching. These difficulties do not necessarily harm the life of faith, rather they can stimulate the mind to a deeper and more accurate understanding of the faith. The recent studies and findings of science, history and philosophy raise new questions which affect life and which demand new theological investigations . . . In pastoral care, sufficient use must be made not only of theological principles, but also of the findings of the secular sciences, especially of psychology and sociology, so that the faithful may be brought to a more adequate and mature life of faith. [39]

To be sure, not all Catholics heralded this rapprochement with joy, and the results of Vatican II continue to be controversial within the Roman Catholic Church today. Nonetheless, it paved the way for a dialogue between Catholic theology and a host of other disciplines, including psychology, and resulted in a mass of integrative work.[40]

---

35. Misiak & Staudt, *Catholics in psychology*.

36. McCarthy, Roman Catholic perspectives.

37. For an excellent history of the topic, see Gillespie, *Psychology and American Catholicism*.

38. See McCarthy, ibid., 46–49.

---

39. Paul VI, *Gaudium et spes*, section 5, ¶3.

40. Several Catholic clergy and laity have written eloquently on psychological topics, in-

Liberal and Neo-orthodox Responses

Liberal and neo-orthodox Christian theologies, given their interest in healing the here-and-now conditions of human suffering, saw in the emerging psychotherapies a powerful ally. "The response of the mainline Protestant churches to the emergence of psychiatry in the United States has been basically favorable."[41] This openness, notes Browning, was a two-way street, encompassing psychologists, such as William James, and theologians, such as Anton Boisen, Paul Tillich, and Reinhold Niebuhr, among others. The response of the theologians, though, was not to swallow the psychotherapeutic enterprise whole. Rather, they sought to assimilate its useful resources and findings, while restraining and correcting elements that they saw as errant or overreaching. This dialogue was both theological and philosophical in nature. As Browning astutely argued, "The [mainline] Protestant response to psychiatry never advanced its case on strictly scriptural or theological grounds. It developed its views always in conjunction with some larger philosophical stance that cleared space, in more neutral philosophical terms, for the possibility of the religious and ethical visions typical of [mainline] Protestant Christian views of life. American philosophical pragmatism

and Continental existential-phenomenology constituted the two principal philosophical sources."[42]

This approach allowed for recognition that biological, behavioral, and psychodynamic aspects of human experience are intimately involved in spirituality. For example, without denying the validity of religious experience, it became possible to acknowledge that social and environmental factors are involved in shaping religious experiences.[43] Likewise, it allowed for dialogue between Protestant theology and other disciplines without resulting in theological reductionism.

While such a détente between mainline Protestantism and the emerging psychotherapies encouraged the theological application of the secularly derived healing arts to religious ends, the relationship came at a cost. In the words of James Wind, "many practitioners of pastoral care quietly (and perhaps unknowingly) shifted their goal from salvation to self-realization."[44] This concern continues to be echoed by those who follow pastoral counseling education today.[45] Yet one

---

cluding William Meissner, Ana-Maria Rizzuto, John McDargh, Adrian Van Kaam, and popularizers such as Henri Nouwen.

41. Browning, *Protestant response*, 21.

42. Ibid., 19.

43. As a pragmatic response, this approach allowed for the rise of the psychology of religion, pioneered by William James.

44. Wind, *Enemies or fellow travelers*, 94

45 As Purves astutely observed, "the history of pastoral care in North America is marked precisely by the movement away from the concern for salvation to the concern for self-realization. This shift represents a serious problem. On the one hand, evangelism is cut off from pastoral work, with the result that it is pushed out to the margins of ministry . . . On the other hand, pastoral work itself without an evangelistic impera-

must not conclude from this concern that the approach is wholly without merit. Rather, one must take care to guard the riches of the Christian faith and calling while engaging the world of our larger culture.

The openness of mainline Protestants to psychology lies in sharp contrast to the reactions of the fundamentalists, who occupied the opposite side of the fundamentalist–modernist controversy. "Compared with conservatives (or fundamentalists), liberal Protestants (or modernists) appear to have been much more open to reflecting on the relation of psychology and the faith."[46] Because modern evangelicalism largely arose out of the fundamentalist reaction to modernism, its reactions to psychology have typically been more guarded and gradual than that of its liberal counterpart.

Evangelical Critiques of Psychology and Integration

In the previous chapter, we noted that evangelicalism is a broad kaleidoscope of Christian traditions and that most of these traditions were shaped by the fundamentalist–modernist controversy of the late nineteenth and early twentieth centuries. The fundamentalist constituency of this movement generally responded to psychology much as it responded to the challenges posed by scientific controversies. Fundamentalists have understandably opposed teachings of isolated psychologists that are at odds with their doctrinal positions. However, rather than limiting their response to specific areas of conflict, they typically opposed the entire field of psychology. Furthermore, in an effort to protect what they perceived as theological orthodoxy, they were very critical of Christians who did not share their distrust of psychology.

Fundamentalism is characterized by an anti-intellectual, anti-social action, and anti-ecumenical stance.[47] Due to its disengagement from liberal-arts education, most fundamentalist critiques fail to address the actual content and source of psychological research or theories. Instead, these critiques reflect biblicism in which church dogma is an unassailable front from which to attack secular, humanistic, modernist, and postmodernist theories. In what is sometimes referred to as the Great Reversal,[48] fundamentalists withdrew from social concerns in the early 1900s, partly because their primary interest was evangelization, and partly because the liberal elements of the church had adopted a social gospel and embraced psychotherapy as a means of ministering to social needs. Thus psychology as a science ran afoul of the fundamentalist disengagement from the intellectual world, and

---

tive, becomes trivialized, concerned increasingly only with care and not with salvation. Pastoral care loses its soteriological and eschatological goal." Purves, *Pastoral theology*, 89–90. See also Holifield, *A history of pastoral care*.

46. Johnson & Jones, A history of Christians in psychology, 32.

---

47. Webber, *The younger evangelicals*, 26–30.

48. Ibid., 29–30; Moberg, *The great reversal.*.

psychotherapy as a treatment method held no interest for fundamentalists because of their withdrawal from social concerns and their lack of interest in collaborating with Christians outside of their own doctrinal fold.

Prior to the 1920's, evangelicals played major roles in social reform in England and the United States, promoting prison reform, humane treatment of the mentally ill, improved working conditions, child labor laws, programs to alleviate poverty and homelessness, efforts to prevent the exploitation of women, and campaigns to point out the negative consequences of alcoholism. In what historians call *the Great Reversal*, evangelicals reacted against the social gospel by abandoning social concerns and focusing almost exclusively on evangelism and missions. But the gospel always sees proclamation of the good news intertwined with concern for tangible human needs.

Evangelical reactions to psychology reflect the diversity of evangelicalism itself. The conservative, fundamental factions usually reject psychology out of hand. Those elements of evangelicalism that have become pro-intellectual, pro-social action, and pro-ecumenical are generally more open to the insights and uses of psychology, but are often characterized by cautious engagement and critique. The evangelical response to psychology can thus be seen as extremely divided. Since it is the division within the evangelical camp—for and against integration—that has occupied much of the integration literature, it is to this division that we will now turn our attention.

Evangelicalism can be credited with pouring tremendous energy into the integration of psychology and Christianity, with several APA-accredited training programs in psychology hosted by evangelical universities,[49] two major journals dedicated to the integration of psychology and theology,[50] and two major Christian professional organizations for individuals in psychology or counseling fields.[51] While some of these efforts originated from liberal Christians, and others stemmed from more conservative Christians, the bulk of these integrative efforts

---

49. The first four explicitly Christian doctoral programs in psychology are currently part of Fuller Seminary, Biola University, George Fox University, and Wheaton College. (Biola absorbed Rosemead School of Psychology in 1977, which had previously been a freestanding institution. Similarly, in 1990, George Fox absorbed a doctoral program in psychology from Western Baptist Seminary.)

50. *The Journal of Psychology and Theology* and *The Journal of Psychology and Christianity*.

51. *Christian Association for Psychological Studies* and *American Association of Christian Counselors*.

have come from solidly evangelical individuals. However, a compelling case can be made that most of the anti-integration critiques have also come from evangelical individuals.[52]

Evangelical interests in psychology, focusing primarily on insights from clinical psychology, began reaching out to the broader Christian community in the form of radio programs (featuring Clyde Narramore) and popular books (by Don Tweedie and Paul Tournier) in the 1950s and 1960s.[53] These efforts soon mushroomed in the 1970s with publications and radio programs by evangelical Christian psychologists (such as James Dobson, Gary Collins, Bruce Narramore, and Larry Crabb). Many parishioners had questions about marital issues, child-drearing, depression, and other concerns addressed by evangelical psychologists who tried to provide practical advice based on Christian teachings and modern psychology.

The popularization of psychology for evangelicals received a divided response. Some saw in these approaches wise counsel and a salve for emotionally wounded people. Others saw this movement as having sold the evangelical birthright for a secular bowl of pottage. Chief among these critics was Jay Adams. In his second major work, Adams directly challenged all nonministerial approaches to counseling.

> Biblically, there is no warrant for acknowledging the existence of a separate and distinct discipline called psychiatry. There are, in the Scriptures, only three specified sources of personal problems in living: demonic activity (principally possession), personal sin, and organic illness . . . All options are covered under these heads, leaving no room for a fourth: non-organic mental illness. There is, therefore, no place in a biblical scheme for the psychiatrist as a separate practitioner.[54]

Adams proceeded to insist that the only place psychiatry legitimately exists is as a medical profession treating organic illness (e.g., brain injuries and dementia). Counseling interventions of any type were exclusively claimed for the domain of the church, and within it, entrusted only to those ordained to Christian ministry.[55]

The debate within the evangelical community about the place of psychology as a clinical method remains virtually unchanged, except new names have gradually begun to replace those of the old guard.[56] A stalemate of sorts

---

52. As the term is used by most historians, the term *evangelical* includes those who retain fundamentalist stances, and many—but not all—of the anti-integration critiques come from the fundamentalist side of evangelicalism.

53. Johnson & Jones, A history of Christians in psychology.

54. Adams, *Christian counselor's manual*, 9.

55. In the fundamentalist tradition, the pastorate is limited to men, and hence only men can perform counseling. Some conservative groups allow women to counsel women.

56. While the debate remains virtually unchanged, anecdotal evidence suggests that

has emerged, in which evangelical practitioners of psychology continue to grow in number and publish articles and books, while largely ignoring the polemical attacks of those evangelicals and fundamentalists who vocally oppose their commitments and efforts. We will return to this topic in a later chapter.

Critiquing Psychological Naturalism and Positivism

Before we turn our attention away from these broad currents in how Christians have responded to psychology, it is important to comment on the pervasive naturalism and positivism that characterized much of twentieth-century psychology. In its quest for natural explanations, many psychologists not only avoided supernatural claims, but also belittled those who believed in supernatural agency. For liberal and neo-orthodox Christians, this was unproblematic, since they had already made compromises with modernism in the wake of Darwinian theory. For evangelical Christians, however, a rejection of supernaturalism is a rejection of Christian orthodoxy. As we will see later, it is important to distinguish between *methodological naturalism* and *philosophical naturalism*, but at this point, we simply want to acknowledge

that the naturalistic assumptions embedded in much of psychology are problematic for evangelicals.

A related issue involves the positivistic assumptions that characterized much of twentieth-century psychology. Failing to recognize their own philosophical assumptions, many secular psychologists embraced the scientific method as the *only* legitimate, or at least the *most reliable*, method for pursuing knowledge. At best such a stance makes religious belief a curiosity; at worst it makes such belief untenable.

Slife and Reber note that the naturalistic assumptions held by most psychologists create an implicit, unacknowledged, and perhaps unconscious bias against theism in psychological research and theories.[57] Naturalistic assumptions can thus lead researchers and clinicians to fail to take a theistic worldview seriously. Researchers who presume that naturalistic theories alone can completely explain religious phenomena will inevitably create reductionistic theories that undermine the reality of genuine spiritual experiences. In clinical practice, there is a danger that if a clinician assumes that there is no God, he or she may consider a client's experience of God as completely explicable in naturalistic terms. In this case, the clinician will treat the client's religious beliefs and experiences as nothing more than biological, psychological, and social constructions which lack any correspondence

---

many conservative churches are increasingly open to the insights of psychology. Thus while vehemently antipsychology rhetoric can still be readily found, it seems to be waning in influence except across a narrow portion of fundamentalism and conservative evangelicalism.

---

57. Slife & Reber, Pervasive bias against theism.

to reality. Consequently, the clinician subtly or overtly may attempt to undermine the client's beliefs.

> From a letter by Sigmund Freud to Oskar Pfister, Feb, 9, 1909. "I am very much struck by the fact that it never occurred to me how extraordinarily helpful the psycho-analytic method might be in pastoral work, but that is surely accounted for by the remoteness from me, as a wicked pagan, of the whole system of [religious] ideas."

Given these twin concerns, Christians who hold to an orthodox faith have found it imperative to critique many of the modernist assumptions that underlie much of secular psychology and to offer an alternative paradigm that can encompass empirical and non-empirical epistemic strategies.

Psychology and Religion: The View the Other Way

The history of psychology includes a few notable theorists who were interested in religion (such as Carl Jung, William James, and Gordon Allport), and many who were vocal opponents of religion (such as Sigmund Freud and Albert Ellis). Yet even many of the opponents of

religion were not as adamant or ardent in their opposition as is sometimes supposed. Sigmund Freud carried on a correspondence of several hundred letters over a twenty-eight-year period with Oskar Pfister, a Swiss pastor. Pfister became a popular guest in the Freud home. Recalling Pfister's visits, Anna Freud wrote: "In the totally non-religious Freud household Pfister, in his clerical garb and with the manners and behaviour of a pastor, was like a visitor from another planet . . . his human warmth and enthusiasm, his capacity for taking a lively part in the minor events of the day, enchanted the children of the household, and made him at all times a most welcome guest, a uniquely human figure in his way."[58] Certainly, not all such meetings between psychology and religion have been respectful or even dialogical, but Pfister and Freud at least model for us the respect and dialogue that can occur.[59]

Turning to the contemporary scene, it is well documented that clinical psychologists as a group are significantly less religious than the general population.[60] It is also well known that the views of many psychologists have historically

---

58. Anna Freud, in Meng and Freud, *Psychoanalysis and faith*, 11.

59. In honor of that dialogue, the American Psychiatric Association's Committee on Religion and Psychiatry, in conjunction with the Association of Professional Chaplains, confers the Oskar Pfister award to individuals who have made significant contributions to the relationship of psychiatry and religion.

60. Bergin & Jensen, Religiosity of psychotherapists.

been anti-religious. For the first half of the nineteenth century, religion was effectively a taboo topic in psychology except as an object of study (i.e., the psychology of religion). However, the past few decades have witnessed a resurgence of interest in spirituality among psychologists. Clinical psychologists increasingly acknowledge the importance of respecting the religious beliefs of clients and current research affirms the potential benefits of religious practices and religious communities for coping with life's difficulties.[61] Many modern psychoanalytic approaches are sympathetic toward spiritual and religious issues, and do not reflect the antagonism that characterized much of Freud's writings.[62] While the contemporary scene allows for more openness between psychology and religion, there are tensions that continue in the present.

Grist for the Mill, or Fuel for the Fire?

Christians should expect that non-Christians will not always be appreciative of Christianity and may sometimes be quite at variance with it. In part this response is simply the result of divergent perspectives, and in part it is a reaction to the real and perceived missteps of Christianity's encounter with other worldviews. For a well-constructed theology, such conflicts should be grist for the mill that stimulates further dialogue and thought. Unfortunately, such reactions sometimes become fuel for the fire, fomenting hostile conflagration rather than resulting in irenic and loving responses. For all the good it has to offer, psychology has, at times, embodied teachings that are an affront to Christian sensibilities. Many therapists adopt more liberal, less religious values than the general population or have little appreciation for spirituality in general; and some are outspoken critics of religious belief.[63] Yet the same could be said of practitioners of medicine or philosophy or history. The issue is not that those fields are inherently non-Christian, but that non-Christians in those fields sometimes believe, teach, and practice things that are at odds with Christian belief, doctrine, and practice. To expect otherwise would be unrealistic.

---

61. The American Catholic Psychological Association existed from 1948 to 1970. It reorganized as a more ecumenical group, Psychologists Interested in Religious Issues, in 1970. This became APA division 36 in 1975. The division was renamed Psychology of Religion in 1992. The most recent (2002) version of the American Psychological Association's *Ethical Principles of Psychologists and Code of Conduct* explicitly recognized the importance of understanding and being sensitive to religious diversity, and APA has recently published several books on religious diversity and spiritual issues in psychotherapy. Religious coping is also a focus of current research.

62. Sorenson, *Minding spirituality.*

---

63. See Cortés, Antecedents to the conflict between psychology and religion.

Summary

The dialogue between psychology and Christianity is a multifaceted one, shaped by historical interactions and tensions between science and Christianity, and developed in response to particular cultural and ecclesiastical concerns. The interaction of psychology and theology is virtually inevitable due to their mutual interest in understanding the ambiguities and mysteries of human behavior, and healing human brokenness. In certain times and places a spirit of cooperation has been evident, while at other times outright hostility has been vented from both sides. Each community, psychological and Christian, is often divided on how much, if any, dialogue should take place. Owing to the dominance of clinical psychology, and the pastoral interest in counseling, more dialogue and more confrontation has taken place at this level than any other, leaving relatively little interaction between nonclinical psychology and Christianity. Ultimately, these interactions are shaped not only by history, as we have seen, but by worldviews and philosophical commitments regarding the nature of knowledge, the nature of the world, and the nature of humanity, as we shall see successively in the next four chapters.

Questions for Reflection and Discussion

1. Recall the conversation between Pam, Ray, and Ian that opened this chapter. Has your own encounter with people from your church background been more similar to the experience of Pam, Ray, or Ian? How have you responded to such encounters? How might you respond to the scenarios that did not mirror your experience?

2. Think about your own background and your experience with people from various denominations. Were there obvious or subtle ways that revealed the views of psychology held by these groups of people? Do your observations fit the patterns discussed in the book (e.g., liberal openness, fundamental opposition)? Can you articulate historical and logical reasons for the pattern in which some denominations embrace and others oppose psychology?

3. The author noted that there were Christians who were suspicious of and opposed to the emergence of experimental psychology. The early experimentalists, like Wundt, dealt primarily with psychophysics and did not deal with metaphysical questions. In what way did their approach seem to threaten traditional theological formulations? Why did Christians of many denominations see the emergence of clinical psychology as a serious threat to the church?

4. Juan Luis Vives (1492–1540) was a Catholic philosopher from Spain and an early proponent of educating women. Vives, encouraging theology to engage philosophical psychology, wrote, "What the soul is, is of no concern for us; what it is like, what its manifestations are, is of very great importance."[64] By this, Vives meant that we cannot define the soul in strict terms, but it is important for us to know how it works in its psychological expressions. In what ways does Vives's statement create an opportunity for dialogue between theology and psychology?

5. As you consider the various reactions of Christians to psychology and psychotherapy, which reactions are most similar to your own? Which reactions are foreign to your way of thinking? Are there concerns voiced in some of the reactions that we should take seriously?

6. How did Vatican II change the nature of theological reflection and the ability for Catholic theology to enjoin other disciplines? How has the Catholic interface with psychology been similar to and different from that of other Christian traditions?

7. How do the reactions of the major traditions (liberal/neo-orthodox, Catholic, fundamentalist, and evangelical) to psychology relate to their reactions to science?

8. The author claims that compared to other Christian groups, evangelicals are more divided about the relationship of theology and psychology. Why might evangelicals be more divided on this issue? What factors in evangelical history and belief compel an interest psychology? What factors in evangelical history and belief have fostered opposition to psychology?

---

64. Quoted in Misiak & Staudt, *Catholics in psychology*, 13.

4

Windows on the World: Assumptions and Worldviews

You can learn a lot from people who view the world differently than you do.
—Anthony d'Angelo

It never occurred to me as a boy that our dinnertime conversations were at all unusual. I just figured that talking about bowel resections and metastatic cancer was what everyone talked about when they passed the mashed potatoes. Of course, not everyone grows up with a father who is a surgeon and a mother who is a nurse. My window on the world was a bit different from those of my peers, but just how different that window was I would only find out as I grew up.

When I was eleven years old my parents decided to spend a summer volunteering at a medical mission station in the country then known as Zaire. My mother had been born to missionary parents, in what was then the Belgian Congo, so it was a homecoming of sorts for her. Our time there would introduce me to a very different world. We left New York by plane, made a brief stop in Iceland, and continued on to Belgium. My uncle was a missionary in Brussels, so we spent some time visiting his family; and after seeing

a bit of Europe, we flew south from Amsterdam. Leaving Europe, we crossed the Mediterranean and traversed more than half the length of Africa before landing at Entebbe Airport near Kampala, Uganda. My mother and sisters all wore full-length dresses on this leg of the trip because a government warning had been issued, cautioning women not to let their knees be exposed. In those days of miniskirts, soldiers had recently shot several women for indecent exposure. In a country where topless women routinely breastfed their children in public, exposure of the thigh was seen as particularly inappropriate and sexually provocative.

Stanley Kline, a missionary, met us at the airport with his driver, who spoke nine languages fluently. After clearing customs and collecting our luggage, we piled into his Land Rover and began the long westerly trip to Zaire. Shortly after leaving Kampala, we left paved roads for a dirt highway that gradually gave way to narrower roads, while the landscape changed from hills to dense forest as we circled around the Ruwenzori Mountains. Whenever we passed another vehicle, which happened very infrequently, we learned to put our hands on the windshield so that it wouldn't crack too badly if we hit a rock that had been thrown into the air. We entered Zaire by putting the Land Rover on a log ferry and crossing the Semliki River while watching hippos lounge in the muddy waters. The rutted red dirt roads become bumpier and muddier, some no more than two tire tracks through the tall grass, and our speed necessarily became slower. Fourteen hours after leaving Kampala, we stopped in Rethy, where my mother had once attended boarding school, and a day later arrived in Nyankunde, a beautiful mission station where missionaries from many different mission organizations had founded Centre Médical Évangélique, a large training hospital where missionaries and nationals worked together to minister to the physical and spiritual needs of the people.

While we were in Nyankunde, a seven-year-old boy was brought to the hospital one day, covered with third-degree burns over most of his body. As had happened many times before, the boy had suddenly begun shaking and had fallen to the ground, but this time he rolled into the fire by his hut. No one would rescue him from the fire, out of fear that the demon that had attacked him would enter the rescuer as well. And so he waited, screamed, and burned. When his tremors stopped, he was taken to Centre Médical Évangélique, where our western doctors had a quite different explanation. The boy was an epileptic and had experienced a seizure. He was the first of two burn victims we saw that summer. The second was a ten-year-old boy whose mother had caught him stealing. She tied his hands together, poured gasoline on them, and set them on fire as punishment. The boy cried for his mother's comfort and forgiveness; his punishment was culturally sanctioned. All of his fingers were fused together, and, even with reconstructive surgery, his hands would remain badly deformed. Clearly, the people of his village had a very different window on the world than the one that I saw through.[1]

Worldviews: What Are They?

Everyone has a worldview—a window through which he or she views the world, framed by the assumptions and beliefs that color what he or she sees. According

---

1. Sadly, the peace and hope in which Nyankunde was founded in 1950 has been shattered by two civil wars—one in the early 1960s and again in 2002. Both times missionaries were evacuated from Nyankunde when it was threatened by violence; but the work of the hospital and the mission was carried on by local pastors and people who had been trained to provide basic medical care. On September 5, 2002, five thousand tribal warriors entered the village of seventeen thousand. Within an hour they killed over fifteen hundred people and looted and destroyed most of the buildings. The Christians in the village I once played in, following in the steps of many, many Jews and Christians over the centuries, began a new diaspora, spreading the gospel as they fled from their homes in loss, pain, and suffering.

to Wolters, "The term *worldview* came into the English language as a translation of the German *Weltanschauung*," which might loosely be translated as "life perspective" or "confessional vision." Worldviews are comprised of the "comprehensive framework of one's basic beliefs about things," or, in other words, the fundamental assumptions that undergird one's understanding of the world.[2] Worldviews shape how we understand our experience in the world, and reflect our expectations about life. As Walsh and Middleton note, "A world view, then, provides a model of the world which guides its adherents in the world. It stipulates how the world ought to be, and it thus advises how its adherents ought to conduct themselves in the world."[3]

Walsh and Middleton suggest that worldviews are built around the answers to four questions.[4] We might summarize these questions as follows:

1. What does it mean to be human? What are the characteristics of human nature? What is the purpose of human life? What duties, obligations, and responsibilities do human beings have?

2. What is the nature of the world?

3. What's wrong with the world, and why do things go wrong? Why does the world contain suffering and evil?

4. How can what is wrong with the world, and what is wrong with my life, be fixed? What gives meaning or hope to human existence?

Each of these questions will be addressed in future chapters of this book, but at this point we are interested in defining worldviews, looking at how they come to be, and why they are important to the topic of integration.

James Sire provided what may be the best definition of a worldview for the present purpose. You might think of it as almost an operational definition that will allow us to define the variables and conduct some experiments. "A worldview is a set of presuppositions, (assumptions which may be true, partially true or entirely false) which we hold (consciously or subconsciously, consistently or inconsistently) about the basic make-up of the world."[5]

To say that worldviews contain assumptions does not imply that these assumptions are unavailable to scrutiny; they can be evaluated and altered or discarded, to some degree. Our worldview assumptions are not always correct, and undoubtedly we each hold some worldview assumptions that are closer to being true, and others that widely miss the mark. Worldviews function somewhat like eyeglasses. If you wear glasses, you might remember how distracting the rims of the glasses were when you first wore them. In a short while, however, you lost your awareness of the rims and

---

2. Wolters, *Creation regained*, 2.

3. Walsh & Middleton, *Transforming vision*, 32.

4. Ibid., 35.

5. Sire, *The universe next door*, 16.

even the lenses. In the same way, world-views serve to focus what we see, but we are strangely ignorant that they exist as a filter between reality and ourselves. Given that they are an inevitable and constant part of our experience, we rarely think about them. We overlook our own worldviews because they are always present and because they make sense of our world. This, of course, underlines the difficulty we encounter in trying to examine our own worldviews.

A friend of mine and I once co-taught a Sunday school series on world-views as a means of helping ourselves to think critically about the assumptions we make. We wanted to evaluate the validity of our assumptions against the witness of Scripture, and we wanted to better understand people who hold different views of the world in order to allow us to engage in informed dialogue with them. My colleague, Pamm Ohlinger, showed a segment from the movie *The Truman Show* to kick off the class. Truman had been raised in a fabricated, self-contained world since his birth. All his experiences were manipulated by a director and tele-vised live; his family, friends, colleagues, and even his wife were merely members of the cast. How could Truman ever doubt that his world was real? It was all he knew. But things didn't always add up. Gradually, ever so gradually, Truman began to notice inconsistencies. He began to experiment with his world, and—little by little—he discovered that his world-view wasn't completely accurate.

We are all a bit like Truman. We tend to assume that the worldviews with which we were raised are correct. We rarely consider that the *Zeitgeist*[6] of our culture has had a major role in fashioning the lenses through which we perceive the world, and in shaping the way we act in it. The *Zeitgeist* of my world led me to expect that everyone in the world would converse with me in English, while the *Zeitgeist* of our African driver led him to acquire fluency in nine languages, because that is the norm in his multilingual tribal setting. When I was young it never occurred to me that my childhood dinner conversations were unusual, or that anyone would doubt a medical explanation for illness. It occurred to very few of the villagers in Zaire that seizures might be anything but the work of demons or that setting a child's hands on fire might be morally wrong. Left to ourselves, we typically assume that our worldviews are correct.

A Worldview Sampler[7]

The young burn victims that came to the hospital in Zaire came from a tribe that practiced a worldview known as *animism*. Animists believe that spirits inhabit the world and impose their wills

---

6. *Zeitgeist* means "the spirit of the times." Its focus is on *the assumptions typical of a particular culture at a particular historical era*; for instance, the assumption of many slave owners in the New World that slavery was an acceptable system sanctioned by Christianity.

7. The worldviews discussed here do not constitute an exhaustive list but are simply a representation of some of the more common worldviews.

upon it, although they can sometimes be placated with sacrifice. The villages where the boys came from had shamans who would try to cure illness or bless the endeavors of the tribe through ancient rituals and sacrifices. Even though Centre Médical Évangélique had been near the villages for many years, and even though many of the local people had been successfully treated there, the shaman was almost always called first when a physical problem occurred.

"Everyone has some kind of philosophy, some general worldview, which to men of other views will seem mythological."

—H. Richard Niebuhr, *Christ and Culture*

Many of the villagers adopted Christian beliefs, but without giving up their animistic beliefs; this is a phenomenon known as *syncretism*. Rather than changing worldviews, syncretists assimilate elements of a foreign worldview into their existing worldview. Thus many missionaries struggle with indigenous peoples who begin praying to Jesus while still worshiping ancestors or utilizing the services of the shaman. Worldviews do not often change easily or suddenly. Our initial reaction upon confronting a worldview different from our own is usually defensive. When worldviews collide, misunderstanding and condemnation are more likely than discernment—not to mention conversion.

A second major worldview is *polytheism*. Many people hold this worldview today, especially in nonindustrialized countries, and it was widely held by people in many ancient civilizations, such as the Greeks in New Testament times and the Egyptians and Canaanites in the period of the Old Testament. Rather than seeing a vast host of spirits as the cause of wind, death, or famine, as animists do, polytheists perceive a hierarchy of gods, each of whom is powerful in a limited domain. The gods can sometimes be played against one another or placated with sacrifice. The Homeric epics constantly set up Athena as a protector of Odysseus against Poseidon, and a draught of wine was never consumed without first "pouring the first drops into their cups, which they then poured onto the ground" as an offering to the gods.[8]

In east Asia, a prevailing worldview is *pantheism*, the belief that everything that exists is part of a great oneness, the one god that is Everything and is in everything. In this view, life is cyclical, with a never-ending succession of birth, death, and rebirth. In many versions of pantheism, reincarnation and assimilation into the grand narrative of the world are the presumed fate of all living objects. Alternatively, in some Eastern religions, our current existence is seen as an illusion that we may transcend through enlightenment and thereby merge into the oneness of the universe.

Animism, polytheism, and pantheism each represent obstacles to scientific

---

8. Homer, *Odyssey*, 84.

thinking. As long as one looks to demons, spirits, forces, and gods to explain the mundane workings of the world, no science can advance. Hippocrates (460–377 BCE), the "father of modern medicine," broke with his contemporaries by rejecting demonic explanations of illness. He believed that both mental and physical illness could be explained based on natural (biological) phenomena. While Hippocrates ushered in a new worldview, it was tied to a pre-Socratic cosmology. His understanding of human personality was thus limited to the categories of the four elements (earth, wind, fire, and water) and their corresponding bodily humors (black bile, yellow bile, phlegm, and blood).[9] Hippocrates's break with the prevailing worldview was incomplete, but it was a starting point from which biological and psychological factors could be considered.

A fourth major worldview is *monotheism*. There are three major monotheistic religions: Judaism, Christianity, and Islam. These religions share not only a common belief that there is only one God, but they also share elements of religious history and literature (for instance, sacred writings about the creation of Adam and Abraham). In all three religions, an all-powerful God is seen as the moving and sustaining force behind the world, and God is without peer. Nothing is seen as having existence that is not derivative from God or ultimately under God's control. Monotheism, while commonly celebrating the goodness of the material world, also holds that there is an immaterial world.

While Judaism, Christianity, and Islam are all monotheistic religions and thus hold a number of worldview assumptions in common, it must be noted that they are also unique from one another, and that each of these religions has various sects whose adherents view the world quite differently. Orthodox, Conservative, Reform, and Reconstructionist Jewish movements share the same Scriptures, but they interpret them in dissimilar ways and see the world and their place within it uniquely. Likewise, Sunni and Shi'a branches of Islam are quite distinct from each other. The same can be said of the many divisions of Christianity. Within all of these groups, local experience and history, political, and economic factors, and a host of other variables shape numerous variations of how the world is seen despite the broad, shared contours of monotheism.

You may recall that the rise of science represented a shift in how the world was understood and of the means through which knowledge was sought. This new worldview became known as *modernism*. Humanity came to see itself as enlightened, and the enlightened populace cast off the constraints of religion. The new worldview ushered in a *Zeitgeist*

---

9. The theory that personality is due to the balance of the four humors, while credited to Hippocrates, was an expansion and adaptation of the views of Empedocles (495–435 BCE). Evangelical author Tim LaHaye in his 1966 book, *Spirit-controlled temperament*, unfortunately resurrected the theory, despite its being nothing but a historical curiosity to contemporary personality researchers.

in which technological progress was widely expected to wipe out war, famine, and illness. The following claim—penned in 1890—is representative of the optimism expressed about modernism:

> Through it [Science] we believe that man will be saved from misery and degradation, not merely acquiring new material powers, but learning to use and to guide his life with understanding. Through Science he will be freed from the fetters of superstition; through faith in Science he will acquire a new and enduring delight in the exercise of his capacities; he will gain a zest and interest in life such as the present phase of culture fails to supply.[10]

These claims ultimately turned out to be hollow. Additionally, modernism embraced an overly optimistic belief in the human capacities for reason and objectivity.

Modernism generally failed to account for the enormous influence of assumptions and worldviews on human thinking. As Alister McGrath pointed out,

> One of the most influential myths of the modern period has been the belief that it is possible to locate and occupy a non-ideological vantage-point, from which reality may be surveyed and interpreted. The social sciences have been among the chief and most strident claimants to such space, arguing that they offer a neutral and objective reading of reality, in which the ultimately spurious truth claims of religious groupings may be deflated and deconstructed in terms of unacknowledged, yet ultimately determinative, social factors.[11]

Modernism's confidence in human objectivity, its unwarranted expectation of human progress, and its rejection of authority (and especially religious authority) are clearly problematic from a Christian standpoint. Because all observation is affected by ideology, integration must begin with the construction of a Christian worldview, which of course represents an appeal to authority. Integrationists affirm that Scripture provides unique and reliable information about the place of human beings (e.g., creation, sin, purpose, salvation, and ethics) that shape how the world should be understood. As a corollary, this necessitates that Christians not merely compare the results of psychology and theology, but that they also explore the underlying influence of assumptions and worldviews on our reasoning and conclusions.

Another assumption of modernism, and especially of empiricism, that we must analyze is the belief that truth claims needed to be independently verifiable. Since knowledge was construed in empirical terms (i.e., "it's true if you can show it to me"), claims about the existence of things that could not be seen were met with skepticism. On the one hand, the focus on empirical knowledge led to immense scientific progress. However, in

---

10. Lankester, Biology and the state, 108–9.

11. McGrath, *Nature*, 17.

an attempt to gain knowledge on rational and empirical grounds alone, modernism rejected all claims of miraculous events and supernatural causes.[12] Cautious skepticism about miraculous claims is, on the one hand, understandable. History is replete with examples of alleged miracles that have very natural explanations, such as a "demon-possessed boy" who actually had seizures. The worldview of the modernist, however, goes so far as to say that *only the material realm exists*, and hence, there is no God, gods, spirits, or nonmaterial forces, a view known as *atheistic materialism*.

Within the last several decades, another worldview, called *postmodernism*, emerged in opposition to modernism.[13]

---

12. Consider David Hume's argument that "no testimony for any kind of miracle has ever amounted to a probability, much less to a proof," and that the Christian who claims to believe a miracle "subverts all the principles of his understanding, and gives him a determination to believe what is most contrary to custom and experience" (Hume, The case against miracles, 41, 44). We will return to a discussion of the possibility of miracles in chapter 6.

13. The term *postmodernism* is an unfortunate one, owing to the fact that its immediate predecessor was called *modernism*; however awkward it may sound, that which follows modernity is, by definition, *post*-modernity. This creates an oxymoron; as Gaggi (1989) noted, "Modern is as new or recent as anything gets, and to declare anything in the present . . . postmodern is to embrace a term that is self-contradictory and, some would say, pretentious" (Gaggi, *Modern/postmodern*, 17). The name perhaps suggests that postmodernism stands less *for* any constructive proposal, than it stands *against* that to which it objects. Despite the unfortunate term for this position, its critique is

Postmodernism is a reaction against several modernist assumptions, such as the unwavering expectation of progress and the belief that knowledge claims can be adequately verified through empirical or rational methodologies. Postmodern critiques have highlighted the potential of individuals and groups who possess political and economic power to install their own views of reality as the "correct" ones and to suppress the voices of the less powerful. Postmodernism reflects "incredulity toward metanarratives,"[14] or a basic belief that all claims to knowledge are dubious because they are shaped by assumptions and written from a one-sided point of view.

Postmodernism has grown in influence, spreading from architecture and literature into the social sciences. Its main impact on psychology, thus far, has been twofold: first, doubt has been cast upon the grand pronouncements of theoretical systems such as modernism; and second, the superiority and usefulness of empiricism as a methodology has been questioned. Postmodern social scientists seek to replace theoretical and empirical systems with qualitative methodologies, particularly narrative approaches in which clients and subjects "give voice" to their own experiences. While postmodernism offers a useful critique of the overreaching pronouncements of the modernist worldview, and while it rightly points out the possibility that people in

---

worth contemplating.

14. Lyotard, quoted in Sire, *The universe next door*, 174.

power can assert as knowledge that which is merely biased conclusion, it is not an unassailable position.[15] Moreover, postmodernists themselves are often guilty of making grand pronouncements, such as the claim that modernism is dead.[16] Even if wounded, the modernist worldview is still very much alive, particularly in scientific communities, and, to paraphrase Mark Twain, the reports of its death are greatly exaggerated.

Implications of Worldviews

Every worldview frames how one understands the world and how one acts in the world. Understanding the phenomenon

of worldviews has implications for our thinking in at least three fundamental ways: 1) understanding what happens when variant worldviews meet, 2) recognizing the degree to which worldviews are inherited, and 3) acknowledging the limited degree to which we can objectively reflect upon and alter our own worldviews.

As we have already seen, elements of different worldviews can be combined syncretistically. Syncretistic combinations are often full of internal contradictions since they fuse elements from different worldviews without an orienting, unified paradigm. On the other hand, when rival worldviews meet, misunderstanding and condemnation are also common. Conflict between worldviews usually stems from incompatibility at the assumptive level. For instance, if one assumes that the material realm is all that exists, then talk of the immaterial seems absurd. Thus the atheistic materialist laughs at the animist, the theist, and the polytheist, seeing them as ignorant and unscientific. Dialogue between individuals who hold differing worldviews must thus begin by talking about the assumptions inherent in their respective worldviews. By way of an example, a Christian might explain to an atheistic materialist why he or she believes in an immaterial, transcendent realm and why these beliefs are not inconsistent with a scientific understanding of the normal workings of nature.

A second implication of the fact that we all hold worldviews is, perhaps, more troubling; it must be admitted that

---

15. While qualitative and narrative methods certainly have advantages, a fundamental challenge is that postmodernism largely replaces knowledge with opinion or conviction, with no suggestion as to how one might determine if a given conviction is in some way better or more accurate than another. Thus my father's medical narrative that the boy in Zaire had a seizure is equally as valid as the tribal narrative that the boy was possessed by a demon.

16. Ironically, some people who critique postmodernism from a modernist perspective believe that the logical inconsistencies and weaknesses of postmodernism will soon lead to its demise. Far from being dead, postmodernism continues to draw a committed following and is spreading in influence. Meanwhile modernism continues to flourish, especially in the sciences. A more accurate picture may be that modernism and postmodernism both have been productive and useful, and that both have significant flaws. Eventually a new paradigm may emerge that recognizes the strengths of both paradigms and deals effectively with their weaknesses. If it ever comes to be, let's hope that they don't decide to call it *post-postmodernism*.

worldviews are less chosen than inherited. From the moment we are born, our views of the world are shaped by the culture and subcultures within which we are raised. Our families, religious traditions, educational institutions, media, and a host of other forces instill within us assumptions about the world and our place within it. We are less aware of these influences than we might imagine or wish. As one astute observer pointed out, "However much each of us may wish to deny it, most of what we know and believe has been given to us by our parents, friends, community, and society. We learn more than we create; we accept more than we reject. In short, we do not develop our own private world views. At most, we refine and reconceptualize (normally the latter) what we have learned from others."[17]

The repercussions of this claim are astounding. Very few people have been able to rise above their cultural prejudices to challenge institutionalized slavery, ethnic conflict, gender bias, or a host of other societal ills. It is humbling to consider how many incorrect beliefs we have adopted—and how many immoral actions we engage in—because of how deeply acculturated they are in our own worldviews.

The fact that so many of our beliefs and behaviors are blindly accepted and ignorantly followed is humbling, but we are not completely without hope, because of our third observation about worldview thinking: we can, to a limited degree, perceive and reflect on our worldviews.

How do we go about this process? First of all, we need to ask what assumptions we make about things such as the nature of knowledge, the nature of human beings, and the nature of the world (the respective topics of our next three chapters).[18] In doing so, we can test our beliefs in several ways. We can ask if our assumptions make rational sense and if our reasoning is sound. We can test claims about observable phenomena by looking at empirical evidence. We can evaluate our beliefs and behavior in light of the biblical message.[19] We can listen to the stories and wisdom of other people, which may help us see things in a new light. None of these methods is infallible; after all, we will invariably consider our own worldviews largely through the lenses of our own worldviews. Willingness to look at our assumptions with humble recognition of our own finitude and failings, though, presents an opportunity for reexamination.

The development of a Christian worldview is particularly important for the integration of psychology and

---

17. Gaede, *Where gods may dwell*, 34.

18. These three areas of inquiry are, as we shall see, foundational to how we approach psychology and Christianity, and hence they are foundational to how we conceptualize the relationship of psychology and Christianity.

19. Note that all of these suggestions themselves reflect worldview assumptions, i.e., that our assumptions should be rational and consonant with observable evidence and biblical teachings. We are all, to a certain degree, like the people in Plato's allegory of the cave, trying to discern reality in the shadows, or, as the Apostle Paul put it, "we see but a poor reflection as in a mirror" (1 Cor 13:12, NIV).

Christian theology. All disciplines—including psychology—reflect the prevailing assumptions of the worldviews and *Zeitgeist* within which they are formed. These underlying assumptions and their influence need to be evaluated in light of a Christian worldview. Thus we must develop the contours of a Christian worldview before we can proceed to explore integration at a disciplinary level.

Forming a Christian Worldview

As we saw in the opening of this chapter, a simple dinner time conversation can reveal a great deal about our assumptions. Imagine that you are sharing a meal with Christians from all over the world. You speak in distinct languages, have been shaped by different religious rituals, and have somewhat diverse ideas about doctrine and about how faith should be lived out. These differences would clearly be expressed in how you think about things like the relationship of Christianity and psychology

In the early days of the integration movement, much of the thinking about the relationship of psychology and theology was cast in terms of Niebuhr's Christ and Culture typologies (against, of, above, in paradox, transforms). The movement was also heavily influenced by Reformed perspectives on Christian higher education. Because we come from diverse Christian backgrounds, though, we need to recognize that there are a variety of ways of thinking about how to live faithfully in the world. However, since

so much of the integration literature has been shaped by the Reformed perspective, we will explore this approach in some detail, and turn our attention to some alternatives later in this book.

You may recall that worldviews ask four basic questions: "Who am I?" "Where am I?" "What's wrong?" and "What's the remedy?" The worldview with which you were raised, modified by your personal experiences and reflection, will inevitably affect your answer to these questions. It will also affect your view of psychology, Christianity, and the possibility of integration. In the Reformed perspective, a prerequisite to integration is the development of a well-conceived Christian worldview, which it constructs around the themes of creation, fall, redemption, and consummation.

Creation

A biblical understanding of creation informs our understanding of who we are, the nature of the world in which we live, and the proper ends toward which we should strive. The biblical account begins not with an anthropocentric focus centered on humanity, but with a theocentric focus centered on God. It is God who creates. It is God who gives graciously and lavishly. It is God who declares the creation to be "good," and after it is completed with the making of an image bearer, it is God who declares it to be "very good."

The Bible provides two accounts of creation. The first account is recorded in

Genesis 1, in which God creates the cosmos in six days, culminating with the creation of humans, male and female, in the image of God, who are given all of creation as a gift of which they are to be stewards. In Genesis 2, we are given a second account of the creation, this time located in the Garden of Eden. Here, we see Adam alone, and God says, "It is not good that the man should be alone; I will make him a helper fit for him" (RSV). When the animals are formed and brought before Adam, no suitable mate is found for him, and so God causes him to fall asleep, and forms Eve from one of his ribs.

"While I know myself as a creation of God, I am also obligated to realize and remember that everyone else and everything else are also God's creation."

—Maya Angelou

Both accounts of creation highlight humanity's connection to the rest of the created order. In the first account, humanity is made on the sixth day of creation, immediately after God made "the beasts of the earth." And yet, there is a significant difference between the creation of Adam and all that has preceded it. The language changes; instead of "Let there be," or "Let the earth bring forth," we now read, "Let us make."

> Let us make man in our image, after our likeness; and let them have dominion over the fish of the sea, and over the birds of the air, and over the cattle, and over all the earth, and over every creeping thing that creeps upon the earth. So God created man in his own image, in the image of God he created him; male and female he created them. And God blessed them, and God said to them, "Be fruitful and multiply, and fill the earth and subdue it; and have dominion over the fish of the sea and over the birds of the air and over every living thing that moves upon the earth." (Gen 1:26–28, NIV)

Humanity, then, is intimately connected to the creation, and yet is set in a unique relationship to the rest of creation.

The biblical sense in which humankind is an "image of God" who is given "dominion" over creation is easily misunderstood. The *image of a god* was a familiar concept within the Ancient Near Eastern cultural context in which Genesis was first read. *Images*, such as idols, were thought to contain the essence of a god, and human beings were thought to have been created to care for the god and the god-image.[20] Politically, however,

---

20. See Gordon and Rendsburg, *The Ancient Near East*; and Walton, et al, *Bible background commentary*. In most Mesopotamian legends, people were seen as created for the benefit of the gods. In at least one Egyptian legend, people are described as "images proceeding from the flesh" of the god, Re. See Currid, *Ancient Egypt*, 71. In *The Royal Instruction of Khety to Merikare* (c. 2160 BCE), we see the creation of humankind in the god's image and for his benefit, as well as the divine appointment of the Pharaoh: "Work for the god, he will also work for You: with offerings that make the altar flourish, with cravings

Ancient Near Eastern religions promoted social stratification, where kings and priests had more access to the gods—and hence more power—than common folk.[21] Kings and idols were both carried before, and venerated by, those who were not royalty. In Egypt, it was not uncommon for kings to claim that they had been suckled by a goddess to buttress their own claims of divinity.[22] The blending of the god-image with the elevation of the king supported an incredible imbalance of social power. It was understood that kings ruled their provinces as the gods' representatives—as the stewards of the land, resources, and people belonging to a local deity. Oppressive kings created and sustained economic, political and educational systems that favored the elite and oppressed the marginalized. In contrast to the surrounding religious cultural context, the God of Genesis reveals that *all of humanity* was created to bear His image. As image bearers, humans are to be God's representatives on earth, to do what God would do: *to lovingly rule and care for the creation* (including not only what we might call "nature," but also all other aspects of God's creation—includ-

ing societal and cultural institutions). The Judeo-Christian belief that humans are the image of God and have dominion over creation is not one in which some people have divine right over others, nor one in which nature is to be pillaged, but rather that all of creation (natural and cultural) is to be tended and developed in loving submission to God's sovereign rule over all things.[23]

The creation story holds two truths in tension, first, that humans are part of the created order, and thus, in many ways similar to the other creatures, and second, that they are made in the very image of God and given a caretaking role over the realm to which they belong. Dietrich Bonhoeffer commented upon these twin truths:

> This freedom of dominion directly includes our tie to the creatures that are ruled. The soil and the animals whose Lord I am are the world in which I live, without which I am not. It is my world, my earth, over which I rule . . . In my total being, in my creatureliness, I belong to this world completely. It bears me, nourishes me, and holds me. But my freedom from it consists in the fact that this world, to which I am bound as a lord to his servant, as the peasant to his soil, is subjected to me, that I am to rule over the earth which is and remains my

---

that proclaim your name. The god thinks of him who works for him! Well-tended is mankind - the cattle of the god: he made sky and earth for their sake, he subdued the water monster, he made breath for their noses to live. They are his images, who came from his body . . . He made for them rulers in the egg, leaders to raise the back of the weak" (280–99).

21. See Oppenheim, *Ancient Mesopotamia*.

22. See Gordon & Rendsburg, *Ancient Near East*.

---

23. I would like to acknowledge the influence of my friend, Bob Robinson, on the development of these thoughts.

earth, and the more strongly I rule it the more it is my earth.[24]

We are part of creation, and yet uniquely set over it to steward it.

The second biblical account of creation, in particular, highlights the fact that we are social beings, and only in community can we completely reflect the image of God. Here we see Adam made of dust by God. We see God place Adam in a garden and declare that it is not good for him to be alone, and that He will make "a helper fit for him." Then God forms the animals of the ground and brings them to Adam to be named, but none of them was "fit for him." Loneliness is not good. God then uniquely makes Eve out of and for Adam (much as Adam was formed out of and for the earth).

It is clear that human beings are viewed as the pinnacle of creation, with the affirmation by God that creation is *very good* occurring only after the creation of humanity. This high view of humanity is echoed in other Scriptures.

> I will give thanks to you, because I am fearfully and wonderfully made. (Ps 119:14a, NASB)

But the goodness of man is always seen as derivative from God, to whom we belong.

> Know that the LORD is God. It is he who made us, and we are his; we are his people, the sheep of his pasture. (Ps 100:3, NIV)

A Christian understanding of human nature begins with the affirmation of an origin in which we were created in the image of God, possessing the intellectual, creative, affective, social, and caretaking capacities with which we were fashioned. We are situated within relationships to our Creator, to each other, and to the rest of creation. While this view highlights the goodness of creation, it also acknowledges that we are limited creatures. It professes that our lives are contingent upon God's care and by right ought to be dedicated to His ends. Christian theology asserts that humans are finite rather than infinite, derivative rather than original, dependent rather than autonomous.

The biblical account sees creation as infused with potential. God's creative power bequeaths power and creativity to the creation. As Andy Crouch points out, God delegates power and creativity to his creatures: "On the successive days of Genesis's story, those empowered creatures will yield seed, bear fruit, rule the day and the night, fly, be fruitful, multiply, creep, and fill the earth."[25]

Humans are told to tend the garden, that is, to develop its potentials. Wolters points out that the presence of the first couple creates the beginnings of social and cultural life, and that through human beings the creation will be shaped as people "bring to fruition the possibilities of development implicit in the work of God's hands."[26] Creation is pregnant with

---

24. Bonhoeffer, *Creation and fall*, 36.

25. Crouch, *Playing God*, 33.

26. Wolters, *Creation regained*, 38.

potential for art, agriculture, education, civil government, science, and literature, waiting to be developed by those who bear the image of God.

A final point about creation must be made: that man, a created being, is given freedom. He can name the animals. He apparently can till and tend and shape the garden as he wishes. But this freedom is also given limits: "And the LORD God commanded the man, saying, 'You may freely eat of every tree of the garden; but of the tree of the knowledge of good and evil you shall not eat, for in the day that you eat of it you shall die'" (Gen 2:16–17, RSV). There is, as Bonhoeffer points out, a paradox in the concept of *created freedom*. Why might God want to create a free creature? C. S. Lewis responds to that question as follows:

> The happiness which God designs for His higher creatures is the happiness of being freely, voluntarily united to Him and to each other in an ecstasy of love and delight compared with which the most rapturous love between a man and a woman on this earth is mere milk and water. And for that they must be free. Of course God knew what would happen if they used their freedom the wrong way: apparently, He thought it worth the risk.[27]

It is the use of free will to transgress against God's will that is the next part of the story, what theologians sometimes refer to as original sin.[28]

---

27. Lewis, *Mere Christianity*, 52.

28. Wiley makes the following observation:

Fall

While Christianity affirms the goodness of creation, it also teaches that this goodness is only part of the story. The next chapter in the story recounts the rebellion of the first human beings against their God-given boundaries and a failure of their responsible to tend the garden faithfully as God's representatives. The result was a fundamental alteration of the entire created realm. As a result of human disobedience, pain was multiplied, relationships were damaged, the ground itself became cursed, and death entered the world (Gen 3:14–19). From that point on, the Bible recognizes a twisted nature within the human condition: "The heart is more deceitful than all else and is desperately sick; who can understand it?" (Jer 17:9, NASB). Moreover, it is precisely because those who were given authority over the creation rebelled that the created realm over which they rule is subject to the curse. Recall, too, that the

---

"In the Christian tradition, the sin of Adam and Eve is described as 'the fall.' The idea of a fall is itself an interpretation of the story. It is not part of the story itself. Within the narrative world of the story itself, there is an 'inside' and an 'outside' and a 'before' and 'after.' Prior to sin, Adam and Eve are inside the garden; after their sin they are outside the garden. Before their disobedience all human needs are met; after their disobedience suffering and toil are their lot and burden of everyone henceforth. The idea of a fall reflects theological speculation about human nature. It takes the external before and after of narrative time and places it into human nature: the state of original righteousness and—after the fall—the state of original sin." (*Original sin*, 34–35).

created realm is not just physical nature, but it also encompasses the potentials for culture and technology, and all of these things are affected by the curse. Thus, art, architecture, politics, science, and every human endeavor is now marred and easily twisted away from their proper ends—bringing glory to God, stewarding the creation in love, and living in peace with each other and with nature.

Traditionally, theologians have tended to focus on the individual aspects of the Fall, perhaps expressed best in the Apostle Paul's lament:

> For what I am doing, I do not understand; for I am not practicing what I would like to do, but I am doing the very thing I hate . . . I find then the principle that evil is present in me, the one who wants to do good. For I joyfully concur with the law of God in the inner man, but I see a different law in the members of my body, waging war against the law of my mind and making me a prisoner of the law of sin which is in my members. Wretched man that I am! Who will set me free from the body of this death? (Rom 7:15, 21–24, NASB)

Anyone who has struggled with trying to overcome a personal vice can easily relate to the distressful tone of these verses. Because we experience the misery of our individual sin and long to be released from its grip and anguish, it is not surprising that the gospel comes as good news to proclaim release from personal sin (see Rom 8:1–2). However, were we to stop here, we would make a tragic error by telling only half the story.

As we read on through the Genesis account, we see that the sin of Adam and Eve leads in quick succession to sibling conflict and fratricide, to an antediluvian culture where God laments "how great the wickedness of the human race had become on the earth, and that every inclination of the thoughts of the human heart was only evil all the time," and where "the earth was corrupt in God's sight and was full of violence" (Gen 6:5, 11, NIV). In this account of human wickedness, we begin to see sin as a corporate phenomenon. Moreover, we begin to catch a glimpse of how sin can become embedded within cultures and institutions, so that its members become blind to the sins of their culture. As Tatha Wiley noted,

> Evil is a feature of our existence prior to our personal choices and decisions. We are born into a world shaped—distorted—by such evils as violence and abuse in families, apartheid, genocide, and discrimination. The doctrine of original sin was one means by which the early Christians named this dimension of human existence and its threat to human well-being.[29]

The antediluvian reference to the wickedness of the human race, though, is certainly not the last time the Bible highlights the corporate aspect of human sinfulness.

---

29. Wiley, *Original sin*, 9.

In the biblical account, having decided to flood the earth and destroy mankind, God saves Noah's family as a remnant, and again we see the caretaking role of humankind as Noah builds an ark in which a portion of the earth's creatures will be saved. But shortly thereafter, we once again see evil swell, this time with the corporate sin of pride. "Come, let us build ourselves a city, with a tower that reaches to the heavens, so that we may make a name for ourselves; otherwise we will be scattered over the face of the whole earth," said the builders of Babel (Gen 11:4, NIV). Throughout the remainder of the Jewish Scriptures we see not just an individual inclination to sin, but the corporate nature of sin, such that the last five of the Ten Commandments focus on social consequences of individual sin (murder, adultery, theft, false witness, covetousness).

In the early twentieth century, the corporate aspects of sin were forcefully exposed by "liberal" Social Gospelers such as Walter Rauschenbusch, while "conservatives" focused on individual sin and the need for individual repentance and individual purity. While critical of "individualistic theology," Social Gospelers did not want to abandon the idea of individual sin, but they did want to expand it. "Sin is not a private transaction between the sinner and God," wrote Rauschenbusch. "We rarely sin against God alone."[30] In this view, sin is not just an individual disposition, but it is also embedded within human culture. "The permanent vices and crimes of adults are not transmitted by heredity, but by being socialized," claimed Rauschenbusch, citing such things as alcoholism, bull-fights, and ethnic conflict.[31]

Rauschenbusch's awareness of the social context of sin was, undoubtedly, influenced by his pastoral work in the Hell's Kitchen district of New York City. While the Gilded Age of the late nineteenth-century industrialization in the United States brought about massive fortunes for some people, Rauschenbush observed its dark underbelly, where poverty and misfortune were the wages of those on whose backs the prosperity of others rested. The industrialist whose material success is built on taking advantage of the environment and of his fellow human being could sit comfortably in church and recite its creeds, oblivious to his own participation in a sinful system. Rauschenbusch's critique still rings painfully true:

> The individualistic gospel has taught us to see the sinfulness of every human heart and has inspired us with faith in the willingness and power of God to save every soul that comes to him. But it has not given us an adequate understanding of the sinfulness of the social order and its share in the sins of all individuals within it. It has not evoked faith in the will and power of God to redeem the permanent institutions of human society from their inherited guilt of oppression and extortion.[32]

---

30. Rauschenbusch, *Theology for the social gospel*, 48.

31. Ibid, 60.

32. Rauschenbusch, *Theology for the social*

While it is entirely appropriate for us to attend to individual sinfulness, doing so is incomplete unless we also focus on our participation in the social and corporate sins of our social practices and social structures.

Conversion, then, as we will see, is not just repenting of individual sin, but also examining our participation in collective sin and prophetically challenging sins that become embedded within a society, including economic systems which disadvantage some and privilege others. Unfortunately, many Christian denominations tend to focus *either* on individual sin and the need for individual repentance *or* on culturally embedded sin and the need for social reform and social justice. A fully biblical picture must acknowledge and address both personal and social dimensions of sin. We will address this issue again in a later chapter.

We must also note that sin has widespread effects throughout the created realm. While sin itself has both individual and social dimensions, the biblical view is that *sin affects the entirety of creation*. The account of the fall includes several consequences, some of which extend to the world in which Adam and Eve would reside:

> Cursed is the ground because of you;
>   through painful toil you will eat
>   food from it
>   all the days of your life.
> It will produce thorns and thistles for
>   you,

and you will eat the plants of the field.
> By the sweat of your brow
>   you will eat your food
> until you return to the ground,
>   since from it you were taken;
> for dust you are
>   and to dust you will return.
> (Gen 3:17–20, NIV)

The effects of the Fall are pervasive, and yet we often fail to notice them, because they are part of the fabric of our lives. As Wolters notes,

> The effects of sin touch all of creation; no created thing is in principle untouched by the corrosive effects of the fall. Whether we look at societal structures such as the state or family, or cultural pursuits such as art or technology, or bodily functions such as sexuality or eating, or anything at all within the wide scope of creation, we discover that the good handiwork of God has been drawn into the sphere of human mutiny against God.[33]

Mark McMinn put the situation in stark terms:

> When sin shattered a perfect creation, everything changed. It's not just that we sin or that we are sinned against, it's that everything is different from the way God intended it to be, and all of these differences can be attributed to the consequences of sin . . . There are weeds in our gardens now, and in our personalities. Since the Fall, creation now groans with birth defects and

---

gospel, 5.

33. Wolters, *Creation regained*, 44.

disease and poverty . . . Everything around us is broken. Things are not the way they are supposed to be.[34]

Cornelius Plantinga paints a picture that contrasts *shalom*, the peace that was intended by God, with *sin*, the cause of the brokenness that surrounds us.

The webbing together of God, humans, and all creation in justice, fulfillment, and delight is what the Hebrew prophets call shalom . . . In the Bible shalom means universal flourishing, wholeness, and delight—a rich state of affairs in which natural needs are satisfied and natural gifts fruitfully employed, a state of affairs that inspires joyful wonder as the creator and savior opens doors and speaks welcome to the creatures in whom he delights. Shalom, in other words, is the way things are supposed to be. Sin is shalom's opposite . . . a sin is any act—any thought, desire, emotion, word, or deed—or its particular absence, that displeases God and deserves blame. Human life is not the way it's supposed to be . . . The real human predicament, as Scripture reveals, is that inexplicably, irrationally, we all keep living our lives against what's good for us. In what can only be called the mystery of iniquity, human beings from nearly the beginning have so often chosen to live against God, against each other, and against God's world.[35]

In this way, it is clear that sin is linked to all that is wrong with the world.

Paul echoes this truth in the book of Romans while discussing the sufferings of this present age:

For the creation was subjected to frustration, not by its own choice, but by the will of the one who subjected it, in hope that the creation itself will be liberated from its bondage to decay and brought into the freedom and glory of the children of God. We know that the whole creation has been groaning as in the pains of childbirth right up to the present time. (Rom 8:20–22, NIV)

Notice that we look forward not only to individuals being released from the consequences of personal sin, as we see in Romans 8:1–2, but now we see that all of the created order is being released from the consequences of the fall. In part, the release of creation from the bondage of the fall comes about when the image bearers begin to rule properly as God intended, rather than in selfishness and idolatry.

Of particular importance for a Christian view of psychology, there is now the terrible possibility of choosing to direct one's life towards that which will glorify God, or toward that which will usurp the role of God by serving any of a myriad of idols. "Where the creature does not find its freedom in responding obediently to the Creator's norms," writes Wolters, "there it enters bondage."[36] This point will have significant implications when we consider that some elements of human distress that come to the attention of clinical psychologists directly or

---

34. McMinn, *Why sin matters*, 51.

35. Plantinga, *Not the way*, 10.

36. Wolters, *Creation regained*, 55.

indirectly stem from living in ways that run counter to God's design for creation.

> "I live now on borrowed time, waiting in the anteroom for the summons that will inevitably come. And then—I go on to the next thing, whatever it is."
>
> —Agatha Christie,
> Epilogue, Autobiography

A final point must be made about the curse that we dare not overlook: the reality of death. Our lives have an expiration date. Some of us live to a ripe old age, some of us die in the prime of life, and some of us die almost at the outset of life; but we all die. We all face the mystery and uncertainty of death. We grieve when others die. The Genesis account does not develop a theology of the afterlife. It simply proclaims at the end of the curse, "For you are dust, and to dust you shall return" (Gen 3:19, NASB). Not surprisingly, this is an issue that is often brought into therapy, whether framed by grief and loss, existential awareness of one's own finitude, relief at the end of suffering, or even suicidal feelings. Decay, suffering, and mortality are among the unavoidable realities that led the author of Ecclesiastes to remark on the seeming futility of life.

In summary, a Christian understanding of human nature affirms our created origin in the image of God, and it recognizes the reality of human sin and its pervasive effects throughout the created realm. While a Christian view insists that we acknowledge the reality of sin—both individual and corporate—the Bible also speaks of God's continuing interest in humankind and recognizes remnants of the splendor in which humanity was created: "What is man that you take thought of him, and the son of man that you care for him? Yet you have made him a little lower than God, And you crown him with glory and majesty!" (Ps 8:4–5, NASB). In the Reformed view, creation and fall both frame important aspects of human nature, but it is the story of redemption that speaks to the deepest hopes of humanity.

Redemption

The biblical story proceeds from creation and fall to the unfolding story of redemption and restoration. It is foreshadowed when God said to the serpent, "I will make you and the woman enemies to each other. Your descendants and her descendants will be enemies. Her child will crush your head. And you will bite his heel" (Gen 3:15, NCV).[37]

---

37. Catholics and Protestants differ on how to translate this verse; my interpretation follows the Protestant tradition. The Catholic position comes from Jerome's translation in the Latin Vulgate, in which he renders the phrase as *ipsa conteret*, and the corresponding English translation thus becomes, "I will put enmities between thee and the woman, and thy seed and her seed: *she shall crush thy head*, and thou shalt lie in wait for her heel" (DR). Prior to Jerome, Latin texts differed on whether the word was rendered *ipse* ("he"), *ipsa* ("she"), or even *ipsum* ("it"). The Hebrew rendering is in the masculine, but interpreters differ on the importance of the grammatical gender to the meaning of the passage. Thus Protestants believe that they are correct

"O Lord, I acknowledge and give thanks that You created in me Your image so that I may remember, contemplate, and love You. But [this image] has been so effaced by the abrasion of transgressions, so hidden from sight by the dark billows of sins, that unless You renew and refashion it, it cannot do what it was created to do."

—Anselm of Canterbury

in insisting on the masculine form (based on the Hebrew, the Septuagint, and other Latin texts), and see it as a foreshadowing of Christ's defeating Satan through his work on the cross. (This last point is forcibly made in Luther's commentary on Genesis.) Roman Catholics, most of whom adopt Jerome's position, understand the verse as referring not to Christ but to Mary, and buttress Jerome's translation with literary parallelism. For the enmity arises between the snake and the woman and between the seed of the snake and the seed of the woman; further, the woman crushes the snake's head while the snake bruises her heel. However, the Latin pronoun *eius* is not gender specific, meaning that the English words *his*, *her*, or *it* must be inferred from the context. Having followed *ipsa* rather than *ipse*, Jerome thus rendered "her," whereas other translators followed the masculine and so rendered "his." The translators of the Challoner Revision of the Douay-Rheims translation included an interesting footnote on *ipsa conteret* (Gen 3:15): "Ipsa, the woman; so divers[e] of the fathers read this place conformably to the Latin; others read it ipsum, viz., the seed. The sense is the same: for it is by her seed, Jesus Christ, that the woman crushes the serpent's head." (Online: http://www.drbo.org/chapter/01003.htm/).

The story advances through God's interactions with characters such as Noah and Abraham and Sarah, and to events such as the deliverance of the Israelites from bondage in Egypt and the giving of the Law to God's people. It includes the progressive history of God's interactions with the Israelites, the proclamations of the prophets, and the rise and fall of the Kingdoms of Israel and Judah. It reaches its climax in the incarnation, life, death, and resurrection of Jesus. It proceeds through the early church, and continues today through God's activity in reconciling all things to Himself (Col 1:20). Throughout these encounters we see redemption cast in both individual and social terms. Individuals are called to turn from their evil ways, and the entire nation of Israel is called upon to enact justice.

The Old Testament prophets confronted individual sin (cf. 2 Samuel 12), idolatry (cf. 2 Kings 17), and corporate sin (cf. Isa 1:1–4). Sin affects the entire people of Israel "as members of the covenant family manipulate, betray, lie to, and deceive one another."[38] Since sin has social consequences and is corporate as well as individual, redemption involves confronting both individual and corporate sin. The book of Isaiah is filled with the theme of confronting corporate sin and pursuing social justice. Early in the book (1:16–18, NIV) we read:

> Wash and make yourselves clean.
> Take your evil deeds out of my sight;

---

38. Doriani, *Sin*, 736.

stop doing wrong.
Learn to do right; seek justice.
Defend the oppressed.
Take up the cause of the fatherless;
  plead the case of the widow.
"Come now, let us settle the matter,"
  says the LORD.
"Though your sins are like scarlet,
  they shall be as white as snow;
though they are red as crimson,
  they shall be like wool."

Interestingly, this last verse is often seen as a resource for those who feel overwhelmed with individual transgressions, but the context is clearly corporate, calling an entire people to repentance and redemption.[39] The theme of social justice in Isaiah culminates in the coming of the messiah who will administer justice. In this context, the Old Testament call to *shalom* is clearly an appeal to social justice, not just the purging of individual sin.

Reconciliation of relationships is clearly a major focus of Christ's redemptive work. When the angel appears to Zechariah to announce that he will have a son who will prepare the way for Christ, he is told that John's ministry will involve reconciliation:

And he will go on before the Lord, in the spirit and power of Elijah, to turn the hearts of the parents to their children and the disobedient to the wisdom of the righteous—to make

ready a people prepared for the Lord. (Luke 1:17, NIV)

But redemption goes well beyond individual and social life. Colossians tells us that *Christ is reconciling all things to Himself*. This means that *every aspect of creation is to be redeemed and restored*: art, music, business, economics, politics, our caretaking role over the environment and our fellow creatures, and so forth. In every conceivable area of life, Christians are called to be agents of redemption.

The redemptive story of the life and death of Jesus is central to the restorative grace that God extends to humankind. This story is the culmination of God's promise of redemption in which God Himself paid the penalty for our sin so that we could be reconciled to Him through faith in His atoning death. In the words of the Apostle Paul:

No human being will be pronounced righteous before God as the result of obedience to Law; for it is Law that shows what sin is. But now, quite apart from Law, the Divine Righteousness stands revealed, and to it the Law and the Prophets bear witness—the Divine Righteousness which is bestowed, through faith in Jesus Christ, upon all, without distinction, who believe in him. For all have sinned, and all fall short of God's glorious ideal, but, in his loving-kindness, are being freely pronounced righteous through the deliverance found in Christ Jesus. For God set him before the world, to be, by the shedding of his blood, a

---

39. However, it must also be noted that the corporate nature of sin does not completely remove individual culpability. See Ezekiel 18.

means of reconciliation through faith. (Rom 3:20–25a, NCV)

The call of Christ, though, is not just a promise that individuals can avoid divine wrath. The ministry of Jesus is one of confronting sin and social injustice with a call to repentance. At the inauguration of his ministry in Nazareth, Jesus read from the prophet Isaiah:

> The Spirit of the LORD is on me,
> because he has anointed me
> to proclaim good news to the poor.
> He has sent me to proclaim freedom
> for the prisoners
> and recovery of sight for the blind,
> to set the oppressed free,
> to proclaim the year of the Lord's favor.
> (Luke 4:18–19; Isa 61:1–2, NIV)

Throughout His ministry, Jesus confronted social injustice and ministered among the poor and the disenfranchised of society. It was also a ministry of healing and restoration.

Redemption entails forgiveness of sin and justification (being declared righteous in God's sight). It removes us from a state of enmity with God, and embarks us on the path of following Christ and becoming more like Him (Rom 8:29). A Christian understanding of redemption, though, is broader than the matter of individual salvation. While personal salvation is important, the Christian understanding of redemption recognizes that the entirety of the created realm was affected by the Fall and is yet to be redeemed. As Paul wrote,

For the creation was subjected to frustration, not by its own choice, but by the will of the one who subjected it, in hope that the creation itself will be liberated from its bondage to decay and brought into the glorious freedom of the children of God. We know that the whole creation has been groaning as in the pains of childbirth right up to the present time. (Rom 8:20–22, NIV)

While Christians are called to participate in the redemption of the created realm, it will only be consummated in the day of "the new heaven and the new earth" (Rev 21:1, NIV).

Consummation

The biblical story as discussed thus far explains why human nature has elements of both good and evil. It explains why the world around us is subject to decay and disease. It introduces God's desire to reconcile humanity and the entire created realm to Himself. If we were to leave the biblical narrative at this point, we would still have an incomplete picture, because it has yet to address questions about our ultimate end and the final shape of God's kingdom. Christians believe that they live in the "now and not yet" of salvation. While a Christian has been saved from the penalty of his or her sin, the struggle with sin and the effects of sin continue. The Christian looks forward to a day when the temporal struggle with individual and corporate sin will be over, when the curses emanating from the fall will be ended and God's rule will be finally and fully realized.

The term *consummation* refers to the *completion* of God's rule over the creation that has been in rebellion against His sovereignty. The concept of consummation is sometimes framed as *re-creation*—that is, that God restores the creation from its fallen state. In the Gospels, we see the coming of the kingdom of God, much like an invasion. Shortly after His baptism and temptation, Jesus began His public ministry with these words: "Repent, for the kingdom of heaven has come near" (Matt 4:17, NIV). People are invited to turn away from following false idols, to repent from their sinful ways, to recognize the coming of the rightful King, and to participate in restoring all of creation to its intended goodness. Throughout Matthew's account, the concept of the kingdom of heaven is unpacked. Pennington notes that, "Matthew's language provided a devastating and subversive critique of this great earthly empire, while providing solace and hope that God's kingdom would eventually come upon the earth."[40] While the invasion of the kingdom has begun, it is incomplete in the present age.

Fulfillment comes in the *eschaton*, the end of the present age, which begins when God's rule is firmly established. Much of what the Bible has to say about this is difficult to interpret because it is often presented in apocalyptic imagery. It is also easily misunderstood, since modern, western, individualistic Christianity often focuses on *the salvation of the individual* rather than on *the restoration of all of creation*. There is, of course, an individual element to restoration, but while the salvation of individuals is crucial to this story, consummation is much broader than this alone.

> Re-creation culminates in the reversal of sin's effects on the fallen, judged creation. The biblical account climaxes with the "new heaven and a new earth, where righteousness is at home" (2 Pet 3:13, NRSV).[41]

It is clear that this picture is not just one of *individuals saved from personal sin*. It is also an image of *the people of God living in community where righteousness reigns*. Thus, the complete reign of Christ offers the solution to both individual and social dimensions of the fall. Moreover, restoration involves the redemption of *all* created things.

Modern Christians tend to embrace one of two forms of eschatology, or views of the end times. The first of these views is found among post-enlightenment Christians who experience a general embarrassment about Christian claims of resurrection and ascension and who cling to beliefs that the church (or, wishing not to be too theologically elitist, "humankind") will gradually fulfill the hopes of progress and renewal within the world. The alternative view is found among fundamentalists and dispensationalists who can display too little

---

40. Pennington, *Heaven and Earth*, 337.

41. Vanhoozer, *Dictionary for theological interpretation*, 438.

concern for the present world, and a corresponding focus on "going to heaven." N. T. Wright contends that both of these views are unbiblical. The post-enlightenment or liberal view tends to neglect the agency of Christ in transforming the world and overemphasize human agency, and it fails to deal adequately with human evil and the pervasiveness of the fall. The second view tends to view "salvation" as primarily personal escape from suffering and neglects the biblical call to participate in the redemption of all things within our present circumstances. The biblical view, in contrast, is one in which we participate in the renewal and restoration of creation *in the here and now, in the power of the risen Christ, while we await the final and complete restoration of all things yet to come.*

Framing eschatology in this way has implications not just for our future hope, but for the present. N. T. Wright makes this point quite explicitly:

> To hope for a better future in this world—for the poor, the sick, the lonely and depressed, for the slaves, the refugees, the hungry and homeless, for the abused, the paranoid, the downtrodden and despairing, and in fact for the whole wide, wonderful, and wounded world—is not something *else*, something extra, something tacked on to the gospel as an afterthought. And to work for that intermediate hope, the surprising hope that comes forward from God's ultimate future into God's urgent present, is not a *distraction from* the task of mission and evan-

gelism in the present. It is a central, essential, vital, and life-giving part of it. Mostly, Jesus himself got a hearing from his contemporaries because of what he was *doing*. They saw him saving people from sickness and death, and they heard him talking about a salvation, the message for which they had longed, that would go beyond the immediate into the ultimate future . . . The whole point of what Jesus was up to . . . was not saving souls for a disembodied eternity but rescuing people from the corruption and decay of the way the world presently is so they could enjoy, already in the present, that renewal of creation which is God's ultimate purpose . . . [42]

Consummation, then, is the final outworking of what God will bring to completion but which He is already beginning to bring about in and through His people in restoring all things to His rule.

The complete rule of Christ is also the occasion of divine judgment. The book of Revelation pictures a great white throne upon which sits God; from Him no one can flee, and before Him all are judged: "And if anyone's name was not found written in the book of life, he was thrown into the lake of fire" (Rev 20:15, NASB). This is a stark image of judgment, highlighting the seriousness of our need to confront our own sin. But it is also a story of divine grace and liberality. Earlier in the book of Revelation we catch a glimpse of the diversity of the redeemed:

---

42. Wright, *Surprised by hope*, 191–92.

After this I looked, and there before me was a great multitude that no one could count, from every nation, tribe, people and language, standing before the throne and before the Lamb. They were wearing white robes and were holding palm branches in their hands. And they cried out in a loud voice: "Salvation belongs to our God, who sits on the throne, and to the Lamb." (Rev 7:9–10, NIV)

Consummation, then, involves both justice and grace.

While understood in different ways by various Christian traditions, consummation is the story of the new heaven and the new earth, when the New Jerusalem (the symbol of God's reign) comes down to earth (Rev 3:12). Salvation, rather than being seen as "going to heaven," as is often assumed, is actually framed as the recreation of earth, where the lines of the Lord's prayer, "your kingdom come, your will be done, on earth as it is in heaven," will finally be consummated. This is pictured in the end of the book of Revelation:

I saw a new heaven and a new earth. The first heaven and the first earth had disappeared, and so had the sea. Then I saw New Jerusalem, that holy city, coming down from God in heaven. It was like a bride dressed in her wedding gown and ready to meet her husband. I heard a loud voice shout from the throne: God's home is now with his people. He will live with them, and they will be his own. Yes, God will make his home among his people. He will wipe all tears from

their eyes, and there will be no more death, suffering, crying, or pain. These things of the past are gone forever. Then the one sitting on the throne said: "I am making everything new. Write down what I have said. My words are true and can be trusted." (Rev 21:1–5, CEV)

In consummation, all things are finally and completely reconciled to God, and restored under His rule.

Finally, we must note that it is a chorus of praise, perhaps more than anything else, that characterizes this final act of the biblical narrative. Christ is recognized as worthy of all honor and glory. We see this first in the book of Revelation when the throne of God is surrounded by creatures who repeat day and night:

Holy, holy, holy
is the Lord God Almighty,
who was, and is, and is to come.
(Rev 4:8, NIV)

A chapter later, we read that thousands and millions of angels proclaim:

Worthy is the Lamb who was
    slaughtered—
    to receive power and riches
and wisdom and strength
    and honor and glory and blessing.
(Rev 5:12, NIV)

And finally, all of creation worships God:

And then I heard every creature in heaven and on earth and under the earth and in the sea. They sang:
    "Blessing and honor and glory and power

belong to the one sitting on the
throne
and to the Lamb forever and ever."
(Rev 5:13, NIV)

Only when all of God's creatures recognize and affirm His sovereignty and goodness is the kingdom truly consummated. And this, of course, is true in our own lives as well.

In summary, a worldview shaped by a Christian understanding of creation, fall, redemption, and consummation is a starting point for integration. The formation of a Christian worldview allows us to pursue knowledge from diverse sources and to seek a holistic viewpoint. In the words of Abraham Kuyper,

> Thinking Christians can arrive at a conception of things that harmonizes with their faith, that supports and strengthens it instead of undermining it, only when Christian learning inducts us into a well-considered, clearly articulated world- and life-view.[43]

While the worldviews of Christians from different cultures and different Christian traditions will vary somewhat, they provide a common set of themes that can inform our understanding of our world and our place within it.

Towards What End?

In our discussion of a Christian worldview, there is an implicit understanding that the narrative of creation, fall, redemption, and consummation has significant implications for how we should live. We see this first in the asymmetrical relationship between God and the creation. He is the Creator, we are part of the creation. Only when we recognize that we owe Him our undivided allegiance can we truly thrive, for in essence, we belong to Him. While God gives us freedom, it is only when we align our will with His will that we will flourish. God has the right to stipulate how we ought to live, and as the creator, He has the wisdom to know the conditions that will foster our wellbeing.

> "There are only two kinds of people in the end: those who say to God, 'Thy will be done', and those to whom God says, in the end, Thy will be done."
>
> —C. S. Lewis, *The Great Divorce*

If we are to follow God's directives, then we must know what they are. Without divine proclamation, most people in most cultures across time recognize that some things promote individual and social happiness (these we usually call virtues), while other things interfere with individual and social happiness (these we usually call vices). Because of prevenient grace, the morality of many courses of action can be discerned by attending to their likely outcomes. Conscience, itself, may also be partly innate, though clearly shaped by culture. But general revelation alone can only tell us so much.

---

43. Quoted in Bratt, *Abraham Kuyper*, 474.

Scripture and other types of special revelation contain (among other things) explicit directions about how we ought to live. Prominent among these are, of course, the Ten Commandments. Note that these commands are designed to promote social well-being as much as individual well-being. Large sections of the Old Testament are dedicated to describing the laws that were to govern the people of Israel. For us, one of the difficulties is determining which of these laws relate to the ceremonial and social structure of Israel, and which are universal. Yet it remains true that to the extent that we follow God's ways, we will be better off than if we choose not to do so. This, of course, is extremely important for clinical psychology, since some forms of distress are related to neglecting or rejecting God's law, and in those cases, true healing must involve repentance—choosing to recognize the error of one's ways and to set a correct course.

While one bookend of the biblical narrative is creation, which frames our relationship to God and to the rest of creation, the other bookend is consummation, which frames our eternal destiny as those who either choose to submit to God's rule or to rebel against it. In the meantime, Christians who are involved in the helping professions can be agents of redemption and restoration as we seek to restore health in the face of personal and relational brokenness. The helping professions can truly be redemptive if they are carried out in ways that emanate from God's call to reconciling all things to Him.

It is well beyond the scope of the present chapter to discuss the hermeneutic and therapeutic issues that stem from these observations, but these are clearly things that Christians who are involved in mental health professions need to think about deeply and carefully. It is also important to note that many forms of distress are not related to personal sin—suffering from the sins of others and simply living in a broken world are also the cause of much distress. Yet we cannot neglect the simple truth that we need to consider whether or not our own behaviors and dispositions (and those of our broader society) are attuned with or opposed to God's call. We would do well to heed the words of the prophet Micah, "He has shown you, O mortal, what is good. And what does the LORD require of you? To act justly and to love mercy and to walk humbly with your God" (Mic 6:8, NIV).

If we acknowledge the influence of worldviews and seek to discern the contours of our own culture, and if we carefully develop a Christian worldview as we grasp the redemptive flow of history and what God requires of us, then we can begin to answer the all-important question of how we should orient our lives. This is crucial if we are to have an accurate Christian understanding of what it means to be human, and implicitly and explicitly, it will affect our engagement with the field of psychology, and perhaps, especially, psychotherapy.

Summary

Inescapably, each of us holds a worldview, a set of glasses that both focus and distort our understanding of the world and our place within it. Worldviews are more learned than they are chosen, and our ability to reflect on them is limited. Some major worldviews were examined including animism, polytheism, pantheism, theism, modernism/atheistic materialism, postmodernism, and syncretism (in which elements from disparate worldviews are merged into one worldview).[44] In evaluating the relative merits of a worldview, it was suggested that we ask if our assumptions are reasonable, if empirical and rational evidence supports or disproves our assumptions, if our assumptions are biblically acceptable, and that we listen to the voices of other people about their own experiences and worldviews. Finally, the paradigm of creation, fall, redemption, and consummation was offered as a way of organizing the basic elements of a Christian worldview. The next three chapters will help to further define a Christian worldview in specific reference to an understanding of the nature of knowledge, the nature of human beings, and the nature of the world.

Questions for Reflection and Discussion

1. Reread the introduction to the chapter. How many times can you identify a clash of worldviews in the author's story? At what points was your own worldview challenged or exposed? How do you think you would react to being exposed to a culture where the prevailing worldview is fundamentally different from your own?

2. Walsh and Middleton define a worldview as something that answers four basic questions that might be loosely summarized as follows: *What does it mean to be a person? What is the nature of the world? What's wrong with the world and why do things go wrong? How can what is wrong with the world, and what is wrong with my life, be fixed?*[45] How would you answer these four questions? Are your answers purely assumptive, or do you have any evidence that you use to support your views?

3. James Sire points out that our presuppositions are not always correct, that we are not always aware of them, and that we do not always hold them consistently. Look back at your answer to the previous question. Can you see elements that support Sire's contention when you reflect on your own worldview assumptions?

---

44. These are not exhaustive categories, nor are they all mutually exclusive.

45. See Walsh & Middleton, *The transforming vision*, 35.

4. How would an animist, a polytheist, a pantheist, a theist, a modernist/atheistic materialist, and a postmodernist answer the four questions posed in question 2?

5. The author claims that "worldviews are less chosen than inherited." Do you think his assertion is correct? Can you give examples of how this is true of your own worldview? How "objective" do you think we can be in evaluating our own worldviews?

6. Both creation accounts (in Genesis 1 and 2) highlight that humans are solidly part of creation and stewards over it. Why is it important for us to affirm both our dependence on and similarity to all of the rest of the created realm? What does it mean to exercise stewardship over creation as the image of God?

7. The author noted that the Fall has both individual and corporate implications. In what ways can you see individual sin as a source of suffering that might be relevant to psychology? In what ways can you see corporate sin as a source of suffering that might be relevant to psychology? Provide specific examples.

8. The author claimed that "every aspect of creation is to be redeemed and restored: art, music, business, economics, politics, our caretaking role over the environment and our fellow creatures, and so forth. In every conceivable area of life, Christians are called to be agents of redemption." Describe several ways that you sense God could call you to be part of the redemption of all of creation. Why is it important to see redemption as broader than just being forgiven for individual sin?

9. In the modern era, Christians tend to frame consummation either as "going to heaven" or as social transformation of this life. Which one of these do you see emphasized in your own religious experience? What would be different if we were to view consummation as "participation in the renewal and restoration of creation in the here and now, in the power of the risen Christ, while we await the final and complete restoration of all things yet to come"?

5

The Pursuit of Truth:
Epistemology—Ways of Knowing

For I do not seek to understand that I may believe, but I believe in order to understand. For this I believe—that unless I believe, I should not understand.
—Saint Anselm

If a man will begin with certainties, he shall end in doubts; but if he will be content to begin with doubts, he shall end in certainties.
 —Francis Bacon

Objective evidence and certitude are doubtless very fine ideals to play with, but where on this moonlit and dream-visited planet are they found?
—William James

I was giving an abnormal psychology lecture on psychosis. As I often do, I used an appropriately disguised clinical vignette to illustrate the material. I recounted the day that I had walked into the patient lounge of the psychiatric hospital, the blue haze and pungent aroma of cigarette smoke hanging heavily in the air. Jimmy sat on the couch, playing some incredibly good licks on his acoustic guitar. "Hey, Jimmy," I said as I sat down, "How long you been playin'?" Jimmy suddenly became wide-eyed and deeply animated. "You ain't gonna believe this, man! I was at a Cat Stevens concert once, and I was

out there singin', an' Cat looked down at me—and I ain't never met the guy—and he says, 'Hey, you! Yeah, you! Come up here an' play guitar for me!' So I hopped up on stage and started playing guitar. I ain't never played before! I was jammin' with Cat, and I been playin' ever since!" After telling my students this story (and explaining that Cat Stevens was a rock and roll star whom most of them had never heard of), I asked, "Now, how many of you *really* believe that Jimmy played guitar with Cat Stevens?" Rebecca's hand shot up in the air. "I do," she said. "You can do all kinds of things when you're possessed by a demon!" I had planned to talk about delusional systems, but the discussion ended up taking a brief detour on the way to understanding psychosis.

Jimmy was convinced that he had learned to play guitar on stage with Cat Stevens. I had read Jimmy's chart; I was convinced that he suffered from delusions caused by a psychotic break and a long history of hallucinogenic drug abuse. Rebecca was convinced that Jimmy was demon possessed. Clearly, we could not all have been right, but we were each convinced that we were.

While Jimmy, Rebecca, and I came to starkly different conclusions, our worldviews were actually similar. We diverged not so much on our understanding of the basic nature of the world as we did in our reality testing abilities and the way we went about evaluating knowledge claims.[1] Unfortunately, drugs and disease had greatly limited Jimmy's ability to evaluate his own claims—which is why his belief system is labeled "delusional."[2]

Rebecca and I differed regarding assumptions that we made about how to evaluate and classify extraordinary claims. Rebecca's lack of experience with the mentally ill, coupled with the beliefs espoused by her church, led her to discount my explanation and to offer the alternate conclusion that Jimmy was demon possessed. My own worldview, shaped by my denominational background, my education, and my experience with the mentally ill, added to the information contained on Jimmy's chart, led me to conclude that Jimmy was delusional and Rebecca was wrong. Despite our conflicting points of view, Rebecca and I shared a common Christian faith, and all three of us possessed worldviews shaped to a large degree by our common culture. Since our worldviews were similar, we must turn in a different direction to explain why our conclusions differed so starkly. It is at this point that we must narrow our focus from broad questions about worldviews, to more specific questions about how we can evaluate knowledge claims.

---

1. For the sake of this discussion I am assuming that my view of reality comes closer to the truth than that of Jimmy or Rebecca. In the final analysis I cannot definitively *prove* that I am correct—after all, my own memory is not infallible, or however absurd it might sound, perhaps I am just a character in someone else's dream! But no one can—or even should—try to live with the far-fetched assumptions of Cartesian skepticism. We must each humbly evaluate the data available to us to the best of our ability, and proceed from there. Thus, while I must humbly admit that the perspective of Jimmy or Rebecca might be closer to the truth than my own view, I retain my view because it seems to me that it more accurately and completely fits the data.

2. Recognizing that clarity of thought is

necessary for rational discourse, philosophers will sometime preface their arguments as applying "under standard conditions." Experimental methodologies must also account for "statistical outliers," events that are so rare as to upset the data set, responses that are errant for other reasons (e.g., misunderstanding directions or survey questions), or errors in data recording that invalidate the statistics.

- The Enlightenment—a period of Western thought and culture, stretching roughly from the mid-seventeenth century through the eighteenth century. Rationalism and empiricism became its major epistemic frameworks, with doubt cast upon reliance on authority and church dogma as sources of truth. It was accompanied by revolutions in science, philosophy, culture, and politics.

- Positivism—a philosophical system that emerged during the Enlightenment which rejects metaphysics and seeks rational or empirical justification of truth claims.

- Empiricism—a method for seeking knowledge based on sense experience, which gave rise to the scientific method. It is a result of positivism.

- Modernism—a philosophical movement in Western society spanning late 19th and early 20th centuries which tended to see knowledge as based on human objectivity and which optimistically expected that technological advances would lead to social progress. Modernism was often accompanied by a shift away from religious belief.

- Post-modernism—although difficult to define, post-modernism is a late-twentieth century western movement that is generally suspicious of the "grand narratives" of modernism, claims of objectivity, and claims of inevitable progress.

Situating Ourselves in History

For many readers, this chapter will contain words that they may be unfamiliar with, words such as epistemology, Enlightenment, positivism, empiricism, modernism, and postmodernism. All of these words relate in some way to the possibilities and difficulties of obtaining knowledge, so it will be instructive to take a few moments to look at our place in the history of ideas. Epistemology is the branch of philosophy that deals with the grounds and nature of knowledge. It would be nice if we could proceed straightaway to cataloging a handful of epistemic methods and—voila!—we could use them to obtain knowledge and be sure of our findings, but the task ahead is a bit more complicated than that.

The Enlightenment was a period in Europe during which the authority of the church had come into question. People began seeking other sources of authority. Gradually, the belief emerged that we could use precise epistemic methods to vouchsafe our certainty. Chief among these epistemic methods were logical reasoning and empiricism. It was thought that we could essentially become our own authorities, knowing with absolute certainty what was right and what was wrong. This became the hallmark of modernism.

The belief in the human capacity to function as an independent authority gave rise to another aspect of modernism: the myth of progress. People began to believe that we could know things with god-like certainty, and that we could solve all human problems. We could solve the problems of starvation and disease. An endless movement toward progress would do away with war and conflict. Modernism was an incredible expression of pride and self-aggrandizement. True, modernism did have many beneficial results, not the least of which was the development of the scientific method and the many things that it provided. But eventually, the naïve belief in inevitable and eternal progress collapsed. World War I and World War II dealt stunning blows to the belief in progress. It also devastated the belief that human nature is essentially good. The deaths of millions of people in combat, concentration camps, and bombing raids stood as a monument to how "progress" could lead to "better" weapons but not necessarily better people.

As modernism collapsed, it did so incompletely and unevenly. Existentialism emerged (or reemerged) as a challenge to objectivism. Postmodernism evolved as a rejection of modernity's epistemic structures. As we will see, the pendulum swung from the modernist belief in authority centered on self to postmodern doubt of all authority. Some postmodernists believe that these vestiges of modernism ought to be dispensed with altogether. They argue that people use knowledge claims to wield power, and that the epistemic methods of modernism have become tools to maintain the status quo. By way of example, it is easy to document "scientific" claims and

rational arguments that have been used to support slavery, racism, sexism, and other social inequalities. Postmodernism has offered a stunning critique of modernism, especially its assumption that we can be completely objective and that we are marching inevitably toward progress.

Postmodernism underscores the degree to which knowledge claims can be abused, as well as the many obstacles that militate against epistemic certainty. Despite the collapse of the modern myth of progress, the epistemic methods of modernism continue to be very influential, and are still the mainstay of most quantitative social-science research. However, faith in modernist epistemic methods as mechanisms to uncover truth with complete objective certainty is in shambles.

Elizabeth Lewis Hall provides a good description of how one can respect many of the valid criticisms offered by postmodernism without completely abandoning the useful methodologies that came from modernism. "The vision presented here begins with . . . [the assumption of] ontological realism, but with epistemological modesty. In other words, this approach will appeal to those who acknowledge the existence of objective truth, but recognize some limitations in our ability to apprehend it. In this way, it differs both from a traditional modernist view, and from a radical postmodern approach which would question the existence of objective truth."[3]

We can no longer sustain the overconfidence promised by modernism,

---

3. Hall, *God as cause*, 200.

but its methods are still useful. A more humble claim seems warranted, namely, that some of the epistemic methods of modernism may be useful, imperfect tools that can aid in our search for understanding.[4]

Tentative Certainty

One of the assumptions that we make about the world involves how well our perception of the world mirrors reality. At one extreme are *naive realists*, who believe that there is a direct one-to-one correspondence between perception and reality. At the opposite extreme are radical *antirealists*, who believe that there is no necessary correspondence between perception and reality; the biases of the individual and community, along with the assumptions of our theories, determine what we see, since "all observation is theory-laden."[5] *Critical realists* take a

middle ground, believing that while assumptions and biases color perception, reality imposes some limitations on interpretation.[6] Critical realists recognize that assumptions and biases affect data interpretation, but they also believe that assumptions and biases can be evaluated (at least to some degree), and that interpretations can be judged by their fitness with the data.

From a critical realist perspective, what we see depends, to some degree, on what we expect and are predisposed to see. As we noted in the last chapter, the window through which we view the world both frames and obscures what we can see. "Our thinking starts from somewhere, and not from absolute objectivity."[7] Our thinking is inevitably shaped by cultural and historical contexts; "all human understanding, including the understanding that engenders the specific social sciences, is based on historically situated and tradition-saturated beginning points."[8] Our ability to know is both dependent upon, and limited by, the assumptions of our worldviews. This being the case, we would be well advised to discern how to evaluate whether or not our conclusions are accurate.

The first thing we might note is that any of us can have errant thinking—whether due to the effects of drugs, delusions, dementia, or deceptive reasoning. Most people would agree that Jimmy's

---

4. Many postmodernists would not accept even this more tentative claim for the utility of the scientific method. Smith and Deemer, for instance, summarize the postmodern conclusion as follows: "There is no possibility of theory-free observation and knowledge, the duality of subject and object is untenable, no epistemic privilege can be attached to any particular method or set of methods, and we cannot have the kind of objective access to an external, extralingual referent that would allow us to adjudicate from among different knowledge claims" (Problem of criteria, 879). While I agree with all of these observations, I still maintain that various epistemic methods are useful and are more than the expression of politics and power.

5. Couvalis, *Philosophy of science*, 11. Van Leeuwen (see next footnote) provided these three categories. For a much more detailed cat-

egorization, see chapter 1, Types of realism, in Niiniluoto, *Critical scientific realism*.

6. Van Leeuwen, Five uneasy questions, 156.

7. Browning & Evison, Introduction, 7.

8. Browning, Psychology in service, 129.

reality-testing abilities were severely impaired by his inability to separate reality from his own delusions. Attempts to convince him that his perceptions were hallucinatory were futile. It rarely makes sense to argue with people who are psychotic or drugged about the nature of reality, because their perceptions seem accurate to them. While medications can sometimes help individuals who are cognitively impaired, regrettably, there are many cases in which the future simply becomes increasingly bleak as a person's cognitive faculties fade. Fortunately, these conditions are the exception rather than the rule, but they must be taken into account. To a certain degree, we are left with the conclusion that unusual claims made by a small percentage of the population are suspect unless sufficient support for those claims exists.[9] Unfortunately, while there is safety in numbers, the crowd can be wrong; things that are commonly believed to be true can be false.[10]

---

9. Suspicion of unusual claims does not, *ipso facto*, make those claims incorrect. For instance, the first claims of Jesus' resurrection were met with incredulity, yet became the cornerstone of Christian faith (Matt 28:1–20; Luke 24:9–11; John 20:24–25; 1 Cor 15:12–20).

10. For instance, in most ancient Eastern and Western traditions, the world was thought to be composed of four basic elements: earth, air, water, and fire. Variations on this view were widely held for thousands of years. This view is no longer tenable, however. The modern periodic table, and all the evidence that supports it, reflects a much more sophisticated and accurate view of the elements of which the world is composed.

Human cognition is amazing, complex, and usually dependable. While our mental processes typically allow us to navigate our world successfully, they are imperfect. Few of us suffer from severe delusions, but we all experience limitations that affect our reasoning abilities. Human memory is imperfect. Reasoning can be flawed. Our experiences prime us to think about the world in ways that influence our conclusions. The frailty of our thinking imposes limitations on our quest for certainty.

The assumptions and beliefs that are widely held in our cultures and subcultures can also impede our attempts to gain knowledge. Rebecca, for instance, was primed by the teachings of her religious group to assume that unusual abilities could be imparted by demons. All of us are affected by assumptions that are entrenched within our cultures. Consider, for example, that prejudice is typically learned from culturally embedded attitudes. In relatively recent times, in the Deep South of the United States, white supremacists concluded that white people were superior to black people, often using a perversion of Christianity to support their conclusions, their message, and their actions. Internet sites still spew their message of hate, often framed in "Christian" language. Black churches were firebombed and burned by church-going whites. African Americans were lynched and shot by white-hooded mobs and beaten by police in the streets. Even the white churches largely failed to stand up for justice. Martin Luther King Jr. once   remarked,   "Well,   the most pervasive mistake I have made was in believing that because our cause was just, we could be sure that the white ministers of the South, once their Christian consciences were challenged, would rise to our aid . . . As our movement unfolded, and direct appeals were made to white ministers, most folded their hands—and some even took stands against us."[11]

> The noetic effects of sin—distortions of human reasoning caused by individual or corporate sin. Classic treatments of this phenomenon assume that sin affects some things less (such as mathematics or chemistry) and others more (such as ethics and theology).

The sins and assumptions of a culture surely affect the sins and the thinking of its resident members. Phillip Yancey, in a remarkably transparent confession of the racism that he was raised with and once practiced, provided this sobering reflection: "Only one thing haunts me more than the sins of my past: What sins am I blind to today?"[12] The sins and assumptions that pervade our culture are blindspots in our moral and epistemic frameworks. Sadly, we must conclude that culture can adversely affect our thinking.

We must also acknowledge that our own human sinfulness affects human thinking. Lack of virtue may be expressed in intentional fabrication. Personal sin can warp our thinking about our own culpability or the effects of our behavior on others. Rationalization, and a host of defense mechanisms, can distort our perception of truth.

Theologians use the phrase *the noetic effects of sin* to describe the ways that sin distorts human thinking.[13] Emil Brunner, for instance, noted that sin affects thinking to greater or lesser degrees. For instance, mathematics and science are less affected by sinful human thinking than are ethics, theology, and the humanities. Sin has a tremendous ability to skew our thinking about our relationship to God and about how we ought to live. Because the social sciences involve our personal and social lives, Brunner believed that we must explicitly consider how the noetic effects of sin can warp our thinking in these areas. This is especially important when we consider the goals toward which we strive. Should we, for instance, encourage people to seek their own happiness above all else? Alternatively, should we encourage them to seek to be faithful to God's call and commands?[14] The purpose of human life is not morally neutral, and personal

---

11. Quoted in Yancey, *Soul survivor*, 38.

12. Ibid., 39.

13. For an excellent discussion of this topic, see Moroney, *Noetic effects*.

14. In the long run, I would contend that seeking to be in right relationship to God and others leads to our greatest good; but in the short term, things like confession and turning away from temptation can be intensely painful.

sin can skew the goals toward which we strive.

It would be bad enough if we only had to concern ourselves with the detrimental effects of personal sin, but the effects of sins that are culturally imbedded also create epistemic problems. The noetic effects of sin are expressed in corporate sins, such as racism, sexism, failure to minister to the plight of the orphan and the widow, and moral laxity. Contemporary American culture may promote materialism, narcissism, and self-aggrandizement to a degree to which we are largely unaware, but which nonetheless affects us in profound ways. Christians in the social sciences need to think carefully about how sin affects our thinking about human individuals and social systems.

The detrimental effects of drugs, disease, cultural bias, and personal sin can distort human thinking. Human thinking is also limited because it is the product of imperfect, finite creatures. We never have access to all the data, and even if we did, we could never comprehend it in its entirety. While our thinking is a remarkable and powerful phenomenon, we must remember that from a Christian perspective, we are frail, fallen, and finite creatures.

How can we know anything? Since all of us begin with worldview beliefs that shape the way we respond to the world, are raised in cultures that mold our thinking through education and everyday experience, and suffer the effects of minds that are finite, frail, and fallen, we must conclude that human beings can never eliminate all error from our thinking. As James Guy concluded, "To recognize that man is unable to fully know the truth is to risk some degree of skepticism. However, in the search for truth such a realization is necessary in order to avoid illusion and fantasy. Dialogue amidst this uncertainty serves as a catalyst for greater accuracy and understanding in conceptualizing truth."[15]

We should react with humility as we grasp the significant limitations placed on our epistemic efforts by our finitude, the frailties of our minds and bodies, and the fallenness of our moral reasoning. This state of affairs should also prompt a deep appreciation that God loves us despite our failings, longs to redeem us, desires to use us to bring restoration to the brokenness of the world, and is Himself actively at work in the world and sovereign over it. As the old hymn proclaims,

> Oh, worship the King, all glorious above.
> Oh, gratefully sing his power and his love;
> Our shield and defender, the Ancient of Days,
> Pavilioned in splendor and girded with praise.
>
> Frail children of dust, and feeble as frail,
> In you do we trust, nor find you to fail;
> Your mercies, how tender, how firm to the end,

---

15. Guy, Search for truth.

Our maker, defender, redeemer, and friend! [16]

The hymn proclaims *human limitations* and *God's goodness*, leading naturally to worship. So, too, our recognition of our limitations should lead to grateful acknowledgement of our dependence upon God and the majesty of His power and His love.

At best, we can humbly try to evaluate our beliefs carefully enough to arrive at a contingent certainty; that is, *if* our assumptions are correct, *and if* we discern a coherent epistemology, *and if* we apply our epistemic methodologies consistently, *then* we can be *tentatively* certain about our conclusions. To hope for (or worse, to claim) more than that is to assert a god-like quality which frail, fallen, and finite creatures cannot attain.

Epistemology and Its Necessary Virtues

Epistemology is the branch of philosophy that considers the nature, possibilities, and limitations of knowledge.[17]

Epistemology is concerned, in part, with whether or not our knowledge claims can stand up to scrutiny in such a way that we can separate mere opinion from justified belief.[18] If our efforts to obtain knowledge are to be fruitful, we will use methods that are appropriate to the type of questions that we ask. For instance, if we want to know if a new medication will decrease the symptoms of dementia, we will not rely exclusively on a rational argument—we will look for empirical data. Likewise, if we want to know about the nature of God, we will turn to methods other than empirical ones.

Before we can discern and apply relevant epistemic methods, though, we must first possess certain cognitive qualities, such as the ability to reason well, and certain virtues, such as perseverance at the difficult tasks of doing empirical research or constructing careful arguments. Additionally, once we have obtained knowledge, we need to know how to use it for appropriate ends. In summary, then the minimum criteria for reasoning accurately and well and for using knowledge for good purposes in order to obtain and make appropriate use of knowledge are: a) that we possess the necessary intellectual qualities, b) that we exercise the crucial virtues, and c) that we competently make use of relevant epistemic methods.[19]

---

16. Robert Grant, 1833.

17. If this were a philosophy text, we would need to discuss what constitutes *knowledge*. For most of intellectual history, knowledge was defined as *justified true belief.* This definition has been much contested in the past fifty years since the publication of Edmund Gettier's short piece, Is justified true belief knowledge? For the present purposes, though, we will concern ourselves with criteria that make it possible for us to *hold beliefs that are true* and that we (at least *reasonably*) *believe to be true.* Any philosopher will quickly see problems with this definition à

la Gettier and others, but it will suffice for the present purposes.

18. Wolfe, *Epistemology.*

19. Aristotle did not have a theory of knowledge in the traditional sense, but he did have

Most institutions of higher education address the requirement of intellectual aptitude by setting admission requirements, such as a minimum high school GPA and SAT scores. We may well question how effectively these requirements function as measures of intellectual aptitude, but let us assume, for the sake of argument, that our college classes are filled with cognitively competent students. If this were the case, could we then simply dispense information and instruct students in correct epistemic methods and be sure that they would be able to obtain and apply knowledge well? Clearly, the answer is *no*. Most professors are aware that students possess *character traits* that either facilitate or inhibit their learning. As one professor laments, "Our frustrations often concern not student's lack of intellectual aptitude . . . but their unwillingness to exercise that aptitude *well*."[20] Some students have cultivated virtues that make it more likely that they will drink deeply from the academic well; others have cultivated vices that make it likely that they

will drop out of school or earn a diploma without actually receiving an education. If we want to avoid such undesirable outcomes, we need to exercise stewardship of our own minds.

I often remind my students that they have been given a rare and lavish gift. This gift requires stewardship on our part if we are to make the most of it. To maximally profit from opportunities to obtain knowledge and to use information for appropriate ends, we need to be both *morally virtuous* and *intellectually virtuous*. Moral virtues help us to moderate our passions rightly and to discern what is right and just, so that we aim towards the right ends. Intellectual virtues are character traits and habits that allow us to think well and, in turn, to employ knowledge well.

So far, we have argued that in order to obtain knowledge and use it for desirable ends, we first need to be a certain kind of person, one who possesses particular habits of thought. Jay Wood highlights the importance of being intellectually virtuous:

> Thinking about epistemology as encompassing the pursuit of intellectual virtue . . . is important . . . for the simple reason that your very character, the kind of person you are and are becoming, is at stake. Careful oversight of our intellectual lives is imperative if we are to think well, and thinking well is an indispensable ingredient to living well . . . If we fail to oversee our intellectual life and cultivate virtue, the likely consequence

---

what you might call a "philosophical psychology"—an account of how the mind comes to know the world, things contained therein, and their causes. In his view, a mind must be suitably prepared or disposed to be able to correctly "know" the object which is affecting it. Aristotle distinguishes between moral virtues, which we must cultivate if we are to live rightly, and intellectual virtues, which enable us to know rightly. In this section, I am not following Aristotle's distinction between the moral and intellectual virtues strictly, but am rather identifying a few characteristics which can affect the clarity and accuracy of our thinking.

20. Floyd, *Education as soulcraft*, 254.

will be a maimed and stunted mind that thwarts our prospects for living a flourishing life.[21]

According to Wood, "Seeking truth appropriately is a matter of seeking it in the right way, for the right reason, using the right methods and for the right purposes."[22] So, what are the intellectual virtues that will allow us to "seek truth correctly"? We will consider a few of these virtues: *studiositas*, intellectual humility, intellectual caution, intellectual courage, intellectual integrity, and intellectual perseverance. [23]

Studiositas

Medieval scholastics made a distinction between the vice of *curiositas,* a vicious intellectual appetite that aimed to privatize and possess knowledge, and *studiositas*, an intellectual virtue that was similar to curiosity in the sense of having a desire to know or understand the world, but framed within the context of seeing knowledge as something that was a gift to be used towards right ends.[24] Griffiths

points out that curiosity was considered to be a vice by Augustine and the early church, whereas today we tend to blindly assume that curiosity is a virtue. Augustine compares curiosity to sexual desire outside of a committed marital relationship, and contends that studiousness, in contrast, is an "appetite for participation in what is given" by God.[25] According to Griffiths, curiosity as a vice seeks possession and ownership of knowledge, much as one buys sex from a prostitute. It is ultimately arrogant and selfish. The studious person, in contrast, seeks knowledge not just to obtain a body of information, but to understand all things as gifts to be explored in appropriate ways and to be used towards godly ends. We are stewards of this gift, not possessors of it. Self-centered curiosity stems from and exacerbates selfishness, arrogance, and possessiveness. On the other hand, if we are studious, we seek knowledge and its connection to God as stewards, and we find our diligence expressed in gratitude, worship, and generosity.

Intellectual humility

Intellectual humility is concerned with the ability to judge oneself accurately and to be open to correction and to

---

21. Wood, *Epistemology*, 17.

22. Ibid., 57.

23. The exact composition of the intellectual virtues is contested. In fact, some philosophers contend that the moral and intellectual virtues are not significantly distinct from one another. The following list is illustrative rather than encyclopedic.

24. In the first two editions of this book, I referred to curiosity as a virtue, a view that I have since come to see as in need of serious revision. My original thought was that curiosity drives us to interest and discovery. However, a book by

---

Paul Griffiths (2006), *The vice of curiosity: An essay on intellectual appetite*, convinced me that what is important in this discussion is not just the desire to know, but the motive for knowing. Griffiths, in turn, led me to realize that Aristotle, Augustine, and Thomas Aquinas had explored the intellectual virtues in great depth.

25. Griffiths, *The vice of curiosity*, 60.

the insights of others.[26] Humility, as all of the virtues, stands in opposition to one or more vices. In this case, humility is opposed to such things as arrogance, conceit, self-righteousness, and selfish ambition.[27] Robert Roberts describes humility as "the ability, without prejudice to one's self-comfort, to admit one's inferiority. . . [or] superiority" in some way.[28] An elite athlete could humbly and accurately say, "I am a very talented basketball player," without being false or self-aggrandizing. Likewise, for a mediocre player to admit that he isn't all that good isn't just false modesty, it's the truth. Humility as an intellectual virtue involves our recognition of our intellectual abilities and liabilities. It allows us to receive correction, feedback, or affirmation appropriately, and to develop and exercise our abilities unencumbered by arrogance or self-deprecation.

---

26. Humility is often considered to be a moral virtue, though some virtue epistemologists such as Jay Wood believe that it is reasonable to see a number of moral virtues as having intellectual applications. To Wood and others, it seems, "perfectly meaningful to speak of intellectual virtues such as 'intellectual humility,' 'intellectual generosity,' and 'intellectual courage,' which combine the operations and ends of the intellect and will. Intellectual humility, for example, is 'intellectual' when it serves the interest of knowledge, understanding, and other intellectual goods, by combatting forms of pride that obstruct our pursuit of truth." Wood, *Faith's intellectual rewards*, 39–40.

27. See Roberts and Wood, *Intellectual virtues*, 236ff.

28. Roberts, *Spiritual emotions*, 83.

Without intellectual humility, our pursuit of knowledge will be seriously impaired. Imagine that you are involved in a class discussion about an assigned reading. One of your peers condescendingly rejects the author's position and claims that it has no merit or evidence in its favor. He confidently proclaims that the author is wrong. Having read the article carefully, you question your peer, thinking that he must have missed something in the article, only to discover that he never read the assignment! Clearly, there are numerous intellectual vices at play here, but surely one of them is a lack of humility, expressed in the belief that he could substantively critique a position that he had never actually considered. While this vice is clear, many of us are guilty of a lack of intellectual humility in less obvious ways. We do not read or listen to other points of view *carefully*. In subtle or overtly arrogant ways, we fail to respect the cultures, experiences, and education that have shaped other people's perspectives. We privilege our own unconsidered opinions. We fail to respect the accumulated wisdom of others. And the list could go on. To guard against these types of errors, we need to cultivate intellectual humility by submitting to instruction. We need to recognize the limits of our intellectual abilities and our knowledge base. We need to admit that our own biases and fallibility can skew our conclusions. These are the first steps in creating the framework of an intellectually virtuous life.

Intellectual caution and intellectual courage

Intellectual humility may lay the groundwork for our ability to profit from instruction and to seek knowledge, but to it we must add several other virtues. Intellectual caution and intellectual courage, our next virtues, are concerned with how we evaluate and respond to the real and imagined threats involved in intellectual pursuits.[29] Allow me to introduce this with an example.

I recently attended a conference where I anticipated that the viewpoints I would encounter would be strongly opposed to some of my own beliefs; I was not disappointed. So why did I go to this conference? I did not go to courageously fight for my beliefs. I went to allow my own beliefs to be challenged, so that I could give an honest hearing to viewpoints that I would otherwise tend to avoid. Doing so was unsettling but good. I found that I understood the beliefs of some people with whom I disagree much better for having listened to them. In fact, I found myself having to reconsider some of my own beliefs and reasoning. Intellectual courage is a virtue that allows us to face situations where knowledge may be unsettling. Clients in therapy and parishioners in confessionals sometimes need intellectual courage to come to know uncomfortable truths about themselves. Education, too, can be unsettling as we face viewpoints that challenge beliefs that we may have never questioned.

On the other hand, one should not rush in where angels fear to tread: there are times when intellectual caution is advised. Intellectual caution requires that we be careful and circumspect in forming judgments. Perhaps in our excitement, we might want to brashly assert more than is justified by the data. In such cases, intellectual caution counsels restraint and discretion.

While intellectual courage calls us to face or overcome fears that ought to be confronted, intellectual caution calls us to appropriately recognize dangers that ought to be avoided or carefully negotiated. Intellectual caution might appropriately cause us to avoid certain quests for knowledge. For instance, given that we have limited intellectual and financial resources, we might appropriately decide that pursuing a particular intellectual path is not worth the costs. Some quests for knowledge could be damaging, for example, if it is likely to be used in ways that are harmful.

So intellectual courage will appropriately push us forward, and intellectual caution will appropriately hold us back. To these, we will now add another virtue which is necessary if we are to think well.

Intellectual integrity

Intellectual integrity or honesty is related to the pursuit of truth in at least two ways—the potential for self-deception, and the intent to deceive others. That we

---

29. For an excellent discussion of this topic, see Roberts and Woods chapter Courage and caution, in their book, *Intellectual virtues*.

can deceive ourselves is one of the hallmarks of Freud's theory of defense mechanisms. For instance, when we do not want to admit that something is morally wrong, we may use rationalization to justify our errant thoughts, feelings, or behaviors. What is particularly damning in Freud's observation is how easily self-deceit takes place automatically and unconsciously. Our own self-deceit naturally leads us to mislead others, but we can also do so quite consciously.

Why might we want to deceive others? Pride and greed are notable vices that come into play in this respect. Pride, of course, can cause us to exaggerate the merits of our own opinions. Greed has certainly been a motive for falsifying data in order to increase the profits of a person or a corporation. A related problem is that we must often rely on the credibility of others for information, and if their intellectual integrity is impaired, our faith in their credibility may be misplaced. When people "lie, exaggerate, or withhold evidence" we are left to doubt the credibility of their truth claims.[30]

Intellectual honesty is one of the most obvious intellectual virtues. We now turn our attention to one more intellectual virtue, which while perhaps not as obvious, is indispensable and cultivated only with great effort.

> "If one has the answers to all the questions—that is the proof that God is not with him. It means that he is a false prophet using religion for himself. The great leaders of the people of God, like Moses, have always left room for doubt. You must leave room for the Lord, not for our certainties; we must be humble."
>
> —Pope Francis

Intellectual perseverance

Intellectual perseverance or *discipline* is another trait that facilitates the attainment of knowledge. Discipline of the mind is much like exercise—it takes time to strengthen muscles, to develop coordination, and to build up endurance. People who give in to the vice of sloth fail to extend adequate energy to attaining goals. By contrast, the disciplined person will put the necessary effort and resources towards developing habits and skills that are necessary to accomplishing worthy objectives.

Academia, again, holds out examples of the difficulties of intellectual perseverance. When I collect term papers, I often ask students what time they finished writing. I suppose you can guess what happens: a few rare souls will have finished a day or two before, while most students finished in the wee hours of the

---

30. Dew and Foreman, *How do we know*, 123.

morning.[31] Procrastination is a vice that affects most of us, and to combat it, we need perseverance. But limitations of time are only one of the obstacles with which we must contend, as we will see.

The quest for knowledge requires that we must be disciplined in applying ourselves to the task of learning. This means, for instance, reading a textbook when you might prefer to play tennis. It may mean needing to read an article over and over and over again to begin to understand the nuances and flow of the argument. It may mean having to struggle with uncertainty and confusion over a long period of time as you attempt to understand complex issues.

There are a number of other moral and intellectual virtues that we need to cultivate and to possess if we are to think well and if we are to make good use of the knowledge that we obtain. The central argument of this section, though, is that the first step in seeking knowledge is to become the kind of people who have the characteristics and dispositions that will allow us to learn and to use knowledge wisely. Without such virtues, the quest for knowledge will be unproductive intellectually and damaging personally. As we turn our attention to look at several epistemic strategies, let us remember

that we must cultivate intellectual virtue if our pursuits are to be worthwhile and maximally effective.

Of Madness and Methodologies

Imagine that your ability to test reality was grossly impaired, as Jimmy's was. You would be what was once called *mad*. The word *mad* comes to us from Old English and Old Saxon words: the Old English *gemad* ("insane") and the Old Saxon *gimed* ("foolish").[32] While most of us are not mad in the delusional sense, we are all quite familiar with being mad in the foolish sense. We make mistakes, draw incorrect inferences, and come to wrong conclusions. Several methodologies can be employed to help us be less foolish. These methodologies provide us with rules to follow so that we can evaluate knowledge claims carefully. An exhaustive discussion of epistemic strategies is beyond the scope of our present concerns, so we will limit ourselves to four that have specific relevance for the integration of psychology and Christianity: authority, logic, empiricism, and hermeneutics. By learning about these methodologies and applying them well, we can avoid being unduly simplistic or excessively foolish in our integrative efforts.

Appeals to Authority

The vast majority of what we know has been handed down to us from

---

31. Operant conditioning helps us understand why procrastination is rewarding. Procrastination is initially negatively reinforced (that is, you feel better by avoiding something unpleasant). Then, if you get a reasonably acceptable grade on the paper that you composed at the last minute, your procrastination is positively reinforced.

---

32. *The Oxford English dictionary*, 9:169.

authorities: parents, teachers, doctors, scientists, theologians, translators, and mechanics, among others. Unfortunately, many falsehoods are also passed down through authority. That any method can go wrong, though, is no reason to get rid of it. Instead, we need to look at how to increase the likelihood that using the method will yield the desired result.

Since the Enlightenment, appeals to authority have been treated with great suspicion. Nevertheless, authority is a powerful means of transferring knowledge from person to person. When a doctor provides a diagnosis and treatment recommendation, she is providing her knowledge (gained in part from the authority of other experts who published their own empirical work, and others who ran lab tests on the patient) to her patient. The patient could accept the diagnosis and the recommendation, or decide to consult his pastor, his plumber, his attorney, his Aunt Irene, or google. Notice, though, that these "authorities" are of vastly different quality. For an authority to be credible the knowledge base of the authority must be relevant; the plumber's knowledge base for designing the water supply and drainage system for a new bathroom is clearly irrelevant to the medical condition of the patient, whereas the doctor's knowledge base is more relevant.

For a relevant authority to be reliable, we need at least three more conditions to be met. First, we need to be able to have a reasonable degree of assurance that the authority accurately discerned the situation (e.g., that the doctor gave the correct diagnosis). This means that the

authority must occupy a privileged position from which she knows things that we do not—she went to medical school, she saw the test results, she is competent in her judgments, and so forth. Of course, the authority can be wrong—misdiagnosis can happen, especially when dealing with probabilities rather than certainties. The second criteria for authority to be credible involves the character of the authority figure, for instance, we need to have sufficient reason to believe that she is honestly representing her knowledge (honesty) and providing it for our benefit and not for personal gain (beneficence). Finally, the usefulness of appeals to authority requires that we accurately understand what the authority is communicating. In the foregoing example, we may need the authority to break down technical terms into language that we can understand. We also might need to make sure that our initial emotional state does not keep us from accurately processing the information given to us.

Although appeals to authority are much maligned, without them we would be utterly lost. There is a social dimension to knowledge that we cannot do without. Of course, we should not blindly trust authority, and authorities can and do err, but authority nevertheless remains one of our most powerful means of seeking knowledge. The social fabric of knowledge requires trust and—under some circumstances—verification. One epistemic method that we can use in verifying some types of truth claims is logic, and it is this method to which we now turn our attention.

"Even in the valley of the shadow of death, two and two do not make six."

—Leo Tolstoy

Logic

The logical approach to epistemology begins from the assumption that we can separate fact from belief by looking at the rational consistency of one's reasoning.[33] Logic can be separated into deductive and inductive types. *Deductive logic* is used to establish truth by combining and evaluating premises based on standard rules and axioms. Similar to geometric proofs, deduction begins with premises that are asserted and then asks what can be concluded if the premises are accepted and combined together. A simple example is the argument, if A = B, and if B = C, then A = C.

Deductive arguments contain three elements: *premises*, *inferences*, and *conclusions*. A *premise* is a statement that must be true or false. In the forgoing example, the first premise was, A = B. Note that a premise is a statement that either is or is not true. If a premise is wrong, the argument is *flawed*. In some cases not everyone will agree that the proposition is true, which highlights the importance of coming up with agreed-upon definitions

and propositions if one's arguments are to be compelling. If you have ever read Socratic dialogues, you know just how much effort can be put into this phase of the exercise!

The second element of a deductive argument is the *inference*. Once the propositions have been agreed upon, a new proposition is created that states an implication that should logically follow from the accepted propositions. It is usually the part of the argument that proceeds from *if* to *therefore*. If the inference (the *if–then* connection) is wrong, the argument is *invalid*.

The third part of a deductive argument is the final inference, which is called the *conclusion*. The conclusion is a new statement that is logically connected to the propositional statements. Conclusions can be true or false based on the validity of the premises and the inferences drawn from them. In order to show how deductive arguments can go wrong and to help us construct them correctly, we make use of a *truth table*. A simple truth table is included below.

TABLE 5.1

Truth Table		
Premise	*Inference*	*Conclusion*
False	Invalid	True or false
False	Valid	True or false
True	Invalid	True or false
True	Valid	True

---

33. Some postmodern critics have argued that knowledge claims are spurious because logic is expressed through language, which is created by humans and changes over time. Therefore, to talk of immutable truth is, by this reckoning, absurd.

In order to be *sound*, the argument must start from true premises, and include valid inferences. If those conditions are met, then we can be theoretically certain that the conclusion is true.[34] Unfortunately, the triple limitations of finitude, frailty, and fallenness restrict how sure we can be of the veracity of our premises and the correct application of the method. Still, logical deduction is a very useful method.

Rebecca's conclusion that Jimmy was demon possessed was the result of logical deduction. The following propositions represent the kind of argument she might have made:

- Rock-and-roll music is often a product of demonic influence.

- People can make Faustian bargains whereby they give their soul to a demonic force in exchange for a supernatural ability.

- Jimmy claims that his guitar-playing ability suddenly emerged during a rock-and-roll concert.

- Jimmy's account is accurate.

- Therefore, Jimmy must have made a deal with a demon to acquire his guitar playing ability.

While Rebecca used logical deduction to conclude that Jimmy was demon possessed, it is obvious that there are numerous flaws in her argument.

Logical deduction is extremely important to experimental psychology, because hypothesis testing involves the application of deductive logic. We evaluate the statistical significance of data by determining whether or not they support the null hypothesis or the experimental hypothesis. Hypothesis testing using statistical analysis would not be possible without deductive logic.

Inductive logic, in contrast to deductive logic, attempts to develop generalizations based on isolated observations. As such, it is probabilistic, inferring how things usually work. Inductive logic is often the initial source of psychological theories. For example, one might notice that a significant portion of special-education students come from economically disadvantaged homes and surmise that poverty contributes to educational problems. At this point the age-old statistical axiom comes into play: *correlation does not imply causation*. While we might observe the correlation of events, we cannot demonstrate cause without manipulating the variables experimentally. It is thus to experimentation that we now turn our attention.

---

34. An example of an unsound argument containing a true statement as its conclusion follows. Imagine that someone is looking at a polar bear and reasons out the following: All bears are white. That animal is a bear. Therefore, that animal is white. Note that the first premise is false, but the conclusion is true.

Empiricism

The words *empiricism* and *empirical* come to us from the ancient Greek root *empiric,* which involved reliance on experience to evaluate knowledge claims. The origin of the word referred to "an ancient sect of physicians who based their practice on experience alone disregarding all theoretical and philosophical considerations."[35] Saint Luke is widely believed to have been a physician, and he exemplified this experiential approach in the opening of his gospel: "Therefore, since *I myself have carefully investigated everything* from the beginning, it seemed good also to me to write an orderly account . . . *so that you may know the certainty of the things you have been taught*" (Luke 1:3–4, NIV, italics added).

Luke was unwilling to trust philosophical speculation alone—he checked out the sources to the best of his ability in order to be sure that what he reported was accurately conveyed and confirmed by investigation.[36]

Contemporary empiricism as an epistemic method is derived from logical positivism, a view in which belief is validated or invalidated solely by the evidence of experience. In the sciences, empiricism proceeds along the familiar lines

of the scientific method. One observes a phenomenon, creates a theory about the nature or cause of the phenomenon, and then generates a hypothesis—a prediction based on the theory about what would happen if certain elements of the phenomenon are altered. An experiment is then created to test the hypothesis. Finally, one observes the results of the experiment and evaluates whether the evidence supports or refutes the theory. Note that *theories can never be proved*, only disproved or supported.[37]

Empirical methods have been central to the development of psychology as a science. By applying the scientific method to human beings, we have increased our understanding of the biological, psychological, and social determinants of human behavior and mental processes. For example, empiricism has drastically improved our understanding of schizophrenia, the disorder that Jimmy suffered from. Inheritance patterns have been determined that may ultimately lead to identification of genes that are implicated in schizophrenia. We have uncovered social factors, such as *expressed emotion* (characterized by criticism, hostility, and emotionality) that are associated with increased risk of relapse. If we were able to study Jimmy's brain, we would likely see characteristic reduction of gray matter in his temporal and frontal lobes. We

---

35. *Merriam-Webster collegiate dictionary.* 408.

36. It is interesting to compare the modernist view of miracles with Luke's view of miracles. The modernist assumes at the outset that miracles cannot exist because they have no basis in nature (which is a circular argument), whereas Luke investigated accounts of miracles and evidently accepted them because no natural explanation sufficiently accounted for them. Note that Luke made use of historical inquiry and appeals to authority as means of seeking knowledge (consulting eyewitnesses), as well as rationally investigating the claims that were made.

---

37. The most basic reason that we can never prove a theory is that we can never observe all possible cases of a population of events, and a single negative case would demonstrate a flaw in the theory.

have greater understanding of the biological changes that take place in the brains of people who have schizophrenia, and of pharmaceutical and psychological interventions that can help them manage their symptoms. Although Jimmy was not cured by his treatments, he was treated more humanely, and he likely had a much better outcome than would have been the case without those treatments.

Since psychology adopted a scientific approach in the late nineteenth century, our understanding of human behavior has advanced considerably. However, psychology, and science in general, have been forced to recognize the limitations of the modernist framework that is usually associated with empiricism. The goal of positivism was irrefutable evidence upon which to base beliefs, but such precision and certainty are never possible. Additionally, scientists do not rely on empiricism alone; for instance, they make use of "the testimony of past witnesses" (appeals to authority), intuition, and reasoning, as well as observation based on sense perception.[38]

While we like to think of science as a way of gathering "facts" about the world, it is better to think of it as an epistemic framework that allows us to view the world through a specific theoretical framework.[39] Each theoretical framework allows us to understand the world through a particular paradigm (e.g., Aristotelian, Neoplatonic, and mechanis-

tic). Each of these paradigms is based on a set of metaphysical presuppositions that "primes its adherents to look for certain kinds of facts and to apply certain [kinds of] interpretations."[40] The most pervasive scientific paradigm today is that of the world-as-machine, yet that paradigm reflects not just brute facts, but philosophical assumptions about the nature of the world (e.g., that it functions like a machine, that it can be calibrated and controlled, and the like.).

Although empirical methods have given us a unique and powerful lens through which to view natural phenomena, we must always remember that they provide a constricted view. Science focuses its attention on a limited domain (the physical world). This intense focus allows it to rigorously investigate material aspects of the world, but it necessarily neglects many other aspects of reality. As theologian Hans Küng noted, "It has become more clear that all the measuring, experimenting, and extrapolating of the highly developed behavioral sciences— as terribly important as it is—rests on a preliminary understanding of human reality that encompasses only certain aspects and dimensions of it."[41] The limited scope of psychology and other sciences allows them to be very productive, but in a very limited domain.

Complicating this picture is the fact that no one develops a theory without first making a series of philosophical assumptions, and in the case of psychology

---

38. Vande Kemp, Sorcerer, 20.

39. See Pearcey & Thaxton, *The soul of science*, 59ff.

40. Ibid., 98.

41. Küng, *Freud and God*, 149–50.

these assumptions go to the very heart of what it means to be human. Sigmund Koch cautioned us about our tendency to overlook these philosophical assumptions.

> Psychology is necessarily the most philosophy-sensitive discipline in the entire gamut of disciplines that claim empirical status. We cannot discriminate a so-called variable, pose a research question, choose or invent a method, project a theory, [or] stipulate a psychotechnology, without making strong presumptions of philosophical cast about the nature of our human subject matter—presumptions that can be ordered to age-old contexts of philosophical discussion.[42]

Furthermore, especially when theories involve human beings, they inevitably involve value judgments. Gordon Allport made this point fifty years ago as he struggled to define what it means to be a "healthy" human being.

> We cannot answer this question solely in terms of pure psychology. In order to say that a person is mentally healthy, sound, [or] mature, we need to know what health, soundness, and maturity are. Psychology alone cannot tell us. To some degree ethical judgment is involved . . . Science alone can never tell us what is sound, healthy, or good.[43]

For this reason, we cannot simply assume that psychology as a science will be "objective" or "self-correcting"—it will always reflect the worldviews and values of its theorists.

To these concerns, some people object that science is a self-correcting discipline because the data we collect force us to reconsider our theories. While there is some truth in this, the degree to which we can be objective is limited: our biases predictably affect our interpretation. Van Leeuwen rightly cautions that recent critiques "have demonstrated the degree to which scientific data are theory-laden, and theories are underdetermined by facts."[44]

Despite these shortcomings, empirical methods can be very useful when they are applied to observable phenomena. However, we need to exercise cautious oversight of our own biases and worldviews. Science has advanced our knowledge of the physical world, but it can only be applied to observable phenomena, and its claims are limited to that domain. Correctly used, empiricism can be a very powerful means of evaluating limited types of claims, notably those which can be observed and tested experientially. To obtain knowledge about non-physical phenomena we need to use other epistemic methods.

Before leaving our discussion of empiricism, we must note that a tumultuous shift has been taking place within the social sciences over the past several

---

42. Koch, *Psychology and human context*, 412.

43. Allport, *Pattern and growth*, 275–76.

44. Van Leeuwen, Five uneasy questions, 150.

decades. Postmodern critiques have resulted in two versions of psychology: one that cherishes empirical research and one that sees empiricism as damaging on political, social, and ethical grounds. One of the first attempts to posit a middle ground was the development of *grounded theory* by Glaser and Strauss.[45] Their approach established the use of qualitative research as a means of giving more latitude and input to research participants, while still yielding quantifiable data. Objectivist grounded theory still maintained "positivistic assumptions of an external world that can be described, analyzed, explained, and predicted."[46] More recently, constructivist grounded theory has rejected these positivistic assumptions. "Constructivism assumes the relativism of multiple social realities, recognizes the mutual creation of knowledge by the viewer and the viewed, and aims toward interpretive understanding of subjects' meanings."[47]

"Science can purify religion from error and superstition. Religion can purify science from idolatry and false absolutes."

—Pope John Paul II

Constructivist-grounded theory and other postempirical approaches to psychology will continue to present epistemic challenges to the field, and by extension, to integration. For the time being, empirical and nonempirical methodologies continue to be influential, competing paradigms within the social sciences.

Revelation and Interpretation

Christians who are committed to historic, orthodox expressions of the faith believe that God has revealed Himself indirectly, through general revelation, and directly, through special revelation.[48] General revelation is invoked by the apostle Paul when he wrote, "For since the creation of the world God's invisible qualities—his eternal power and divine nature—have been clearly seen, being understood from what has been made, so that men are without excuse" (Rom 1:20, NIV). Special revelation refers to unique acts whereby God discloses Himself in word or deed, such as in theophanies, miracles, dreams, and visions.[49] Orthodox

---

45. Glaser & Strauss, *Discovery*.

46. Charmaz, Grounded theory, 524.

47. Ibid., 510.

---

48. Some integrative theorists have suggested that psychology is an expression of general revelation, while scriptural teachings about human beings are derived from special revelation. While the attempt to ground integrative efforts within this paradigm is well intentioned, the language is misleading. Technically both general and special revelation refer to what can be known *about God* through natural or revelational means, not what can be known about created things through those means. Alternatively, understanding that we can attempt to discern truth through studying both God's Word and His Works is a more accurate—and useful—paradigm.

49. Alexander & Rosner, *New dictionary of*

Christians accept the Old and New Testament books as God's special revelation, preserved as His written Word. While all of God's Word is true, Christians do not see Scripture as containing all truth. For instance, a car-repair manual will be more useful than the Gospel of John if you need instructions about changing the oil in your car. As Arthur Holmes remarked, "The Christian regards the biblical revelation as the final rule of faith and conduct, but he does not think of it as an exhaustive source of all truth . . . Moreover, if all truth is God's truth and truth is one, then God does not contradict himself, and in the final analysis there will be no conflict between the truth taught in scripture and truth available from other sources."[50] Harmony must thus exist between truths obtained from the biblical message and truths that God has made known through other channels.

Scripture contains numerous accounts of people who experienced psychological distress. These accounts help us understand the experience of human anguish and they remind us of our responsibility to help those who suffer. However, the Bible does not provide extensive information about the etiology and treatment of mental disorders. Failing to understand the natural causes of psychotic behavior, some Christians, especially in the Middle Ages, misinterpreted delusions and hallucinations as having demonic origins. Some contemporary Christians, such as Rebecca, continue to misconstrue the causes of psychosis because they have not adequately considered alternative explanations.

While God's Word is without fault, human understanding and interpretation of the Scriptures are fallible. Our theologies and Christian beliefs are shaped by human thinking and human reflection on the Word of God. We must be careful to distinguish between what Scripture says and what we *think* it says (or worse, what we want to make it say). To aid us in this task, we make use of hermeneutics.

Hermeneutics are rules of interpretation. Once again, we are indebted to the ancient Greeks for an English word. The word "hermeneutics" originates from the name of the Greek god *Hermes*, whose job was to deliver messages between the gods or from the gods to human beings. The task of the messenger is to make sure that the plain meaning of the message is accurately communicated. Hence, *hermeneutics* is the science and art of making sure that the message is accurately understood. It is concerned with how we derive meaning from spoken or written words. For help in elucidating some hermeneutical principles, we will turn to what may seem an unlikely source at first: William Shakespeare.

---

biblical theology.

50. Holmes, *The idea of a Christian college*, 18.

Hermeneutics:
An Introduction in Two Acts

A Shakespearean Example

In the English language perhaps one of the most commonly quoted lines—and one of the most commonly misunderstood—is this: "Romeo, Romeo, Wherefore art thou Romeo?" It is often construed as if a love-struck teenager is either waiting for a hot date or wishing she had one. *Just where is this lover boy anyway?* Perhaps, if we take a look at the original source, we might learn what William Shakespeare really meant, and it might help us learn to read our Bibles more carefully too.[51] To accomplish this, we have to set the scene. Romeo and Juliet have been smitten with each other

and only learn as the story unfolds that they are members of rival families whose quarrel threatens any relationship they might wish to have. It is shortly after this that we pick up the story. Romeo (a Montague) has just scaled the wall surrounding the Capulets' home, seeking to catch a glimpse of Juliet. Juliet (a Capulet) appears above at a window. After brief monologues, Romeo overhears Juliet, and a dialogue breaks out.

Romeo and Juliet, Act 2, Scene 2: Capulet's orchard[52]

JULIET: O Romeo, Romeo! wherefore art thou Romeo?
Deny thy father and refuse thy name;
Or, if thou wilt not, be but sworn my love,
And I'll no longer be a Capulet.

ROMEO [*Aside*]: Shall I hear more, or shall I speak at this?

JULIET: 'Tis but thy name that is my enemy;
Thou art thyself, though not a Montague.
What's Montague? it is nor hand, nor foot,
Nor arm, nor face, nor any other part
Belonging to a man. O, be some other name!
What's in a name? that which we call a rose
By any other name would smell as sweet;
So Romeo would, were he not Romeo call'd,
Retain that dear perfection which he owes
Without that title. Romeo, doff thy name,
And for that name which is no part of thee
Take all myself.

ROMEO: I take thee at thy word:
Call me but love, and I'll be new baptized;
Henceforth I never will be Romeo.

---

51. The assumption taken here is directly counter to the assumption of postmodernists such as Kenneth Gergen. In his 1991 book, *The saturated self*, Gergen claimed that "we can no longer sustain the presumption that individual minds operate as mirrors of external reality" (103) and that, as a result, every reading of a text is correct within the context of the reader's interpretive framework. "This argument is not a happy one for most teachers of literature, for it means that all readings of a text or poem—including those of neophyte students—are equally valid as insights into 'true' meaning" (105). I disagree. While subjective meaning may be created by the interface of the text and the reader, it does not logically follow that such meaning is "valid." To the extent that one can correctly discern an author's intent from contextual cues, some interpretations will be more accurate than others. The alternative is a cacophony of conflicting meanings that need have no evidentiary basis whatsoever, a chaos in which communication would be impossible.

---

52. Shakespeare, *Romeo and Juliet*.

"Romeo, Romeo! wherefore art thou Romeo?" To understand the line, we need to ask several questions. What is the immediate context of the line? What is the overall context of the passage? Are there any words whose meanings are unclear?

First, the immediate context: The line we are considering occurs while Juliet is on the balcony, unaware that Romeo is listening. (Perhaps we should avoid giving Romeo any psychiatric labels at this point!) The surrounding lines seem to suggest that more is going on here than the longings of a love-struck adolescent. She dwells on the meaning of names, calls for Romeo to deny his name, and offers to give up her own name. When Romeo speaks, he offers to be "new baptized," at which point a child being christened is given his or her new or "Christian" name. Whatever Juliet is lamenting, it would seem to have more to do with names than with the absence of her lover.

Second, the overall context: Romeo and Juliet come from rival families, the Montagues and the Capulets. Their family rivalry runs so deep that neither can see any way of pursuing their relationship in the open, so Romeo and Juliet decide to run away together, and through a tragic set of circumstances, both end up committing suicide, and their families are left to confront the feuding hatred that Romeo and Juliet had overcome through their love, but which then contributed to their deaths. Again, the overall context makes untenable the reading of the neophyte that this line expresses Juliet's pining because she misses Romeo.

Third, the question of language. Looking at Juliet's line, the one word that seems most awkward to the modern reader is "wherefore." It is a word that was common in Shakespeare's day but is not in ours. Rather than meaning *where* it actually means *why*.[53] So, if we were to update the language, the line would read, "Romeo, Romeo, why are you Romeo?" Putting the clues together helps us uncover an utterly different meaning than we might have expected. Far from listlessly waiting for the absent Romeo, Juliet is asking why Romeo, the man she loves, is by definition of his name, the enemy of her family.

The common misinterpretation of Juliet's soliloquy is due to careless analysis. In the same way, carelessness in our approach to Scripture can lead to misunderstanding and misapplication. To avoid such problems, we need to try to understand the author's intent, and to aid us in this task we can utilize a variety of hermeneutical principles.

An Evangelical Example

The hermeneutical approach adopted by most evangelicals rests on the belief that the Scriptures are God-given and are trustworthy as a guide for faith and practice (2 Tim 3:16).[54] With a strong

---

53. Compare a reading of Isa 55:1–2 in the KJV and a modern translation to see how this principle of interpretation is relevant in scriptural interpretation.

54. There are clearly many other hermeneutical systems available. I present evangelical

belief in the value of Scripture for personal application, evangelicals are—at least ideally—committed to understanding Scripture as fully as possible. In this ideal, they seek to discern the meaning of Scripture in the context of its original audience, culture, language, and history. From this perspective, it is best to try to understand what the biblical author intended to say to the original audience as the first step in determining how Scripture might apply to our contemporary situation. Several hermeneutical principles are utilized in the quest to discern the intent of the author. A few of these principles follow in the form of questions that may be asked as we look at Scripture.

- What does the Scripture say? *Approach the study of Scripture with an open mind in an attempt to see what it says rather than trying to make it agree with your own preconceptions.*

- Who wrote the book?

- To whom was it written?

- Why was it written? What was the stated or implied purpose?

---

hermeneutics here because they are the ones to which I am most committed and with which I am most familiar. As a resource to delve into this matter more thoroughly from an evangelical perspective, I would recommend: Fee, *How to read the Bible*; Kaiser & Silva, *An introduction to biblical hermeneutics*; and Osborne, *The hermeneutical spiral*. For other hermeneutical approaches, you might consider looking at: Brueggemann, *Texts under negotiation*; Grant & Tracy, *A short history*; and Kee, *The Bible in the twenty-first century*.

- What was the current situation of author and audience (culturally, historically, etc.)?

- In what *genre* is it written (apocalyptic, historical, narrative, poetic, prophetic, etc.)? The genre will influence how interpretation should proceed.

- Are there words that are unclear to us, or that may carry a different meaning in today's language? (This is especially important if you are using a translation with archaic language. Even when using modern translations, it is often helpful to look at the Scripture in the original language, if possible.)

- What is the immediate context of a passage of Scripture? How does the context of a verse make sense of the passage under consideration?

- What is the overall context of a passage? How does it fit in with the argument or teaching of the whole book?

- How does it relate to other Scriptures? "*Scripture interprets Scripture.*" (Less clear Scriptures must be understood in the light of more clear Scriptures; uncommon themes are secondary to primary scriptural themes.)

- How is the passage understood by other credible sources? (Church tradition and biblical commentaries, while not infallible, are helpful interpretive aids. Novel interpretations that depart from those of reliable sources must meet a higher burden of proof before they can be accepted.)

Many more principles could be elucidated, but the foregoing questions provide a good basis for Scripture study by the average layperson. The danger in not being rigorous in the application of hermeneutical principles is that it may result in misunderstanding and misapplication. Admittedly, this makes study a bit more work than simply opening a Bible and haphazardly reading whatever is there, but it also opens up the possibility of gaining a deeper understanding and appreciation of Scripture as one attempts to grow as a Christian.

Only after the hermeneutical task is accomplished can one effectively ask the interpretive question of how Scripture applies to our contemporary situation.[55] A significant difficulty in applying Scripture is how to deal with culturally embedded aspects of the text. All of Scripture is shaped by the culture and experience of the original audience. Every

Scripture was communicated through the language, culture, worldview, and knowledge base of the authors through whom God spoke and the people to whom His message was addressed. The message of Scripture, though, provides an unfolding picture of God's redemptive acts in human history and expresses timeless truths that are not culturally relative. Application of the text to our cultural situation requires that we struggle to determine not just what the text meant to the original audience, but how it should be understood and applied to our contemporary situation given an understanding of cultural matters and the flow of redemptive history.

A Theocentric Unified Model of Knowing

After exploring worldviews, human finitude and frailty, the place of virtues in seeking knowledge, and various means of seeking knowledge, we must ask ourselves how these all fit together. Listed below, in outline form, are several propositions that bring together a theory of knowing based on a Christian worldview. (Figure 5.1 presents these propositions schematically.)

1. There is a real world, whose normal workings ("scientific laws") human beings can perceive with some reasonable degree of correspondence to the external world.

2. God is the transcendent creator, Who not only created the world, but also upholds and sustains it, and is

---

55. A consideration that is not addressed in the following discussion is the role of the Holy Spirit in guiding interpretation. Scriptural interpretation is to be guided not just by hermeneutics, history, and tradition, but by the illumination of the Spirit (1 Cor 2:9–14). Unfortunately, while most evangelicals admit that such illumination is necessary, theological discussion of the topic is underdeveloped; "The illumination of the Holy Spirit is regularly mentioned in theological literature; yet detailed discussion of this subject is rare." Klooster, The role of the Holy Spirit, 451.

FIGURE 5.1: A Theocentric Unified Model of Knowing

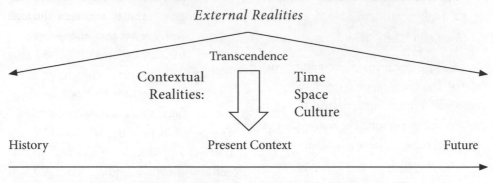

External Realities

Transcendence

Contextual Realities: Time Space Culture

History   Present Context   Future

Embedded Realities: Rational, Relational, Spiritual, Biological

Historical Inquiry	A Christian Theocentric Worldview	Prediction
Archeology, Geology, Written records, Oral tradition, Etc.	1. The essential unity of truth is recognized as grounded in a transcendent God who created an orderly world. 2. Human capacities are seen as God-given, to be guided by intellectual and moral virtues and resulting in adoration of God. 3. Reality is seen as a holistic unity composed of physical, social, psychological, and transcendent phenomena. 4. Human finitude, frailty, and the individual and corporate (communal) effects of sin are recognized as limiting factors in the pursuit and acquisition of knowledge. 5. Various means of epistemic inquiry (e.g., rational discourse, empirical investigation, etc.) are recognized as means of evaluating truth claims, though each has unique strengths, limitations, and areas of application that make them relevant to different forms of epistemic application.	Limited prediction possible, based on observation of past trends and reasoned outcomes

Rational discourse
Experimentation
Hermeneutics
etc.

capable of intervening within it (i.e., miracles, revelation, Scripture).

3. We are situated within a context of time, physical locale, and culture. These contextual realities shape our perceptions, limit our access to information and thereby limit our objectivity.

4. Human beings are rational, relational, spiritual and biological beings, (created as good, though finite, frail, and now fallen).

5. A Christian worldview recognizes that

   a. all truth is grounded in the transcendent God who created an orderly world, and whose truths can often be known through rational, experimental, or revelational means;

   b. the creative and intellectual abilities of human beings are God-given, to be guided by intellectual and moral virtues and exercised in adoration of God.

   c. reality is physical and spiritual. Our experience is social and psychological in nature;

   d. our ability to know is limited both by our finitude and by the effects of personal and corporate sins (e.g., lack of personal virtue, cultural bias); *the noetic effects of sin*;

   e. various means of epistemic inquiry can be used to evaluate truth claims, though each has unique strengths, limitations, and areas of epistemic application. These methods include (but are not limited to)

      i. Rational discourse

      ii. Experimentation

      iii. Hermeneutics

6. Historical events can be explored using a variety of methods and sources (e.g., archeology, geology, written records, oral tradition), with a recognition that our investigations are guided and limited by the assumptions made and the materials found.

7. The future is not completely determined, but a limited degree of predictive accuracy is possible based on past trends and reasoned outcomes.

A major implication of this model is that psychology and theology can be seen as united under a common set of assumptions about the world. Given that their sources are rooted in the truths of God's world, the fundamental unity of their domains is assumed. The limitations of their respective methodologies and of human thought in general guarantee that the conclusions in each field will not always fit nicely together, but the framework itself suggests that harmony is conceptually possible. Moreover, an approach informed by both psychology and Christian theology is desirable if we seek a more complete picture of human nature and functioning. In order to continue developing this picture, it is necessary for us to ask about the nature of the world in which human beings reside, and that is the topic of our next chapter.

To bring this chapter to a close, recall the discussion about Jimmy (the man who claimed to have learned to play guitar on stage with Cat Stevens). Jimmy's story highlights the importance of epistemic justification. If we are to evaluate whether Jimmy was sane, demon possessed, or delusional, we must look at the quality and consistency of the evidence used to justify each of those conclusions. Jimmy's conclusion ("I really did learn to play guitar on stage with Cat Stevens") seems hard to believe because it is such an extraordinary claim: people just don't learn to play guitar on the spot; rock-and-roll stars rarely invite people on stage that they don't know, and they certainly don't let people whose musical skills are unknown play with the band! Rebecca's conclusion ("Jimmy had a demon who gave him supernatural guitar-playing ability") is internally consistent but is advanced with no evidence to corroborate her conclusion, and it fails to take into account other possible explanations or the evidence in favor of those explanations. My explanation ("Jimmy was delusional, and his guitar-playing abilities were learned through years of practice") is internally consistent, fits the data on his chart (the history of drug abuse, previous psychotic diagnoses, and a positive history of favorable response to neuroleptic medications), and is consistent with a theology that understands disease

and infirmity as a result of the Fall.[56] Whether evaluated on the basis of logic, empirical evidence, or scriptural evidence, my position offers an explanation that is consistent, comprehensive, and which stands up well against alternative hypotheses. While I could still be wrong, I'll stick with my hypothesis, because I haven't been confronted with sufficient evidence to compel me to replace it with an alternative one.

Summary

The desire to know and understand God's world is a God-given capacity, but the pursuit of knowledge is affected by worldviews, human finitude, human frailty, individual and communal sin, assumptions, methodological limitations, and the availability of data, among other things. Our ability to know is contingent, limited, and fallible. If we approach the quest for knowledge with an awareness of our limitations and guided by intellectual virtues to appropriate ends, this quest is worthwhile and partly attainable. Given this epistemic framework, it is possible to use various methods to understand human experience, including psychological theory, psychological science, and Christian theology. While our findings must be held tentatively and humbly, this

---

56. In this view, infirmity can be viewed as a generic result of living in a fallen world (disease in general, whether inherited or environmentally induced); the effects of personal choice (such as drug abuse); or the effects of other people's choices (such as growing up with abusive parents).

framework makes integration conceptually possible and intellectually appealing.

Questions for Reflection and Discussion

1. Identify some of the assumptions that you have acquired from your culture and subculture which shape the way that you view the world. To what degree do you think you can become aware of such assumptions? How easy do you think it is to challenge assumptions that are deeply embedded in a culture? If you had been born into an overtly racist family in a culture permeated by racism, do you think that you would have been more likely to accept or reject the racist values of your culture? Why or why not?

2. The author stated his belief that "at best, we can humbly try to evaluate our beliefs carefully enough to arrive at a contingent certainty" and that "to hope for (or worse, to claim) more than that is claiming a god-like quality which frail and finite human beings cannot attain." Do you agree or disagree? Why?

3. The author discussed several intellectual virtues: studiositas, intellectual humility, intellectual caution, intellectual courage, intellectual integrity, and intellectual perseverance. Which of these characteristics are the most difficult for you? What can you do to develop and strengthen this capacity?

4. How do human finitude, human frailty, and human fallenness (the individual and corporate effects of sin) affect and limit the quest for knowledge?

5. Think of several examples in which you discovered that you had come to an incorrect conclusion. In retrospect, what roles did culturally based assumptions, intellectual virtues, self-deception, lack of information, and methodological errors play in each situation?

6. Look at the argument that Rebecca used to conclude that Jimmy was demon possessed. Identify the elements of the argument (premises, inferences, and conclusion), and identify potential flaws in the premises and whether or not the argument itself is valid.

7. For most of its modern (post-1879) history, psychology has been conceptualized as an empirical discipline. Outline what you know about the modernist assumptions of empirical psychology and of postmodern critiques and alternatives. (Note that this chapter introduced this issue in brief; the point of this question is to help you and your instructor to think about what you know about these issues and to spark discussion about them.)

8. What kind of hermeneutics do you use when you read Scripture? Are there specific hermeneutical principles that the author noted that you want to adopt? Are there specific

hermeneutical principles that the author noted with which you disagree? Why?

9. The author described four methodologies for seeking knowledge: authority, logic, empiricism, and hermeneutics. Give one example of how someone might make use of each of these methods to attain knowledge.

10. The author presented an outline and diagram of how he conceptualizes the task and possibility of knowing within a Christian worldview. Create your own diagram that reflects how you currently conceptualize the task and possibility of knowing within your worldview. Are there things in your model that you need to reconsider? Within your framework, is faith-learning integration possible or desirable?

6

The Nature of the World: Metaphysics

Nature is too thin a screen; the glory of the omnipresent God bursts through everywhere.

—Ralph Waldo Emerson

There is nothing which God hath established in a constant cause of nature and which therefore is done every day, but would seem a miracle, and exercise our admiration, if it were done but once.

—John Donne

It was a mild April day when my flight arrived in Colorado. I spent the next two days in Colorado Springs sitting through conference presentations at the Holiday Inn, exercising my mind while my body suffered from inactivity. It was definitely time to reverse the paradigm. Still functioning on East-Coast time, I awoke early in the morning, jumped into the Dodge Stratus that I had rented, stopped at a bagel shop where I bought a large coffee and a pesto bagel with sun-dried-tomato cream cheese, and headed up Route 24, winding through the mountains towards Pike's Peak. Heading west, I found a place where I could park the car by a trailhead. I hiked along the trail for an hour before the thin, cold air drove me back to the car.

I was starting to feel rejuvenated, and I continued to drive up the mountain, enjoying the silence and the scenery. The higher I drove, the colder it became. Suddenly I found myself surrounded by white-capped mountains in every direction. I found a place to park and got out of the car, as the bitter wind reminded me that I had no coat. I stared in silence, captivated by the vista: blue sky, white clouds, the sun illuminating the brightness of the snow, and mountains as far as the eye could see. Reflexively, without thinking, I uttered aloud, "God, this is beautiful!" I did not try to pray; rather awe and praise simply flowed through me.

Awe is a fascinating affective state, and only recently has it been the object of scientific study. Although awe is a common emotion, it is hard to define. It can encompass surprise, wonder, joy, and even

121

dread—so much so that the word "awful" is related to the word "awe." Humans, it seems, are primed to look for agency (e.g., a belief in God) when they experience awe.[1] Seeing ourselves as finite in the face of vast beauty seems to lead to a sense of anxiety because so much is beyond our personal control, and this anxiety is reduced by belief in divine agency. This may be a new idea in experimental social science, but it is easily found among poets and philosophers and psalmists.

Think about a time when you experienced wonder and awe. Did it result in praise of God or a sense of connection to God? Would a lack of awe reveal a deficiency (such as being a mere "brute" or lacking common sense or wisdom)?

My friends who grew up in flat wheat fields or painted deserts may disagree with me, but I think mountains proclaim that there is a God better than any other landscape.[2] Even so, I have had similar experiences of awe-filled praise while listening to lively South American music, watching giraffes loll across the Serengeti Plain at dusk, seeing the sunset reflected off a frozen Indiana lake,

walking on New England cliffs above the ocean, strolling along a California beach at night, or gazing at a star-filled sky.

According to C. S. Lewis, "Men of sensibility look up on the night sky with awe: brutal and stupid men do not."[3] In his view, sensible people look at the stars with humility, and the wonders of nature elicit their awe. In contrast, those who gaze upon the beauty of nature with indifference have a character flaw. Their ignorance or apathy prevents them from having the appropriate response to their experience.

The point that Lewis made has a long tradition, stretching back at least to Plato and Aristotle. One of the great tragedies that modernism has foisted on contemporary education is that we have severed the *development of character* from the *attainment of knowledge*. Classically, education focused on character formation *and* knowledge acquisition. In fact, Aristotle believed that a central purpose of education is to shape character so that our desires are correctly ordered. "Hence we ought to have been brought up in a particular way from our very youth, as Plato says, so as both to delight in and to be pained by the things that we ought; for this is the right education."[4]

Aristotle, Plato, and Lewis all assumed that some things *ought* to elicit awe, that some things *ought* to elicit desire, and that some things *ought* to revolt us. This brings us to the heart of an important issue: What is our proper place in

---

1. See, for example, Valdesolo & Graham, *Awe, uncertainty, and agency.*

2. Our understanding of the geological forces that are the proximal causes of the mountains that we see today does not diminish our experience of beauty, or the awe we feel when we recognize God's immanence and creativity.

3. Lewis, *Miracles*, 72.

4. Aristotle *Nichomachean ethics* II,3.

the world? In order to answer this question, we first need to understand the nature of the world we live in. In this chapter, we will explore this issue by looking at the nature and origins of the physical world (cosmology) and proceed to explore the ultimate nature of reality (metaphysics). This will pave the way for us to discuss human nature itself in chapter 7.

Some readers may initially think that the topics of this chapter are dull philosophical issues or that they are irrelevant to integration. Partly this reaction stems from the unfortunate effect of modernism on contemporary education. Contemporary politicians, parents, and students often fall into a trap of seeing only the instrumental values of education (e.g., "How will this help me get a good job?"). At its best, though, education is a process of character formation that seeks to shape the kind of person one is becoming, and it is a mechanism to hone critical-thinking skills. Lack of interest in these issues may also be a result of the postmodern stance that truth, beauty, and goodness are largely matters of subjective opinion. Contrary to these views, you may find that exploring the nature of the world and of ultimate reality can be important and interesting. In fact, the topic of this chapter has much to do with how you understand your experience, and we will begin by looking at your own experience of awe.

Thin Places

Think back to a time when you experienced a feeling that was something like a mixture of amazement, joy, and gratitude. Perhaps you were picking wild blackberries while walking along a mountain trail in early summer. Maybe you were drifting lazily downstream as the currents lapped the sides of your boat. Or you could have been staring through a microscope, gazing with fascination at protozoa that are invisible to the naked eye. Many people express overwhelming feelings when they see the birth of a child. Some people see such events as having deeply spiritual meanings, a view that has a long and venerable tradition.

Celtic Christianity, which began to flourish in the fifth century in the British Isles, embodied deep respect for God's creation. Prior to this period, though, nature was understood through pagan beliefs and celebrated through druid practices. When Christianity came to the Isles, reverence for nature took its rightful place as a signpost to its Creator. In the words of the psalmist:

The heavens declare the glory of God;
    the skies proclaim the work of his
        hands.
Day after day they pour forth speech;
    night after night they display
        knowledge.
There is no speech or language
    where their voice is not heard.
      (Ps 19:1–3, NIV)

Celtic Christians believed in the existence of *thin places*, where the gap between the natural and supernatural worlds was more transparent than usual. In this view, when I sensed God's presence as I looked at the snow-capped mountains surrounding me in Colorado, I was in a thin place. The idea of thin places resonates with me. In the modern world, though, we are prone to try to explain everything with scientific formulas, and some people believe that everything can be reduced to natural explanations that remove God from our picture of the world. Can scientific explanation coexist with belief in transcendent thin places? The answer to that question depends on one's view of cosmology, the nature of the world. Cosmology, narrowly defined, is "the science of the nature, structure, and origin of the universe as a whole."[5] The questions modern cosmologists attempt to answer reflect ancient *metaphysical* issues, although framed in scientific rather than philosophical terms.

Does the fact that we are so small and the world is so large mean that we are insignificant?

Modern cosmology is written in the words of mathematics, theoretical physics, and astronomical terminology. The creation account of Judaism and Christianity is written in narrative: "In the beginning God created the heavens and the earth" (Gen 1:1, NIV). Much of the ancient Hebrew cosmology meshes well with modern cosmology, and much of it seems foreign.[6] An especially difficult

point of contrast in these cosmologies is the place of humankind. Are humans central to the created world, or are they a peripheral accident at the edge of insignificance? Consider the following claim:

> The cornerstone of modern cosmology is the belief that the place which we occupy in the Universe is in no way special. This is known as the cosmological principle, and it is an idea that is both powerful and simple. It is intriguing, then, that for the bulk of the history of civilization it was believed that we occupy a very special location, usually the center, in the scheme of things.[7]

That our physical world is not the center of the universe is no longer in doubt. Our sun does not rotate around the earth, the sun itself is not in the center of our galaxy, and our galaxy is not in the center of the universe.

Our world is not only less central to the universe than we might have once thought, but the size of the universe is larger still by many magnitudes than most of us can even conceive. The light of our nearest celestial neighbor, Proxima Centauri, travels 4.2 years across the expanse of space to reach us.[8] The speck

---

5. Audi, *Cambridge dictionary of philosophy*, 489.

6. As we saw in chapter 2, the diverse Christian traditions favor different ways of reconciling the words of the ancient text to the findings of modern science, ranging from "demythologizing" the text at the one extreme to emasculating science on the other. A key issue is determining when to interpret the language of the ancient texts literally, and when to take it figuratively, an issue over which there has been, is, and will continue to be much controversy.

7. Liddle, *An introduction to cosmology*.

8. Silk, *A short history of the universe*, 6.

of light that we currently see as the North Star originated seven hundred years ago,[9] shortly before the founding of the Ottoman Empire, the start of the Hundred Years' War, or the beginning of the bubonic plague.[10] Our planet resides in a galaxy that covers an expanse of over 45 thousand light-years, and the *observable* universe is at least one thousand times that size, a distance of 10^{23} kilometers.[11] Yet no matter how old or how large the universe is, how small our little corner of it is, or how remote we are from its geographic center, one still wonders if our place within it is of any eternal and existential significance.

When we look at the stars, are we faced with the cold, hard truth that this world is all that there is, or are we encountering a thin place that hints that nature herself is upheld by a kind and loving God? Our answer to this question

9. Padmanabhan, *After the first three minutes*, 3.

10. Our world is not only older than we often imagine but bigger than we can really conceive. The North Star is 700 light-years distant from us, or seven quadrillion kilometers (7,000,000,000,000,000)—and it is one of our relatively close neighbors.

11. Padmanabhan, *After the first three minutes*, 3–5. If my understanding of mathematical notation is correct, the length of the observable universe can be expressed as 100,000,000,000,000,000,000,000 kilometers, or one hundred sextillion kilometers *across*. If we assume that the area covered by that distance is spherical, and apply the formula: $v = 4/3 \times \pi \times r^3$, we would estimate its size as 5.23596×10^{68} cubic kilometers—and that number merely estimates the size of the *observable* universe! (My thanks to Dr. John Williams for help with the mathematics.)

depends on several metaphysical issues to which we now turn our attention.

From Cosmology to Metaphysics

Aristotle lived more than three centuries before the birth of Christ. His writings covered subjects as diverse as physics, biology, poetry, and ethics. Aristotle was the first person to create a comprehensive philosophical system in the Western world. According to tradition, the task of cataloguing Aristotle's writings fell to his student, Andronicus of Rhodes.[12] Aristotle's first fourteen books concerned the elements that compose the world, optics, and causes. These books were grouped together and catalogued as having to do with nature—*ta physika*. When his remaining books were cataloged, they were identified as the books coming *after nature: ta meta ta physika*.[13] These writings dealt with many topics, including the ultimate nature of reality and the nature of being.

Metaphysics involves "the philosophical investigation of the nature, constitution, and structure of reality."[14] We have already engaged in metaphysical exploration when we looked at *worldviews* in chapter 5. Every worldview attempts to answer basic metaphysical questions about the world. Our task here is not to revisit the worldview questions. Instead,

12. Coreth, *Metaphysics*.

13. Jaegwon & Sosa, *A companion to metaphysics*, 311.

14. Audi, *The Cambridge dictionary of philosophy*, 489.

we need to ask how Christian answers to several specific metaphysical questions can be reconciled with a world understood in scientific terms, and what implications these answers have for the pursuit of integration.

In their thinking, scientists cannot avoid making metaphysical assumptions, since the scientist "investigates questions science does not address but the answers to which it presupposes."[15] For instance, if a scientist makes the metaphysical assumption that everything that exists is knowable as a part of nature (an assumption known as *metaphysical naturalism*), he or she may reject supernatural claims as being without merit.[16] This rejection is based on a metaphysical assumption, not on an established scientific "fact." Many apparent contradictions between science and Christianity are the result of differing metaphysical premises and interpretations based on those premises. As we will see, the metaphysical assumptions that one makes have implications for

one's understanding of truth, goodness, and beauty. We have already addressed the first of these topics in chapter 5. Our discussion will now proceed by exploring three specific metaphysical issues: the nature and origin of the world, the nature and source of ethical values, and the nature and source of beauty.[17]

Does Anything Outside of Nature Exist?

In the Western world, most people are either naturalists or supernaturalists.[18] Naturalists believe that nothing other than the material world exists; supernaturalists believe that the material world exists, but that it came into existence at some point when God created it. Naturalism is defined by two propositions: there is no God, and matter is all that there is. We will thus refer to holders of this view as *naturalists* or *atheistic materialists*. Supernaturalism, at least as expressed in orthodox Christianity, agrees with the naturalist that matter exists, but supernaturalists do not view the world as a self-existent material realm. Christianity teaches that the material world is a derivative realm created by God.

Peter Van Inwagen compares two metaphysical positions, which we shall

---

15. Ibid.

16. It is important to distinguish *methodological naturalism* from *metaphysical naturalism*. Methodological naturalism merely states that the application of empirical methodologies are the best way of obtaining knowledge about some subjects, but it makes no assumption that things that are not observable are untrue. Metaphysical naturalism (or ontological naturalism), on the other hand, is a comprehensive worldview in which the world is seen as being exclusively composed of things that are empirically knowable. In the former view, supernatural claims are seen as outside the domain of science; in the latter view, they are seen as *a priori* impossibilities. The atheistic materialist is by definition a metaphysical naturalist.

17. Whole books have been written on each of the following questions. My intention here is simply to introduce the topics and to provide some preliminary thoughts from a Christian vantage point.

18. The views expressed in this section build on the ideas that C. S. Lewis developed in his classic book *Miracles*.

refer to as *naturalism* and *supernaturalism*. Naturalism has been prevalent since the nineteenth century, while supernaturalism was the commonly held view in the Middle Ages. Van Inwagon summarizes the views of naturalism and supernaturalism with three points of difference, as illustrated in table 6.1 on the following page.[19] While we might want to debate or expand some of Van Inwagen's characterizations of naturalism and supernaturalism, several points of contrast are immediately evident.

Most naturalists presume that the world is a self-existent material realm that at some point or other exploded from a tiny singularity into the wide expanse that is now the universe. Perhaps it cyclically expands and contracts, perhaps not; beyond the Big Bang theoretical physics cannot peer. In this view, the world is self-contained; nothing is responsible for its existence. Atheistic materialism posits that no God, gods, or forces exist outside of nature. Nature is the sum total of all there is. If this view is correct, then when I gaze at stars or snowcapped mountains and feel impelled to praise God, I am, in a sense, delusional. Over the past few decades, several neurological imaging studies have identified brain regions involved in religious experiences. To someone who believes that the physical world is all that there is, my religious experience is nothing but the activation of specific regions of my brain, which I misinterpret as having some external reality.

TABLE 6.1 (adapted from Van Inwagen)

Naturalism	Supernaturalism
"The World consists of matter in motion. There is nothing but matter, which operates according to the strict and invariable laws of physics. Every individual thing is made up of matter, and every aspect of its behavior is due to the workings of those laws."[20]	"The World consists of God and all He has made."[21] God is not a material being; God is eternally existent.
"Matter has always existed."[22] Because it has always existed, it is meaningless to ask why it exists.	All things other than God exist because God brought them into being, and they continue to exist because He sustains their being.
"Human beings are complex configurations of matter."[23] Humans have no meaning or purpose for existence. They have no soul, and they will cease to exist when they die.	"Human beings were created by God to love and serve Him forever."[24]

---

19. Van Inwagen, *Metaphysics*, 5–6. The table is my own construction. Van Inwagen does not use a table; he has two lists with three points each.

20. Ibid., 6.

21. Ibid., 5.

22. Ibid., 6.

23. Ibid., 6.

24. Ibid., 5.

Christianity takes as its starting point a different premise: "In the beginning God" (Gen 1:1). God is seen as distinct from, independent of, and superior to nature. He is the creator of nature and the eternal "I am" (Exod 3:14). Supernaturalists believe that God is self-existent, and all other things are derivative from His creative acts. However, Christians differ greatly in how to reconcile the model proposed by modern cosmology with the teachings of Scripture. Some seek to see Genesis as a metaphorical expression of eons of cosmic and local evolution, while others hold to a literal understanding that must either negate modern cosmology or collapse it into a much shorter timeline punctuated by multiple acts of God. For all their differences, both expressions of Christian thinking emphasize *Who did it* while diverging on *how it was done*. The main point of the Genesis account is to proclaim God as the personal originator and upholder of a material creation that He affirmed was good. Theologians may disagree on whether to take this account literally or not, but the scriptural position as understood by the church across the ages does not allow for solely naturalistic explanations that exclude God's activity as the Sovereign of creation.

In the Christian view, there is a supernatural world in addition to a natural world. Physical processes will mediate my experience of God, although God exists independently of my experience. Philip Yancey provides an apt illustration of the connection between the natural world and our experience of the supernatural: "Because we are material beings, God must deal with us on that level. Every spiritual experience depends on the cooperation of our very mundane bodies. A stroke can put an end to a saint's prayer life. Stop all intake of food and water, and a mystical state will soon come to an end. Nearly everything we know about the supernatural world comes filtered through the ordinary, natural world—which makes it easy for skeptics to dismiss or disbelieve."[25]

Ultimately, one may not be able to prove that the Christian view is correct, but it is at least a consistent, defensible position. Atheistic materialism, likewise, can be viewed as a position that cannot be proved but that can be defended. The divergent implications of these two worldviews are enormous.

If the viewpoint of the atheistic materialist is correct, then all our questions have materialistic answers, and any talk of the supernatural is merely superstitious and unscientific. If the theistic view is correct, then the material realm owes its existence to a superior Being and expresses the designs and purposes of its Creator. In the later view, we may sense what Philip Yancey referred to as *rumors of another world*: things that gently suggest that there may be more than meets the eye.

G. K. Chesterton was fond of pointing out the differences in how these two views make us think about nature. If nature is all that there is, then it makes sense to think of her as our mother. She controls everything. She is the answer to

---

25. Yancey, *Rumors of another world*, 39.

everything. She runs the whole show. But if the Christian view is correct, then nature is our fellow creation. Nature is then not our mother, but our sister. In Chesterton's words:

> Unfortunately, if you regard Nature as a mother, you discover that she is a step-mother. The main point of Christianity was this: that Nature is not our mother: Nature is our sister. We can be proud of her beauty, since we have the same father; but she has no authority over us; we have to admire, but not to imitate. This gives to the typically Christian pleasure in this earth a strange touch of lightness that is almost frivolity . . . To St. Francis, Nature is a sister, and even a younger sister: a little, dancing sister, to be laughed at as well as loved.[26]

Thus for the atheistic materialist, nature is all that there is, and all meaningful questions ultimately have material answers. For the Christian, nature contains thin places that beckon us to look beyond nature and to stand in awe of the Creator.

Tied closely to the question at hand is an important observation. Both the atheistic materialist and the Christian agree that there is a material realm; they can both look at the data and come to identical conclusions about the mechanistic functions of the material. The dividing lines are the origin, purpose, and trajectory of the material realm. Van Inwagen's summary of naturalism included

the belief that humans have no meaning or purpose for existence, and their existence will end when they die.

Thus far, we have seen that atheistic materialists and Christians disagree about the ultimate nature of reality. There are many implications of their divergent beliefs that we will explore throughout the remainder of this chapter. First, though, we need to address a potential objection by the atheistic materialist against the Christian.

Supernaturalism and Science

A common criticism of theism by atheistic materialists is the accusation that the theist cannot be scientific and believe in a supernatural realm. C. S. Lewis addressed this criticism in *Miracles*. Lewis argued that the ability to identify something as a miracle actually depends upon knowledge of the normal rules of nature, precisely because the miraculous does not fit the normal and expected pattern. In his view, a miracle is not something that breaks the rules of nature, but it is an intervention by which something new is introduced into nature, which nature then accommodates. "The moment [a miraculous intervention] enters her realm it obeys all her laws. Miraculous wine will intoxicate, miraculous conception will lead to pregnancy, inspired books will suffer all the ordinary processes of textual corruption, miraculous bread will be digested."[27]

---

26. Chesterton, *Orthodoxy*, 112.

27. Lewis, *Miracles*, 81.

Lewis referred to the birth of Christ as "the Grand Miracle," because "every other miracle prepares for this, or exhibits this, or results from this."[28] Nature could not have brought about the virgin birth of Jesus Christ; but once the conception had taken place within the Virgin Mary, the gestation and birth of the holy child proceeded along natural lines. For the Christian, the divine source of this miracle is foundational to Christian faith. For the naturalist, a Virgin Birth is impossible (since nothing beyond nature exists), so either Jesus was born out of wedlock, or His disciples embellished the story as the religion that sprung up around Him developed.

Miracles are by definition rare events, exceptions to the norm and to what we expected—the Virgin Birth was a one-time event, and it certainly wasn't readily accepted or believed. However, miracles are not violations of scientific realities. The material world is celebrated in a theistic worldview as the handiwork of God. It was created by God and is sustained by God. The Creator endowed the creation with order that allows us to discern the normal rules by which it operates. God can intervene in nature when He sees fit to do so. Of course, if He did so routinely, the rules by which nature operates would constantly seem to be in flux, which is one of the reasons that miracles are, of necessity, very rare events.

Miracles do not contradict natural laws for two reasons. First, nature, as creation, merely accommodates miraculous events into its ordinary realm. Second, science describes how reality typically acts, but it cannot state that it is the way it *must* act. In fact, one of the most influential views of science was that of the positivist Ernst Mach (1838–1916), who believed that "laws are nothing more than concise summaries of past experience, useful in predicting future observations."[29] Thus they "do not explain phenomena; they merely describe them. To say that a successful theory expresses some kind of truth behind the phenomena is to indulge in metaphysical speculation, for such a statement cannot be tested by observation or experiment."[30]

Understood in this way, science merely provides a *descriptive account* of nature based on prior observations, not a *normative account* of how nature must behave. Given this understanding, miraculous events, while not open to empirical inquiry, would not be incompatible with a scientific viewpoint.

On the other hand, as Lewis pointed out, every claim of a miracle must be observed within nature, and one can always explain miracles away by looking only at the natural *effect* and ignoring the supernatural *cause*. The reality that supernatural interventions must be expressed in natural (and hence, material) circumstances highlights the difficulty of determining whether something is a mere coincidence or a miracle. If one presumes at the outset that miracles cannot exist, claims of miracles will be

---

28. Ibid., 143.

29. Layzer, *Constructing the universe*, 11.

30. Ibid.

dismissed as coincidences, rejected in favor of naturalistic explanations, or the need for more data to "clear up the misconception" will be invoked. Conversely, we can see how easy it is to wrongly label coincidences as miracles. Some claims of "miraculous healing" clearly fail to account for the effects of medical intervention and spontaneous remissions due to natural but poorly understood factors. The difficulty of separating coincidences from legitimate miracles should make us cautious of rejecting miraculous claims out of hand, and equally cautious of accepting them uncritically.

The *a priori* rejection of supernatural explanations by atheistic materialists can only proceed on debatable metaphysical grounds. When science is understood as a descriptive rather than a normative process, and when it is understood that supernatural events are not violations of scientific laws, it becomes evident that Christian and scientific understandings are compatible. This state of affairs has tremendous implications for psychology and integration. First of all, we must be aware of the metaphysical assumptions that we bring to the table. Secondly, it means that we need to be careful to avoid materialistic reductionism. While psychological phenomena may be expressed biologically, and especially neurologically, it does not then follow that human functioning can be completely explained based on deterministic neurobiological findings. Thirdly, it means that psychological explanations and theological explanations are not mutually exclusive. In fact, it suggests that both explanations

are useful: the one stemming from an attempt to understand human functioning within its natural context, and the other recognizing that human nature and functioning, though expressed in nature, have their origin and purpose rooted in the designs of the Creator.

The Nature of God

If we accept the Christian proposition that the physical world is a created realm, we must then ask about the nature of its Creator. A brief survey of Christian teachings would illustrate that God is omnipotent, omniscient, omnipresent, holy, relational, personal, immutable, faithful, just, creative, and transcendent.[31] Many of these attributes have tangible implications for some of the deepest questions of human existence, such as whether or not there is purpose to living, whether or not there is right or wrong, and so forth. They also generate certain intellectual difficulties. For instance, as C. S. Lewis pointed out, Christianity "creates rather than solves, the problem of pain, for pain would be no problem unless, side by side with our daily experience of this painful world, we had received what we think a

---

31. This list is not exhaustive, and no attempt is made here to support each of these claims scripturally. For those who are interested in pursuing this further, you can easily use a concordance to look up scriptural passages having to do with God's character. You might then look up "Attributes of God" or "God, Doctrine of" in a good dictionary or encyclopedia of theology as a starting point.

good assurance that ultimate reality is righteous and loving."[32]

The problem of why a good God allows suffering is called theodicy. Many people struggle with how to relate to God in the midst of their suffering. Because psychologists deal with suffering people, it should not be surprising that this is an issue that is often encountered in psychotherapy.

While God's nature is of considerable importance to the integrative enterprise, one of the crucial implications is that God is interested in human beings. He created us. He loves us. He sacrificed Himself for us. Perhaps John 3:16 is such a well-known verse because it summarizes this truth so well: "God loved the world so much that he gave his one and only Son so that whoever believes in him may not be lost, but have eternal life" (NCV). And, as our Creator, He also has the ability and right to tell us how we ought to live.

Ethics

No worldview can survive without an ethical system that maintains a cohesive set of guidelines for determining which behaviors are acceptable and ethical, and which are not. Lewis argued that an understanding of nature that reduces everything to a material level fails to account for the phenomena of *reason* and *morality*. If thinking is nothing more than a biologically determined phenomenon,

then our belief in the accuracy of our thinking is biologically determined, and, being *determined*, it offers no room for evaluating the merits of reason. The case is similar for moral judgments: unless there is something outside of nature that provides a basis for morality, then what we perceive as "moral" or "immoral" is simply a matter of biologically and sociologically determined belief. Atheistic materialism cannot ground reason or morality in anything beyond the material realm because it believes that there is nothing other than the material realm.

Lewis argued that reason and morality must be grounded in something beyond nature, because nature itself could not give rise to them. In his view, God is ultimately the ground of reason and of morality. They are, however, expressed through material substances, and we can only observe their appearance in the natural realm. "The various and complex conditions under which Reason and Morality appear are the twists and turns of the frontier between Nature and Supernature. That is why, if you wish, you can always ignore Supernature and treat the phenomena purely from the Natural side . . . What we call rational thought in a man always involves a state of the brain, in the long run a relation of atoms. But . . . Reason is something more than cerebral bio-chemistry."[33]

For Lewis, human thought and morality are inexplicable by nature alone, reflective of a divine origin, yet expressed

---

32. Lewis, *The problem of pain*, 21.

33. Lewis, *Miracles*, 56–57.

in the material stuff of neurons and neurotransmitters.[34]

Christianity has much to say about how we ought to live, as do philosophical systems that stem from non-Christian worldviews. Aristotle, for instance, is a tremendous resource in our attempts to understand the good life. Consider the wisdom of just a single section of the *Nicomachean Ethics*:

> None of the virtues of character arises in us naturally . . . the virtues arise in us neither by nature nor against nature. Rather, we are by nature able to acquire them, and we are completed through habit . . . Further, the sources and means that develop each virtue also ruin it, just as they do in a craft. For playing the harp makes both good and bad harpists . . . It is the same, then, with the virtues. For what we do in our dealings with other people makes some of us just, some unjust . . . That is why we must perform the right activities, since difference in these imply corresponding differ-

ences in states. It is not unimportant, then, to acquire one sort of habit or another, right from our youth. On the contrary, it is very important, indeed all-important.[35]

The wisdom of Aristotle, coming from a non-Christian worldview, is nonetheless instructive for Christians.[36] Aristotle aids us in understanding that the habitual practice of virtue, the living out of one's ethical system, is the manner through which character is shaped, for good or for ill. Thus we clearly cannot say that non-Christian worldviews are devoid of legitimate ethics, nor that we have nothing to learn from non-Christians regarding character and ethics.

The worldview posed by atheistic materialism, however, gives rise to a difficulty regarding how an ethical system can be construed as obligatory. No ethical system can be imposed transcendently from without, for there is no one or nothing outside of the system. One solution to this situation—although by no means the only possible solution—is to construe ethics as purely based on the material value of survival, relative to individual desire, or based on a social pact in which individuals somehow agree on the contours of utilitarian beneficence.[37]

---

34. The belief that reason and morality exist at the frontier between Nature and Supernature has as an important implication in our understanding of normal and diseased states of mind. "The rational and moral element in each human mind is a point of force from the Supernatural working its way into Nature, exploiting at each point those conditions which Nature offers, repulsed where the conditions are hopeless and impeded when they are unfavorable . . . [They] are conditioned by the apparatus but not originated by it." Thus a damaged brain impedes good thinking, and deficiencies in societal ethics impede personal morality. The quotation is from Lewis, *Miracles*, 56.

---

35. Aristotle *Nicomachean ethics* book II,1 (Irwin translation), 18–19.

36. In fact, Aristotelian ethics are a major source of at least one dominant strand of ethics within the Christian tradition: Roman Catholicism.

37. These are not the only possible ethical systems that could be adopted by atheistic materialists. It is, however, one that is philosophically

None of these are without difficulty. A society in which every member was simply motivated to "look out for number one" would hardly be more welcoming or safe than a dark alley. The drive for survival may perhaps help in the propagation of species, but offers relatively little ground for determining what is right.

Evolutionary psychologists have posited several theories about how moral reasoning might have evolved as a result of the survival value it conferred upon the human species. Machery and Mallon described three particular types of moral evolution theories. Some theorists contend that increased cognitive capacities evolved, which in turn gave rise to "emotions, dispositions, rule-based reasoning systems, or concepts."[38] A second approach argues that normative cognition (a system composed of beliefs about what we should or should not do) evolved, and as norms emerged, so did the tendency to punish those who violate societal rules.[39] A third approach suggests see that moral norms themselves emerged as a particular type of normative cognition.[40] However, even if one accepts the premise that a moral sense evolved in human beings and that it conferred a survival advantage on the species, at best that would help us understand the process of moral reasoning. It would not help us in any

way actually determine what is objectively right or wrong.

For instance, consider the following example. Imagine that Jean discovers that she is pregnant. She is in her third year of college and recently broke up with her boyfriend. She discusses her situation with friends and makes an appointment to talk to someone at the college counseling center. She considers having an abortion, but decides instead that she will keep the child, and that she will not inform her ex-boyfriend that he fathered her child. Jean has just engaged in decision-making that involved making several moral judgments. The first moral issue involves whether or not abortion is morally acceptable. (Note, however, that we don't know whether or not Jean's decision to keep the child rested on this issue or not—she may view abortion as morally acceptable or not. In fact, Jean could have believed that abortion was morally wrong and still had one, or believed that abortion is morally acceptable and chose not to have one. Moral reasoning does not necessarily mean that we will choose to do what we believe to be right.) Jean also decides to withhold information about her child's paternity from the father. Again, we don't know why Jean made this choice (perhaps he was abusive, an alcoholic, unfaithful, or they just decided to go their separate ways). But once again, Jean makes a decision that involves a moral element (does she have a moral duty to tell the father about the pregnancy?). In this example, we can clearly see where several branches of psychology might help us understand

consistent and that can easily be documented historically.

38. Machery and Mallon, *Evolution of morality*, 5.

39. Ibid., 11ff.

40. Ibid., 20ff.

a myriad of factors that were involved in Jean's moral reasoning. However, the evolutionary forces that are thought to undergird these factors, as well as the contemporary forces that influence Jean's thinking and behavior, tell us absolutely nothing about whether or not a particular course of action is actually morally acceptable.

Whether or not one accepts the idea that a moral sense evolved as an evolutionary adaptation, it leaves open the question of how (or even if) anything can be shown to be morally compelling or morally delinquent. Christianity, on the other hand, views morality as being grounded in God's design and intention. "You mortals, the Lord has told you what is good. This is what the LORD requires from you: to do what is right, to love mercy, and to live humbly with your God" (Mic 6:8, GW). As others have pointed out, God did not give us "The Ten Suggestions" on Mount Sinai. Rather, we are given commandments; there are some things that we should do (e.g., Sabbath-keeping, honoring one's parents) and some things that we should not do (e.g., make idols, bear false witness, commit adultery, etc.). Of course, it goes without saying that our moral sense can be incorrect: people with obsessive-compulsive disorder may believe that there are things they must not do (like walking on the lines of a tiled floor), and people may fail to see errors within their moral reasoning. However, to be reliable, universal, and compelling, more is needed than just a history of how a moral sense and an ethical code evolved.

One might argue that if the survival of the species is the ultimate good, then controlled breeding to maximize the most "fit" and minimize the most "undesirable" members of society should be the basis of human ethics.[41] That proposal was expressed supremely in Social Darwinism. The American eugenics movement took Social Darwinism to its natural conclusion.[42] On the grounds that some families were "more fit" than others, recommendations to control population through involuntary sterilization of "degenerates" were codified into laws, some of which were ultimately upheld by the United States Supreme Court. In a majority opinion that is now stunning in the light of the Holocaust, Justice Oliver Wendell Holmes Jr. wrote, "It is better for all the world if, instead of waiting to execute degenerate offspring for crime or to let them starve for their imbecility, society can prevent those who are manifestly unfit from continuing their kind."[43] The ruling overturned a Virginia Supreme Court decision that had prevented the involuntary sterilization of Carrie Buck, a seventeen-year-old girl who, the State argued, had inherited traits of

---

41. Here too, however, there is the problem of determining on what basis a trait or a person is "fit" or "undesirable." Again we are pushed back to metaphysical questions of what is "good."

42. Unfortunately, the policies advocated by social Darwinists were adopted not just by atheists but by religious people as well. May God forgive us for our blindness and our failures to confront the injustices of the past, and may we refuse to be blind and silent in the present.

43. *Buck v. Bell.*

imbecility and sexual promiscuity from her mother,[44] who had been institutionalized in an insane asylum. Unfortunately, "psychological" and "scientific" views based on social Darwinism were a major impetus to the development of American eugenics laws.[45] Certainly, not all atheistic materialists sanctioned the eugenics movement. What is troubling, though, is that there was little political opposition to Social Darwinism. Most troubling of all, is the relative lack of dissent offered by Christians to this movement, and worse yet, the outright support given to it by others.[46] The extremes of the eugenics movement, the use of "scientific" and "psychological" testimony in its behalf, and the historical silence of the church in the face of this issue clearly highlight the necessity of developing a moral system that is both *reliable* and *valid*.

It would certainly be wrong to suppose that all atheistic materialists are social Darwinists or Nazis. Whether or not they have logical grounds for their ethics, many atheists and other non-Christians are deeply ethical people. Alternately, it is humbling to recount how often the church of Christ has been silent in the face of injustice or has actually been used as a vehicle to promote injustice.[47] Yet the ideals taught by the Christian tradition stand in stark contrast to these failings.

---

44. She had given birth to a child out of wedlock; the court failed to note that the pregnancy was a result of rape rather than "promiscuity."

45. We should all be humbled at the degree to which prejudice can become expressed in "professional opinion" or "scientific findings" when we recall that Dr. Albert Priddy testified that Carrie and her mother belonged "to the shiftless, ignorant, and worthless class of anti-social whites of the South." The result of *Buck v. Bell* was that in excess of sixty thousand Americans underwent forced sterilization. The 1907 Indiana law that first legalized forced sterilization served as a model for Germany's 1937 law that resulted in the sterilization of three hundred fifty thousand people during the Nazi régime, and which presaged its subsequent eugenics laws and the attempt to wipe out entire classes of "undesirable" human beings. In 2002, the Commonwealth of Virginia passed a resolution honoring Carrie Buck and repudiating the errors that had led to her wrongful labeling and sterilization. The text of the resolution ironically noted that Carrie's daughter, Vivian (who died of a childhood illness), far from being an "imbecile," had made the honor roll in school. Shortly before her death in 1983, Carrie Buck Detamore, who had married but never had additional children due to her sterilization, said, "I tried helping everybody all my life, and I tried to be good to everybody. It just don't do no good to hold grudges" (quoted in Santos, Historic test case, B1). Information about the case can be found in Lombardo, Carrie Buck's pedigree.

46. See Durst, Evangelical engagements with eugenics. The author had hoped to find evidence of significant opposition to eugenics by Christians, but he found instead, "on the whole the evangelical mainstream in the decades following the turn of the century appeared apathetic, acquiescent, or at times downright supportive of the eugenics movement" (45).

47. While Christians rightly celebrate the heroism of a few Christians like Dietrich Bonhoeffer who risked and sacrificed their lives to oppose evil, we often turn a blind eye to the way Christianity has been distorted in the past and present to support hostilities against Muslims, Jews, or those of African ancestry. Records from the Nazi concentration camp Auschwitz revealed that 42.4 percent of the camp staff claimed to be Roman Catholic, and 36.5 percent claimed to be Protestant (Lasik, Structure and character, 53).

These ideals can form the basis of a valid Christian ethical system, but intentional reflection is necessary for us to reliably apply these ideals to current situations; moral awareness demands moral obedience.

One of the classic confessions of the Catholic church is the recitation, "I confess to almighty God, and to you, my brothers and sisters, that I have sinned through my own fault, in my thoughts and in my words, in what I have done, and in what I have failed to do." As we seek to live out the ethics of loving God and our neighbor, why is it important to confess our continual failures to do so?

The Christian understanding of goodness is that moral obedience is an obligation, but it also results in well-being. This does not mean that Christians never suffer, but it means that behaving ethically creates optimal conditions for human living. Doing what is good (or moral) is motivated by an appreciation of right action and it results in the deep satisfaction of doing things well.[48] With

moral law seen as built into the fabric of the world, Christians and non-Christians alike can discern the good and be motivated to follow it, albeit imperfectly.

The duty to love God and neighbor is seen by the Christian as having been built into the fabric of creation and expressed in divine commandment. Jesus was once asked what the greatest commandment was. "The most important one," answered Jesus, "is this: 'Hear, O Israel, the Lord our God, the Lord is one. Love the Lord your God with all your heart and with all your soul and with all your mind and with all your strength.' The second is this: 'Love your neighbor as yourself.' There is no commandment greater than these" (Mark 12:29–31, NIV).

It is not enough to recognize that the world includes ethical ingredients; we must follow the ethical duties conferred upon us. This too is fundamental to integration: that we do all things as an expression of our love of God and love for our neighbor. If we fail to recognize and act on the command to love God and to love our fellow human beings in our integrative efforts, then we must agree with the Apostle Paul, "I gain nothing by doing these things if I do not have love" (1 Cor 13:3, BBE).[49]

---

48. For instance, the psalmist revels in the goodness of God's law in Ps 19:7–11, appreciating the law as being "more precious than gold" and "sweeter than honey," yet also recognizing that in the keeping of the law is pleasure "giving joy to the heart" and "in keeping them there is great reward" (NIV).

49. While the text certainly does not have integration in mind, the principle would seem to apply to the life of the mind exercised without love just as much as to any act of service done in the same manner.

From Duty to Beauty

A Christian understanding of the nature and origin of the universe not only imposes a basis for ethical action, but it also provides an impetus for the creation and appreciation of beauty. The world was proclaimed to be "good" by God, and "very good" when it was completed with the creation of humankind. The psalms are full of praise compelled by wonder at and awe of the beauty that surrounds us.

How many are your works, O LORD!
In wisdom you made them all;
    the earth is full of your creatures.
    (Ps 104:24, NIV).

Yet beauty serves not as an end in itself, but as a reminder that the hand from which it comes is divine. In fact, the Scriptures caution us about the ephemeral nature of earthly beauty:

But the wicked will perish:
The LORD's enemies will be like the
        beauty of the fields,
    they will vanish—vanish like smoke.
    (Ps 37:20, NIV)

Your beauty should not come from outward adornment, such as braided hair and the wearing of gold jewelry and fine clothes. Instead, it should be that of your inner self, the unfading beauty of a gentle and quiet spirit, which is of great worth in God's sight. (1 Pet 3:3–5, NIV).

I have seen the burden God has laid on men. He has made everything beautiful in its time. He has also set eternity in the hearts of men; yet they cannot fathom what God has done from beginning to end. I know that there is nothing better for men than to be happy and do good while they live. (Eccl 3:10–12, NIV).

While we are to enjoy beauty, we are called to recognize that the beauty of the material world is transient. Our observation of the wonders of human nature and functioning, while tempered by sadness and grief over human fallenness and frailty, should draw us to an experience of wonder and awe that culminates in praise.

For the Christian every good thing in life should lead to awe, gratitude, and praise, tempered by the awareness that the material world is transient. This sacramental view of life helps us to recognize that all of life is sacred, and all of its wonders are an impetus to gratitude. G. K. Chesterton understood this. Writing about expressing gratitude for God's goodness ("saying grace"), he wrote: "You say grace before meals . . . But I say grace before the concert and the opera, and grace before the play and pantomime, and grace before I open a book, and grace before sketching, painting, and swimming, fencing, boxing, walking, playing, dancing, and grace before I dip the pen in ink."[50]

An integrative paradigm that neglects beauty has ignored one of the most fundamental realities of a Christian worldview. And so it is for the Christian who is engaged in any activity, or any

---

50. Although this statement is widely quoted, its original source is unknown, but it is alleged to be from one of Chesterton's journals.

area of study. As we explore the wonders of the creation, we cannot help but be grateful, and to praise and stand in awe of our Creator.

Summary: Let There Be Light

On Christmas Eve 1968, black-and-white images of earth, taken from Apollo 8, flickered on television screens around the world. Astronauts Frank Borman, Jim Lovell, and William Anders, who had left their solid footing on Earth for the first manned lunar orbit, were broadcasting a live feed to the distant earth. William Anders initiated the closing moments, his voice punctuated by the extraneous sounds of the transmission: "For all the people on Earth the crew of Apollo 8 has a message we would like to send you: 'In the beginning God created the heaven and the earth. And the earth was without form, and void; and darkness was upon the face of the deep. And the Spirit of God moved upon the face of the waters. And God said, Let there be light: and there was light. And God saw the light, that it was good: and God divided the light from the darkness.'"[51]

The astronauts took turns reading the passage, taken from the first chapter of Genesis. Mission Commander Frank Borman read the last few verses, and ended the broadcast with the words, "And from the crew of Apollo 8, we close with good night, good luck, a Merry Christmas, and God bless all of you—all of you

on the good Earth." From a lunar orbit the ancient words had been broadcast with state-of-the-art technology. According to the ancient text, God had declared that the creation was *good*. Viewed from space by the modern eye, we simply had to agree: this blue-and-white shimmering jewel shining in the vastness of space is indeed *good*.

For all of human history we could look at space in awe, and now we can gaze at Earth from space. We know more about the workings of the material world than at any time in human history. Naturalists (or atheistic materialists) see our increased knowledge as an indication of inevitable progress that can ultimately reduce every experience to material explanations. Supernaturalists agree that we have made incredible leaps in understanding material causation, but they claim that *rumors of another world* persist. *Thin places* still produce amazement, joy, and gratitude that beckon us to look beyond the material realm.

Naturalism and supernaturalism lead to different understandings of the nature of the world and of the ultimate nature of truth, goodness, and beauty. In this chapter, we compared some of the implications of Christian answers to metaphysical questions about the existence and nature of God, the relationship of God to the created order, the nature of the world, ethics, and aesthetics. Each of these considerations has implications for an integrative paradigm, both in making such models conceptually possible (i.e., scientific and Christian understandings are compatible) and in pointing to

---

51. National Aeronautics and Space Administration, "Apollo 8 Christmas Eve Broadcast."

the ultimate ends of human purpose and activity (praise of God and love of neighbor).

One might wonder why so much time has been spent on philosophical issues in a book that is about Christian approaches to psychology. Quite simply, it is because these philosophical issues change how we understand the world and our place in it. Alan Tjeltveit put it succinctly:

> Psychologists' ethical and metaphysical assumptions profoundly shape their psychologies . . . Explicit articulation and thinking about those underlying beliefs would improve psychology and certainly improve efforts to articulate the optimal ways to draw on both psychology and Christian faith in seeking psychological understanding.[52]

While this is true of epistemology and metaphysics, it is even more central to our discussion as we turn our attention to the assumptions that we make about human nature.

Our next chapter will bring us closer to the mutual subject of Christian theology and psychology as we turn our attention to the nature of humanity.

Questions for Reflection and Discussion

1. The cosmology of Genesis points to the creation of humankind as the crowning achievement in which the creation is completed and it is declared to be "very good." Modern cosmology demonstrates that our planet is relatively insignificant and peripheral on a cosmic scale. Can human life be both eternally and existentially significant, and yet at the physical periphery of the universe? (You might want to consider Psalm 8 as you think about this.)

2. Summarize the differences between naturalism and supernaturalism regarding the ultimate nature of the world and the purpose of human life.

3. Can one be scientific and still believe in the supernatural (the existence of God)? Why or why not?

4. The author noted that miracles do not contradict science but are simply events that originate externally from nature but are accommodated by nature. Do you agree or disagree with this?

5. In discussing miracles, the author suggested that a difficulty exists in that it is *too easy to dismiss miraculous claims by explaining their effects on a purely naturalistic basis*, or alternatively, *too easy to claim as miraculous things which are statistically uncommon but readily explicable in natural terms*. Which of these extremes is most evident in your own thinking? Do you too readily accept or too readily reject claims of the miraculous?

6. What difference does it make to view nature as our sister rather than as our mother?

---

52. Tjeltveit, *Lost opportunities*, 18.

7. What do you believe about how the world came to be? What evidence supports your belief of the origin of the world? Note what kind of evidence you utilize in your answer (e.g., biblical, experiential, philosophical, etc.) and what methodology you utilize in evaluating that evidence (e.g., what kind of hermeneutics do you use?).

8. In his discussion of ethics, the author pointed to Jesus's admonition to love God with all our being and to love our neighbors as we love ourselves. How are these ethical ideals related to the pursuit of integration?

9. Describe at least two times when you have experienced thin places. (If you are not a Christian, describe times when your experience of nature elicited feelings such as awe, amazement, joy, or gratitude.) Contrast this to times when you failed to be awed by nature. Do you think that Lewis was correct in stating that we are somehow brutal or stupid when we are indifferent to the majesty of nature?

7

The Nature of Humanity: Philosophical Anthropology

So complex is the human spirit that it can itself scarce discern the deep springs which impel it to action.

—Sir Arthur Conan Doyle

Love every man in spite of his falling into sin. Never mind the sins, but remember that the foundation of the man is the same—the image of God.

—John of Kronstadt

Psychology and theology confront a complex task in attempting to understand human nature. Consider the diverse perspectives on this topic offered by two literary authors. First, the oft-misunderstood lines of Shakespeare's *Hamlet*:

> What a piece of work is a man! how
>   noble in reason!
> how infinite in faculties, in form and
>   moving
> how express and admirable! in action
>   how like an angel!
> in apprehension how like a god! the
>   beauty of the
> world! the paragon of animals; and yet
>   to me,
> what is this quintessence of dust? Man
>   delights not me:
> no, nor woman neither . . .[1]

Yet another perspective is offered by Samuel Clemens (a.k.a., Mark Twain) in the words of the Old Man in his essay *What Is Man?*

> Man the machine—man the impersonal engine. Whatsoever a man is, is due to his *make*, and to the *influences* brought to bear upon it by his heredities, his habitat, his associations. He is moved, directed, COMMANDED, by *exterior* influences—*solely*. He *originates* nothing, not even a thought.[2]

Hamlet is not praising the virtues of human beings, as is often supposed; he is sarcastically mocking such a high view of humanity in the face of his own exposure to the baser side of human nature.[3] The

1. Shakespeare, *Hamlet*, act 2, scene 2.

2. Twain, *What is man?* 7.

3. "Here is a young intellectual who once

Old Man has also rejected the high view of humanity, instead perceiving human nature in purely mechanistic terms.

> "The line separating good and evil passes not through states, nor between classes, nor between political parties either —but right through every human heart—and through all human hearts. This line shifts. Inside us, it oscillates with the years. And even within hearts overwhelmed by evil, one small bridgehead of good is retained. And even in the best of all hearts, there remains . . . an unuprooted small corner of evil."
>
> —Aleksandr Solzhenitsyn, *The Gulag Archipelago*

With Hamlet, we struggle to understand how human beings can be the recipient of incredible abilities and prone to great evil. We try to reconcile how human beings are saints *and* sinners. Humanity has spawned those in the fashion of Mother Teresa and those in the style of Adolf Hitler. If we are honest, though, our deeper struggle is that *good and evil reside in every human heart*, including our own. With the Old Man, we struggle to understand humanity as an emancipated being and as a machine. While we cherish the notion of human freedom, with the Old Man we must admit that many things influence our actions: the externals of heredity, habitat, and associations.

Like Shakespeare's Hamlet and Clemens's Old Man, we all possess assumptions about the nature of human beings, many of which are shaped by our worldviews, as we saw in chapter 4. When we try to evaluate beliefs about human nature, we rely on the epistemic sources and methods that were the topic of chapter 5. Our beliefs about human nature are also affected by our assumptions about the kind of world we live in (e.g., the contrasting views of naturalism and supernaturalism that we explored in chapter 6).

When psychologists and theologians attempt to understand *human behavior*, their insights are inevitably affected by their previously held assumptions about *human nature*. In assessing the validity of such assumptions, we embark on an investigation of *philosophical anthropology* (the study of the character, disposition, qualities, and inclinations of human beings).[4]

---

embraced the Renaissance view of an ordered and moral universe in which man, endowed with reason, was the noblest of creature . . . But Hamlet has learned that mankind has a terrifying capacity to reject reason, to descend to the bestial level: subjects may murder kings, brother may kill brother; wives and mothers may hasten to incestuous sheets; boyhood friends may permit themselves to be used as spies, rejecting the sacred principles of friendship" (Hillegass, *"Hamlet": Notes*, 41).

---

4. The term *philosophical anthropology* carries several meanings. In its narrowest sense, it refers to the question of what makes human beings different from other creatures or objects.

Psychology and theology are both concerned with philosophical anthropology. Psychology draws its name from the root ψυχή (*psychē*), a Greek word whose use can encompass the physical, the psychological, and the immaterial (i.e., "soul") aspects of humanity. In both clinical and experimental expressions, the nature and functioning of human beings is the central concern of psychology. The word *theology* comes from the root word θεός (*theos*), or "God." In its most restrictive use, the word *theology* is concerned with the nature of God and with God's relationship to the world. As the word is now used, the discipline of theology encompasses all of the beliefs or doctrines of a given religion.[5] Scripture, of course, holds a central place in the development of doctrine. Since the place of human beings is a major focus of Christian revelation, and since much of Scripture is explicitly concerned with the condition and nature of human beings, philosophical anthropology is a central concern of Christian theology. The manner in which psychology and theology approach their

common subject is a point that we will now develop further.

One Subject, Two Perspectives

A foundational assumption for the integration of psychology and Christianity is that we can gain knowledge about the nature and functioning of human beings both from Scripture (as we develop a biblical anthropology) and from science (as we look at the theories and findings of psychology and other social sciences). Although psychology and theology have a common interest in human beings, they approach the topic with different assumptions (implicit and explicit), methodologies, hypotheses, and goals. Table 7.1 provides a summary of these differences, followed by an extended discussion of how these differences allow us to develop a more complete philosophical anthropology.

Psychological Perspectives

Psychology as a science is based on the premises that the world is an orderly place in which observation can lead to awareness of the regularities of phenomena (including human behavior) and that some degree of predictability is possible given these regularities.[6] As a science, psychology employs *methodological naturalism*, that is, it seeks natural explanations for the

---

It also refers to an early twentieth-century philosophical school that sought to ground understanding of human character in phenomenology and biology. The term is used here in the broadest sense of the totality of one's assumptions about the nature of human beings.

5. Theology is developed from numerous sources. In addition to its scriptural basis, Christian theology is developed through reason, church tradition, archaeology, history, and other means of analysis. Christian traditions differ somewhat in their theologies based on their unique histories and their interpretations of Scripture.

---

6. This premise is characteristic of the dominant models of psychology. Postmodern approaches to psychology do not necessarily accept this premise.

TABLE 7.1: Psychological and Theological Approaches to Philosophical Anthropology

	Assumptions & Exemplar Categories	Methodologies	Organization of findings	Ideals & Goals
P S Y C H O L O G Y	The world is knowable and predictable Methodological Naturalism Bio-psycho-social perspective	Empiricism Rational Inquiry	Theories	Understanding Improving life by reducing suffering and optimizing ideal conditions
T H E O L O G Y	God's revealed word (the Bible) is discernible, and is the guide for faith and practice Natural and supernatural explanations Humans are created in the image of God, finite, and fallen	Hermeneutics Natural Theology Rational Inquiry	Systematic Theology	Understanding Salvation Sanctification Meaning Stewardship Worship

phenomena it investigates. This does not rule out explanations other than naturalistic ones. However, the use of methodological naturalism limits the focus of its questions and its explanatory hypotheses to natural explanations.[7]

> "Psychology is the study of the mind and behavior. The discipline embraces all aspects of the human experience—from the functions of the brain to the actions of nations, from child development to care for the aged. In every conceivable setting from scientific research centers to mental healthcare services, "the understanding of behavior" is the enterprise of psychologists."
>
> —American Psychological Association

While much of modern psychology is built on a scientific approach to studying behavior, it is also built on the metaphysical assumptions of those who study and practice psychology. To say that psychology utilizes scientific inquiry does *not* mean that it is free from bias or that it leads to incontrovertible proof. To think scientifically is simply to utilize the "perceptions, inferences, and memories of a community examining reality from a particular point of view," notably, one that makes use of the scientific method.[8] Psychologists primarily utilize two epistemic frameworks for understanding their subject: empiricism and rational discourse. Psychologists do not rely solely on the scientific method. We have already seen that they rely on reason to develop theories and analyze data. Their worldviews, their personal experiences, and their education (including the historical development of ideas in academia) shape their theories.

Psychologists rely on *reason* to develop and analyze ideas. Psychologists use reason to develop theories, primarily through inductive logic, as we saw in chapter 5. Empirical studies produce data that are analyzed with rational thought, primarily utilizing deductive logic. However, we would be naïve to overlook the influence exerted by the assumptions of the theorist's worldview, epistemology, cosmology, metaphysics, and philosophical anthropology. Such assumptions impact how theories are created and evaluated. *Every psychologist grounds his or her psychology in a philosophical system, whether or not it is explicitly articulated or carefully considered; every psychology is done from an antecedent worldview perspective.* Yet psychology, as a science, rigorously attempts to rely on *observable* data in developing and evaluating theories.[9]

---

7. Even those areas of psychology that are more philosophical than empirical still tend to cast things in naturalistic terms, although there are some notable exceptions.

8. Hodges, Perception is relative, 105.

9. Recall from chapter 5 that empiricism, the method of science, is based on an approach to

Research approaches to psychology attempt to learn about human and animal behavior and mental processes by collecting and evaluating quantifiable data. Researchers describe phenomena using case studies, surveys, and naturalistic observation. They quantify data that can be systematically evaluated. Non-experimental theorists typically use observational methods to gather data, but they organize their observations utilizing rational inquiry (for instance, a personality theorist may logically infer the functions that meaning plays in organizing and motivating behavior). Experimental and nonexperimental approaches result in theories that organize the observations of the theorist.

Experimental methods take this a step further. Theories guide the development of hypotheses that attempt to predict what will happen under certain conditions. The hypothesis is tested by manipulating a variable of interest (such as level of frustration). Other variables are held constant (such as age of the subject). The experimenter creates a situation in which the effects of the manipulation can be observed (such as exposing some subjects to frustrating circumstances and others to a control condition), and then coding and comparing the number of aggressive behaviors that occurred in each group. The hypotheses must be posited in falsifiable terms (i.e., predictions must be framed in such a way that the results can be seen to either support the hypothesis or not).

It is important to note that not all psychological theories are experimentally verifiable, and some psychological methodologies are non-empirical. Furthermore, although experimental data help us to test theories, other theories may emerge that explain the data more accurately or more completely. In fact, scientific advances often occur when new theories challenge existing theories; such challenges help us to accept or modify useful theories and to discard theories that are less effective, elegant, or parsimonious.[10]

Finally, we need to know the goals of psychology. Its principal goals, ideally, are increased *knowledge* and the *improvement of human life* by the reduction of suffering or the optimizing of conditions under which human beings flourish. The first goal is motivated by *curiosity* and the desire to understand the world. The second goal is motivated by *compassion* (for instance, concern for people suffering from depression or dementia) and by the desire to optimize human potentials (e.g., to help organizations develop cultures that foster productivity and employee satisfaction). Yet we must hasten to add that vices such as arrogance, pride, desire for recognition, and other failings are the constant nemeses of the ideals for which psychologists strive.

---

knowledge that relies on the observation of experience to test ideas rather than relying solely on philosophical speculation.

---

10. This does not mean, though, that science *inevitably* leads to progress. Even when science increases our knowledge, it can be used for good or for ill.

Christian theology is the study of Christian belief and practice. Its primary sources include the Christian Bible, as well as Church tradition. Rather than just being an intellectual endeavor, Christian theology is expressed through how Christians conceptualize God's activity in the world and, in turn, how we understand ourselves and God's call for how we should live in the world.

Christian Perspectives

Christian theology, like psychology, proceeds from its own foundational assumptions. Christian theology sees God's revealed Word as discernible, and views it as the guide for faith and practice.[11] While most psychologists are committed to methodological naturalism (investigating phenomena by looking for naturalistic explanations), Christians assume that both natural and supernatural explanations may be helpful in understanding phenomena. For instance, Leviticus 13 contains extensive instructions for determining whether a skin infection is leprous or not based on naturalistic observations.[12] While leprosy was typically understood as a natural phenomenon (leading to ceremonial uncleanness and expulsion from the community to quarantine disease), there were occasions when leprosy was seen as a supernatural curse (e.g., the leprous condition of Miriam (see Numbers 12), Gehazi (see 2 Kings 5), and Uzziah (see 2 Chronicles 26).

Christian theology is developed and organized around concepts such as creation, sin, grace, redemption, and revelation. Knowledge about such topics is sought through interpretation and application of source materials (notably the Bible), utilizing hermeneutical methods. Theologians also draw on natural theology, attempting to discern theological truths from the observation of the created realm. Additionally theologians, like psychologists, make use of rational inquiry;[13] this is especially evi-

---

11. The means of discernment differ in theological systems, but most emphasize some combination of guidance by the Holy Spirit and the application of logically deduced hermeneutical principles.

12. Hansen's disease is the medical name given to a condition that is commonly known as leprosy. However, this disease is probably not the same as the disease that modern translations of the Bible refer to as leprosy. Milgrom argues that the conditions mentioned in Leviticus 13 should be translated as "scale diseases" to avoid confusing them with Hansen's disease. He also notes that these conditions were most likely not contagious but they were regarded as ritual impurities. See Milgrom, *Leviticus*, 127–33.

13. The theologian cannot honestly claim that all his or her theology comes "straight from the Bible." As Coe observes, "the theologian also depends upon the natural disciplines with respect to methodology. For example, the exegete and biblical theologian depend upon the disciplines of philology, literary criticism, his-

dent in medieval scholars such as Thomas Aquinas, whose *Summa Theologiae* is as much a dialogue with Aristotelian and Neoplatonic philosophy as it is an exegesis of Scripture. Various theological systems reflect the historical development of Christian thinking from within diverse Christian traditions (e.g., Roman Catholic, Reformed, Anabaptist, Wesleyan, etc.). *Every theologian grounds his or her theology in a philosophical system, whether or not it is explicitly articulated or carefully considered; every theology is done from an antecedent worldview perspective.* While theological studies certainly can (and often should) alter one's worldview perspective, it is naïve to deny that we possess epistemic, cosmological, and anthropological assumptions at the outset that influence how we construct our theological understanding.[14]

The corpus of theological findings is arranged into systematic theologies that, much like theories, attempt to organize the observations of the theologian about a variety of topics. Each systematic theology represents the viewpoint of a particular theologian or school of theology. Some of these perspectives carry the consensus of "orthodoxy," some of them diverge from orthodoxy, and others focus

on issues that are seen as speculative or peripheral to the core doctrines of the faith. Theology, like psychology, is motivated by a quest for *understanding*. Theology, like psychology, is motivated by *compassion*, but it has a longer view that includes eternal concerns in addition to temporal concerns. It expresses a quest for spiritual wholeness and reconciliation in considering topics like salvation and sanctification. Christianity supplies meaning and purpose for life, as well as a motivation to meet tangible temporal needs.[15]

While Christian theology undeniably contains cognitive elements, it is crucial to remember that Christianity is also incarnational. Doctrine that is not lived out in relationship and identity is not fully Christian. Christian theology seeks to understand how human beings can be reconciled to God, how human beings can deal with sin, and how human beings can find meaning in life. Theology, and any undertaking for the Christian, should be motivated by stewardship and worship. Unfortunately, arrogance, pride, desire for recognition, and other vices that tempt the psychologist,

---

tory and archeology." Coe, An interdependent model, 112.

14. Such assumptions are, to some degree, able to be identified and evaluated, as we saw in chapter 5. The reading of Scripture and the urging of the Holy Spirit can both aid us in evaluating our assumptions. Nevertheless, we can never fully rise above our own assumptions, and none of us can completely rise above our cultural and historical conditioning.

15. While Christianity sees temporal suffering as able to produce spiritual benefits (Jas 1:2–4), it does not see suffering as an end in itself, and it commends us to seek to reduce suffering by ministering to those in need (e.g., Acts 2:45; Rom 12:15; 1 Tim 5:3; Jas 1:27; 5:14). In this tradition, Christian missions continue to establish hospitals *and* churches, ministering to physical *and* spiritual needs (Jas 2:15–16). Likewise the integration of psychology and Christianity paves the way for holistic ministry that takes seriously temporal *and* eternal conditions.

likewise hinder the theologian; we are all sinful human beings with mixed and impure motives.

"We cannot know the whole truth, which belongs to God alone, but our task nevertheless is to seek to know what is true."

—Wendell Berry

Psychology and Theology: Variations on a Theme

It is important to note that psychology and theology study different variations of the same topic when they look at human nature. As Malcolm Jeeves wisely cautioned: "The psychologist researching human behavior can only take us as he finds us. Any questions of what we might have been like, had there never been a Fall, sit firmly in the domain of the theologian. He writes about our fallen nature, our sinful nature, our unregenerate nature, and so on."[16]

Another British pioneer in the interface of theology and psychology put it this way: "We cannot discover, by inspection of large numbers of specimens of humanity as it exists, still less by introspection, what is 'normal' or 'proper' human spiritual functioning. There are no unspoiled specimens of the species available for inspection."[17]

This reality constrains psychology to observe humanity as it currently exists.[18] Christian theology reflects on humanity as it is, but it also has access to some information about how humanity was intended to be before the Fall, and on the moral decrees of how we ought to live.

Rather than being antithetical or irrelevant to each other, psychology and Christian theology can be of use to each other. By using both disciplines, we can gain a more complete view of humanity than we can from just one vantage point. In the Introduction to this book I described a tree that looked perfectly healthy from one perspective but was obviously diseased when seen from another perspective. Likewise, theology may tell us about certain aspects of humanity (created in the image of God, fallen, tainted by sin), but psychology may be able to tell us how this fallenness is expressed in distorted thinking and relationships (defense mechanisms and unhealthy patterns of relating). Conversely, psychology may be able to describe human beings as they are, but only Christian theology can describe them as they were intended to be. Again, only theology can answer questions of ultimate concern (e.g., how did we come to be, what is our purpose, what is our

---

16. Jeeves, *Human nature at the millennium*, 103.

17. Lake, *Clinical theology*, 30.

18. While psychology can explore how various human behaviors affect human well-being (e.g., finding that premarital sex and cohabitation are associated with higher divorce rates), it cannot—in and of itself—supply a normative view of human nature (that is, a statement of the ideal behavior and purpose of human beings). Christianity provides a normative framework, thus offering to psychology a crucial piece of the human puzzle.

destiny?). Having painted the broad contours of the two disciplines, we can begin to ask how both of them can contribute to the creation of a sound philosophical anthropology.

"The biopsychosocial model is both a philosophy of clinical care and a practical clinical guide. Philosophically, it is a way of understanding how suffering, disease, and illness are affected by multiple levels of organization, from the societal to the molecular. At the practical level, it is a way of understanding the patient's subjective experience as an essential contributor to accurate diagnosis, health outcomes, and humane care."

—Borrell-Carrió, Suchman, and Epstein

Philosophical Anthropology: Psychological Perspectives

In recent years, the phrase "bio-psycho-social perspective" has become a convenient rubric under which to organize the complexity of the myriad factors that influence human behavior. We are biological beings, shaped by genetic inheritance and the organization and health of our neurological structures. We have rich inner lives of diverse dispositions, motivations, cognitive abilities and processes, intrapsychic dynamics, and reinforcement histories. We are also social creatures, affected by our social and cultural environments. Together these elements help us understand normal phenomena (like memory construction, neurological function, and social attraction) and abnormal psychological occurrences (such as pseudo-memories, Alzheimer's disease, and dysfunctional relationships).

Unfortunately, much of the work on the integration of Christianity and psychology has focused narrowly on what we know about human functioning from the perspective of clinical psychology while neglecting the majority of the discipline of psychology (e.g., neuropsychology, social psychology, developmental psychology, learning, sensation and perception). A brief outline of the contours of the discipline of psychology will help us to shape a fuller understanding of psychological approaches to human nature and functioning. Drawing loosely on David Myers's enumeration of the current perspectives through which psychology is studied, we will look at biological, behavioral, cognitive, sociocultural, evolutionary, and psychodynamic approaches.[19]

The realization that psychological events are simultaneously biological events is the foundation of modern biological psychology. The human nervous system is a wonderfully complex system that we are beginning to understand not

---

19. Myers, *Psychology*, 9. For the sake of convenience, I have collapsed Myers's neuroscience and behavior genetics approaches into the more generic "biological psychology" category.

only at the gross anatomical level (where we can discern the workings of the sensory and motor strips, and the effects of damage to Broca's and Wernicke's areas) but also at the neuroanatomical level (where we can determine the mechanisms of neural transmission and the consequences of functional deficiencies of serotonin). Behavioral genetics, likewise, has given us a key to understanding the heritability of traits ranging from shyness to schizophrenia. We can, to some degree, separate the origins of biological structure and function into their antecedent sources (nature and nurture). For the unwary, however, it is easy to fall into a trap of biological reductionism by assuming that every psychological event is exhaustively explicable in biological terms. While we must admit that the biological paradigm is a powerful one, we must also resist the temptation to see it as all encompassing.

Psychology's behavioral perspective is concerned with analyzing how external factors, such as rewards and punishment, influence the acquisition or extinction of behavior. Behavioral psychology studies learning under a variety of models utilizing both human and animal subjects. The major models of behaviorism are classical conditioning (originating in the work of Ivan Pavlov), operant conditioning (à la B. F. Skinner), and observational learning (from Albert Bandura's social-learning theory).

On another cutting edge of psychology is cognitive psychology (which should not to be confused with cognitive therapy). Cognitive psychologists study how information is processed, stored, and retrieved. Obviously, there is some significant overlap with the biological perspective, since such processing, storage, and retrieval are biological events. The difference, however, is that cognitive psychology focuses less on the biology of these phenomena and more on the circumstances under which they occur, the internal processes that facilitate or inhibit information processing (e.g., attention, perception, memory, learning), the content of cognition as mental representation, and so forth. There is also overlap with the behavioral perspective, but whereas most behaviorists are principally concerned with identifying external stimuli and reinforcers of behavior, cognitive psychologists are interested in the *processes* that lead to such connections and in what happens within the *mind*.

The sociocultural perspective of psychology is interested in how behavior is shaped by social phenomena, such as culture, affiliation, or awareness that one is being observed. Here too there is overlap, particularly with Bandura's social-learning theory. Human beings are, by nature, social creatures, and we are both the shapers of societies and shaped by our societies, able to influence the behavior of others, and influenced by others in our own thoughts and actions. Religious belief is sometimes studied as a social phenomenon, but it can also be studied as an intrapsychic phenomenon, or its effects on mental and physical health evaluated. Conditions that foster or inhibit religious belief and change can also be considered.[20]

The relative newcomer to psychology's perspectives is the evolutionary perspective. Utilizing an evolutionary paradigm, this perspective asks how various behaviors, biological processes, and cognitive mechanisms may have been influenced by their survival value. This perspective has some unique obstacles, not the least of which is that its theories are necessarily post hoc and thus typically untestable by scientific means.

Perhaps the oldest of psychology's perspectives is the psychodynamic approach. While the name *Sigmund Freud* springs to mind, the word *psychodynamic* is here used in a broader sense than applying to Freud's theories alone, although he is the major figure associated with this approach in modern times.[21] The psychodynamic approach asks about the role of intrapsychic phenomena such as unconscious conflicts, innate drives, defense mechanisms, and so forth. It is also concerned with intrapsychic experiences, such as one's image of God, beliefs about the world, and so forth.

Within and between each of the perspectives from which the study of psychology is approached, competing theories vie with each other to offer the best or most comprehensive theory of how a given psychological phenomenon works. Theories differ regarding explanatory processes, how evidence is gathered and evaluated, and on presuppositions that the theorists bring to the table. As an example, in personality theory, theorists differ on their assumptions about whether human nature is basically good or bad; whether nature or nurture is more important; whether human beings are free agents or largely determined; whether behavior is governed more by past events or future goals; and so forth. These are largely assumptive issues that theorists bring to the study of personality. Of course, our observations can confirm both sides of the issues in most cases, because human beings are exceptionally complex and exasperatingly inconsistent. Theologians must also confront the complex and inconsistent nature of human beings, though they frame the issues on different grounds, as we shall see.

Psychology has so many diverse perspectives not only because theorists differ regarding their assumptions, but also because its subject matter is so complex. An appreciation of this complexity leads to the conclusion that psychology's perspectives are more *complementary* than *incompatible*. The mysterious twists and turns of human behavior form a Gordian knot that can be viewed in terms of biology, environmental reinforcement, cognitive processes, social influences,

---

20. Psychology of religion is a very worthwhile field for psychologists and theologians to consider. While the veracity of religious experience cannot be evaluated by psychology, the intrapsychic, social, and behavioral expressions of religious belief and commitment can profitably be explored.

21. This is not a new perspective; a casual reading of ancient Greek philosophy or of Shakespeare will serve to demonstrate that it is a very ancient and venerable approach to understanding human behavior.

adaptive value, and psychodynamic processes.[22] Each of these domains has a place in shaping human behavior, and hence only a comprehensive understanding of them can satisfactorily account for the complexities of our subject.

"Truth is truth, whether it is spoken by the lips of Jesus or Balaam's donkey."

—attributed to George MacDonald

You might notice that clinical psychology is not even included as one of the major perspectives of psychology. While clinical psychology is a subfield of psychology (as are industrial and organizational psychology and neuropsychology), it is not itself a perspective through which the entire field is viewed. Rather, clinical psychology asks how the methods and findings of the major psychological perspectives help us to organize our understanding of psychological disorders, to explicate the factors that facilitate or harm psychological health, and to evaluate the efficacy of interventions for people who have psychological disorders.

Given that clinical psychology is the area that dominates the field of psychology (at least in terms of the number of doctorates awarded), and that its subject matter often brings it into contact with theological issues, it is not surprising that the integrative literature has been spurred heavily by this important but small subfield of psychology. Nonetheless, we are well advised to heed the counsel of Malcolm Jeeves: "Any claim to talk about the integration of psychology and Christian belief must deal with psychology as it actually is today. It will not do to confine our discussion to some small section . . . and fail to take account of the vast majority of the psychological landscape."[23] In heeding Jeeves's advice, we should recognize the importance of clinical psychology to our discussion, but not allow it to dominate the conversation.

What does psychology provide us in terms of philosophical anthropology? Psychology provides a framework from which to think about the complexity of human nature and functioning. It encompasses theories developed from a variety of perspectives, utilizing diverse epistemic methods, all in an attempt to provide a fuller picture of humans as biological, psychological, and social beings.

---

22. In Greek mythology, a peasant named Gordius arrived in Phrygia on an ox-cart just after an oracle had announced that the new king would be the next person who came into town on an ox-cart. Gordius then tied his cart with an intricate knot, and the belief spread that whoever could untie it would rule Asia, as Alexander the Great is said to have done when he severed the knot by the stroke of his sword. One interpretation of the myth was that Gordius actually wound the rope around the tongue of the cart, spliced the two ends together, and then hid his handiwork with a series of knots. The analogy here to the psyche is significant—the living human being knows no distinction between body, mind, spirit, and so forth—and once these "parts" are severed, we are left with naught but a dead body. Yet we can profitably explore various "parts" of the single, knotted rope.

23. Jeeves, *Human nature*, 21.

Psychology also provides data about human beings that can only be gained from empirical inquiry. Although the methods and source materials of theology differ from those of psychology, it shares many of the same goals and limitations. Theology, instead of organizing its observations around a bio-psycho-social framework, will arrange its observations of human nature in terms of a finite creature, fashioned in the image of God, and corrupted by sin.

Philosophical Anthropology: Theological Perspectives

Although psychology has much to teach us about human behavior, it cannot provide the larger context that gives meaning and direction for life itself. Pope Benedict XVI in his encyclical *Caritas in Veritatate* (*Charity in Truth*) put it succinctly: "Without God man neither knows which way to go, nor even understands who he is."[24] Theological reflection thus provides us with access to a dimension that is essential to understanding who we are, our relationship with God, and how we ought to live, among other things.

A Christian view of humanity begins with wonder and awe. J. Gresham Machen, reflecting on the personhood of the first created man, marveled at the mystery: "What a stupendous mystery that is! Here is man, a finite creature, product of God's creative hand, walking here upon this earth in a body made of the dust of the ground . . . [and he] possesses the strange and terrible gift of personal freedom, and is capable of personal companionship with the infinite and eternal God."[25] Whatever else it may offer, a Christian view of humanity provides a sense of awe that must result in praise of our Creator.

> "The self is curved inward, cut off from God and from the neighbor, and therefore ultimately cut off from true self-understanding as well."
>
> —Brian Gregor,
> *A Philosophical Anthropology of the Cross*

When theologians turn their attention to the study of human nature, they confront the same obstacle faced by psychologists: they become both the investigator and the object of investigation. Theology professor Millard J. Erickson notes the unique problems that this creates for the theologian: "The doctrine of humanity has an unusual status. Here the student of theology is also its object . . . Our anthropology will determine how we understand ourselves and, consequently, how we do theology, or even

---

24. Benedict, *Caritas in Veritate*, sec. 78, ¶1.

25. Machen, *The Christian view of man*, 169–70. It is worth noting that Machen was rather dubious about the possibility of a science of psychology apart from a Christian understanding of the soul, though in fairness he was recoiling against the excessively reductionistic tendencies of the early behaviorists, whose claims often exceeded their data.

what theology is, that is, to the degree that it is thought of as a human activity."[26]

The critique that psychology is "sinful human beings sinfully thinking about sinful human beings" applies equally to theologians who are concerned with philosophical anthropology. As such, careful consideration of the assumptions that are brought to the table by theologians is also required.

Theological perspectives on philosophical anthropology, like their psychological counterparts, are diverse interpretations based on the data available for inspection. In this case, the diverse interpretations represent various theological traditions in the way that biblical sources are understood. As Johnson and Webber put it, "While the Scriptures are unequivocal about the pervasive nature of sin in all human persons, a precise theory about sin is not fully articulated within the pages of the Bible. One will look in vain through the prophets, the Gospels, or the epistles to find a theological explanation regarding the nature of man. The Scriptures proclaim, they do not explain. The proclamation is everywhere the same: man is fallen and in desperate need of grace."[27]

Theological understanding of human nature reflects foundational Scriptures about human nature and the historical development of various theological traditions as they have attempted

to come to grips with the teachings of Scripture.[28]

The primary biblical texts regarding the nature of humanity are contained in the first three chapters of the book of Genesis. There are, however, many additional texts that are significant to the topic because they comment on such things as the purpose of human life (e.g., to glorify God; Isa 43:7), the capacity of human beings for evil and self-deception (e.g., Jer 17:9), the position of human beings in the created order (e.g., Ps 8:3–8), and so forth. The accounts of Creation and Fall found in Genesis introduce a number of important concepts. First, human beings are created, and are therefore a part of the creation; they owe their lives and allegiance to the Creator. That human beings are finite, limited, and related to the rest of the created order is taken as a given. This includes the ideas that they are created as social beings ("male and female"), interdependent, given a procreative mandate, and granted stewardship over all of creation. Second, although they are creatures, they uniquely bear the image of God, the *imago Dei*. Third, they are fallen creatures, tempted by sin, having willfully chosen to act on forbidden desires. What follows is a brief compendium of some core conclusions

---

26. Erickson, *Christian theology*, 481.

27. Johnson & Webber, *What Christians believe*, 212.

---

28. For a brief survey of biblical teachings on the topic, see What Christians believe about man and sin: The biblical revelation, in Johnson & Webber, *What Christians believe*. For a brief survey of the theological development of the topic, see What Christians believe about man and sin: The historical development, in the same book.

about human nature and functioning organized around the understanding of humanity as finite creatures, image-bearers, and fallen beings.[29]

Humans as Finite Creatures

Most theology texts deal extensively with the conceptualization of human beings as made in the image of God and as sinners, but provide relatively little attention to the conceptualization of human beings as finite creatures. Whatever the reason for this oversight, it is an onerous one. As C. Stephen Evans noted, "No Christian view of man can afford to ignore the fact that man is solidly part of nature. That man is dust, a bodily creature, makes this especially evident. It is bodily existence which serves as a forceful reminder of man's general creatureliness and the limitations which go with that status."[30]

Niebuhr too pointed to the importance of human creatureliness: "The obvious fact is that man is a child of nature, subject to its vicissitudes, compelled by its necessities, driven by its impulses, and confined within the brevity of the years which nature permits its varied organic form, allowing them some, but not too much, latitude."[31]

There is an unwarranted tendency to view this creatureliness in a negative light. Niebuhr argued that the built-in limitations of our creatureliness should be understood as part of the design of human nature that was declared "good" by our creator: "The Biblical view is that finiteness, dependence, and the insufficiency of man's mortal life are facts which belong to God's plan of creation and must be accepted with reverence and humility."[32]

One of the few evangelical theologians to deal extensively with the meaning of our creatureliness, Millard J. Erickson, posited nine implications of this doctrine, which are summarized below.[33]

1. Human beings are designed to praise and serve their Creator, and are dependent upon God for all that they are and all that they have.

2. "That we are part of creation also means that we have much in common with the other creatures. This commonality means that there is some validity in [psychology's] attempt to understand humanity by studying animals. For just like animals humans and their motivations are subject to the laws of creation."[34]

---

29. Reinhold Niebuhr presented a threefold description of human nature as 1) made in the image of God, 2) a finite, dependent creature, and 3) a sinner. While not unique to Niebuhr, his explicit categorization and development of this theme is helpful and will be the organizing paradigm utilized in this discussion. See Niebuhr, *The nature and destiny of man*, 150.

30. Evans, *Preserving the person*, 143

31. Niebuhr, *The nature and destiny*, 3.

32. Ibid., 167.

33. Erickson, *Christian theology*, 510–16.

34. Ibid., 512.

3. Humans exercise a unique place of stewardship within the created realm.

4. We are all part of one human family, which calls us to care for and empathize with one another.

5. The wonder and complexity of the human creature and human achievements are not ends in themselves, but are to be used to glorify God.

6. Human finitude means that there are limitations of our abilities and our knowledge.

7. Limitations are not necessarily bad; having made humanity with limitations, God yet pronounced His creation "very good."

8. Awareness of our finitude is necessary to healthy adjustment and should result in humility.

9. "Humanity is, nonetheless, something wonderful. Although they are creatures, humans are the highest among them, the only ones made in the image of God."[35]

The awareness that we are finite creatures, dependent upon God for our abilities and for our very being, should cause us to stand in awe of our Creator, to be grateful to Him, and to willingly offer our praise and service to Him. We should recognize our similarities to the creation over which we are to exercise stewardship. We should appreciate our interdependence as a human family. We should

humbly acknowledge our finitude, even as we acknowledge that we alone among the creation are created in the image of God.

Christian theology provides a unique view of our creatureliness that adds to our understanding of human nature. It helps us see that we our dependent on God and that having a proper relationship with Him is integral to our well being. Christian theology also helps us see our relatedness to each other and to the larger created realm, with all of the responsibilities that entails. Our limitations and our abilities should be used to recognize our dependence on God and to give Him praise. While Christian theology informs us about our status as creatures, it also enlightens us about our unique status within the creation as bearers of God's image, as we will now see.

Humanity as Imago Dei

The exact meaning of the *imago Dei* has been the subject of much theological reflection and debate. To understand it accurately, we must take into account the literary, symbolic, and cultural context of the relevant passages (Gen 1:26–27; 5:1; 9:6; 1 Cor 11:7; Jas 3:9, and a handful of ancient extrabiblical texts). The implications of the biblical claim that we are created in the image of God is a difficult task because of the sparse context that the relevant passages provide. Major interpretations of the *imago Dei* can be categorized as structural, functional, and relational views. In the structural (or substantive) view, the focus is on a characteristic that

---

35. Ibid., 515.

we might share with God, such as reason, spirituality, or existence. In the functional view, human beings are seen as those who act as God's representatives in the creation, naming and caring for the other creatures, for instance. In the relational view, the focus is on the social characteristics that God and human beings share; the Trinity is an expression of God's relationship, and human beings are made male and female, and flourish best when they are in right relationship with each other and with God.[36]

The medieval Scholastics, following Augustine, understood the *imago Dei* as reflecting both *image* and *likeness*. "According to Augustine, image relates to the *cognitio veritatis*, and likeness to the *amor virtutis*; the former to the intellectual, and the latter to the moral faculties."[37] In other words, Augustine and those who followed in his tradition understood the image of God as the human capacities of *reason* and *moral agency*. Hodge believed that the words *image* and *likeness* were mutually explanatory ("an image which he is like"), making Augustine's distinction superfluous, but nonetheless accurately portraying the content of the *imago Dei*.[38]

The *imago Dei* must be understood as corporately reflected by all of humanity and individually displayed in each of its members. Acknowledging that human persons are the very image of God has important implications for how we ought to regard each and every human being, and our responsibilities to the entirety of our human family. "The distinguishing mark of humanity, which is designated by the expression 'the image of God,' is far-reaching, extending to all humans. In the sight of God, all humans are equal. The distinctions of race, social status, and sex are of no significance to him (Gal 3:28). Salvation, eternal life, and fellowship with God are available to all persons. And because this is the case, Christians should show the same impartial interest in and concern for all humans, regardless of the incidentals of their lives (James 2:9)."[39]

Wayne Grudem expresses the viewpoint that to be *the image of God* means that we *represent God* and that we, in ways unspecified by the text, are *like God*. These likenesses might possibly include such things as moral accountability, spirituality, intellect and language, and relationality.[40]

Christian theology informs us about our uniqueness within the creation in a way that no other perspective does. Knowing that we are created in the image of God should cause us to be humble at the position that we occupy within the creation as God's image-bearers. It

---

36. Erickson, *Christian theology*, 520–36. The functional or "royal view" is essentially that human beings are God's representatives to rule over the creation, not usurping His rule, which would be idolatry, but cultivating the physical and social world with creativity and justice. See Middleton, *The liberating image?*

37. Hodge, *Systematic theology*, vol. 2, 96.

38. Ibid.

39. Erickson, *Christian theology*, 575.

40. Grudem, *Bible doctrine*.

should cause us to treat one another with respect, and to carry out our responsibility to care for one another, for, no matter how sinful we might be, we are still the bearer of God's very image.

Humanity as Fallen Being

We are finite creatures, connected to the dust of the earth and the rest of creation. We are the very image of God. And we are sinful, fallen human beings. Christian theology insists on all three of these truths. In the Genesis account of the Fall, Adam and Eve transgressed God's command by performing the only act forbidden to them, thus setting themselves up as an authority superior to God, a position for which they were ill equipped. In Hodge's view, the immediate effects of Adam and Eve's willful disobedience was *shame* and *dread* of God's displeasure, leading them to hide.[41] The ultimate consequence was not only their personal expulsion from paradise, but the imputation of their sin upon all of their offspring.[42]

> "To love someone means to see him as God intended him."
>
> —Fyodor Dostoevsky

Grudem, as well as many other theologians, believes that the image of God was not destroyed by the Fall, but the effects of the Fall were widespread. "As a result of the Fall, however, the

image is distorted, though not destroyed. His moral purity has been lost and his sinful character certainly does not reflect God's holiness. His intellect is corrupted by falsehood and misunderstanding; his speech no longer continually glorifies God; his relationships are often governed by selfishness rather than love, and so forth. Though man is still in the image of God, in every aspect of life some parts of that image have been distorted or lost."[43]

Neo-orthodox and liberal theologians typically deny the historicity of the Fall but still maintain its depiction of a world torn asunder. Paul Tillich, for instance, denied the existence of a utopian creation. He conceptualized the Fall not as an actual event but as the pervasive human experience of alienation. Whether or not one finds Tillich's theological position compelling, he effectively described this existential estrangement: "The state of existence is the state of estrangement. Man is estranged from the ground of his being, from others, and from himself. The transition from essence to existence results in personal guilt and universal tragedy . . . Man as he exists is not what he essentially is and ought to be."[44]

Tillich, the quintessential existentialist, pointed out the guilt and despair of finding ourselves separated from God, from our fellow human beings, and from our selves.

Emil Brunner expressed the essential estrangement that gave rise to Tillich's existential experience in describing what

---

41. Hodge, *Systematic theology*, 2:129.

42. Ibid., 192.

---

43. Grudem, *Bible doctrine*, 190.

44. Tillich, *Existence and the Christ*, 44–45.

he called the "contradiction of man," that is, "that he is at one and the same time created by God for God, and has turned away from him."[45] This "turning away" has radical consequences in one's relationship to God, oneself, and one's neighbor. As Erickson observed, "Sin has very serious consequences when it comes to the relationship between the sinner and God. These results include divine disfavor, guilt, punishment, and death. Physical death, spiritual death, and eternal death flow from the consequences of sin. Sin also has consequences that affect the individual sinner. These include enslavement, flight from reality, denial of sin, self-deceit, insensitivity, self-centeredness, and restlessness. These effects on the sinner also have social implications in competition, inability to empathize, rejection of authority, and inability to love."[46] Additionally, we must acknowledge that sin is not only *individual*, but also *corporate* or *communal*.

Individual sin is something with which each of us is all too familiar. The ancient Christian church summarized the seven deadly sins as lust, gluttony, greed, sloth, anger, envy, and pride. Several scriptural passages provide a list of individual sins. For instance, the epistle to the Galatians warns against "acts of the sinful nature" such as "sexual immorality, impurity and debauchery; idolatry and witchcraft; hatred, discord, jealousy, fits of rage, selfish ambition, dissensions, factions and envy; drunkenness, orgies, and the like" (Gal 5:19–21, NIV).

It is obvious that most of the sins listed above are committed by individuals. However, some sins are practiced so widely that they become corporate sins that are embedded in one's culture. Idolatry, for instance, can become so common in a culture that few individuals realize that it is a sin. Someone who grew up in a pagan culture may never question whether ancestor worship is wrong. Likewise many of us who grew up in materialistic cultures may never question whether our attachment to money and material objects is idolatrous. Communal sins are particularly hard to notice because one's peers comfortably practice them: "We may be so conditioned by membership in a group that our very perception of reality is colored by it . . . This conditioning is something so subtle and thoroughgoing that we may not be aware that there is a given side of a given issue, or even that there is an issue at all."[47]

Things such as racism, prejudice, materialism, discrimination, loosening of sexual standards, and many other sins are hard to see when they are embedded within one's culture. The Roman Catholic Church, in particular, has done a good job of pointing out the social and cultural dimensions of sin. "The Church forcefully maintains this link between life ethics

---

45. Brunner, *God and man*, 153. Brunner believed that understanding this fundamental estrangement could allow a "Christian psychology" to regulate the concerns and findings of secular psychology by providing an orienting compass from which to view the complexities and contradictions of human nature.

46. Erickson, *Christian theology*, 618.

47. Ibid., 659.

and social ethics, fully aware that 'a society lacks solid foundations when, on the one hand, it asserts values such as the dignity of the person, justice and peace, but then, on the other hand, radically acts to the contrary by allowing or tolerating a variety of ways in which human life is devalued and violated, especially where it is weak or marginalized.'"[48] The Roman Catholic Church expresses grave concern about individualism, sexual ethics, respect for human life, economic oppression, and a host of other issues that are shaped by social attitudes.

Whether individual or communal, the effects of sin are pervasive. Sin affects our relationships to God. Sin has negative consequences for the individual. Sin alienates us from each other and causes suffering among those who are caught in the wake of other people's sins. The entire created realm has been marred by sin through sickness and death. Christian theology helps us see this aspect of human nature with sobering clarity, but it also proclaims the solution to our terrible situation.

While there is tremendous diversity of theological interpretation regarding the nature of human beings, "there is at least a consensus that man is made in the image of God, that Adam's Fall has resulted in disastrous consequences for the entire human race, and that Jesus Christ is the Second Adam" through whom we can be reconciled to God.[49] We are creatures, we are image bearers, and we are sinners living in a broken world. We are, indeed, complex and contradictory creatures.

Summary

In the Christian view, human beings are, quite literally, works of art, composed by the hand of God. Throughout this book we have seen how Christian theology and other disciplines, including psychology, can help us view the world from different but complementary perspectives. To change the metaphor somewhat, we might want to think of Christian theology and psychology as instruments in an orchestra. It is not surprising that, despite their differences in methodology, psychological and theological perspectives on philosophical anthropology have a considerable degree of harmony. Sometimes they share the melody, although the sounds of each instrument are distinct. Sometimes one instrument plays the melody, while the other offers a complex harmony that weaves around the unadorned, central tune. Occasionally one instrument or another has a solo part, allowing it to play a score unique to the resonance of its instrument. Unfortunately, sometimes one player or another in the orchestra misreads the score, and the momentary cacophony upsets the music. The score itself is complicated, reflecting the majesty and wonder of a creation made in the image of the composer

---

48. Benedict XVI, *Caritas in Veritate*, sec. 15, ¶2. The quotation within the quotation is from John Paul II's encyclical, *Evangelium vitae*.

---

49. Johnson & Webber, *What Christians believe*, 230.

and proclaimed by the master to be very good, with built in limitations of a finite creature, but with the dissonant and somber sounds of sin and disease.

A psychological perspective provides an understanding of humans as bio-psycho-social beings. Our biology is complex, awe-inspiring, but sometimes broken. We have incredible, awe-inspiring abilities, but we also have built-in limitations. These capacities *and* limitations express the goodness of creation. The fall, and the effects of our own sin and the sins of others, have altered human nature, adding personal distress, brokenness, and alienation to our experience. We are relational beings, with social capacities and needs. A biblical anthropology serves to ground human value in the acknowledgment that we are bearers of God's image, fearfully and wonderfully made. We have limitations as creatures and are dependent on God for our existence. We suffer from the damaging effects of the Fall and from personal and corporate sin. Just like the musical score of an orchestra, the score of our lives is complex. Only through reading it to the best of our ability can we hope to obtain an inkling of understanding of who we are.

Questions for Reflection and Discussion

1. Look back at the quotation from *Hamlet*. How can one reconcile the incredible faculties of humanity with the realities of human evil? (Reading footnote 3 may help you to understand the complexity of Hamlet's monologue.)

2. The Old Man in Clemens's story compares a man to a steam locomotive, his behavior solely attributable to his heredities (genetics), habitat (environmental reinforcement), and associations (culture and socialization). Identify some of the factors that determine or influence behavior. How determinative do you think these factors are? How much freedom do you think human beings have in regulating their own behavior?

3. How do the different assumptions, methodologies, organizational structures, and goals of psychology and theology provide opportunities for integrating psychology and Christianity? In what ways do these differences create obstacles to integration?

4. The author pointed out that *every psychologist and every theologian grounds his or her psychology or theology in a philosophical system, whether or not it is explicitly articulated or carefully considered; every psychology and every theology is done from an antecedent worldview perspective.* Do you consciously attend to the way that your philosophical assumptions and worldview shapes your psychological and theological positions? How can you become more aware of these assumptions?

5. How has reading this chapter helped you to identify or change your philosophical anthropology?

6. What are some of the implications of a philosophical anthropology that views human nature from a bio-psycho-social perspective combined with a theological view of humans as limited creatures, image bearers, and fallen sinners?

7. Pope Benedict XVI claims that "without God man neither knows which way to go, nor even understands who he is." What are the implications of this statement for the possibilities and limitations of psychology absent this grounding?

8. Compare the psychological and theological understandings of philosophical anthropology. Identify several commonalities between their viewpoints. Identify several distinct contributions offered by psychology that are absent (or not offered in detail) by Christian theology. Identify several distinct contributions offered by Christian theology that are absent (or not offered in detail) by psychology.

9. Do you think that psychological and theological perspectives on philosophical anthropology are ultimately opposed to and irreconcilable with each other, or can they be reconciled by noting fruitful commonalities and complementary relationships between them? Defend your answer.

8

Understanding and Making Models

*The proponents of competing paradigms practice their trades in different
worlds . . . Practicing in different worlds, [they] see different things . . . Before
they can hope to communicate fully, one group or the other must experience the
conversion that we have been calling a paradigm shift.*

—Thomas Kuhn, *The structure of scientific revolutions*, 150

When I was a boy, I loved to make models
of airplanes, automobiles, ships, and even
of the Starship Enterprise.[1] My earliest
efforts were of the "snap-fit" variety—I
simply had to snap the pieces together—
no glue required! Over time, I graduated
to more complex models, with decals and
paint. I remember, in particular, a beautiful model of an SR-71 Blackbird. The
real SR-71 was a military aircraft whose
length was in excess of 107 feet, with
graceful, sweeping wings that spanned
over 55 feet. With distinctive black paint
and two huge Pratt and Whitney J-58 engines, the SR-71 is breathtaking, able to
travel at Mach-III—*three times the speed
of sound.*

When I finished my model, I "flew"
my model around the room, making all
the requisite sounds, imagining myself
commanding the plane through sunlit
skies. Yet, for all my enthusiasm, it was a
model. It *represented* the original, reflecting crucial details in miniature, made of
different materials, and without working
engines or instruments. Had I thrown it
in the air, the result would have been disastrous. No one would mistake my model for a real SR-71, but it clearly, though
imperfectly, *represented* the real thing.

We make extensive use of models as
we try to understand our world. As children, we create mental representations
of our parents. As we grow we begin to
use language to symbolize concrete objects, and later on, we use language to
describe abstract concepts. We use symbols to represent sounds and numbers.
We use maps to represent geographical
features of the natural world and clocks

---

1. The only *Enterprise* when I was a kid was
the NCC-1701, launched in 2245 and destroyed
in 2285 (or 1984 if you prefer the movie date). It
is interesting to note how realistic a model of a
fictional object can seem.

to represent the passage of time. Without models, our ability to understand our world would be severely limited.

Every scholarly discipline makes use of models. We make *theological models* to represent the truths found in God's Word and His Works.[2] We make *biological models* of the anatomy and physiology of kidneys and the transport mechanisms of chloride ions. We make *psychological models* of memory and depression, and *economic models* of how people accumulate wealth, what they do with their money, and the factors that contribute to economic inequity. Sometimes our models are more descriptive than illustrative, like those of Keynesian or Marxist economic theories. Sometimes the models are physical, like the anatomical models found in doctors' offices and science classrooms. Whenever human beings try to understand their world, though, they create models of reality that imperfectly represent the objects of their interest. Such models may be *useful*, and they are often *accurate* in many details, but they are inevitably *imperfect*.

When we look at the relationship of psychology and religion (or Christianity), we are concerned with *models based on models*; that is, we express our understanding of religion, Christianity, and Christian theology in various models, we express our understanding of psychology in other models, and we then conceptualize their relationship in yet more

models. Thus, to understand a theorist's model of the relationship of psychology and theology, we must first understand his or her conceptualization of psychology and theology.

Take a minute to think about how often you use models— clocks, diagrams, language, maps, theories, and so forth. Are your maps always accurate? How much does their accuracy affect their usefulness? What would be life without such models?

Asking the Right Questions

As we saw in chapter 4, worldviews focus our perception of the world, but they also distort our perception inasmuch as the world is seen through the lenses of our assumptions. Similarly, people have different beliefs about psychology and theology, and these differences are reflected in their models of how the two disciplines relate to one another. As we explore different models about the relationship of psychology and Christianity in the next several chapters, we need to remember that these models emerge in part from different assumptions about psychology and Christianity. Sometimes a theorist will explicitly state his or her assumptions and goals. Often, though, we will find that assumptions exert their influence in the subtleties of how things are phrased, evidence that is admitted or

---

2. Examples include dispensational theology, Calvinistic theology, Arminian theology, and so forth.

overlooked, the way that terms are defined, and so forth. In a similar way, the goals of a model may be explicitly stated, but sometimes the goals are subtle, unacknowledged, or even deliberately hidden.

It is extremely important for us to be aware of—and to evaluate—the presuppositions that we bring to any subject. In the words of Mr. Pond, the main character in G. K. Chesterton's short detective stories, "Once assume the wrong beginning, and you'll not only give the wrong answer, but ask the wrong question."[3] Different presuppositions cause us to ask different questions. As we begin to explore different models of the relationship of psychology and theology, we must carefully examine our presuppositions and those of the theorists that we will consider.

Models of the Relationship of Psychology and Theology

In the late 1990s, Brian Eck identified and critiqued twenty-seven models for relating psychology and theology.[4] Perhaps the most influential models of the relationship of psychology and Christianity were developed by Carter,[5] and expanded upon by Carter and Narramore.[6] The models were loosely based on Niebuhr's *Christ and Culture* models.[7] Attempting

to create a framework for understanding the various ways in which psychology and religion can be related, Carter defined four secular models (*Psychology against Religion*, *Psychology of Religion*, *Psychology Parallels Religion*, and *Psychology Integrates Religion*) and four sacred models (*Christianity against Psychology*, *Christianity of Psychology*, *Christianity Parallels Psychology*, and *Christianity Integrates Psychology*).[8]

In the next three chapters, I will develop a framework composed of six models: *Enemies*, *Spies*, *Colonialists*, *Rebuilders*, *Neutral Parties*, and *Allies*.[9] For the most part, four of these categories build on Carter's ideas while reframing them in a different metaphor. The models that I am developing are analogous to the ways that nations interact with each other.

Psychology and theology obviously differ in the source materials that they

---

3. Chesterton, Ring of lovers, 88.

4. Eck, Integrating the integrators.

5. Carter, Secular and sacred models.

6. Carter & Narramore, *The integration of psychology and theology*.

7. Niebuhr, *Christ and culture*.

8. In his original (1977) description, Carter referred to the four sacred models as *Christianity* against, *Christianity* of, *Christianity* parallels, and *Christianity* integrates psychology. His summary tables referred to them as *Scripture* against, *Scripture* of, *Scripture* parallels, and *Scripture* integrates psychology. The change in terminology is not explained but probably reflects the desire to clarify that what is being related takes place at a disciplinary level. My choice of terminology likewise emphasizes disciplinary relationship.

9. The names of these models should be understood descriptively rather than pejoratively. They merely describe the way that someone tries to relate two systems of thought. In each case, the person employing the model believes that his or her way of relating the two systems is appropriate and correct.

consult, as well as the methodologies that are appropriate to study those materials. Theology utilizes Scripture as its primary source, though it also uses linguistics, philosophy, history, archeology and many other sources of knowledge as it tries to understand Scripture. Psychology, like many other extrabiblical disciplines, utilizes reason and observation of nature as its primary source, but like theology, it must rely on many other disciplines as it attempts to understand the natural world. These two different source materials—Scripture and nature—are not completely separate. Historic, orthodox Christianity holds that both Scripture and the natural world have their origins in God's creativity and revelation. One of the earliest scientists, Francis Bacon, described these two different sources as two books authored by God. "There are two books laid before us to study, to prevent our falling into error; first, the book of God's Word, which reveals the will of God; and the book of God's Works, which express His power."[10] In Bacon's terminology, the book of God's Word referred to the Bible, and the book of His Works reflected His deeds written throughout creation.[11] The models

that we will explore represent how different people think about the book of God's Word and the book of God's Works as means of learning about human beings.

The six models also differ in their *telos*: the ends, purposes, and goals that they hope to achieve. Imagine that you are at a train station. It is not enough to know how the train works; you also want to know where the train is going. Although the trains are similar in many respects, they are headed to different places. Similarly, the six models will have many things in common—for instance, they all make assumptions, use logical arguments, and accept or reject various propositions. However, they have different goals in mind as to what they want to accomplish. As a result, they conceptualize and use theology and psychology in different ways. The six models will be introduced in this chapter, and explored in more detail and illustrated with examples in the next three chapters.

Before we begin our exploration of these models, we need to make a distinction between models and the procedures used within the models.[12] The six models represent different ways of conceptualizing the relationship between psychology and religion in general, or psychology and Christianity, in particular. *Procedures* are the specific techniques that are used in constructing the models. Different model builders may begin with different conceptualizations, but they often

---

10. This is a common paraphrase of Francis Bacon. For the exact quotation and citation, see the suggested assignments for chapter 3 in the appendix of this book.

11. Creation here should be broadly construed as not only the physical word but also the order and logic with which it is endowed. Thus, the primary source of theology is the book of God's Word, and the primary source of every other discipline is the book of God's Works.

---

12. Brian Eck is credited with making the distinction between paradigms and procedures. See: Eck, Integrating the integrators.

use the same procedures (cutting things away, gluing things together, etc.), but to different degrees and for different ends. Thus, the models that we consider will diverge much more at the conceptual level, and less at the procedural level. Their procedural differences reflect the larger paradigmatic designs toward which they aim. Finally, in exploring models about the relationship of psychology and Christianity, keep in mind that they are abstractions of general trends. Reality does not always afford clear-cut categories; sometimes people will vacillate between different models or blend their elements in such a way that singular categorization is not possible. Nevertheless, the models are useful if they accurately reflect the procedures and goals that different people employ.

A mnemonic device that may help you remember the six models for relating psychology and Christianity: Ending Spurious Conflict Requires New Alternatives (Enemies, Spies, Colonialists, Rebuilders, Neutral Parties, Allies).

Enemies

Antagonistic models are based on the belief that psychology and theology are mutually exclusive. They are adversaries that are always in skirmish and never far from an all out war. They are sworn enemies, and the adversary must be vigorously attacked to protect truth. Historically, the *Enemies* model emerged with force during the Enlightenment. Ecclesiastical authority, which had been paramount throughout the Middle Ages, was largely rejected by Enlightenment thinkers, who sought to establish *reason* as the principal epistemic authority. They cherished the ideals of individuality, liberty, and the right of self-governance. Truth claims based on religious proclamation were of dubious merit to Enlightenment thinkers. As we saw in chapter 2, the Enlightenment gave rise to the fundamentalist-modernist controversy within the Church. Those who adopted the fundamentalist stance retreated from serious academic inquiry and expressed suspicion of most extrabiblical sources of knowledge. For much of the past two hundred years, modernists and fundamentalists have taken a stance of mutual rejection.

Holders of the *Enemies* model take an *either/or* position on the psychology of human beings *versus* the theology of human beings. Such model builders seemingly grasp either a mechanistic view *or* a spiritual view, but not both. People who depict the relationship of Christianity and science (or Christianity and psychology) through the *Enemies* model primarily employ procedures that sever and segregate the parts of one discipline from those of the other. Those who follow an *Enemies* model either neglect or disregard the book of God's Word or the book of God's Works. In less extreme cases this may simply be a matter of neglect. In more extreme cases the animosity of this model can erupt into the flames of book burning by those who wish to suppress other points of view.[13]

There are two versions of the *Enemies* model: *Secular Combatants* and *Christian Combatants*.[14] People who are committed to the field of psychology and who have a worldview that is antagonistic toward religious belief are *Secular Combatants*. The telos of the *Secular Combatants* is rooted in the modernist rejection of authority in general, and of religious authority in particular. Their aim is thus to exalt the autonomous exercise of human reason. In direct opposition to this are the *Christian Combatants*, whose worldview makes them suspicious of all human reason. Their telos is to protect religious authority and religious pronouncements against corruption by human reason.

Secular Combatants and *Christian Combatants* are more alike than they are different in terms of how they approach the interface of psychology and Christian theology. They each begin with the assumption that the relationship between psychology and theology can only be seen in inimical terms, a state of affairs that is as irreconcilable as it is inevitable. The adherents of these models construe the foundations and teachings of the two disciplines as antithetical to one another. Thus, *Secular Combatants* see religion as incompatible with mental health and honest intellectual discourse. Meanwhile, *Christian Combatants* see psychology as an enemy which is opposed by sound doctrine, and they see the use of psychotherapy (and sometimes psychotropic medication) as incompatible with (and unnecessary for) those who live victorious Christian lives. The difference between these two versions of the *Enemies* model is simply a matter of which discipline is seen as the bearer of truth and which is seen as heretical.

The public voice of the *Secular Combatants* has become less volatile in recent years. This may reflect two incongruent trends. The first trend, taking place within clinical psychology and a larger culture that increasingly values tolerance, reflects recent findings that support the contention that there may be psychological benefits of religious belief and practice.[15] Additionally, the American Psychological Association's *Code of Ethics* explicitly recognizes the need to respect the religious beliefs of clients and

---

13. This can occur literally or figuratively on either side. Figuratively it is seen in animosity expressed toward divergent viewpoints. Literally, it can be observed when ecclesiastics order that books be suppressed or burned, and when secularists try to expunge religious discourse and influence from public and academic spheres.

14. Carter's term for this approach is *the against model*, which he subdivided into secular and sacred versions. The *secular against* version describes the view held by psychologically committed persons who are opposed to religion; holders of this version of the *Enemies* model are *Secular Combatants*. The *sacred against* version focuses on Christian opposition to psychology; holders of this version of the *Enemies* model are *Christian Combatants*.

---

15. See, for example, Pargament, et al., God help me: I; and Pargament, et al., God help me: II.

to attempt to eliminate religious and other bias from psychological practice and research.[16] Further, there has been a resurgence of interest in spirituality among psychologists themselves, which has resulted in an increase of pro-religious literature and research within mainstream clinical psychology.[17] This shift, while in large measure pragmatic, is remarkable, given that it could hardly have been imagined a few decades ago.

The second trend, which is seemingly the reverse of the first, is that in other contexts, religious bias has gone underground or, in some cases, is simply so unquestioned that it is merely presumed that religious belief and scientific progress represent rival worldviews.[18] This trend appears to be more prevalent in the nonclinical areas of psychology, as well as in the way overtly committed Christians are regarded in both clinical and nonclinical settings.[19] Within Christian circles, the *Christian Combatant* view is less pervasive than it was a decade or two ago, but it is still very entrenched within some circles, as we will see in chapter 9.

While the antagonism of the *Enemies* model may not be as pervasive as it was a few years ago, it is still influential. Central to this approach is the rejection of anything that comes from the domain of the "enemy camp." Eck classified models of this type as being *nonintegrative paradigms that utilize a process of rejection*; psychology rejects religion or theology rejects psychology.[20] The *Enemies* model precludes meaningful dia-

---

16. Principle E of the American Psychological Association's Code of Ethics reads, in part, "Psychologists are aware of and respect cultural, individual, and role differences, including those based on age, gender, gender identity, race, ethnicity, culture, national origin, *religion*, sexual orientation, disability, language, and socioeconomic status and consider these factors when working with members of such groups. *Psychologists try to eliminate the effect on their work of biases based on those factors, and they do not knowingly participate in or condone activities of others based upon such prejudices*" (American Psychological Association, *Ethical principles.*, principle E.; italics added).

17. The former can be seen in the increasing popularity of psychology conferences on "spirituality" (broadly construed). The latter can be seen in the publication of books such as Richards and Bergin, *Handbook of psychotherapy and religious diversity*.

18. Consider the following quotations from a recent textbook on cognitive psychology: "Part of the supernatural perspective of medieval Europe included the idea that humans have a unique place in the world of creation. According to this supernatural perspective, God created the world for humans, who are God's most important creation. Supposedly we are made in God's image" (Guenther, *Human cognition*, 2). "Human origins are not a consequence of divine intervention but of a natural process intrinsic to the nature of reproductive and developmental mechanisms and the interaction of living things with the physical environment" (ibid., 4). Notice how the author's assertions are simply stated as fact and are not viewed as presuppositions. In this case, the *Enemies* model is simply proclaimed as a fait accompli.

19. This would appear to have been the experience of many of my nonclinical colleagues who studied psychology in secular settings, particularly of those whose disciplinary specialization makes use of reductionistic and mechanistic assumptions. Neither is it an uncommon experience of clinicians who train in secular programs or work in secular settings.

20. Eck, Integrating the integrators, 114.

logue because it presupposes a mutual exclusivity and repudiation.

As we noted earlier, different presuppositions lead us to ask different questions, which in turn leads us to different answers. We could summarize this model and some of its representative questions as follows:

Enemies—General assumption: Psychology and Christianity (or religion in general) are fundamentally opposed to and incompatible with each other.

Secular Combatants: Psychological health is incompatible with religious practice. Enlightened people cannot believe in religious nonsense.

Telos—Secular combatants, reflecting their commitment to modernism, reject authority in general, and religious authority in particular. Their aim is to exalt the autonomous exercise of human reason.

- Why do religious people have higher rates of mental problems than nonreligious people?

- In an age of reason, how can people still believe in religious myths and superstitions?

- How does a religious upbringing harm children?

- How does religion foster and trap people in unhealthy marriages and abusive relationships?

- How can we help people who have been harmed by the restrictive and repressive sexual mores of

religion develop views that are more enlightened?

Christian Combatants: Christians who turn to psychology for help are denying the sufficiency of Christ. Only Christians can fully understand the soul and only Scripture can provide the true remedy to the human condition. Psychologists are misleading people and undermining their faith through their theories, methods, and so-called therapies.

Telos—suspicious of all human reason, the Christian Combatants aim to protect religious authority and religious pronouncements against corruption by human reason.

- What are the secular, antireligious foundations of modern psychology that make it incompatible with Christian faith and practice?

- Why are Christians embracing a field that is and always has been antithetical to Christianity?

- What sinful actions or beliefs cause people to have personal and interpersonal problems?

- How can the Bible and Christian practices be used to bring people to truth, repentance, reconciliation and restoration?

Many of the questions listed above are legitimate and useful. However, note that the framework from which the questions are asked tend to lead toward particular answers to those questions. Likewise, the models themselves have different goals. As we look at the remaining models, we will note that similar questions may sometimes be asked by holders of different models, but often with a different emphasis, although they will often ask quite different questions. The next model that we will explore recognizes that truth can be found in both psychology and religion (broadly construed), but followers of this model will hold a primary commitment to one camp, while reconnoitering in the territory of the other camp in order to identify things that might be useful for their own ends. Although most individuals who adopt this approach do not intend to be subversive, the net result of their approach is to remove from one of God's books only that which they see as useful based on their "scientific" or "theological" commitments.

Spies

Religious systems inevitably contain psychological content. As people gather in faith communities, they forge social connections, they find existential meaning, they seek forgiveness and comfort through prayer, and so forth. The potential psychological benefits of religious belief and behavior are considerable, and of considerable interest. For most people, these benefits are byproducts of the religious system. Other people, either from outside of the religious system as researchers, or from within the congregation itself, become interested in harnessing the power of the religious system

to foster psychological benefits as an end in itself.

Religion, on one level, is an expression of human belief and activity. Religious beliefs and behaviors contain elements that may be useful (or harmful) psychologically. When someone becomes more interested in the effects of religion independent of the doctrinal teachings of religion, they have, in effect, participated in espionage. They either reject or minimize many of the tenets of religious belief, focusing their efforts instead on how religious belief can assist people with coping, happiness, prosperity, or other tangible benefits. This can be done from the perspective of *foreign spies* (psychologists who pragmatically seek to identify religious elements that have psychological benefits), or of *domestic spies* (those who practice a watered-down religion and are interested in proclaiming its psychological benefits). In both cases, those who followed the *Spies* model are more interested in uncovering the psychology of the religious system rather than holding on to orthodox theology.

The telos of the *Spies* models is a pragmatic desire to use any means at their disposal to aid human well-being. People who depict the relationship of religious belief and science (or psychology) through the *Spies* model primarily employ procedures of severing what they see as "useful" or "beneficial" aspects of religion from the beliefs or practices that they see as incidental to mental health. [21]

---

21. Carter and Narramore's *of* model is similar to what I have called the *Spies* model. Carter

Using this approach, one can peruse religious teachings or practices in an attempt to extract their embedded psychological content. The *Spies model*, unlike the *Enemies* model, does not reject religion, but its primary focus is on religion as a repository of psychological truths dressed in priestly robes; thus, this model is not characteristic of orthodox belief. Using this approach, "theological findings [are revised] from the perspective of psychological findings . . ."[22]

Eck classified models of this type as *manipulative integration paradigms that utilize a reconstruction process.*[23] This reconstruction is manipulative in that it is premised on a belief "that the truth from the other discipline is [not] directly admissible into the integration process" and "must be altered to become acceptable . . . for the process of integration"

to proceed.[24] They do not represent real integrative efforts in that they fail to recognize the integrity of each discipline. Implementing this approach involves a process of *reconstruction* in which either the supernatural elements of religion are expunged (psychology reconstructs theology), or psychology is construed as an expression of theological truths (theology reconstructs psychology).

When the *Spies* model is applied by *foreigners* (psychologists who pragmatically seek to identify religious elements that have psychological benefits), it proceeds without (or, at least, does not require) religious commitment.[25] When *domestic residents* employ this model, religious teachings are watered-down in order to harvest psychological benefits. This can be done from a liberal or neo-orthodox perspective in which theology is seen as valuable but in need of modernistic or scientific reformation.[26] It also occurs among those whose general theological framework is more conservative, but who emphasize a gospel of health and wealth.

The *Spies* model is summarized below, along with the types of questions that domestic and foreign spies might ask.

Spies—General assumption: All religious systems (Christian and non-Christian) are psychological

---

and Narramore do *not* include the psychology of religion (as a subdiscipline of psychology) in this model. Psychology of religion, as an academic discipline, investigates the psychological forces that contribute to religious belief (or nonbelief) and practice, and the psychological effects of religious belief (or nonbelief) and practice. Narramore clarified the distinction that he and Carter maintain between the *psychology of religion* and the *of* model as follows: "John and I do not include the academic discipline, Psychology of Religion, in our *of* model. It seems to me that the work done in that academic discipline can be from an *integrates*, *of*, or *parallel* model, depending on the basic epistemological and methodological assumptions of the researcher" (Personal communication, November 11, 2002; minor changes made for clarity).

22. Farnsworth, *Whole-hearted integration*, 99.

23. Eck, Integrating the integrators, 115.

24. Ibid., 104.

25. This is similar to Carter & Narramore's *secular of model.*

26. This is similar to Carter & Narramore's *sacred of model.*

phenomena. The primary emphasis is not on the religious content of a religion as much as it is on its effects on human welfare. Religious systems may be helpful or harmful.

Telos—Spies have a pragmatic desire to use any means at their disposal to aid human well-being. They may lack deep commitment to a religious system, or they may water down core doctrines as they seek to improve human well-being. Domestic Residents and Foreigners differ in whether they are working from within a religious system or are observing it from the outside.

Domestic Spies: In a liberal version of this model, the specific content of one's own religion may be seen as largely mythic, useful for illustrating things about human nature and human needs. In a conservative version of this model, one may acknowledge core doctrines of the faith, but the bulk of one's efforts focus on personal well-being. The primary purpose of faith is to offer tangible benefits to those who practice the religion.

- How can the religious beliefs of my tradition help people cope with the problems of life?

- How can belief in God's love be harnessed to help people feel good about themselves, to bring about positive thinking and self-esteem?

- How can I affirm the truth of my religious system without taking its teachings (especially about supernatural or miraculous claims) literally? (liberal version)

- How can I use the teachings and stories of the Bible to help people find health and happiness in the here and now? (conservative version)

- What things in my religious tradition need to be challenged, deemphasized, or rejected so that its positive benefits can flourish?

Foreign Spies: Religion, in general, can be useful or harmful. In the interest of advancing human welfare, the benefits of religion should be studied and harnessed; detrimental effects should be identified so they can be eliminated or minimized.

- How can a person's spirituality exert a positive influence on mental and physical health?

- Are particular beliefs, practices, or modes of religious expression associated with detrimental psychological or physical consequences?

- What mediating variables can be identified that can help explain the natural mechanisms through which religion and spirituality exert positive and negative influences on health (e.g., affiliation, hope, context for suffering, etc.)?

Our next model, while sharing some similar characteristics with the *Spies* model, takes place from the perspective of someone who is openly committed to

Christian orthodoxy, but who sees psychology as a foreign territory to be captured for Christ and brought under the flag of theology.

Colonialists

For much of human history, powerful empires arose that conquered other nations and forced them into subservience. During the Age of Exploration, explorers "discovered" new lands, and European countries scrambled to exert their economic and military power over these territories, often thinking that they were divinely appointed to rule these new lands. In 1494, Pope Alexander VI divided newly discovered lands between Spain and Portugal. Other European nations, especially Britain, France, Belgium, the Netherlands, and Germany, joined in the lust for expansion. Colonial empires competed with one another to secure foreign lands. They did not own the territories by historic entitlement or by working the land; they simply claimed them as their own.

A number of Christians have approached psychology from a similarly colonial mindset. Holders of the *Colonialist* model borrow *selective* findings from psychology, but they do so as outsiders and pilferers. Colonialists differ from *domestic spies* in that they adhere to a conservative or orthodox Christian theological system rather than a liberal, neo-orthodox, or more broadly "religious" position. The primary allegiance of the colonialist is to his or her theological system; while the colonialist sees psychology as valuable, it is foreign soil. Psychology can be useful only to the degree that it can be forced to conform to the theological system. Conservative Christians who have a passing interest in psychology often hold this model. Christians with training in psychology who embrace this model usually harbor deep suspicions about the field. Colonialists selectively accept, reject, or modify isolated findings from psychology based on their prior religious presuppositions, without adequately evaluating the evidentiary support for the psychological findings or the soundness of their theological commitments.

The telos of the *Colonialists* is the appropriation of psychological methods or findings that can illustrate or buttress the claims of their theological proclamations. Most colonialists have no deep commitment to—or even understanding of—the discipline of psychology. As such, the interaction between psychology and theology is severely limited. Few colonialists invest their energies in reading psychological theories or studies outside of those that are popularly available. Nor do most of them attempt to pursue psychological training, much less contribute to the discipline of psychology in any meaningful way. Clinicians and counselors who adopt this approach typically work with Christian clients, write for Christian audiences, and attend Christian conferences, segregating themselves from mainstream psychology in their own enclaves. The word "enclave" is quite apt—it refers to an area that is surrounded by another area—much as Vatican

City is completely surrounded by Italy. In this view "Christian psychology" could be its own little region surrounded by—but not truly engaged in—the discipline of psychology.

Colonial powers profited from colonization by removing goods from the colony. In a similar way, the *Colonialist* model involves selectively *including, rejecting,* and *relabeling* psychological findings to reflect the theological perspective of the model builder. Psychology, as an independent discipline, is thus forced into theological categories and subjugated to theological dominion. The colonialist carries out no real psychological research or theorizing; he or she simply removes from psychology whatever seems to be of interest, rejects whatever he or she cannot bring into alignment with his or her theological assumptions, or tries to convert the discipline to reflect those assumptions.

This is a hierarchical model that places the book of God's Word over the book of God's Works, and theology over psychology. It often results in psychological findings being accepted or rejected based on scattered scriptural proof-texting, with inadequate exegesis and insufficient attention to psychological data or methods. Eck classified models of this type as *manipulative integration paradigms that utilize a transformational process.* They presume that "psychological truth must either pass through a particular theological filter" or psychological truth must be "altered to stay in keeping with

a particular theological worldview . . ."[27] We can summarize this model and its questions as follows:

Colonialists—Christianity embodies the true revelation of God to humankind about the human condition and God's plan of salvation. Psychology, to the degree that it correctly understands human problems, can be useful to illustrate what Scripture tells us. The colonialist typically has a superficial acquaintance with psychological theories or findings. The colonialist does not exert significant effort towards understanding how psychology and Christianity can both express truth, or how the two can be used to gain a larger picture of human nature and functioning.

Telos—*Colonialists* desire to appropriate psychological methods or findings that can illustrate or buttress their theological beliefs. There is usually no deep commitment to, or engagement in, the broader discipline of psychology, and they often prefer to segregate themselves in enclaves with like-minded people.

- How can the Bible be used in counseling as a means of bringing truth, repentance, and reconciliation?

- What psychological findings or theories should be rejected based on religious beliefs?

---

27. Eck, Integrating the integrators, 106–7.

- How can some psychological findings or theories be brought into conformity with religious beliefs?

- How can statistics about marital satisfaction and its relationship to church attendance be used to illustrate the importance of a Christian understanding of marriage?

- How can rates of depression and anxiety highlight our need for relationship with God?

Rebuilders

Jerusalem, the capital of Judah, was captured by Nebuchadnezzar after the Battle of Carchemish in 605 BCE. As a result, Judah had to pay tribute to Babylon. After four years, Jehoiakim, King of Judah, refused to pay the annual taxes which had been levied against it, leading to another siege of Jerusalem. Its defeat was followed by several waves of deportations of its inhabitants into captivity in Babylon. Many years later, Artaxerxes, who now controlled the empire, allowed captives to return to their homeland. In a series of repatriations, many Jewish people, including Nehemiah, returned to their ancestral homeland, only to find that Jerusalem, its wall and its temple, lay in ruins, and its current occupants had fallen into pagan practices. With God ordained favor and much effort, the returning exiles rebuilt the temple and the walls of the city, and reinstituted the proper worship of the God of Israel.[28]

In a similar way, *Rebuilders* look at psychology as something that belongs to God, but which has been overrun and occupied by people who do not acknowledge or serve God. They believe that Christians are at risk of compromising with the dominant secular values found in modern psychological paradigms. To counteract this, they believe that we must rebuild psychology—or at least, a particular type of psychology—on solid Christian assumptions while still interacting with mainstream psychology.

Christianity is fundamentally psychological in nature, that is, Christianity tells us about *who we are* and *how we ought to be*. For the Rebuilders:

> Scripture is the normative and formative foundation for what Christian psychologists think and do. God's view of reality, as presented in the Bible, is the ultimate perspective. Every theory, method, or understanding that is considered important with regard to psychology and soul care is held under the microscope of God's illuminating Word.[29]

Calling their approach *Christian psychology*, those who follow this approach want to rebuild psychology on explicitly Christian assumptions. Their telos is to use the insights and practices of Scripture and Christian history and theology to create

---

28. The biblical accounts of this can be found in the books of Ezra and Nehemiah.

29. Vassiliades, Kim, and Kwon, Report, 8.

methods of *soul care*. That is, they are not simply content to relieve suffering, but they want to aid people in becoming the kind of people that God desires us to be.

Unlike the *Colonialists*, however, *Rebuilders* have a great deal of respect for modern psychology, but they see it as severely truncated, and they offer a compelling critique of its secular and modernist philosophical underpinnings. In its effort to be scientific, modern psychology has often neglected its own philosophical roots. Much like a modern Ezra surveying the broken walls of Jerusalem, these rebuilders see modern psychology easily slipping into idolatry, especially in its emphasis on empiricism as the prescribed way to find truth, its rejection of divinely revealed truths, and in its adoption of modern sensibilities about self-determination of human morals. The Rebuilders want to draw on God's proclamations as the starting point for a new, Christian psychology. With this accomplished, they proceed to develop methods of soul care, primarily for Christian clients. In regards to the larger academy, though, they aim to critique assumptions of secular psychology, and to offer alternatives based on explicitly articulated Christian beliefs. They can also conduct research on topics that draw on Christian theology and on the findings and methods of modern psychology.

The attempt to transform psychology is not new.[30] The current emphasis on rebuilding psychology in the *Chris-tian psychology* movement, though, tends to be far more sophisticated in its critique of and engagement with modern psychology from a largely postmodern, post-structural perspective. Unlike the other models represented in this chapter, it is not comfortable following the modernist division of academia into discrete fields, but rather sees all forms of knowledge as interrelated. Thus, its primary aim is not to relate "psychology" and "theology" so much as to develop a theologically-informed view of persons and how to aid them in flourishing holistically. In essence, they want to recognize Christ as the Lord of psychology, and to discern the means by which we ought to be transformed into the kinds of people God desires us to be.

Because their aims are quite different from those of the other models, they engage Christina theology, church tradition, and modern psychology much differently than other models. As we have seen, they draw deeply on Scripture and church tradition in forming their view of personhood and personal transformation. They are vigilant about the assumptions made by "secular" psychology, in theory and research. For the most part, they are conversant with contemporary psychology and willingly engage the field with a sophisticated understanding of philosophy, theory, and research. But their primary aim is *soul care*, shaped by Christian theology and Christian tradition. This approach is summarized below.

Rebuilders—Christianity is fundamentally psychological—Christianity

---

30. See, for example, Collins, The rebuilding of psychology.

tells us about our origins, our nature, about how we ought to be, and about soul care that transforms us into becoming more Christ-like. Modern psychology neglects its philosophical roots, and often operates under assumptions and values that run counter to those of Christianity.

Telos—*Rebuilders* want to rebuild psychology, recognizing the Lordship of Christ, on a firm foundation of Christian assumptions about human beings: our creation, our fallen nature, our ultimate purpose, mechanisms of change, and so forth. *Christian psychology*, as it currently exists, rejects modernist distinctions between disciplines but encourages dialogue with contemporary psychology, desiring to express Christian viewpoints within the academy.

- What does Scripture tell us about the origin, nature, and value of persons?

- What does Christian tradition tell us about soul care, how to be transformed into the kind of people that God wishes us to be?

- In what ways has contemporary psychology rejected foundational assumptions that Christians hold to be true? How can we win a hearing for Christian perspectives within the modern academy?

- How can Christians be faithful to their tradition and engage

contemporary psychology theory and research?

Neutral Parties

To this point, all of the models we have considered breach the boundaries of one of the disciplines involved either by trying to annihilate it, to remove its fundamental character, or to force it into subservience. A fifth approach represents a truce between the two disciplines. It is prefaced on the idea that the two do not need to be in conflict as long as they simply respect each other's territory.

Christians who follow the *Neutral Parties* model have as their telos the accumulation of knowledge and the protection of disciplinary sovereignty. They typically acknowledge the influence of worldviews on the pursuit of knowledge, but they also tend to accept the modernist division of knowledge into discrete disciplines that are relatively autonomous. In a sense, they attempt to follow two masters—when in Athens, they do as the Athenians, and when in Rome, they do as the Romans. Like a person with dual citizenship, they see themselves as obligated to the laws of whichever country they happen to be in at the moment. They may gladly tell their Roman neighbors about how things work in Athens, and they may willingly share Roman insights with the Athenians. But they are always obligated to follow the sovereignty of the territory that they happen to be in at any given time.[31]

People who depict the relationship of Christianity and science (or Christianity and psychology) through the *Neutral Parties* model primarily employ procedures that serve to segregate the parts of each discipline from each other, and—perhaps—to compare the findings of the one model to the findings of the other model. The *Neutral Parties* model follows the tactic of noting the distinctiveness of psychology and the uniqueness of theology, while identifying their similarities of content or function. Because it focuses on finding similarities between psychology and theology, Carter and Narramore designated this approach to the relationship of psychology and Christianity *the parallels model*.

The *Neutral Parties* model allows psychological theories and findings to exist on their own merits. One version of this model emphasizes the need to keep all psychological and theological reflection completely separate in order to protect the disciplines from being contaminated by ideas or beliefs from the other discipline. In essence, they are trying to protect disciplinary sovereignty. In this version, psychology and theology are seen as nonintersecting perspectives from which a subject can be viewed; psychological and theological reflection

are carefully segregated from one another through *disciplinary isolationism*. The second version of this model also insists on disciplinary sovereignty. However, once the disciplines have been allowed to run independently, it recognizes that they may have independently come to some conclusions that can be compared, correlated, or seen in parallel terms. This version allows someone "to correlate or align certain psychological and spiritual concepts" (*isolated correlationalism*).[32] Eck classified such approaches as *nonmanipulative integration paradigms that use a correlates process*. Adherents of this view accept "the legitimacy of truth from both disciplines" without needing to alter their data prior to relating the two.[33] The *Neutral Parties* model and the questions it gives rise to is summarized below.

Neutral Parties—Psychology and theology are completely independent disciplines, with their own sources, methodologies, and findings. They need to be carefully segregated to keep either from infecting the other (*disciplinary isolationism*). However, there may be parallels between the findings of psychology and theology that can be discerned (*isolated correlationalism*).

Telos—people who follow the *Neutral Parties* approach seek to accumulate knowledge and protect disciplinary sovereignty. They typically acknowledge the influence of worldviews on the pursuit of knowledge, but they also

---

31. Brian Eck shared another useful analogy with me. Someone who adopts this model is somewhat like a soldier serving a U.N. mission as a member of the United States military. There are divided loyalties that are not always easily resolved.

---

32. Eck, Integrating the integrators, 108–9.

33. Ibid., 108.

tend to accept the modernist division of knowledge into discrete disciplines that are relatively autonomous. Thus, they are always obligated to follow the sovereignty of whichever discipline they are operating in at a given point in time.

- How can I make sure that my religious beliefs do not bias me in my scientific or clinical work?

- If psychological and theological teachings appear to conflict, can the differences be explained as simply reflecting the different languages and methodologies of the two disciplines?

- How does one determine if a problem is primarily a spiritual issue or a psychological issue?

- In what ways do psychology and theology seem to be saying the same thing in different words?

Allies as Subjects of One Sovereign

The final model that we will consider recognizes the underlying unity of human nature and the legitimacy of both theological and psychological investigation. The *Allies as Subjects of One Sovereign* (*Allies*) model recognizes that all truth is known by God, who is Sovereign over all things. It acknowledges that various methods can be used to learn about the world in general, and human beings in particular. Compared to the other models, it has a stronger recognition that worldviews exert an enormous influence on human thinking, so it emphasizes the importance of forming a Christian worldview from which to approach all of life, including psychology.

One proposition that undergirds this perspective is *the unity of truth*. From God's perspective, all truth fits together cohesively. All truth is ultimately under God's sovereignty. However, due to human error and human limitations, our understanding is imperfect, and sometimes flawed. Nonetheless, if something is true, it cannot contradict other things that are true. This does not mean, however, that all truths are equally important. For instance, I believe that the proposition, "For God so loved the world, that He gave His only begotten Son, that whoever believes in Him shall not perish, but have eternal life" (John 3:16, NASB) is just as true as the proposition that—at the time of this writing—I own a red minivan. However, the truth of John 3:16 is far more foundational to my life than the fact that I own a red minivan.

This perspective affirms that psychology and Christian theology are both subject to God's sovereignty. God gave birth to the subject of psychology (human behavior) when he created human beings. God granted us the foundations of Christian theology when He gave us His Word. Psychology and theology are His subjects, both in the sense that He is sovereign over them and that they should serve His ends. "For from him and through him and to him are all things. To him be the glory forever" (Rom 11:36, NIV).

The *Allies* model acknowledges the sovereignty of Christ as the creator and sustainer of all things: "For by him all things were created: things in heaven and on earth, visible and invisible, whether thrones or powers or rulers or authorities; all things were created by him and for him. He is before all things, and in him all things hold together" (Col 1:16–17, NIV).

The christocentric nature of this model is one of its distinguishing features, as is its recognition of human error and finitude. Carter and Narramore called this the *Integration Model*, because it seeks to integrate psychology and theology by discerning their underlying unity. Discerning the underlying unity of truth and using it for godly ends are the chief disciplinary goals of the *Allies as Subjects of One Sovereign* model. However, its telos is larger than disciplinary integration alone. Instead, the *Allies* model recognizes that human purpose is ultimately expressed when we see ourselves in proper relationship to God. This includes, for example, recognizing and submitting to God's sovereignty, serving him completely with heart, soul, mind, and strength (Mark 12:30), giving him praise and thanks in all things (Col 3:17), and loving our neighbor (Mark 12:31). The telos of the Allies model aims at being faithful to God in all of our lives, including studying the book of His Works *and* the book of His Word as we attempt to discern the underlying unity of truth, serving and praising God, and loving our neighbor.

Eck classified such approaches as utilizing a *non-manipulative paradigm* with a "unifies process." In his words,

> the truth to be integrated from each discipline is brought together to create a unified set of truths that mirror the wholeness and unity of God's created and revealed truths. This process seeks to use the data gathered through the best methods each discipline has to offer while recognizing that we are "looking through a glass darkly" (I Cor. 13:12, NIV). This approach recognizes the limitations of human understanding that impact our ability to know and understand the truth from both disciplines, yet seeks to live out a unified set of truths in one's life and practice of psychology.[34]

Psychology and theology, rightly understood, are thus seen as allies, both of which are subjects of One Sovereign God. For those of us who follow this model, we will respect the "laws" of Jerusalem and Athens, but our ultimate allegiance is to the God who is Sovereign over all things.

The *Allies* model will use many of the same procedures utilized in the other models, but its goals are uniquely shaped by acknowledging God's sovereignty. It will utilize segregation, but only for the purpose of disciplinary distinctiveness and methodology. It will be interested in looking at the psychological functions of religious belief and practice, and the theological soundness of psychological

---

34. Eck, Integrating the integrators, 109

concepts and assumptions. It will be concerned with comparing and contrasting psychological and theological concepts and findings. In seeking to understand the holistic and unified nature of its subject—human behavior—those who use the *Allies* model will sometimes find that parts of one model or the other are incompatible, and we will undertake a more thorough analysis to discern which model is more accurate and which is in need of correction.[35] Above all, however, the *Allies* model recognizes God's sovereignty.

In this model, our allegiance is neither to psychology nor to theology, but to God who reigns over all spheres of which we are subjects. It is our Christian duty to engage psychology in such a way that we are faithful in discerning truths about God's world, utilizing and applying the unique methods of psychology in full recognition of their limitations. It is our Christian duty to study Christian theology in such a way that we are faithful in seeking and following the truths of God's Word, utilizing the unique methods of theology in full recognition of their limitations. It is important to highlight that this is not just an intellectual exercise: psychology and theology are not just about abstract beliefs—they are also about how we live. Finally, by being

aware of the human limitations of finitude, frailty, and fallenness, and of the methodological limitations of our disciplines, we can proceed to seek a holistic and unified understanding of humanity, and to apply our knowledge in ways that honor God and minister to the needs of our fellow human beings. We can summarize the *Allies as Subjects of One Sovereign* model and the kinds of questions it asks as follows:

Allies—God is the author of all truth, and all things are "by him, for him" and "hold together" in Him. Although psychology and theology are separate disciplines, with their own sources, methodologies, and findings, they both express truth about human nature and functioning. They are both dependent, to some degree, on human thinking, and to the degree that human thinking is errant, our psychological and theological conclusions can be wrong. Apparent contradictions between psychology and theology suggest that we need to reconsider our reasoning and data to see if we can identify logical, methodological, interpretive, or other errors in our thinking.

Telos—Allies strive to be faithful stewards of all that God has entrusted to us, including studying the book of His Works *and* the book of His Word. Our ultimate goals include serving and praising God with all of our being, and fulfilling our call to love our neighbor. At the disciplinary level, the *Allies* model aims to discern the underlying

---

35. We must be careful, however, not to reinterpret Scripture based on the current whim of scientific or psychological opinion. When biblical and scientific interpretations are at odds, one must carefully review the bases upon which those interpretations are made. More will be said of this in later chapters of this book.

unity of truth and to use it for godly ends.

- How can we discern the nature of human beings using both psychology and theology?

- How can a Christian worldview help us evaluate fundamental assumptions about our place in the world, especially as they are reflected in academic disciplines?

- How can we maintain the disciplinary distinctives of psychology and theology as we seek to understand human nature holistically?

- How can psychology and theology help us to minister God's love to the many needs that people have?

- How can all that we do be an expression of love of God and love of our neighbor?

Apparent Conflict and the Six Models: An Example

Let us turn our attention to a situation in which a theological teaching seems to be at odds with contemporary psychology. A significant amount of psychological research highlights the destructive potential of anger, but modern psychology also suggests that anger has adaptive value.[36] It is often noted that forgiveness is a process that involves dealing with anger and other reactions to having been harmed.[37] Forgiveness might be defined psychologically as a process that "takes place over time," and involves the choice to release an offending person from resentment by the extension of compassion and generosity.[38] In contrast, some contemporary Bible teachers proclaim that it would be sinful to go to bed with unresolved anger since the Bible says, "Do not let the sun go down on your anger" (Eph 4:27a). An example of this is seen in the following advice. "Develop ways of dealing with anger. Chief among these is the old Biblical injunction, 'do not let the sun go down on your wrath.' In other words, if you have to stay up all night talking in order to resolve differences, do so. Do not go to bed angry."[39]

On similar grounds, some pastors teach that forgiveness is a decision made once for all, and that once forgiven, an offense should be forgotten. Some psychologists teach that forgiveness is best conceived as a process rather than a point-in-time decision, and that the offense may still need to be discussed and worked through even after the offender has been forgiven. How ought we to understand the apparent conflict between these claims?

Holders of the *Enemies* model would view this apparent conflict as solvable by rejecting the claims of one discipline or the other; *Secular Combatants* would reject the religious claim, and *Christian*

---

36. See, for example, Novaco, The functions and regulation. See also Ellis & Malamuth, Love and anger in romantic relationships.

37. See, for example, Enright & Fitzgibbons, Empirical validation.

38. Konstam, et al., Toward forgiveness, 26.

39. AllSands, *Healthy marriage*, ¶7.

TABLE 8.1: **Models of Disciplinary Relationship**

Model	Telos	Description
Enemies *Secular Combatants* *Christian Combatants*	Allegiance to a worldview that excludes (or greatly restricts) either religious belief or the insights of human reason. The autonomous exercise of human reason. Protection of religious authority and religious pronouncements against corruption by human reason.	Rejection of one perspective or discipline. *Non-integrative paradigm, Rejects process*
Spies *Foreign Spies* *Domestic Spies*	Pragmatic desire to use any means to aid human well-being. They lack deep commitment to any religious system, have little investment in religious doctrine, or tend to water down doctrine in favor of promoting their vision of temporal well-being.	Selective rejection and selective plundering. Rejection of orthodox theological perspective, but recognition of the potential for religion to promote well-being. *Manipulative Integration paradigm; Reconstructs Process*
Colonialists *Biblical Psychology*	Primary allegiance to a religious system that accepts the importance of Christian doctrine and behavior; appropriation of psychological methods or findings that can illustrate or buttress the claims of their theological proclamations.	Filtering isolated psychological findings through proof-texts or worldview; accepts or rejects findings without engaging discipline or methods of psychology. *Manipulative Integration paradigm; Theology Transforms Psychology*
Rebuilders *Christian Psychology*	Recovery of psychological views from Christian scripture and tradition, especially in terms of wise counsel for living; interaction with contemporary psychology with an aim towards building a unique Christian psychology perspective.	Criticism of modernist definition of psychology and its claims of objectivity. Primacy of Christian framework and perspective. Recognition of the value of empirical approaches to psychology. *Postmodern, post-structural paradigm; Theology Transforms Psychology*
Neutral Parties *Levels of Analysis*	Accumulation of knowledge, and the protection of disciplinary sovereignty. They tent to accept the modernist division of knowledge into discrete disciplines that are relatively autonomous.	Asserts the legitimacy of psychology and theology as independent domains. The emphasis is on distinctiveness rather than unity. *Non-Manipulative Integration Paradigm, Correlates Process*
Allies	Recognition that human purpose is ultimately expressed when we see ourselves in proper relationship to God. Discerning the underlying unity of truth and using it for godly ends are the chief disciplinary goals of the model.	Psychological and theological methods are used to gain a more holistic and unified understanding of truth. *Non-manipulative Integration Paradigm, Unifies Process*

Combatants would reject the psychological claim. Individuals who adhere to the *Spies* model would ignore data that does not fit with their preexisting assumptions, and borrow only data that support their beliefs. *Colonialists* would attempt to reform psychology by filtering secular concepts through religious categories (thus rejecting the psychological viewpoint on this issue). *Rebuilders* would attempt to reorient the field of psychology by infusing it with Christian values. The *Neutral Parties* approach would be to admit that there was an apparent discrepancy, but to either relegate this discrepancy to differences of perspective (*disciplinary isolationism*), or to look for other areas where parallels between theological teachings and psychological findings are more compatible (*isolated correlationalism*). Finally, believing that the apparent conflict was based on misunderstanding or misinterpretation, the *Allies* model would suggest that we need to revisit our *interpretations* of Scripture and of the psychological data, as we will see in the following paragraphs.[40]

Following the approach of the *Allies* model, we might first note that the advice that Christians should not to go to bed angry is not an easy fit with the context of the verse (Ephesians 4). The first theme of the surrounding verses highlights the importance of *unity within the body of Christ*; anger that is not resolved over time will destroy unity. The second theme of the surrounding verses is the need to *mature into a Christ-like image*. Children do not manage their anger well, but—ideally—through socialization and development we gradually learn to restrain our anger and express it appropriately. In a similar fashion, Christians are to "grow up" so that their behavior is more mature and Christ-like.

The language employed by the biblical author appears to have two sources: Psalm 4:4 and an ancient social custom. The first source is a psalm in which David cries out to God in distress, but then interrupts his lament with the phrase, "In your anger do not sin; when you are on your beds, search your hearts and be silent" (Ps 4:4, NIV). In its original context, the injunction appears to function as a warning to be silent before God and circumspect in judgment.[41] It also appears that the apostle Paul might have drawn upon a common saying, attributed to Plutarch, that men who were angry at each other should "shake hands before the sun set."[42] Paul may thus be using an ancient, sacred teaching and attaching it to a contemporary maxim to illustrate the need to resolve anger appropriately, not necessarily intending a wooden interpretation of doing so before going to bed.

---

40. Note that we do not assume in advance which interpretation is more likely to be correct; we simply use the apparent conflict as an impetus to reconsider the data and the interpretive processes on both sides of the issue. More will be said of this in chapter 12.

41. Schnackenburg suggested that the original context of Psalm 4 had as its purpose "to prevent sinning against God through ill-humour" (*Ephesians*, 207).

42. Moule, *Ephesian studies*, 232.

A final question is what is to be put aside. The words for "anger" in Ephesians 4:26, while related, are not identical. Most modern translations treat the words identically: "In your *anger* do not sin: Do not let the sun go down on your *anger*." However, the second word for *anger* includes a preposition that could alter its meaning; the King James Version recognized this by translating the second word as *wrath*. Marvin Vincent suggested that Paul's injunction was against the passionate impulses of *exasperation*.[43] Another commentator believed that "the term used in the second clause suggests the idea of embitterment or exasperation . . . The injunction not to let the sun go down on your wrath signifies irascibility rather than ire."[44] Jamieson, Fausset, and Brown concurred: "Our natural feelings are not wrong when directed to their legitimate object, and when not exceeding due bounds . . . The sense is not, Your *anger* shall not be imputed to you if you put it away before nightfall; but 'let no *wrath* (that is, as the *Greek,* personal 'irritation' or 'exasperation') mingle with your 'anger,' even though, the latter be righteous."[45]

Thus, anger itself is not the problem, but rather anger that is nursed, vengeance that is cultivated, or conflict that breeds contempt.

When faced with such apparent conflicts, we need to allow our interpretation of Scripture to serve as a touchstone for reevaluating our psychological conclusions in the light of scriptural and psychological data. If a psychologist were to argue that giving full reign to one's anger was good, or that there is no need to try to resolve interpersonal conflict, we would certainly have some theological objections to these claims. We would also find that the psychological data would not support such claims.[46]

A comparison of these perspectives allows for a process of mutual critique that may help us identify errors in psychological interpretation or theological interpretation. In this case, it may be that a rightly understood psychology of forgiveness could here provide a corrective impetus to a wrongly understood theology of anger. While well intentioned, the advice to never go to bed with anger (that is, with interpersonal tension) may actually be counterproductive in *some* circumstances. Such advice has the potential to promote repression of emotion and suppression of conflict,

---

43. Vincent, *Paul*, 396. Vincent further noted that the first anger is an enduring sentiment; thus one may rightly persist in anger at sin and injustice, but the passion for vengeance must be quelled.

44. Simpson & Bruce, *Commentary on the epistles to the Ephesians and the Colossians*, 108.

45. Jamieson, et al., *A commentary*, 72–73.

46. A recent meta-analytic study found that process-based forgiveness interventions were effective in promoting forgiveness and emotional well-being, while decision-based forgiveness interventions were not effective. See Baskin & Enright, Intervention studies on forgiveness, 82. Another recent meta-analytic study found that the efficacy of various approaches to anger management differ according to the type of anger involved. See Del Vecchio & O'Leary, Effectiveness of anger treatments.

all in the name of harmony that it does not necessarily achieve. There are times when an issue must be addressed immediately, but there are also occasions when a temporary impasse in a relationship is better served by a good night's sleep and calm reflection and discourse the next day. The theological data, however, serve as a strong caution that interpersonal wounds and conflicts ought to be resolved in a reasonably brief period of time and should not be nursed or allowed to fester indefinitely.[47]

As the forgoing example illustrates, the six models bring about different ways of thinking about apparent conflicts between psychology and theology. In the next three chapters, we will gain a deeper understanding of these models.

Summary

When we look at the relationship of psychology and theology, we are concerned with *models based on models*; that is, *models* of how to understand the *model of psychology* and the *model of theology* that a theorist has constructed, and the realities that they represent. Six models for various ways of relating psychology and theology were proposed (*Enemies, Spies, Colonialists, Rebuilders, Neutral Parties,* and *Allies as Subjects of One Sovereign*), and comparisons were made to other models that have been proposed.

Table 8.1 summarizes each of the six models and provides a comparison to previously proposed models. In the next two chapters, we will explore examples of these models and elaborate on them conceptually.

Questions for Reflection and Discussion

1. Why is it important to recognize that models about the relationship of psychology and theology are *models based on models*? Given this recognition, how can your comprehension of a theorist's *model of psychology* and his or her *model of theology* help you to understand the model that the theorist creates to understand the relationship of psychology and theology?

2. The author noted that conflict regarding how to view the relationship of psychology and theology sometimes reflects worldview presuppositions. He then quoted G. K. Chesterton's detective, Mr. Pond: "Once assume the wrong beginning, and you'll not only give the wrong answer, but ask the wrong question." In what ways do the presuppositions of the *Enemies, Spies, Colonialists, Rebuilders, Neutral Parties,* and *Allies* models lead their adherents to ask different questions, for which they supply different answers?

3. Do you agree or disagree with the statement that, "*Secular Combatants* and *Christian Combatants* are more alike than they are different in terms

47. Here too psychological observation confirms the dangers of failing to bring reconciliation to wounded or broken relationships in a reasonable space of time.

of how they approach the interface of psychology and theology." Why or why not? Do you think members of the secular and sacred *against* models would be likely to engage each other in genuine dialogue? Why or why not?

4. Summarize the relationship of psychology and theology as understood by holders of the *Enemies*, *Spies*, *Colonialists*, *Rebuilders*, *Neutral Parties*, and *Allies* models.

5. How are *Rebuilders* different from, and similar to, *Colonialists*?

6. How is the *Spy* different from, and similar to, the *Colonialist*?

7. What can you see as some of the advantages and disadvantages of adopting a *Neutral Parties* approach?

8. How does the telos of each of the six models shape the way they understand and approach the relationship of psychology and Christianity?

9. The author claimed that "God gave birth to the subject of psychology (human behavior) when he created human beings. God granted us the foundations of Christian theology when He gave us His Word. Psychology and theology are His subjects, both in the sense that He is sovereign over them and that they should serve His ends . . . Psychology and theology, rightly understood, are thus seen as allies, both of which are subjects of One Sovereign God." How is this model different from the other five models?

10. What are the implications of the claim that "our allegiance is neither to psychology nor to theology, but to God who reigns over all spheres of which we are subjects"?

9

Antagonistic Models of Disciplinary Relationship: Enemies

Indeed, it is a strange-disposed time: But men may construe things after their fashion, Clean from the purpose of the things themselves.[1]

–William Shakespeare

People suffer and die every day because of territorial conflicts. Combatants wage war with each other while innocent bystanders suffer. Western news media often fail to report these conflicts even though they occur on a massive scale. Ethnic and religious conflicts lead to bloodshed in places as diverse as Afghanistan, Chechnya, China, Iraq, Israel, Pakistan, Palestine, Rwanda, Sri Lanka, Somalia, and Sudan. In many of these conflicts, the core issue is *territory*. The *Enemies* model of the relationship of psychology and Christianity (or religion) is largely a territorial dispute. Like all such disputes, territory often becomes a background issue once hostilities break out. One group of people identifies another group as dangerous infidels, "unfaithful ones." The warring sides perceive each other as hostile and combative. Each side

sees its own attacks as justified by the antagonistic behavior and infidelity of the other side. After several rounds of self-justification and escalating assaults, both sides become convinced that the other side started the conflict, and that their own side is the only one that has merit. Unfortunately, such conflicts cause untold suffering among the people that are caught between the warring factions.

To understand the roots and supporting factors of any conflict, it is necessary to comprehend the worldviews of the adversaries, and to understand the history of the conflict. We have already discussed some of the issues that created antagonism between psychology and religion in chapters 2 and 3. Having introduced the *Enemies* model in chapter 8, the way is paved for us to continue to develop an understanding of this perspective.

People who subscribe to the *Enemies* model assume that psychology and religion (or Christianity) are fundamentally

---

1. Shakespeare, *Julius Caesar*, act 1, scene 3.

incompatible with each other. This model is carried out through *rejection* and *erad-ication*. On the one side, there is a whole-sale rejection of the system to which one is opposed. On the other hand, efforts are exerted to eradicate anything in one's own system that has its roots in the ex-ternal system.

Two versions of the *Enemies* mod-el exist. In the first version, religion is seen as the enemy of psychology; this is the perspective of *Secular Combatants*. In the second version, psychology is seen as the enemy of Christianity; this is the perspective of *Christian Combatants*. We will explore each of these in turn in this chapter.[2]

Religion as the Enemy of Psychology: Secular Combatants

Christians who are opposed to psycholo-gy often single out Sigmund Freud as the central figure of psychology and as the epitome of its antireligious bent (both of these propositions are debatable). Freud is an enigmatic and complicated figure. As the recipient of anti-Semitic preju-dice, and as a member of an ethnic group

long persecuted by Christians, "he was bound to feel prejudiced against Chris-tianity in general, the religion that had inflicted such untold suffering on his people through the centuries."[3]

Freud personally encountered anti-Semitic discrimination as a child and in his adult life. As a young child he lived in a largely Catholic area where anti-Semi-tism was rampant. His family employed a Catholic nanny for him, and she often took him to mass. Samuel Slipp provid-ed an interesting interpretation of this event:

> An added confusion beclouded young Sigmund's first two years of life. He was raised by two mother figures. Besides his biological mother, Amalie, he was cared for by an elderly Czech nanny named Resi Wittek (also called Monika Zajic by other writers). To add to the confusion, Resi, who was Catholic, was allowed to take little Sigmund to church with her. At Catholic church he learned about sin, heaven, and hell. Amalie was clearly aware that the nanny was taking Sigmund to church with her, but she expressed a cavalier attitude about it. Amalie related with amusement how Sigmund would come home from church and preach to the family. Why was this Jewish mother amused that her son was attending church? Was she encouraging Christian assimilation as a way of dealing with anti-Semitism? Assimilation was not an uncommon path followed by many Austrian and German Jews. Was she angry at her

---

2. What I am calling the *Enemies* model was called the *against model* by Carter, which he separated into *secular and sacred* versions. These were later developed by Carter and Narramore, *The integration of psychology and theology.* Carter and Narramore described two versions of this model, a *secular-against model*, in which psychologists are opposed to religion, and a *sacred-against model*, in which Christians are opposed to psychology. My nomenclature largely re-names their model and contextualizes it in a different analogy.

---

3. Jones, *The last phase*, 352.

religious Jewish husband who had gone bankrupt? Allowing Sigmund to go to church might have been her way of acting out her defiance and her anger against her husband.[4]

"Because of our commons roots, a true Christian cannot be anti-Semitic."

—Pope Francis

"Every day, I pray with the Psalms of David. My prayer is Jewish, then I have the Eucharist, which is Christian."

— Pope Francis

"Looking to the future of relations between Jews and Christians, in the first place, we appeal to our Catholic brothers and sisters to renew the awareness of the Hebrew roots of their faith. . . . At the end of this Millennium the Catholic Church desires to express her deep sorrow for the failures of her sons and daughters in every age. This is an act of repentance . . ."

—*We remember: A reflection on the Shoah*; Vatican archives, 1998

The nanny was dismissed for stealing from the family, and one wonders if this event colored Freud's view of religion. In any event, the anti-Semitism he and his family experienced created much bitterness.

For many years building up to the holocaust, anti-Semitism was rampant throughout Europe. Jacob Freud tried to console Sigmund by sharing his own experiences. Sigmund, however, seems to have reacted with disappointment that his father tolerated the abuse to which Jews were regularly exposed. He recounts one particular incident that left an indelible impression on him.

I might have been ten or twelve years old when my father began to take me with him on his walks, and in his conversation to reveal his views on the things of this world. Thus it was that he once told me the following incident, in order to show me that I had been born into happier times than he: "When I was a young man, I was walking one Saturday along the street in the village where you were born; I was well-dressed, with a new fur cap on my head. Up comes a Christian, who knocks my cap into the mud, and shouts, 'Jew, get off the pavement!'"— "And what did you do?"—"I went into the street and picked up the cap," he calmly replied.[5]

Freud related this story while explaining that he never intended to study medicine. He had wanted to study law

---

4. Slipp, *The Freudian mystique*, 66–67.

5. Freud, *The interpretation of dreams*, 70.

and enter government service, but as a Jew, this path was not open to him.

When he was compiling his autobiography at the age of sixty-nine, Freud recounted his experience as a university student: "Above all, I found that I was expected to feel myself inferior and an alien because I was a Jew. I refused absolutely to do the first of these things."[6]

While his personal experiences may have left him jaded toward religion, and especially Christianity, his chosen profession also played a role in his anti-religious sentiments. Medicine in the late 1800s was influenced by the mechanistic physiology of a German school of medicine that sought to reduce the human being to chemical and physical forces. "In this way physicalist physiology . . . eliminated all traces of 'vitalism' of the Aristotelian and Scholastic tradition, which assumed that organisms had been endowed by the Creator with immaterial factors . . ."[7]

Despite these forces impelling Freud's antagonism toward religion, he was very well educated in Judaism as a child and very familiar with other religions as an adult.

Freud was unusually well read in the religious literature not only of Jews and Christians, but also of the ancient Greeks, Egyptians, Indians, and Chinese, and he could quote at will from the Hebrew and Christian Scriptures.[8] His

theological views are largely revisionist, offering psychological explanations for religious phenomena.[9]

Freud clearly viewed religion itself as having neurotic origins that ought to be outgrown: "Religion is comparable to a childhood neurosis, and [a psychologist who does not deceive himself] is optimistic enough to suppose that mankind will surmount this neurotic phase, just as so many children grow out of their similar neurosis."[10]

While Freud correctly noted that *some* religious practices may serve neurotic functions, his contention that neurosis *created* religion is clearly speculative. Furthermore, as the theologian Hans Küng pointed out, Freud's conclusion was based on a logical error. Even if religious belief expresses wish fulfillments, it does not mean that God does not exist. "For psychological interpretation alone, from its very nature, cannot penetrate to the absolutely final or first reality . . . the existence of God remains an open question."[11]

In Freud's view, though, psychological and sociological forces are responsible for our belief in God, who is "nothing but an exalted father."[12]   For Freud, the only god that existed, the only god worth serving, and the only one who

---

6. Quoted in Küng, *Freud and the problem of God*, 12.

7. Ibid.,14.

8. Jones, *The last phase*, 350–51.

9. This can be seen in both his clinical cases and in his more "theological" works, notably *Totem and taboo, Moses and monotheism,* and *The future of an illusion.*

10. Freud, *Future of an illusion,* 87.

11. Küng, *Freud and the problem of God*, 80.

12. Freud, *Totem and taboo*, 90.

offered hope or "salvation" was *truth*, or, as he put it, "our God, logos." For Freud, truth could relieve some of our anxieties and offer us a sense of earthly hope and comfort. In his view, though, truth is a cold reality. We cannot hope for the loving arms of God, or for justice or mercy. "Our God, logos, is perhaps not a very almighty one, and he may only be able to fulfill a small part of what his predecessors have promised."[13]

The only realistic hope, in Freud's view, was for humans to overcome the superstitions and empty promises of primitive religious belief. Toward this end, Freud viewed psychoanalysis as a means to a more scientific understanding of reality:

> The final judgment of science on the religious Weltanschauung, then . . . [is that] it cannot achieve its end. Its doctrines carry with them the stamp of the times in which they originated, the ignorant childhood days of the human race . . . The ethical commands, to which religion seeks to lend its weight, require some other foundation instead, since human society cannot do without them, and it is dangerous to link up obedience to them with religious belief. If one at-

tempts to assign to religion its place in man's evolution, it seems not so much a lasting acquisition as a parallel to the neurosis which the civilized individual must pass through on his way from childhood to maturity.[14]

Freud's faith in scientific progress, though, was misplaced. Modernism was unable to deliver on its promises. Freud's god, logos, "turned out to be an idol."[15] Human rationality and the hope of scientific advancement have not changed human nature, and they can as easily cause human suffering (e.g., creating "better" weapons, destroying the environment) as relieve it (alleviating famine and lessening psychological distress).

Surprisingly, Freud's antagonism toward religion did not prevent him from collaborating with religious individuals, such as Oskar Pfister, a Swiss pastor.[16] Nor did Freud consistently see his meth-

---

13. Freud, *The future of an illusion*, 89. The word λόγος (*logos*) is transliterated in this quotation for ease of reading. It is worth noting that on the following page Freud pointed out that "science" (within which he included psychoanalysis) "has many open *enemies* . . . among those who cannot forgive her for having weakened religious faith and threatening to overthrow it" (italics added).

14. Freud, quoted in Jones, *The last phase*, 360.

15. Küng, *Freud and the problem of God*, 83.

16. Freud seemed alternatively amused by, impressed with and irritated at Pfister; his irritation is revealed in Freud's letters to Jung. Freud and his family evidently shared a warm relationship with Pfister, which can be seen in the tenor of their correspondence and the reflections of his daughter, Anna. Freud's perplexity at Pfister's interest in psychoanalysis and his theological convictions sometimes come to the fore in their letters: for instance, when Freud praised Pfister's book on the Apostle Paul, or his comment, "That you should be such a convinced analyst and at the same time a clerical gentleman is one of the contradictions that make life so interesting." The quotation is from Freud's letter to Pfister, November 25, 1934, reprinted in Meng & Freud, *Psychoanalysis and faith*, 142.

od or theories as *necessarily* opposed to religious belief or practice; in one letter he wrote, "In itself, psychoanalysis is neither religious nor the opposite, but an impartial instrument which can serve the clergy as well as the laity when it is used only to free suffering people."[17] One might legitimately challenge how "impartial" any therapeutic approach can be. It is widely recognized that—even if we strive for "technical" or "therapeutic" neutrality—our own values are inevitably expressed in the psychotherapeutic situation. Nonetheless, the fact remains that Christians can benefit from the insights of secular individuals. While some techniques or admonitions may clearly violate Christian values, there are others, which, stemming from a discernment of the workings of God's creation, are equally applicable to Christians and non-Christians alike.[18] Thus Freud was personally committed to atheism while maintaining a warm dialogue with religiously committed people. He saw religion as based on infantile needs that could be supplanted by science and truth, and yet did not see his method as requiring or encouraging an atheistic bent.

Closer to the contemporary scene, one of the most outspoken critics of religious belief has been Albert Ellis. Some of Ellis's more dogmatic statements against religion include the following:

If religion is defined as man's dependence on a power above and beyond the human, then as a psychotherapist, I find it to be exceptionally pernicious. For the psychotherapist is normally dedicated to helping human beings in general, and his patients in particular, to achieve certain goals of mental health, and virtually all these goals are antithetical to a truly religious viewpoint.[19]

In most respects religion seriously sabotages mental health.[20]

In the final analysis, then, religion is a neurosis . . . What then is the role of psychotherapy in dealing with the religious views of disturbed patients? . . . [T]he sane and effective psychotherapist should not . . . go along with the patients' religious orientation and try to help these patients live successfully with their religions, for this is equivalent to trying to help them live successfully with their emotional illness.[21]

Ellis's assumptions clearly reflect the *Secular Combatants* version of the *Enemies* model.

In 1980, the *Journal of Consulting and Clinical Psychology* published an article in which Alan Bergin proposed that psychology needed to take a more inclusive stance toward religious belief.[22] Ellis

---

17. Quoted in Jones, *The last phase*, 352.

18. The same, it might be noted, applies to the counsel of a pastor or a friend; we simply cannot divorce ourselves from our own biases and beliefs, nor should we.

---

19. Ellis, *The case against religion*, 2

20. Ibid., 5.

21. Ibid., 15.

22. Bergin, Psychotherapy and religious values. This is a pivotal article, which, along with the responses to it, is a "must read" for anyone

continued his diatribe against religious belief in response to Bergin's article, proposing that "devout, orthodox, or dogmatic religion is significantly correlated with emotional disturbance,"[23] challenging religious assumptions about the value of "fidelity or loyalty to any interpersonal commitment, especially marriage,"[24] and suggesting that people would be better off "without their belief in the intervening variable of religion or god."[25] While Ellis claimed that agnosticism was the healthiest choice, he believed that people who couldn't give up the crutch of religion could live comfortable and reasonably healthy lives with suitably undogmatic religious beliefs. In his later writings, Ellis softened his rhetoric considerably, and even coauthored *Counseling and Psychotherapy with Religious*

Are the negative views of psychology expressed by Freud and Ellis based on empirical evidence? To what degree are their conclusions the result of their assumptions? Where did these assumptions come from?

Persons, a book on adapting his techniques for use with religiously committed clients.[26]

The approach taken by Ellis and his coauthors in *Counseling and Psychotherapy with Religious Persons* seems strangely incongruent with most of Ellis's previous statements about the supposed harmful effects of religious belief. For instance, the authors admonish therapists to guard against antireligious sentiments that could impede therapeutic success:

> Antireligious sentiments could lead psychotherapists to discount or disparage client religious beliefs. Psychotherapists may assume that religious beliefs and practice cause psychopathology. No such link is supported by research. Rather, a growing body of research reveals a positive relation between religious commitment and physical health; summaries of studies examining a link between mental illness and religion find that religion is either a neutral factor or there may be a positive relation between mental health and religious commitment . . .[27]

This view of religion is completely at variance with many of Ellis's former statements,[28] and his essential stance has

---

interested in integration. Bergin is a member of the Church of Jesus Christ of Latter-day Saints and spent his academic career as a professor at Brigham Young University. His article unleashed a firestorm of criticism and debate but paved the way for a more conducive atmosphere of dialogue that currently prevails.

23. Ellis, Psychotherapy and atheistic values, 637.

24. Ibid., 638.

25. Ibid.

---

26. Nielsen, et al., *Counseling and psychotherapy with religious persons.*

27. Ibid., 6.

28. For example, consider the following statement. "So will the therapist, if he himself is not too sick or gutless, attack his patient's religiosity . . . [and] vigorously and forcefully question, challenge, and attack the patient's irrational beliefs that support these disturbed traits"

remained at odds with the idea that one may benefit psychologically from strongly held religious beliefs.

Shortly before his death in 2007, Ellis issued another attack against religious commitment. Ellis argued that survey results that find that religiously committed people express higher levels of happiness and life satisfaction than nonreligious people are simply artifacts of self-deceit or social desirability bias. He claimed that "moderate" religious belief may be benign, so long as the believers "mainly run their own lives and rarely damn themselves (and others) for nonreligious observance."[29] He ended with the admonition: "Try to avoid a doctrinal system through which you are dogmatically convinced that you absolutely must devote yourself to the one, only, right, and unerring deity . . . Otherwise, in my view as a psychotherapist, you most probably are headed for emotional trouble."[30]

Ellis, one might say, concluded that we are better off without religion, but religious belief can be benign as long as you aren't too sure about it, you don't care whether anyone else believes it, and it exercises relatively little influence in your life.

Freud and Ellis should be commended for having stated their beliefs about religion explicitly. At the very least, by putting their cards on the table, they were honest about their assumptions and

they created a possibility for dialogue. On the other hand, when someone is largely unaware of his or her assumptions, honest dialogue is impeded. This situation is, unfortunately, very common in psychology. People in general tend to be largely unaware of the degree to which the prevailing *Zeitgeist* shapes their worldviews. Psychologists are particularly at risk of this trend because the modernist mindset that underlies empirical psychology is largely unacknowledged. Psychological training tends to be extremely weak regarding philosophy generally, and metaphysics and epistemology specifically (other than training in the scientific method). Furthermore, every counseling theory makes assumptions about human nature and the ideals towards which we should strive (e.g., happiness, personal satisfaction, autonomy, etc.), many of which are infused in the broader culture. Although these assumptions are unacknowledged, they nonetheless exert incredible influence in how psychology is carried out and the goals toward which it is directed.

An even more dangerous situation exists when someone deliberately conceals his or her antireligious bias. Perhaps no clearer example of this can be found than Abraham Maslow. Throughout his life Maslow kept a journal of his private thoughts, many of which are startling to anyone who is familiar only with his published work. The following quotations, taken from his posthumously published journal, are illustrative of the carefully concealed views that lurked beneath the façade of his public

---

(Ellis, *The case against religion*, 16).

29. Ellis, No: Dogmatic devotion doesn't help, 363.

30. Ibid., 365.

pronouncements. The first quotation is in reference to a presentation he gave at Brandeis University.

> First time I ever spoke qua atheist in public . . . I didn't dare mention my elitist conception that educated people need "churches" far less than average & low-IQ people. Maybe morons *need* rules, dogmas, ceremonies, etc., as Eleanor Wembridge claimed long ago—that her feebleminded clients behaved much better and felt better being Catholic and following all the rules.[31]

> It's possible now to make a completely coherent & comprehensive psychological & naturalistic theory of religion—far more clear and real than any theology or religion has ever been . . . I think we can save everything worth saving in religion, everything real and true, without swallowing any of the crap. A new, true religion would certainly change things. Something really good to harness all the good impulses now wasted on nunneries & churches & Bibles.[32]

> Very "successful" lecture last night before hundreds of Catholics. Left me exhausted & weary. They shouldn't applaud me—they should attack. If they were fully aware of what I was doing, they would. But maybe not.[33]

Maslow's views on sexuality, dominance, eugenics, and other topics were sequestered in his private journals, but obviously flowed from assumptions that influenced his theories. In evaluating any psychological theory, it is imperative that we examine the underlying assumptions—explicit and implicit—that shape the theory and the ideals toward which it directs us. The influence of assumptions may be of crucial importance if the theorist is ignorant of them or if he or she is deliberately concealing them.

The explicit assaults upon religion by Freud, Ellis, and others have clearly been a setback to the relationship of psychology and Christianity. The attacks themselves are based on a dubious presupposition of the incompatibility of "scientific" thinking and religious commitment.[34] More subtly and more profoundly, any implicit assumptions that deny the legitimacy of a Christian worldview must be addressed for fruitful dialogue to occur between psychology and Christian theology at a disciplinary level.

Some people, including several psychological theorists, reject religion because of bad personal experiences with religiously committed individuals. A prime example is Freud's personal experience and his awareness of historical "Christian" anti-Semitism. Yet, in fairness, we must admit that any religious system can be hijacked by people who endorse errant doctrines that cause physical, psychological, and spiritual problems. Regardless of how far out of the

---

31. Lowry, *The journals of Abraham Maslow,* 7:710–11, entry of February 25, 1967.

32. Ibid., 6, entry of March 12, 1959.

33. Ibid.

---

34. See chapters 1–4.

mainstream they are, religious teachings (such as, that true believers should forgo medical care; raise their children with callous, iron-fisted discipline; or practice extremes of asceticism) give nonreligious people a very skewed view of religion. My own experience suggests that people raised under the influence of rigidly authoritarian religious practices disproportionately come to the attention of medical and mental health professionals. For whatever reasons, though, the fact is that a *psychology against religion* view is alive and well, even if the assumptions upon which it is based are neither compelling nor productive.

Looking Back: *What are some of the reasons that some psychologists might see religion as an enemy of psychology?*

Psychology as the Enemy of Christianity: Christian Combatants

The animosity of some Christians toward psychology is easy to document, such as the Catholic notion at the outset of the twentieth century that practicing or undergoing psychoanalysis was a mortal sin.[35] The acrimony of the *Enemies* model within the church has a long history, and it continues to attract a committed following in some circles. The idea that mixing psychology and theology together is heretical has many roots, including the fundamentalist–modernist

controversy that we have previously discussed. Understandably, *Christian Combatants* have reacted against the antireligious sentiments of some secular psychologists. *Christian Combatants* are also concerned that advice given by secular mental health professionals may diverge significantly from scriptural views, a concern that is not unwarranted.

Some *Christian Combatants* are opposed to psychology as an academic discipline but more commonly, they focus their opposition on clinical psychology. The *Christian Combatants* view is typified by the condemnation leveled by Jay Adams:

> the psychiatrist has usurped the work of the physician, but mostly the work of the preacher. And he engages in this work without warrant from God, without the aid of the Scriptures (in almost every case), and without regard to the power of the Holy Spirit. Thus he seeks to change the behavior and values of people in an ungodly manner. Insofar as he succeeds, the results may be feared. The work of changing men's lives belongs to the Christian ministry in particular and to Christian people in general; not to some self-appointed caste of humanistic priests that has moved into the Church's territory . . .[36]

Adams clearly perceived psychology as the enemy of the church in a territorial dispute. While Adams included some in-house psychological critique by referencing Thomas Szasz and Hans Eysenck,

---

35. McCarthy, Roman Catholic perspectives.

36. Adams, *The big umbrella*, 8.

(both of whom have expressed views that are clearly outside of mainstream psychology), his critique was largely polemical and presuppositional.[37] The nature of his critique requires us to evaluate the bases for his theological argumentation and his presuppositions, and the merits advanced in their favor.

Adams's beliefs were formed in a cauldron in which, as a pastor, he had "learned little about counseling in seminary" and began pastoral ministry "with virtually no knowledge of what to do."[38] He tried to provide impromptu counsel, sought to explore the counseling literature (which at the time was primarily Freudian and Rogerian), and finally became convinced that "the more directive I became (simply telling counselees what God required of them), the more people were helped."[39] His conviction was reinforced when, after spending a summer studying patients in psychiatric hospitals with psychologist O. Hobart Mowrer,[40] Adams became convinced that most of the patients "were there . . . not because they were sick, but because they were sinful."[41]

Following his study with Mowrer, Adams began a study of scriptural references to "counseling" and developed "Nouthetic Counseling,"[42] the conclusions of which "are not based upon scientific findings. My method is presuppositional. I avowedly accept the inerrant Bible as the Standard of all faith and practice."[43] While the Bible clearly is the standard of Christian faith and practice, stretching this concept to mean that Scripture contains *all information relevant to psychological health* is a dubious assertion. Furthermore, Adams's hermeneutical case for "Nouthetic Counseling" is contestable. Carter, in a theological and psychological critique, offered this criticism: The biblical rationale of choosing "*noutheteo* and its cognate *nouthesia* as a model of counseling" is never provided by Adams, despite the fact that it is an infrequent word, occurring only thirteen times in the New Testament. Furthermore,

> While Adams links *noutheteo* to preaching and discipline, its position in the network of biblical concepts

---

37. Adams, like most of those Christians who hold an *Enemies* model, focus his attacks almost exclusively on counseling.

38. Adams, *Competent to counsel*, xi.

39. Ibid., xiii.

40. While Adams claimed that his nouthetic Counseling model was derived from Scripture, the degree of largely unacknowledged overlap between Adams's system and Mowrer's teachings is remarkable. Mowrer is remembered not only for his critique of mainstream psychology but also as a major contributor to it. He was a president of the American Psychological Association, a coauthor of the classic text *Frustration and aggression*, and is remembered as the inventor of the alarm system—based on Pavlovian conditioning—that is still used in the treatment of enuresis.

41. Adams, *Competent to counsel*, xvii.

42. Adams coined the name from the Greek word νουθετέω (*noutheteō*), a word which occurs only about a dozen times in the New Testament, and which means "to put in mind; to admonish, warn" (Moulton, *Analytical Greek lexicon*, 279).

43. Adams, *Competent to counsel*, xxi.

is neither basic nor central. On the other hand . . . *parakaleo* and its cognate *paraklesis* make a much more adequate model of counseling from a biblical perspective. These words or concepts are more central biblically. Together they are translated in the King James Version 29 times as 'comfort,' 27 times as 'exhort,' 14 times as 'consolation,' and 43 times as 'beseech,' and infrequently as 'desire,' 'entreat,' and 'pray.' Furthermore, and perhaps of greater import, *paraklesis* is listed as a gift to the church (Romans 12:8) . . . The concept [of *paraklesis*, calling or coming beside] is broad enough to support a variety of therapeutic techniques from crisis intervention to depth therapy, and it is a gift given to the church which is clearly different than the gift of prophet or teacher. On the other hand, *nouthesia* represents a rather narrow range of functioning which Christians are to engage in but does not have the status of a gift to the church and does not have the centrality that Adams wants to give it.[44]

Thus, while premised on a reading of Scripture, Adams's *Christian Combatants* approach is not above theological critique.

The tradition of Jay Adams's nouthetic counseling has been sustained and modified by David Powlison and others through the National Association of Nouthetic Counselors and the books and journal articles generated by its devotees.[45] (Powlison has moderated some

of Adams's antagonism, as we will see in the next chapter.) Many conservative pastors share Adams's opposition to psychology. For instance, one pastor indicated that he became concerned that his own ministry had allowed psychology to seep into his preaching. While comparing a popular Christian self-help book to Calvin's *Institutes of the Christian Religion*, he concluded that he needed to repent of Christian Psychology.

> I have grown more certain of the evil of blending Christianity and psychology. Just as in Israel of old, men both 'feared the Lord and served their own gods according to the custom of the nations' (2 Ki. 17:33), so I believe many American Christians have fallen into a synchretistic blending of Christianity and worldly psychology. But the two do not mix.[46]

In his view, the use of psychology is essentially idolatrous. Because it has infected the church, we must repent of it and eradicate it wherever it is found in our churches.

Lay authors Martin and Deidra Bobgan have written numerous self-published books in which they attack psychology within the church. The Bobgans

---

44. Carter, Adams's theory, 152–53.

45. For a good introduction to current

thinking in Nouthetic Counseling, see Powlison, Biblical counseling view. Due to several changes, I have classified Powlison as following a *Colonialist* model (see chapter 10) rather than an *Enemies* model, although these changes do not appear to be consistent across all his writings, and less so among others in the "biblical counseling" camp.

46. Cole, How John Calvin led me to repent, 32.

coined the term "psychoheresy" to refer to any admixture of psychological theory and scriptural views. Their website, psychoheresy-aware.org/, features a logo of a snake with a ψ as its head (representing psychology) twisted around an open Bible. They have published diatribes against integrative efforts in general,[47] as well as against James Dobson,[48] Larry Crabb,[49] 12-Step programs,[50] and others.

By far the most influential and recent popularizer of the *Christian Combatants* movement is John MacArthur. MacArthur is the pastor of a non-denominational church in Southern California, which was once ranked in the top 70 largest churches in the United States. He hosts "Grace to You," a radio ministry that broadcasts his sermons up to a thousand times per day in English and 900 times in Spanish per day in twenty-three countries. He has published over 400 study guides and books.[51] MacArthur's influence among some conservative Christians is far-reaching and significant.

MacArthur is a fierce defender of what he sees as Christian orthodoxy, and he has taken aim against the charismatic movement, Roman Catholicism,[52] egal-itarian gender roles in church leadership, as well as secular forces that he sees as dangerous to the church, including psychology. In his view, psychology is dangerously subversive to true Christian faith. Consider the following quotation: "The rush to embrace psychology within the Church is frankly mystifying. Psychology and Christianity have been enemies from the beginning."[53] Note that MacArthur began with a presupposition—a statement that is presumed to be true, but for which no evidence is offered.[54] Even if his contention were historically true, it would not logically follow that psychology and theology are *necessarily* enemies. Absent in his reasoning is the possibility that a Christian worldview could ever allow for, or even offer a corrective to, psychology as a science or psychotherapy as a discipline.

Another of MacArthur's presuppositions mirrors Adams's contention that the care of the soul belongs solely to the church, and that psychology is a mere trespasser in its territory.

> The word psychology is a good one. Literally it means "the study of the soul." As such it originally carried a connotation that has distinctly Christian implications, for only some-

47. Bobgan & Bobgan, *Psychoheresy*.

48. Bobgan & Bobgan, *James Dobson's gospel*.

49. Bobgan & Bobgan, *Larry Crabb's gospel*.

50. Bobgan & Bobgan, *12 steps to destruction*.

51. https://www.masters.edu/president, March 5, 2015.

52. "The fact is, the most formidable, relentless, and deceptive enemy in Satan's long war on the truth has been Roman Catholicism. It's an apostate, corrupt, heretical, false Christianity—a thinly veiled façade for the kingdom of Satan" http://www.gty.org/blog/B130221.

53. MacArthur et al., *Introduction to biblical counseling*, xiii.

54. Also note that MacArthur's statement is aimed at the counseling portion of psychology, but his wording is leveled against the entire field of psychology.

one who has been made complete in Christ is properly equipped to study the human soul. But psychology cannot really study the soul; it is limited to studying human behavior. There is certainly value in that, but a clear distinction must be made between the contribution behavioral studies make to the educational, industrial, and physical needs of a society and their ability to meet the spiritual needs of people. Outside the Word and the Spirit there are no solutions to any of the problems of the human soul.[55]

MacArthur's proposition regarding the definition of psychology is both simplistic and etymologically and historically inaccurate.[56] Given his view, MacArthur proceeded to offer a dualistic proposition that psychology can only be done by Christians and that specifically Christian resources are sufficient to do such work. "True soul-study cannot be done by unbelievers. After all, only Christians have the resources for comprehending the nature of the human soul and understanding how it can be transformed."[57] "It is inane and dangerous to believe that any problem is beyond

the scope of Scripture or unmet by our spiritual riches in Christ."[58]

Similarly, in the preface to *Introduction to Biblical Counseling*, MacArthur and Mack identified their presuppositional commitments, including the conviction that "God's Word should be our counseling authority."[59] Mack makes this point even more explicitly in another book in which he makes the following claim: "Secular psychology has nothing to offer for understanding or providing solutions to the non-physical problems of people. When it comes to counseling people, we have no reason to depend on the insights of fallen men."[60]

This perspective is problematic at three points. First, it presumes that the effects of the Fall are so drastic that non-Christians cannot have any insight into the problems or solutions of human suffering. Secondly, it assumes that the Christian resources *sufficient for faith and practice* include all that is *necessary for psychological well-being*, and for which Scripture functions as a counseling authority. Thirdly, it engages in theological reductionism by viewing the psyche primarily as immaterial ("soul").

MacArthur's contention that Christian faith is sufficient for psychological well-being is premised on the belief that "Scripture itself claims to be a sufficient resource for meeting emotional and spiritual needs" and that "those who are saying

---

55. MacArthur, *Our sufficiency in Christ*, 30. Also note the errant reasoning that the word held "distinctly Christian implications." The etymology of the word does not trace its roots to Christianity (although Scripture uses the word ψυχή, *psychē*) but to Greek language and philosophy.

56. For a more complete history of the term, see Vande Kemp, *The tension between psychology and theology*, 105–12.

57. MacArthur, et al., *Introduction to biblical counseling*, 8.

58. MacArthur, *Our sufficiency in Christ.*, 31.

59. MacArthur et al., *Introduction to biblical counseilng*, ix.

60. Mack, What is biblical counseling? 53.

it is not are in serious error."[61] While MacArthur provides numerous Scripture citations, none of them actually make the claim that Scripture is a sufficient resource for meeting all of our emotional and psychological needs. An examination of two texts cited by MacArthur is instructive. First, a common element in MacArthur's approach is to cite a portion of Scripture, out of context, and to read into it broader implications than the context allows. Examples of this can be seen in the three times that he cited 2 Corinthians 12:9 in *Our Sufficiency in Christ*. The first time he simply wrote, "His grace is sufficient for every situation (2 Cor. 12:9)."[62] Two pages later he wrote, "'My grace is sufficient for you,' the Lord said to the apostle Paul (2 Cor 12:9)," following which MacArthur chastised people for turning away from God's resources and toward "hollow human teachings."[63] Finally, he quoted the verse in its entirety on the facing page of a chapter.[64] On three other occasions MacArthur elaborated on the verse in context, in which Paul related that *God's grace was sufficient when He chose not to remove Paul's thorn in the flesh*. When put in context, MacArthur largely limited his claims to those that fit the text (e.g., the need for humility and dependence on God, recognizing that God does not always choose to remove suffering but is present and sufficient in our suffering, the need for

contentment, recognition of God's power, etc).[65] Yet elsewhere, he construed the verse in terms that do not fit the context.

Does MacArthur's interpretation of the passages noted here reflect careful use of sound hermeneutics? Why or why not? To what degree are his conclusions the result of his assumptions? Where did these assumptions come from?

As a second example, MacArthur recounted 2 Corinthians 9:8–11, used as a proof-text, which he abbreviated as follows: "God is able to make *all* grace *abound* to you, that *always* having *all* sufficiency in *everything*, you may have an *abundance* for *every* good deed . . . You will be enriched in *everything* for *all* liberality, which through us is producing thanksgiving to God."[66] The meaning of the passage is skewed by the adjectives that MacArthur chose to italicize, and by the material deleted within the ellipses. While the larger passage emphasizes the *purpose and context* of God's sufficiency, MacArthur's emphasis forced it to be incorrectly read as a *scope* of sufficiency *that does not fit the text*. If we look at the context, it is clear that Paul was concerned with encouraging the Corinthian churches to be generous in their *financial*

---

61. MacArthur, Preaching in biblical counseling, 324.

62. MacArthur, *Our sufficiency in Christ*, 18.

63. Ibid., 20.

64. Ibid., 240.

65. See especially ibid., 245–52.

66. Ibid., 244. MacArthur failed to mention the version of the Bible translation used in this passage. Italics are as per MacArthur's rendering.

giving, and his message essentially served as a reminder that their giving to support his ministry was *in response to God's provision* for them. Furthermore, the point of the passage does not revolve around *emotional sufficiency*; rather, it builds to a crescendo in proclaiming that we are given sufficiency to accomplish *good deeds* that culminate in *thanksgiving*. Read in context, Paul simply could not have had in mind the implications that MacArthur forced upon the text. In their extensive critique of MacArthur's view, de Oliveira and Braun concluded that the "rejection of psychology on the grounds of biblical sufficiency reflects poor exegesis, theology, and logic."[67]

Similarly, MacArthur's assumption that Scripture can effectively function as a counseling text is premised on an unorthodox understanding of the sufficiency of Scripture in matters of faith and practice. The term "faith and practice" is not itself a biblical one, but it is a concept that is biblical. "All Scripture is God-breathed and is useful for teaching, rebuking, correcting and training in righteousness, so that the man of God may be thoroughly equipped for every good work" (2 Tim 3:16–17, NIV). The concept is that all Scripture is inspired and useful in all areas of Christian faith (doctrine) and practice (comportment). "Paul never prohibits, or calls others to forsake, good resources on the flowed grounds that the Scripture *alone* is

sufficient."[68] An orthodox understanding does not twist this to mean that Scripture provides all of the answers for every life problem, whether it is medical, psychological, or vocational.

While MacArthur allowed for the use of "the scientific disciplines" and medicine, he characterized psychological needs as spiritual needs: "Every so-called psychological need that is not traceable to physical causes is, in reality, a spiritual problem, and Scripture does indeed claim to be the only sufficient guide in handling spiritual problems."[69] This view is evidently rooted in a dichotomous view of human nature, in which "people are composed of two distinct elements, body and soul," such that all nonphysical problems are viewed as spiritual problems.[70]

In MacArthur's view, since all nonphysical problems are understood as spiritual problems, God's sufficiency must be understood as meeting a spiritual need. MacArthur taught that God is sufficient not by giving us what we want, but "by supplying sufficient grace" for us to endure our situation.[71] Thus the

---

67. De Oliveira & Braun, "Jesus didn't need a shrink," 20.

68. Ibid., 15.

69. MacArthur et al., *An introduction to biblical counseling*, 368.

70. Sarles, Frequently asked questions about biblical counseling, 376.

71. MacArthur, *Our sufficiency in Christ*, 249. I heartily agree with MacArthur that it would be an error to suggest to people "that Scripture offers no answers to the issues that trouble them" (MacArthur, Preaching in biblical counseling, 323). I would also agree with him that it is tragic when pastors begin to preach

psychological attempt to relieve suffering is viewed as a threat to the process of sanctification. In this vein, MacArthur construed psychology as a pseudo-science and a rival gospel; in fact, he identified psychology as one of "three deadly influences that undermine . . . spiritual life," which together he perceived as constituting "neo-gnosticism's attack on the contemporary church."[72] Yet, even if his handling of the previously cited texts is accepted, they cannot mean that we are prohibited from making efforts to alter our situation in accord with the abilities, civil rights, and tools available to us, *provided that they are exercised in a manner consistent with Christian faith and practice.* For instance, it would clearly be absurd to say, "I will not buy, make, or eat food, because God's grace is sufficient for me." Likewise, only strained reasoning could lead a person who is severely depressed due to the effects of abuse, the severing of a relationship, or biological factors to say, "I will not seek the counsel or medical intervention available to me because God's grace is sufficient for me." In fact, it may well be that God grants human companionship and the insights

garnered from observation of His World, along with the truths of His Word, as means through which He demonstrates and provides His grace and sufficiency.

Regarding the proposition that MacArthur engaged in theological reductionism, it is notable that he did not portray the psyche in holistic terms that could be seen as biological, psychodynamic, or social. He primarily perceives a *soul* that must be sanctified by *moral obedience.* While moral obedience is crucial for spiritual health, and while sinful behavior certainly bodes ill for psychological functioning, it is erroneous and injurious to see morality as the only determinant of psychological health.[73] Psychological health and spiritual health may be related, but they are not identical. Furthermore, MacArthur's reductionism tends not only to neglect the biological, psychodynamic, and social sources of distress, but it puts the onus of responsibility for personal well-being solely on personal righteousness, while failing to recognize the importance of corporate sin, the effects of being sinned against, or the effects of living in a fallen world.[74]

---

psychotherapy instead of the Bible. However, neither of these propositions necessarily provokes conflict between the truths of Scripture and insights from extrabiblical sources.

72. The first quotation is taken from the subtitle of *Our sufficiency in Christ.* The second is taken from the subheading (on page 29) of the same book's first chapter, Resurrecting an old heresy. The other two "deadly influences" grouped with psychology by MacArthur are pragmatism and mysticism.

73. Immoral behavior can at least temporarily lead to exhilaration, and moral behavior can lead to despondency. As the wise man of Ecclesiastes reminds us, "The heart of the wise is in the house of mourning, but the heart of fools is in the house of pleasure" (Eccl 7:4, NIV). For an interesting discussion of this phenomena applied to self-serving bias, see Moroney, Thinking of ourselves.

74. A tragic consequence of this emphasis is that it easily lends itself to a theology of legalism and works rather than a theology of grace.

Nally vs. Grace Community Church

MacArthur and his Southern California congregation of nearly 20,000 attendees, Grace Community Church (GCC), were drawn into the national spotlight in a lengthy court case. Sadly, a young man named Kenneth Nally, who had received "biblical counseling" from several church pastors committed suicide. Nally had also seen medical doctors and mental health professionals in the weeks prior to his suicide. He was hospitalized following a failed suicide attempt less than a month before he committed suicide. Kenneth's father, Walter Nally, tried to understand what drove his son to suicide and became convinced that "the church and its pastoral counselors . . . [and] John MacArthur in particular" were responsible for his son's suicide.[75] The family initiated a landmark case against GCC and four of its pastors for clergy malpractice.

An important subtext to the case was the conflict between fundamentalism and Catholicism. Ken's mother, Maria, had once attended church with him at GCC where a hostess asked her if she was a Christian. Maria said, "Yes, I am Catholic." The hostess "quickly told her that she was not a Christian, that as a Catholic she had not been born again, and that until she was born again, she was destined to go to hell."[76] Differences in teaching were also central areas of conflict. Traditionally, Catholicism taught that suicide was a mortal sin, a view which Grace's pastors

did not share, and which they discussed with Kenneth Nally.

The case went to trial a year after Nally's death, and stretched on for nearly nine years through the appeals process. MacArthur framed the relevant legal issues as follows:

> In 1980, Grace Community Church was hit with a lawsuit charging that the pastors on our staff were negligent because we tried to help a suicidal young member of our church by giving him biblical truth . . . One of the key issues raised was the question of whether churches should have the legal right to counsel troubled people with the Bible . . . Not only did the courts view the issue as a First Amendment right of religious freedom into which government should not intrude, but all three times we won the case, the judges also expressed the opinion that the church had not failed in its responsibility to give him proper care.[77]

Suicide is devastating to family members, friends, and to those who are involved in trying to treat emotional disorders. Mental health professionals are all too familiar with the grief and anguish of suicide. One assumes that MacArthur and his colleagues endured similar loss and anguish. The court case that ensued following Nally's suicide was momentous in its personal dimensions for the appellants (Nally's parents) and for the defendants.

---

75. Weitz, *Clergy malpractice*, 5.

76. Ibid., 19.

77. MacArthur, *Our sufficiency in Christ*, 55–56.

For the plaintiffs, the issue was not whether the church was negligent because it "tried to help" a man by "giving him biblical truth." The wrongful death lawsuit alleged that GCC and its pastors were implicated in Kenneth Nally's suicide on three grounds: clergy malpractice, negligence, and outrageous conduct.[78] The plaintiffs asserted that the church was negligent in several ways including discouraging Nally from receiving psychological or psychiatric care, failing to meet a standard of care for pastoral care, failure to obtain adequate psychological training, and infliction of emotional distress.[79] The defense lawyers retained by GCC filed eight defenses including First Amendment issues, among others.[80]

The negligence issues were raised in part because one of Grace Community Church's pastors told Nally "he would still be accepted into heaven" if he committed suicide.[81] Three weeks before he completed suicide with a firearm, Nally had made a previous suicide attempt by overdose. According to evidence presented in the trial: "On the afternoon of March 12, Pastors MacArthur and Rea visited Nally at the hospital. Nally, who was still drowsy from the drug overdose, separately told both pastors that he was sorry he did not succeed in commit-

ting suicide. Apparently, MacArthur and Rea assumed the entire hospital staff was aware of Nally's unstable mental condition, and they did not discuss Nally's death-wish comment with anyone else."[82]

Following the suicide attempt, Nally's arm was paralyzed, evidently because he had lain on it for an extended time while unconscious from his overdose. "The pastors told him that this was a sign that God was punishing him."[83] Following his release from the hospital, Nally moved into MacArthur's home and was encouraged to see a medical doctor from the church and to keep an appointment the hospital had scheduled for an outpatient psychiatric evaluation. Nally later moved home when the MacArthurs left for a planned trip to Scotland. He committed suicide by a self-inflicted shotgun blast to the head a few days later.

Nally's parents, who brought the suit, "introduced evidence from an expert witness that the defendants increased Nally's despair and anguish" and that "the attitude and naïveté of the members of GCC toward someone as severely disturbed as Nally was incomprehensible."[84] Testimony provided by a GCC pastoral counselor affirmed that GCC's counselors: "treated all kinds of emotional problems, from severe depression, alcoholism, and sexual problems to phobias and schizophrenia. Sin lay at the root of these problems and each

---

78. Weitz, *Clergy malpractice*, 58.

79. Bullis & Mazur, *Legal issues and religious counseling*.

80. Weitz, *Clergy malpractice*, 66.

81. Bullis & Mazur, *Legal issues and religious counseling*, 25.

---

82. 47 Cal.3d 279, Opinion II-B.

83. Ibid., 26.

84. Ibid.

had a corresponding biblical answer."[85] Throughout the case, GCC and its pastors remained adamant in their testimony that Kenneth Nally had been given competent, biblical counsel.

The Nally case is extremely complicated. It began with the Nallys filing a one-million-dollar negligence and clergy malpractice suit against GCC and four of its pastors in 1980. It was dismissed for insufficient evidence in 1981. In 1984 the California Second District Court of Appeals overturned the dismissal, sending it back to trial. After four weeks of plaintiff arguments in 1985, the trial judge dismissed the case when the defense requested a motion of nonsuit before the defense began its arguments. In 1987 the California Second District Court of Appeals again reversed the trial judge's ruling. Before it could return to trial, the California Supreme Court agreed to hear the case in 1988.[86]

The California Supreme Court (referred to as "Nally III" because it was the third court to review the case) dismissed the case against Grace Community Church. It avoided the First Amendment issue altogether, instead arguing that the case did not meet the legal requirements for malpractice. The majority opinion concluded that "plaintiffs have not met the threshold requirements for imposing on defendants a duty to prevent suicide . . . Plaintiffs failed to persuade us that the duty to prevent suicide . . . should be extended to a nontherapist counselor who offers counseling to a potentially suicidal person on secular or spiritual matters."[87]

A successful lawsuit against GCC and its pastors would have required the plaintiffs to demonstrate that the defendants had a special relationship with Nally, that they had a duty to Nally that met a standard of care, that they breached this duty, and that the breach of this duty caused harm to Nally. The court ruled that the plaintiffs had not proved that all of these requirements were met, so the case could not proceed. Nearly ten years after the death of Kenneth Nally, the case against Grace Community Church ended when the United States Supreme Court declined to take it up on appeal.

In 2005, twenty-five years after Nally's suicide, and fifteen years after the case against the church was dismissed, MacArthur was interviewed regarding the tragic events of the case. MacArthur affirmed that "sin is the reason anything goes wrong" and denied that he had any regrets about the way the church approached Nally.

> Interviewer: "Do you think the counseling he received was appropriate and good?"
>
> MacArthur: "Yes, I think it was exactly the kind of counseling we always do. We've done it with thousands upon thousands of people."
>
> Interviewer: "But what if a person is mentally ill?"

---

85. Weitz, *Clergy malpractice*, 122.

86. Ibid., 213–14.

87. *Walter J. Nally et al. v. Grace Community Church of the Valley et al.*

MacArthur: "We simply approach the issues spiritually. We don't refer them to psychologists or psychiatrists or whatever. We don't attempt to deal with them in those terms. The only real transforming, life-changing guidance is that which God provides through His Word to his people. Anything else is going to be the wisdom of man, not the wisdom of God."[88]

MacArthur's comments suggest that he is convinced that "mental illness"—unless it has a physical cause—is ultimately and exclusively a spiritual issue.

For MacArthur, the lawsuit likely solidified his antagonism toward positive engagement between Christianity and psychology. In his words:

Unfortunately, the privilege of counseling people with biblical truth may be in jeopardy anyway—not because of any legal barrier imposed from outside the church, but because of the attitude toward Scripture within the church. During the trial, a number of "experts" were called to give testimony. Most surprising to me were the so-called Christian psychologists and psychiatrists who testified that the Bible alone does not contain sufficient help to meet people's deepest personal and emotional needs. These men were actually arguing before a secular court that God's Word is not an adequate resource for counseling people about their spiritual problems![89]

The Master's College & Seminary

MacArthur is the president of The Master's College and Seminary (its motto is, "For Christ and Scripture"). The college, needless to say, does not offer an undergraduate psychology degree. Among other degrees, it offers undergraduate and master's degrees in "biblical counseling." According the school's website: "This emphasis consists of a study of the principles and aspects of biblical counseling, and is designed to prepare God's people to meet counseling related needs wherever they exist with the sufficient and superior resources God provides. The course of study trains students to counsel people in the local church. It emphasizes the proper interpretation and specific application of Scripture in ministering to people."[90] From his pulpit, in his books, and through The Master's College and Seminary, MacArthur's views influence hundreds of people who assume the title "biblical counselor" and thousands of people who sit in their pews or seek their counsel.

John Street is one of MacArthur's followers, and a professor at The Master's College and Seminary. Street rejects psychology as a discipline on several grounds. First, he claims that psychology and Christianity hold rival worldviews. "The historical distrust and innate hostility between psychology and theology exist because each calls

---

88. Public Broadcasting Service. *Christian counseling.*

89. MacArthur, *Our sufficiency in Christ*, 57.

90. The Master's College, *Biblical studies*, n.p.

into question the legitimacy of the other's Weltanschauung."[91] Street asserted that psychology's foundations (which he identifies with modernism, materialism, and evolutionism) are incompatible with Christianity. Street is correct to point out the enormous influence exerted by worldview assumptions. However, it is simply untrue that all psychologists accept each of the foundations that he claims are essential to psychology. He ultimately fails to see any way that Christianity could constructively engage psychology or profit from its resources. Street fails to recognize that Christians who promote integration are cognizant of the worldview concerns that he raises. He belittles the assumption on which integration (and in fact, the entire Christian liberal arts approach) is grounded. "While it is certainly true that 'all truth is God's truth,' it is equally true that 'all error is the devil's error.' The truism that 'all truth is God's truth' reduces their arguments to *reductio ad absurdum* and begs the question when used simplistically by integrationists."[92] The *Christian Combatants* approach is thus opposed not only to "secular psychology," but to any attempt by Christians to productively engage the academic discipline of psychology.

While Street is suspicious of psychology as a discipline, his more serious concern is with counseling based on "secular psychology." Echoing Adams and MacArthur, Street claims that, "psychology trespasses and seeks to

usurp spiritual authority. Only the Word of God can effectively instruct believers how to glorify Him."[93] As a result, "using psychology for soul-care is like treating cancer with aspirin. It may temporarily relieve the pain or even mask the symptoms, but it will never penetrate the issues of the heart like God's Word."[94]

It should be evident that the *Christian Combatants* typically see only spiritual and physical causes of what others would call psychological problems. Sanctification is their goal, and evidently in their view, with sanctification comes complete emotional, psychological, and interpersonal health. So the cure for emotional distress in this view is limited to medicine and repentance.

In what can only be described as ironic but strangely consistent, MacArthur and his colleagues have been attacked by Martin and Deidre Bobgan as having compromised the Bible in the pursuit of "Biblical Counseling."[95] The

---

91. Street, Why biblical counseling and not psychology?, 204.

92. Ibid., 216.

93. Ibid., 219.

94. Ibid., 217.

95. It is ironic in that one member of the *against* camp condemned another of its members for not being sufficiently *against*. It is consistent inasmuch as the biblical-counseling view utilized a framework for "an organized method of gaining information" from counselees, that includes items that would be a standard part of any psychological interview, including information about sleep, diet, exercise, physical illnesses, medications, affect, history, etc., and methods for developing a counseling relationship, instilling hope, etc. that are broadly "psychological." The Bobgans see the adoption of such methods as "psychological" heresy because those methods are not, strictly speaking, "biblical." [The quotation in this footnote is from Mack, Taking

Bobgans' *PsychoHeresy Newsletter* proclaimed that some of the material in *Introduction to Biblical Psychology* "reeks of the psychological way."[96] They further warned against the efforts of the National Association of Nouthetic Counselors, the conservative Christian Counseling and Education Foundation, and the Biblical Counseling major at MacArthur's Master's College. Of the latter, they said, "We hope that MacArthur will realize how unbiblical it is and call a halt to it."[97]

Adams, MacArthur, and the Bobgans represent a small sampling of the *Christian Combatants* version of the *Enemies* model. While one may disagree with their conclusions, we must recognize that their views are partly based on honest intellectual differences founded upon differing presuppositions. Furthermore, it is undeniable that psychology has had a hand in creating these animosities, both by isolated attacks on religious belief and through the promulgation of specific techniques and positions that are an affront to Christian conscience. Additionally we must admit that the modern era has created a turf war in which care of the psyche has become partly decentralized from the church and increasingly fragmented, with pastors caring for "souls" and psychologists dealing with "psyches," and with neither typically dealing with the holistic unity that is the human person.

It is also worth noting that the motivations behind the *Enemies* model within the church stem from the historical opposition of the conservative branch of the Church to modernism, liberalism, and neo-orthodoxy and the Church's current preoccupation with "culture wars." In these contexts the adherents of the *Christian Combatants* version of the *Enemies* model see themselves as defenders of the faith, an assertion that is not wholly without merit. It is worth considering, though, if part of the problem may stem from what Mark Noll identified as *the scandal of the evangelical mind*, that is, that evangelical culture is one of "intense, detailed, and precise efforts . . . to understand the Bible. But it is not a culture where the same effort has been expended to understand the world or, even more important, the processes by which wisdom from Scripture should be brought into relation with knowledge about the world."[98] The failure to create a truly Christian worldview in which all of life is sacramental, from the arts and sciences to politics and prayer, has left us with a situation in which Christians too easily polarize themselves against the world rather than engaging it in a constructive and uniquely Christian fashion.

For whatever reasons, the fact is that the *Christian Combatants* view is alive and influential. While one might reject this model because of its progenitors' "lack of understanding of psychology, their unique or limited Christian world

counselee inventory, 210.]

96. PsychoHeresy Newsletter. Dr. John MacArthur, Jr., and biblical counseling. n.p.

97. Ibid.

98. Noll, *The scandal of the evangelical mind*, 14–45.

views, their inadequate biblical hermeneutics, their logic, or their factual distortions, the fact remains that they do
continue to influence the thinking of a
significant portion of the more conservative wing of the Church."[99] We must understand and interact with this position
because of its effects on people who seek
help and healing from psychologists and
religious counselors.

Looking Back: *What are some
of the reasons that some Christians might see psychology as
an enemy of Christianity?*

Summary

The *Enemies* model describes two versions of an antagonistic relationship between psychology and Christianity: the
polar opposites of the *Secular Combatants* and the *Christian Combatants*. Adherents of these models reject or neglect
one of the two books of God: His Word
or His Works. They utilize a process of
rejecting the entire discipline of the opposing camp, and of rooting out any of
its practices that may have seeped into
their own camp. These are nonintegrative
models in which "acceptable data are believed to come from only one discipline,"
resulting in the inevitable outcome that
"each discipline must reject the other as a
source of truth."[100] Even given this mutual antagonism, it is worth reminding our-

selves that those with whom we disagree
often have things to teach us. In the
words of the seventeenth-century English poet Joseph Addison, "A man must
be both stupid and uncharitable who believes there is no virtue or truth but on
his own side." Thus, whether or not one
chooses to adopt either of the *Enemies*
positions, it is important to ask ourselves
what is to be learned and appreciated
from them. However, these are not the
only models for our consideration, as we
will see in the following chapters.

Questions for Reflection and Discussion

1. Since models of integration are *models
   of models*, one must first understand
   a theorist's models of Christianity
   and psychology before one can understand his or her model of their
   relationship. Compare the model of
   psychology offered by theorists who
   adopt a *Secular Combatants* version
   of the *Enemies* model to the model of
   psychology offered by theorists who
   adopt a *Christian Combatants* version of the *Enemies* model. Compare
   the model of religion offered by theorists who adopt a *Secular Combatants*
   version of the *Enemies* model to the
   model of theology offered by theorists
   who adopt a *Christian Combatants*
   version of the *Enemies* model.

2. In what ways do the presuppositions
   of Albert Ellis and Jay Adams lead
   them to ask different questions? How

---

99. Narramore, Barriers to the integration of
faith and learning, 119.

100. Eck, Integrating the integrators, 103.

do the questions they ask end up promoting antagonistic answers?

3. Summarize the argument of the *Secular Combatants* version of the *Enemies* model. Other than presuppositional concerns, what factors might encourage a secular psychologist to be opposed to religion?

4. Given what you know about Abraham Maslow's theories (e.g., the hierarchy of needs), how did you react to his views toward religion? Does his deception in intentionally hiding his views make you wary of anything in his views?

5. Summarize the argument of the *Christian Combatants* version of the *Enemies* model. Other than presuppositional concerns, what factors might encourage a committed Christian to be opposed to psychology?

6. As you reflect on the Nally case, what concerns do you have about its potential implications for freedom of religion? Do you think that there should be a legal standard to evaluate the competence of pastoral counseling? Why or why not?

7. In your education and your personal experiences, how have you encountered the different versions of the *Enemies* model?

8. The author ended the chapter by noting that "those with whom we disagree often have things to teach us" and issued a challenge to "ask ourselves what is to be learned and appreciated from" those with whom we disagree. Identify at least three things that you appreciate or can learn from those who adopt the *Secular Combatants* version of the *Enemies* model. Identify at least three things that you appreciate or can learn from those who adopt the *Christian Combatants* version of the *Enemies* model.

9. After reading this chapter, what concerns, if any, do you have about the influence of secular assumptions on the field of psychology? What concerns, if any, do you have about the claims and counsel of the biblical counseling movement?

10. The author separated the wholesale opposition of the *Enemies* model from the process of rejection that it utilizes. Do you think that the process of rejection can have a necessary or beneficial purpose if it is used reflectively and selectively rather than reflexively and indiscriminately?

10

Intermediate Models of Disciplinary Relationship: Spies, Colonialists, Rebuilders, and Neutral Parties

The problem to be faced is: how to combine loyalty to one's own tradition with reverence for different traditions.

—Abraham Heschel

One of my favorite pastimes is traveling. My travels have allowed me to sample exotic food, ranging from hippo stew in Africa (it tasted just like beef and was quite good) to frog legs in Florida (it did not taste like chicken and I will never try it again!). I have seen huge variations in architecture, from mud huts, to castles, to communist block-style apartments, to cities obliterated by war, to quaint European towns with centuries-old buildings. What intrigues me most in my travels, though, is the people. All over the world, despite our differences, we share the same struggles: finding love, making a living, raising children, failing to live up to the moral standards we believe in, and so forth.

On one excursion, I visited Germany during the Cold War. Germany had been partitioned into two separate countries following World War II. East Germany was controlled by the USSR, and West Germany was mostly sovereign but

with American, British, and French influence. Berlin, the historic capital of Germany, sat in the middle of East Germany, divided into four sectors—American, British, French and Russian. For fifteen years following the war, East and West Berlin were in a state of relative neutrality. Every day, half a million people traveled between the different sections of the city, relatively unimpeded. Over two and a half million Germans fled from East to West in the fifteen years following World War II. The Russians, fearing defections to the West, closed the border. With no announcement, the border between East and West Berlin was sealed on August 15, 1961. All of the streets between East and West Berlin were closed, except for a few checkpoints. The Berlin Wall, separating East from West, was erected overnight, first as a heavily guarded perimeter with barbed wire, and later with concrete slabs. West Berlin—which was in East

Germany—was completely cut off from the rest of the world.

When I visited Berlin, the differences between East and West were astounding. West Berlin was a modern city with steel and glass buildings. East Berlin was full of concrete structures—square, functional, drab. To pass from one side to the other we went through Checkpoint Charlie. On the West side, soldiers looked at our documents, smiled, and waved us through. Walking through the narrow passageway along Friedrichstrasse, we passed through an opening in the concrete wall. Barbed wire, guard dogs, and armed soldiers patrolled the Eastern side. Somber officials in drab uniforms carefully examined our documents and stamped our passports, while soldiers in the street put mirrors under the buses and cars, especially those leaving East Berlin. Supposedly, they were looking for spies, trying to keep the West Germans from infiltrating the East. But the real story was that they were trying to prevent East German escapes. People tried climbing or flying over the wall, digging tunnels beneath the wall, or being smuggled in hollow spaces hidden in cars whose gas tanks had been removed. One hundred and seventy-one people died attempting to escape, and countless others were arrested and imprisoned.

The German experience following World War II illustrates several themes that are relevant to our present concerns. Different kinds of relationship can be posited between psychology and Christianity, and the nature of that relationship can change over time. While it would be convenient to have models that contain only two extremes—*Allies* and *Enemies*—it would also be misleading; there are a number of ways of thinking and behaving that fall between these two outermost categories. Intermediate models recognize that there is something valuable in both psychology and theology (or religion), but they fail to discern any fundamental unifying structure that is common to both disciplines. I have identified four intermediate models. There are *Spies* who scope out the territory of the other camp, but who rarely engage in overt hostilities. There are *Colonialists* who try to claim foreign land under their flag. There are *Rebuilders*, who believe that the psychological landscape needs to be rebuilt on specifically Christian foundations. And there are *Neutral Parties* who are content to live in peace with each other, perhaps even exchanging emissaries, so long as their own sovereignty is respected. In the following sections we will examine these three models in greater detail.

Espionage: The *Spies* Model

Let the king who sees everything through his spies discover the two sorts of thieves who deprive others of their property, both those who show themselves openly and those who lie concealed.

–Guru Nanak

One of the staples of popular literature and movies is the spy story. In one variation of the genre, the spy is a good guy who is doing his job—engaging in espionage—for a greater good. In another variation of the genre, the bad guy steals secrets from the good guy. In either case, the spy is committed to one cause while trying to obtain something from another organization.[1]

A sort of espionage occurs when psychologists become interested in appropriating the benefits of religious belief and practice for psychological well-being. Imagine that someone in a white lab coat showed up in your place of worship one Sunday. She asked you to talk about your beliefs, she observed your behavior, and she assessed your physical and mental health. When you ask her what this is all about, she informs you that she is interested in studying connections between religion and health. When you ask about her own religious beliefs, she informs you that she is just there as an observer. She does not intend any harm toward you; she just wants to enter your world to see if it has anything useful or interesting to her as a researcher. In a sense, she is functioning as a *foreign spy*. *Foreign spies* are not committed to a religious system, but

they want to understand it so they can make use of its resources. For instance, a psychologist might encourage a client to pray, knowing that prayer has psychological benefits, even if he or she does not share the client's religious beliefs.

Imagine another person who joins a church or synagogue. Over time, she becomes part of the congregation. People care about her, and she finds that her affiliation brings her meaning and happiness. She gets to know one of the leaders of the congregation, and one day she asks him why he decided to take on a ministerial role. "It's a great way to help people," he says. As she continues to talk to him, she learns that he sees the role of the clergy as helping people to find comfort, peace, and fulfillment. In a sense, the religious leader is a *domestic spy*. When espionage is an inside job, individuals are primarily interested in the psychological benefits of their own religious system. They are *domestic spies* who participate in a religious community, but they have a greater commitment to the psychological benefits of the religious system than to its core theological positions. This approach was common among theological liberals, who saw the specific content of religion as largely mythic, but as useful for illustrating things about human nature and human needs. More recently, conservative versions of this model have emerged among televangelists and "prosperity gospel" adherents who may acknowledge core Christian doctrines, but their primary emphasis is on personal well-being.

---

1. Spies are not always enemies; "friendly" nations spy on each other, as do rival nations. The goals, however, are different. The former seeks to steal secrets that may be of benefit to his or her nation, but with no malice intended toward the nation from whom those secrets are stolen; the latter engages in espionage with the intention of undermining its rival. For those who hold the latter view, elements of the *Enemies* model can be seen, but there is the added notion that they see value in religious concerns and admit that religion can have psychological benefits.

"Everybody does it. . . . Espionage is part of our lives. . . . Let us assume someone is listening—with purely professional intentions—in order to know, what is being said. For that is the essence of espionage: Gathering information. . . ."

—Helmut Müller-Enbergs

How can spying (gathering information) be a good thing?

The foreign spy and the domestic spy both compromise the integrity of the religious system, and its psychological content is appropriated for purposes that are not directly related to the core of the theological system. In the *Spies* model, religion is construed as an expression of psychological forces and its beliefs and rituals are valued to the degree that they have psychological benefits.[2] Eck referred to such models as *reconstruction models*, and described them as follows: "Although there is a beginning acceptance that some admissible truth resides in both disciplines, the data of one discipline are reconstructed in such a way that the outcome is similar to the rejects models in that it yields only one acceptable body of knowledge."[3]

Both the foreign and domestic versions of the *Spies* model attempt "to find 'good' psychology in religion."[4] In the following two sections, we will explore the two variations on this theme: *psychologically committed espionage*, and *religiously committed espionage*.[5]

Foreign Spies: Psychologically Committed Espionage

Psychologically committed espionage occurs when a person who has a primary commitment to the field of psychology becomes interested in appropriating religious contributions to psychological or physical health. Religious systems inevitably either foster or inhibit psychological well-being, and the psychologist is understandably interested in this phenomenon. Likewise, a host of research demonstrates positive and negative associations between physical health and religious beliefs and practices. A psychologist or health professional need not be personally committed to a religious system to recognize its potential benefits. This approach emphasizes clinical pragmatism, a single-minded focus on things that should be recommended based on their pragmatic effects. Whether or not the psychologist or health professional

---

2. The reason this perspective is feasible is because religion makes use of psychological forces (e.g., the need to feel loved and forgiven) and carries out psychological functions (e.g., socialization). However, in this model, religion is *reduced to* those psychological forces and functions.

---

3. Eck, Integrating the integrators, 104.

4. Carter & Narramore, *The integration of psychology and theology*, 81.

5. These are essentially identical to Carter and Narramore's *secular and sacred of models*.

personally accepts or rejects the theological tenets of the religion is irrelevant to the therapeutic effects of the religious system.

Carter and Narramore described this approach as one in which the religious content and supernatural claims of religion are dismissed. Instead, the model emphasizes the psychological content of religious narratives and teachings, so that religion "becomes a vehicle for the expression of psychological truth."[6] Carter and Narramore identified Erich Fromm as an example of this view. Born and raised in an Orthodox Jewish family, Fromm studied sociology and became a psychoanalyst. As an adult, he professed no religious belief, but he believed that the *concerns* of religion are relevant. In his own words, Fromm wanted "to show . . . that it is not true that we have to give up the concern for the soul if we do not accept the tenets of religion."[7]

Carl Jung is another exemplar of this approach. While he saw religious belief as primitive and unscientific, he saw its symbols and meanings as having psychological value. We can easily discern Jung's disdain of the "trappings" of religion when he criticized the "medieval view" in which: "Men were all children of God under the loving care of the Most High, who prepared them for eternal blessedness; and all knew exactly what they should do and how they should conduct themselves in order to rise from a corruptible world to an incorruptible and joyous existence. Such a life no longer seems real to us, even in our dreams. Science has long ago torn this lovely veil to shreds."[8]

The denial that religious systems contain divine revelation did not prevent Jung from seeing them as bearers of truth. To be acceptable to the modern mind, however, Jung believed that useful content had to be severed from religious faith. His proposal for the reconstruction of religion runs along these lines: "Modern man abhors faith and the religions based upon it. He holds them valid only so far as their knowledge-content seems to accord with his own experience . . . [but he] is willing to make use of all the existing assumptions as a means to this end, including those of the recognized religions . . ."[9]

Jung was thus a *foreign spy* who engaged in *psychologically committed espionage*; he possessed no genuine interest in the veracity or survival of any given religion, but he wanted to preserve the psychological benefits that religion supplies.

Many other examples of spying out the psychological value of religious systems could be given, including Rollo May's rejection of religion, but his valuing of Jesus' teaching to "love your enemies."[10] Common to all such approaches is a desire to abstract from religion those teachings and concepts that have "psychological significance," but to

---

6. Carter & Narramore, *The integration of psychology and theology*, 82.

7. Quoted in ibid., 83.

8. Jung, Civilization in transition, 464.

9. Ibid., 468.

10. May, *Power and innocence*, 256–58.

leave behind the "religious baggage of primitive belief."

Domestic Spies: Religiously Committed Espionage

Espionage can also be an inside job, however; a *domestic spy* who steals from his or her employer clearly has divided loyalties. When *religiously committed espionage* takes place, it proceeds not from psychologists, but from religious congregants. This approach is sometimes adopted by people "from theologically liberal traditions that, like their secular counterparts, reject the supernatural elements of Christianity and take a strongly humanistic and/or naturalistic attitude toward religion."[11] This can be seen in popular books and religious broadcasts that peddle views that are light on religion and full of "pop psychology." They often promote positive thinking and feel-good theology. Norman Vincent Peale is an apt example of a simplistic version of the *religiously committed espionage* model. In the preface to *The Power of Positive Thinking*, Peale affirmed his religious commitment, claiming that his book was based on the teachings of Christ and of Christianity: "I need not point out that the powerful principles contained herein are not my invention but are given to us by the greatest Teacher who ever lived and who still lives. This book teaches applied Christianity; a simple yet scientific

system of practical techniques of successful living that works."[12]

Peale's conclusion is that "positive thinking" (which is evident in such things as choosing to be happy, expecting the best, and having faith) is taught by Christianity and contains good psychology. For example, he claimed that reading the New Testament and memorizing verses on faith would transform a person's mind. As a result, he claimed, "You will have new power to get what God and you decide you really want from life. The most powerful force in human nature is the spiritual-power technique taught in the Bible."[13] Notice that Peale's emphasis is devoid of any deep theological teaching or doctrine; it is not *Christianity as salvation from sin* so much as it is *Christianity as salvation from low self-esteem*. Likewise, the "scientific system" of Peale's psychology is largely devoid of science and of psychology as a discipline.

While the liberal version of this model traces its roots to the fundamentalist-modernist controversy, a conservative version of the model began to emerge with the advent of televangelism in the 1970s, and before that, in healing ministries that focused on temporal healing to the point that they neglected the core message of the gospel. Many televangelists focus their preaching on how God can help you unlock your potential, how He can help you become a happier, more confident person, and how you can find health and wealth by putting yourself

---

11. Carter & Narramore, *The integration of psychology and theology*, 85.

12. Peale, *The power of positive thinking*, ix.

13. Ibid., 109.

in the position to receive His blessings. There is a grain of truth here, but to make the grain the whole harvest is a mistake. Jesus did not die to make you and me happy and successful by earthly standards—He died to offer redemption to sinners.

Those who promote the gospel of health and wealth often have deeply flawed exegesis, not only of Scripture, but of the stories and research that they cite as well. For instance, the author of a popular religious self-help book tells a story about a man who froze to death while locked in a refrigerated boxcar, scrawling a note to his family that he was going to die of hypothermia, which he did. But the refrigeration unit wasn't on, and he "froze" to death on a night when the temperature never went below sixty-one degrees! The author used the story to support his claim that we get what we expect.[14] Does the story sound suspicious? It should. There is no documented evidence that it ever happened, and variations of the story are rampant on the Internet and easily debunked by checking out one of the urban legends websites. The same author's biblical exegesis is often just as lacking. For instance, he interprets Jesus' statement that no one puts new wine into old wineskins as meaning that we cannot experience our full potential unless we enlarge our vision and rid ourselves of negative thinking.

---

14. Osteen, *Your best life now*, 72–73. The story—complete with assurances of its truth, has also been told by John Hagee on *John Hagee Today.*

While *religiously committed espionage* is common among feel-good religious authors and televangelists, their teaching, at best, often represents superficial psychology and shallow theology. At first glance, they appear to be helpful and religious, but upon closer inspection, one is struck not only by the lack of sophistication and empirical verification on the psychological side, but also by the inadequacy of the theological conceptualizations and solutions offered in these populist approaches.

On a more sophisticated level, numerous liberal and neo-orthodox theologians adopt a similar approach. Abraham Maslow, who expressed his disdain for religion in his journals, was sought out by liberal pastors. His comments about this dynamic are informative:

> What functions are left for a minister or rabbi who has given up dogmas, churches, & supernaturals, but who is interested in the godlike within human nature and cultivating it? . . . How to help men become godlike or transcendent or whatever the word will turn out to be that will catch on? Virtuous? Noble? Good? Fully human? Fully functioning? . . . A few years ago I would have had no respect for them or their job. I would have urged them to stop wasting their lives—and get into a useful occupation. Now I'm a hero for them & I think probably justly. I think my psychology could give them the doctrine of man which would permit them to live a useful & important life right where they are. What an ironic thing!

. . . What kind of lectures-sermons will they give? It might very well be the old "religious" questions, hitherto thought to be supernatural, but now snatched away from the priests and brought back into the natural world. Humility & pride, good & evil, the good life, the good man. How much "cognitive therapy" is possible , i.e., doing these things by lecturing, writing, teaching, exhorting, preaching?[15]

A religious leader who adopts this kind of approach has replaced the uniquely salvific message of the Gospel with a smattering of questionable psychological insights.

According to Eck, a liberal theologian who follows this course "reinterprets theological data to make it consistent with a scientific view."[16] In doing so, the reconstructionist may, perhaps, have identified some psychological truths within a religious system, but more likely he or she has simply forced a psychological theory upon isolated texts. The means for doing so may involve "demythologizing" the text to make it more "scientific," and "psychologizing" religious teachings by rendering theological language into psychological terms.[17]

The specifically religious and orthodox content of a religious system is lost, watered down, or overlooked in both versions of the *spies* model; the theological

birthright is thus sold to secure a psychological pot of porridge.[18] Both versions of this model are reductionistic, forcing the content of one discipline to "be altered to become acceptable" within the view of the other discipline.[19] For this reason Eck classified them as *manipulative paradigms*. While such approaches allow for a relationship between psychology and theology, they typically result in the loss of a genuinely psychological science and the abdication of orthodox theology. The nature of espionage is such that, by definition, the spy removes what he or she sees as valuable, and leaves the rest behind.

Theological Dominance: The *Colonialist* Model

It is in the nature of imperialism that citizens of the imperial power are always among the last to know—or care—about circumstances in the colonies.

—Bertrand Russell

Devout congregants do not knowingly participate in the *Spies* model because they value not just the psychological content of their religious system, but they are

---

15. Lowry, *The journals of Abraham Maslow*, 405–6, entry of September 17, 1964.

16. Eck, Integrating the integrators,105.

17. Eck credits Farnsworth for this model. See Farnsworth, *Whole-hearted integration*.

18. While genuine psychological insights are of value, in a system that lacks empirical and theoretical sophistication, the psychological insights are apt to be trite and limited. Worse, a theological system that loses sight of divine and eternal significance has abandoned not only the currency of its commerce, but its very reason for being.

19. Eck, Integrating the integrators, 104.

committed to the larger theological system itself. Many of them do, however, recognize that there is value within psychology that could be brought into (or, perhaps, restored to) the church. When they look at psychology as a secular discipline, they see it as foreign territory. Some colonists learn to work the foreign soil of the new land. More often, however, colonialism leads to plundering the resources of the foreign land. Guided by their theological commitments, they remove from the foreign territory of psychology things that might be of use to religiously committed people. In a sense, colonialists function as religious spies in the psychological world. This model has a long history, and is essentially the model held by the inquisitors who saw Galileo's science as legitimate, so long as his theories did not transgress their theological proclamations.

While colonialists see selective portions of psychology as valuable, most of them are not trained in the methods of psychology, nor do they engage in productive research. The *Colonialist* position is embodied in the "new" Nouthetic Counseling movement. While Jay Adams adopted an *Enemies* model, some of his followers have moderated his anti-psychological bent somewhat. For instance, Welch and Powlison claimed that "Nouthetic Counseling is not opposed to the use of psychological data, especially when it is used to illustrate and describe rather than explain."[20] They distinguish themselves from integrationists as follows: "Many integrationists maintain that there are two authoritative books: the book of nature and the book of Scripture. One book is not better than the other; each is unique. The books have different topics. Such a position gives theoretical warrant for an autonomous discipline called 'psychology.' We believe, however, that the Bible does not stand beside the book of nature; rather, the Bible is creation's authoritative interpreter."[21]

In practice, colonization rarely leads to a complete reading of both books, and even less commonly to actually doing psychological research. Most of the writing that has ensued from this model relies primarily on scriptural citation and theological interpretation.[22] From this perspective, psychological theory and research are seen as secondary, or more often, inconsequential, sources of information. At best, this approach leads to an engagement with isolated psychological *findings*, but it does not promote engagement with *psychology as a discipline* or with its *methods*.

---

20. Welch, and Powlison, Every common bush afire, 303.

21. Ibid., 310.

22. *The Journal of Biblical Counseling* sometimes deals with "psychological issues" such as obsessive compulsive disorder or self-mutilation, but it rarely, if ever, cites the results of epidemiological or efficacy research. In fact, it far more often includes diatribes against psychology. These facts stand in sharp contrast to Welch and Powlison's claim that "Nouthetic Counseling is not opposed to the use of psychological data," and support the contention that a *Colonialist* mindset rarely leads to a productive interchange between psychology and theology.

Colonization of psychological findings can be done either by selectively filtering psychological conclusions by comparing them to Scripture verses,[23] or by aligning psychological findings to a Christian worldview.[24] Both of these approaches have significant strengths. Scripture is an invaluable source of information about human nature, and there are presuppositions within psychology that need to be critiqued from a Christian perspective. We cannot approach any discipline without taking our worldviews with us, and these models affirm the importance of a theologically informed worldview. The limitation of the *Colonialist* model, however, is that it begins with a confusion of categories. Rather than seeing psychology and theology as *disciplines* that owe their allegiance to Christ, they see psychology as a collection of findings and theories that must be filtered through their interpretation of Scripture.[25] Unfortunately, this often leads to scattered proof-texting rather than solid exegesis as well as to an unsophisticated understanding of the methods and findings of psychology. These limitations prevent any deep engagement between psychology and theology.

While colonialists may value isolated psychological insights, their ultimate allegiance is to theology. Recall that Welch and Powlison argued that the Bible is the authoritative interpreter of nature. They are legitimately concerned that nature can be misinterpreted. Their solution is to place "Scripture" over nature. However, people who adopt this solution typically fail to distinguish *scriptural authority* from *theological interpretation*. Failing to appreciate the influence of interpretation on theological reasoning, they unwittingly attempt to infuse their own beliefs with the same degree of authority vested in Scripture itself. An unfortunate byproduct of this confusion is that it leads to "theological imperialism" in which *theological interpretation* is presumed to trump *psychological interpretation*, without an adequate understanding that one's interpretation may need to be reconsidered.[26] Both theological and psychological interpretation can be wrong; our assumptions, methodologies, and theological or psychological data sampling can lead us to errant conclusions.

How was colonialism good— and bad—for colonial powers and for their colonies? In what ways is this similar to a colonialist view of theology and psychology?

Another weakness of this model is that most colonialists lack a sufficient understanding of psychological methodologies. Thus, when a psychological theory

---

23. Farnsworth's *Credibility Model*.

24. Farnsworth's *Conformability Model*.

25. For an excellent article on a constructive model that is integrative rather than colonial, see Johnson, Christ, the Lord of psychology.

26. Farnsworth, *Whole-hearted integration*, 102.

or finding is discrepant from their theological beliefs, they simply dismiss out of hand those conclusions that conflict with previously held theological *interpretations*. A more productive response would be to see discrepant results as an opportunity to reevaluate the data, methodologies, and interpretations that lie behind the psychological and theological conclusions. This could lead to fruitful new research, but the colonialist risks intellectual foreclosure by avoiding the emotional discomfort and the hard work of directly dealing with apparent contradictions. Finally, since this approach tends merely to borrow selectively from the *contents* of psychology, it fails to produce significant involvement with the *discipline* of psychology or to utilize its *methods* to produce useful research.

Recall Francis Bacon's claim—made over four hundred years ago—that God has given us two books to study, His Word and His Works. Bacon pointed out that God's Works can help us to understand God's Word, and vice versa. In contrast, holders of the *Colonialist* model see the book of God's Word as superior to the book of God's Works. They read primarily from the book of God's Word, and rarely have fluency in reading the book of His Works (i.e., they lack competency in psychology as a discipline).

While the *Colonialist* model may result in a co-mingling of psychological and theological thought, it fails to be integrative because it presumes that the book of God's Works must be viewed through the book of God's Word. This is problematic on two levels. First, we cannot view the world *directly* through God's Word, but only *indirectly* through our own thinking as it is shaped by our interpretations of God's Word. Secondly, God's Works and God's Word exist on an equal footing. Of course, from our perspective, God's Word and God's Works are seen through fallen eyes. Given this situation, we cannot discern *how the world ought to be* by examining *the world as it is*. Even so, we recognize that God's Works were spoken into existence by His Word; while our deeds and our words are sometimes inconsistent, God's Works and His Word are always uniform. Thus it may be that we sometimes gain a better understanding of His Word by exploring His Works, and vice versa.

While colonialists may not read the book of God's Works with much sophistication, they at least recognize that it is of some value. The colonialists also remind us of an important truth: it is essential that integration proceed from a worldview shaped and informed by Christian presuppositions. However, when psychology *as a discipline* is subjugated to theological *interpretation*, the unique content and methods of psychology are needlessly sacrificed on the altar of personal or shared religious interpretation.[27]

---

27. For example, consider a common interpretation of 2 Corinthians 10:5, which reads, in part, "take captive every thought to make it obedient to Christ" (NIV). Some pastors make use of this verse to teach a practice of getting rid of "bad" thoughts. However, the context makes it clear that Paul is admonishing us to contend for the truth against false teachings, not promoting a form of cognitive-behavioral therapy.

In a sense, we might say that the *Colonialist* is half-right. We do need to compare the conclusions of our psychology to the conclusions of our theology, but we cannot *a priori* assume that theological *interpretation* trumps psychological *interpretation*. Rather, both of God's books lie side by side, and it is our job to try to comprehend the truths of both books and allow them to lead us to a more complete understanding than can be found with either alone. Where there appears to be conflict, it is a conflict of *interpretation*. Thus, we need to exercise epistemic humility, reread *both* books, and resolve discrepancies in a nonimperialistic manner when we can. When such resolution is not apparent, we must be content to live with the ambiguity and uncertainty that is part and parcel of human experience.

One Firm Foundation: The Rebuilders Model

Do you wish to be great? Then begin by being little. Do you desire to construct a vast and lofty fabric? Think first about the foundations of humility. The higher your structure is to be, the deeper must be its foundation.

—Saint Augustine

Furthermore, a theology that is informed by dynamic psychotherapy should recognize the pervasiveness of sin—in our conscious and unconscious mental lives—such that any claim to the possibility of sinless perfection should be extremely dubious.

Christian psychology, which is currently the main expression of the *Rebuilders model*, has several origins. It can be traced, in part, to the efforts of two Christian philosophers, Robert Roberts and C. Stephen Evans, who espoused a much broader definition of "psychology" than that which would be accepted by most people within contemporary, mainstream psychology. This is understandable, given that psychology was considered to be part of philosophy prior to its emergence as a separate discipline in the late nineteenth century. Along with a number of other people, they argued that Christianity contains an implicit psychology that is found in Christian tradition and Scripture. Eric Johnson, another key figure of this movement, pointed out that twentieth-century psychology, framed by modernism, "seemed to be leading Western culture's turn away from the God of Christianity."[28] The Christian psychology view has gained a foothold among some Christians who are skeptical of the modernist conceptualization of discrete disciplines and who embrace a broader definition of psychology and who wish to explicitly draw on Christian resources to undergird a Christian view of persons and Christian counseling. The Society for Christian Psychology has spurred the development and influence of this approach.

The Christian psychology view has a different starting point from most of the other models that we have explored.

---

28. Worthington, Johnson, Hook, and Aten, *Evidence-based practices*, 326.

Most of the models are primarily concerned with a dialogue between the religious formulations of personhood and the theories and findings of the "secular" discipline of psychology as it is practiced today.[29] Christian psychology, on the other hand, begins with the assumption that psychology is more generically defined as the study of human beings, much as it was defined prior to the late 1800's. This definition allows psychology to be found in religious traditions and philosophy as well as within the modern academic discipline which goes by that name. Within the Christian tradition we can discover a "rich treasure of insights, themes, and foundational assumptions upon which to ground the project of a Christian psychology."[30]

While it does not reject empirical science or modern theories outright, Christian psychology is suspicious of the degree to which modernism frames our current understandings of psychology. The Christian psychology approach advocated by these authors begins with a deep grounding in scripture and Christian tradition in an attempt to recover the Christian psychology of the past, and then proceeds to dialogue with contemporary psychological theories and findings. In many cases, they assume that they will be able to learn from and contribute to the field of psychology as it is practiced today. However, they also assume (as do most other models), that there will be areas where Christian and secular views are in tension. In such instances, they propose an ambitious goal of developing uniquely Christian approaches to psychological phenomena. In other words, they want to develop Christian psychology as a specific type of psychology. The Society for Christian Psychology explains its goals as follows:

> [We] also seek to produce distinctively Christian theories, research programs, and soul-care practice, where appropriate, in areas that are more world-view dependent (e.g., motivation, personality, psychopathology, therapy, and social relations), where a Christian perspective would be expected to yield qualitatively different ways of interpreting human beings. Recognizing and utilizing one's communal perspectives will likely become increasingly important in the general field of psychology in the future, because of the growing recognition that a community's world-view assumptions affect not only what we can see in the human sciences, but also the

---

29. Adherents of many of the models would acknowledge—along with the Christian Psychology camp—that psychology existed prior to the late 1800's as a branch of philosophy and as careful reflection on human nature, often within religious contexts. Most of the models would also acknowledge that psychological views are influenced by world-views and philosophical assumptions, and that modern psychology is not driven by empirical findings alone. To a much greater degree than most of the other models, though, Christian Psychology asserts that the starting point for Christians who wish to "do" psychology must be intense reflection on God's normative view of humanity as expressed in scripture and as developed in Christian theology.

30. Society for Christian Psychology, *About the Society*, ¶1.

development of the objects under investigation.[31]

The Christian psychology perspective has an intense focus on the way that assumptions affect our observations and it is given shape by an intentional and extensive attempt to develop a specifically Christian view of persons.

The Christian psychology view begins, of necessity, with an attempt to discern a Christian view of human nature.

Our task as Christian psychologists. . . is in large part to retrieve the Christian psychology of the past, understand what these writers have to say, sift it for what has enduring importance and present it to our contemporaries as a form that can be understood and used.[32]

Much of the foundational work in Christian psychology will therefore require a careful rereading of Scripture, in the light of some of the great Christian psychologists of the subsequent past (Augustine, Aquinas, Pascal, Kierkegaard), by people who are familiar with contemporary psychology and can therefore sniff out a biblical psychology that effectively speaks to current circumstances.[33]

Importantly, this view explicitly affirms that Christianity tells us how we should orient our lives. While psychotherapy is a normative discipline (that is, it tells us how we ought to be), it often fails to acknowledge that it is implicitly enacting value judgments. For instance, if a cognitive-behavioral therapist tells a client that his catastrophizing statements are reinforcing his depression, there are clearly some normative, value judgments being made—catastrophizing is bad for you, and it is better to be happy than to be depressed. Yet few therapists are in the habit of laying their assumptions about normative goals bare for consideration. The Christian psychology view, in contrast, assumes that behavior, thoughts, and feelings which deviate from God's design for human beings will be harmful for our well-being. A corollary, then, is that we should develop psychotherapeutic techniques which help produce Christian character as a context for helping people deal with psychological issues.

Christian psychology criticizes the degree to which secular psychological models of "health" may deviate from Christian views of health. Johnson, for instance, noted that:

Throughout the past 100 years, unbelieving individuals in psychology have been living out their lives in largely unconscious yet fundamental opposition to God, and *the field of psychology has been shaped to some extent by this underlying anti-spiritual agenda.*[34]

---

31. Ibid., ¶3.

32. Roberts, A Christian Psychology View, in Johnson and Jones, *Psychology and Christianity: four views,* 184.

33. Roberts and Watson, A Christian Psychology View, in Johnson, *Psychology and Christianity: five views,* 155.

34. Johnson, Christ, the Lord of psychology, 14.

Secular psychology does not recognize the sovereignty of God over the things that it studies, nor does it recognize the authority of God to say how we ought to live. For the Christian, these fundamentals cannot be mere additions to secular psychology. Thus Johnson argues that we must begin by recognizing the Lordship of Christ over psychology and over human life. Christian psychology, then, requires that we dig deeply into Scripture and Christian tradition to understand what is wrong with humanity (most fundamentally, that we are, at core, in rebellion against God), the ideals towards which we should strive, and the means to attaining the goal of being more Christ-like.

What are the main concerns of Rebuilders about secular psychology? How do they propose to build "Christian psychology"?

Once a normative framework for human well-being has been recovered from Christian Scripture and Christian tradition, the Christian psychology approach proceeds to empirical research. Doing so requires that we carefully ascertain whether our measures accurately operationalize our concepts, that we explicitly acknowledge our assumptions in our research, that we conduct empirical analysis of our hypotheses, and that

we enter into dialogue with mainstream psychology.[35]

The degree to which such dialogue occurs, or is desired, is a point worth considering. Roberts, for instance, defines Christian psychology as something that:

> starts with ideas and practices already established by centuries of Christian tradition, and it develops psychological concepts and practices from these *with a minimum of reference to or influence from the psychologies of the twentieth century.*[36]

Roberts is suspicious of modern psychology because it all too easily promotes ideals of well-being that are alien to Christian teachings and sensibilities. Poorly done integration, he warns, can easily encourage us to adopt secular, anti-Christian ideals as the goal of psychotherapy and can damage the psychological and spiritual well-being of those we claim to be helping. Moreover, since most psychotherapy outcome research shows similar effectiveness regardless of the therapeutic technique used, Roberts argues that we are better off sticking with explicitly Christian psychology rather than trying to "integrate" secular psychology and Christianity.[37] In fact, he

35. See Roberts and Watson, A Christian Psychology View, in Johnson, *Psychology and Christianity: Five Views*, 155, italics mine.

36. Roberts, Pauline psychotherapy, in McMinn and Phillips, *Care for the soul*, 133.

37. See Roberts, Psychotherapy and Christian ministry.

goes so far as to argue that we ought to have:

> a moratorium on the integration of establishment techniques and explanatory frameworks into Christian thought and practice until we Christians have a firmer understanding and appreciation of the psychology of our own tradition. Only such deep understanding can protect us from promoting the narcissism, individualism, consumerism, egoism, emotivism, instrumentalism, victimism, irresponsibilism and atheism that the modern therapies tend to promote.[38]

Note, however, that Roberts is not opposed to engaging secular psychology per se. Rather, he thinks that we need to be better grounded in our own Christian tradition before we are adequately equipped to do so.

At this point, it is evident that the Christian psychology approach shares elements of both the Colonialist and the Allies paradigm. Like the Colonialist, the Christian psychology approach places primacy on the theological data. Like the Allies approach, the Christian psychology approach values mainstream psychology and empirical research. It clearly lends itself well to an exploration of "soul care," or looking at the potential for the Christian tradition to have meaningful things to offer about human well-being within a therapeutic context. It is less

clear how well this model works for areas of psychology that are not as deeply tied to "soul care" and deep engagement with mainstream psychology.

Live and Let Live: The *Neutral Parties* Model

People who demand neutrality in any situation are usually not neutral but in favor of the status quo.

—Max Eastman

Recognizing that theological imperialism has the potential to impede scientific inquiry, some religiously committed people try to segregate science and faith. They see psychology and theology as *Neutral Parties*. The *Neutral Parties* model allows for a level of interaction that is absent in the *Enemies* model, and, unlike the *Spies* or *Colonialist* models, it encourages the exploration of the unique content of both disciplines and the methodologies that they employ. This approach also emphasizes the point that psychology and religion may say similar things, but they are perpetually distinct. Like the two rails of a railroad track, they run alongside each other, but they never merge. Carter and Narramore referred to such models as *parallels models*.

Carter and Narramore noted that the *parallels* model has two versions: one that emphasizes the distinctiveness of psychology and theology, and one that emphasizes their similarities. You might think of the first version as being like a person who looks at a railroad track and

---

38. See Roberts, A Christian Psychology Response to integration, in Johnson, *Psychology and Christianity: Five Views*, 133.

focuses on the fact that there are two separate rails. This version attempts to protect the independence of psychology and theology through *disciplinary isolationism*. Thus, holders of the *isolation* version are people who essentially compartmentalize their occupational commitments and their religious faith. They recognize each as valid in its own domain, but see little overlap between them. The second version is like a person who focuses on the fact that the railroad ties serve to connect the rails, and on how the rails are similar in function. Holders of the *correlation version* intentionally seek to identify unique areas of overlap between psychology and theology, allowing for limited interaction between complementary findings of the two disciplines.[39]

Both the *isolation* and *correlation* versions of the *Neutral Parties* model assert that there can be no actual conflict between faith and psychology because they occupy distinct and noninteracting spheres. They are completely different perspectives that cannot be combined because each view requires a different vantage point. Experientially, however, conflicts are virtually inevitable at the interpretive level, and the need to exercise

two distinct ways of thinking tends to break down. Writing about this tendency among those who see faith and science in parallel or *compartmental* terms, Bube noted that one of the two disciplines tends to become primary and the other secondary: "Because of this inherent instability in the compartmentalization approach, it frequently develops that one of the descriptions comes to take on primary practical significance, with the consequence that the other description is retained only as a useful fiction or as a cultural attachment."[40]

Thus, while ostensibly recognizing the value and independence of both scientific and theological approaches, in practice, holders of this model may not always be able to maintain such autonomy. The *Neutral Parties* model can be carried out through *psychological neutrality* or through *Christian neutrality*.[41] Their distinctives will be addressed in the following two sections.

Psychological Neutrality

Psychological neutrality occurs when a person who is committed to the profession of psychology simultaneously holds religious, but not necessarily Christian, beliefs. Both the *isolation* and *correlation* views are described by Allport, the eminent psychologist and devout Episcopalian[42] who grew up with "plain Prot-

---

39. Limited interaction between disciplinary content is possible in the *Spies, Colonialist*, and *Neutral Parties* approaches. The first two models assume that the truth of one discipline is subsumed by the truth of another discipline, while the *Neutral Parties* model assumes that both disciplines have autonomous methods and content. While the *Spies* and *Colonialist* models are reductionistic, the *Neutral Parties* model tends to be dualistic.

40. Bube, *Putting it all together*, 97.

41. Carter and Narramore's *secular parallels* and *Christian parallels* models, respectively.

42. Pettigrew, Gordon Willard Allport: a

estant piety and hard work."[43] Allport clearly had the *isolationist* in mind when he wrote: "The axioms on which a scientist proceeds while he is acting scientifically are at odds with the axioms on which a person proceeds when he is acting religiously . . . Clearly we are accustomed to keep our axioms in logic-tight compartments."[44]

Nicholas Wolterstorff, a Christian philosopher, describes the cost of such an approach:

> The Christian who is a scholar finds himself in two communities: the community of his fellow Christians and the community of his fellow scholars . . . Without a doubt a person can simply live in the two different communities, doing as the Athenians do when in Athens and as the Jerusalemites when in Jerusalem. But if one who is a scholar as well as a Christian wants coherence in life—or even if he only wants self-understanding—he cannot help asking, how does my membership in these two communities fit together?[45]

Allport suggested that people employ various ways of reconciling their divergent commitments, one of which is simply to keep them independent of each other. Another way of reconciling psychology and religion is to serve as a linguistic translator. Such translation is readily accessible, for as Allport observed, "the vocabulary of religion and of modern science differ markedly, though their meanings are essentially the same . . . It would be difficult, I suspect, to find any proposition in modern mental hygiene that has not been expressed with venerable symbols in some portion of the world's religious literature."[46]

Allport thus perceived psychology and religion as having similar content and function, but with no attempt to explain the ground of that similarity. Allport's approach expresses *psychological neutrality* in that there is no effort extended to discern ultimate truth; it is interested in religious or spiritual principles in the abstract rather than Christian truth in particular.

When a person recognizes psychology and theology as distinct disciplines, and is at the same time concerned with intentionally drawing connections between psychological and religious findings, we have a situation that is similar to the *Spies* model, but with better respect for disciplinary independence. However, *psychological neutrality*, like the approach of the *foreign spy*, lacks a commitment to Christian orthodoxy, and is often simply "spiritual" or "religious."

With the increasing search for meaning and openness to spirituality in the larger American culture, books that seek to leverage the value of such parallelism have become quite common in

tribute.

43. Allport, *The person in psychology*, 379.

44. Allport, *The individual and his religion*, 115.

45. Wolterstorff, *Reason within the bounds of religion*, 17.

46. Allport, *The individual and his religion*, 86.

recent years. M. Scott Peck's 1978 best-seller, *The Road Less Traveled*, can be seen in this light. It is broadly spiritual, but not Christian. Peck credits the book's memorable beginning to the first of "Buddha's Four Noble Truths." "Life is difficult. This is a great truth, one of the greatest truths. It is a great truth because once we truly see this truth, we transcend it."[47]

Another representative of this approach is the one-time Catholic monk and Jungian psychotherapist Thomas Moore. At first glance his approach sounds integrative: "I have also taken the Renaissance approach of not separating psychology from religion."[48] "Psychology and spirituality need to be seen as one."[49] Upon closer inspection, however, there is no *fundamental* integration and it is more spiritual than Christian: "Although I am borrowing the terminology of Christianity, what I am proposing is not specifically Christian, nor is it tied to any particular religious tradition."[50] Furthermore, where Moore does combine psychological and spiritual matters, it comes across as Jungian mysticism in which the unique contributions of psychology as a science and theology as a discipline are blurred, resulting in a loss of psychological science and of specifically Christian theology. None of these observations should be taken to mean that the insights of Allport, Peck, Moore, and others are totally without merit; we

have much to learn from them. However, while their conceptualizations of the relationship of psychology and theology allow for disciplinary independence and interaction, they tend to be of limited scope, neglect scientific and/or doctrinal specificity, lack a well thought-out epistemology, and suffer from worldview conceptualizations that lead to compartmentalization or to a superficial meshing of religious and psychological constructs. Furthermore, *psychological neutrality* tends to foster an instrumental view of religion, and to either ignore or strip religion of its revelational, soteriological, and moral significance.

Christian Neutrality

Christian neutrality occurs when a person who is committed to the profession of psychology simultaneously holds Christian beliefs. It differs from its secular counterpart primarily in that it is specifically Christian rather than broadly spiritual or religious in orientation. As in the secular model, it can be accomplished either through *isolation* or through *correlation*.

Relatively few Christians explicitly adopt an isolationary approach to relating Christianity and psychology, although it is probably far more common in practice than many people realize. In this model, Christian commitments are compartmentalized from disciplinary concerns and practice. Carter and Narramore identified Clement as a fitting example of this model. The isolationism of

---

47. Peck. *The road less traveled*, 15.

48. Moore, *Care of the soul*, xii.

49. Ibid., xv.

50. Ibid.

Clement's approach can be seen in the following quotation.

> Students of inferential statistics learn a concept which is very useful in solving a fundamental problem in the integration of psychology and theology. It is the concept of orthogonal relationships. Two factors are orthogonally related, if they are independent or uncorrelated . . . As with all orthogonally related disciplines, psychology and theology are complementary. Both add to a more complete picture of man's experience. Logically they cannot contradict each other, since contradictions can only take place within a perspective. Clashes between perspectives can only produce pseudo-contradictions.[51]

Carter and Narramore commented that this model works "by carefully relegating each discipline to the confines of its own methodology, language, and perspectives" so that any conflict is resolved by stressing their independence.[52] The isolationist solution, however, comes at a substantial cost: it "rules out the possibility of integration. Such isolation destroys integration; for if psychology and theology are orthogonally related, there can be no meaningful interaction."[53]

Christians who follow a *Neutral Parties* model by isolating the two disciplines

do not rule out the possibility that there will be limited areas of overlap between psychology and theology. The work of the psychologist and the work of the theologian, however, are seen as taking place in relative isolation from each other, with few areas of overlapping content. In this view, it should make no difference if a researcher is a Christian or not; the data are what they are, or, as the old phrase from experimental psychology has it, "the rat is always right." One of the major drawbacks to this approach is that it fails to recognize the degree to which worldview assumptions shape psychological and theological viewpoints. The isolationism of the *Neutral Parties* model embraces modernism's myths of objectivity, neutrality, and independence.

A Christian who adopts a correlational approach to the *Neutral Parties* model goes a step further than his or her isolationist colleague. While emphasizing the unique scope and methods of psychology and differentiating them from the unique scope and methods of theology, the correlationalist intentionally looks for comparable findings of the two disciplines. In this view, the psychologist and the theologian may well come to similar conclusions, and parallels can be identified. For the correlationalist, however, this is as far as the process can go. The assumption behind the model is that there may be limited parallel concerns or findings between two distinctly separate spheres of knowledge.

The correlational approach affirms the idea that "God has written two books—nature and the Bible," but it sees

---

51. Clement, quoted in Carter & Narramore, *The integration of psychology and theology,* 94–95.

52. Ibid., 95.

53. Ibid.

the two books as very independent from each other, so that "it is the task of professional scientists and biblical scholars to help us discern these two revelations."[54] This approach stresses the need for disciplinary independence because of "the dangers of subjecting science to theology or theology to science."[55] Instead of attempting to see how psychology and theology are integrally related, this view stresses that the two disciplines pose different questions so that "religion takes over where science leaves off."[56] Despite protestations to the contrary, in the end, this view promotes compartmentalization, since the domains of science and theology are seen as largely segregated from one another.

This view allows for psychology and Christian theology to be related as parallels between them are discovered, but it prevents any fundamental interaction. People who adopt this view tend to underplay the degree to which our observations reflect our assumptions, especially in their conceptualization of theology and psychology as autonomous disciplines. They are thus content to describe different perspectives of human nature, without searching for "unifying . . . truths that could conceivably embrace both disciplines."[57] As we will see in our discussion of integration, the idea that there could be unifying or overarching truths

does not mean that one must make psychology subservient to theology or vice-versa. Rather it means that both disciplines reflect truths that are larger and more fundamental than either discipline can contain.

Christian psychologists whose fields of specialization are less clinical and more empirical tend to favor this approach to relating Christianity and psychology.[58] Malcolm Jeeves[59] and David Myers[60] exemplify this approach. One of the assumptions that they make is that human behavior can be described at different levels, each of which involve different kinds of questions and answers.

> Since each of us is a complex system, simultaneously part of a larger social system and composed of smaller systems which in turn are composed of ever smaller subsystems, any aspect of human behavior and cognition chosen for investigation may be analyzed at different levels. Each level

---

54. Myers, Social psychology, 218.

55. Ibid.

56. Ibid.

57. Carter & Narramore, *The integration of psychology and theology*, 98.

58. The science/faith relationship is usually defined in conflict, compartmentalization, and complement theories. The *Neutral Parties* model is similar to the *compartment theory* of science and faith in that both see science and religion as occurring in different domains between which there can be no direct interaction. The more science-oriented psychologist may be well served by examining the seven models for relating science and faith reviewed by Richard Bube, *Putting it all together*.

59. Myers & Jeeves, *Psychology through the eyes of faith*; Jeeves, *Mind fields*; and Jeeves, *Human nature at the millennium*.

60. For an excellent summary, see Myers, Levels-of-explanation. See also Myers, *Human puzzle*.

entails its own questions and appropriate methods for answering them. While the account given at each level may be complete within itself that does not mean that by itself it constitutes a full account of the phenomenon under investigation. Each level complements the others.[61]

In the words of David Myers, the parallelism of the disciplines allows us to relate "psychological and religious descriptions of human nature. We can map human nature from two directions, asking how well psychological and biblical understandings *correlate*."[62] This correlating can only be done with a strict respect for disciplinary peculiarity.

Without searching for unifying concepts and underlying foundations, this approach remains one of identifying parallels and discerning correlations rather than being truly integrative. Although the people who hold this view are usually aware of the impact of worldview assumptions on thinking, they tend to embrace modernist assumptions about objectivity and the "self-correcting" nature of science.[63] While they are insistent on maintaining disciplinary independence, holders of the correlational view heartily endorse the idea that psychology and theology can profit from dialogue.

David Myers, Malcolm Jeeves, and Fraser Watts are prominent psychologists who readily acknowledge their Christian commitments, and they have each encouraged dialogue about the complementary findings of psychology and theology. Myers and Jeeves, for instance, preface their book, *Psychology through the Eyes of Faith*, by saying that the book: "Identifies major insights regarding human nature that college and university students will encounter in a basic psychology course and ponders how the resulting human image connects with Christian belief."[64]

Following a few introductory chapters, the book gives a basic overview of scientific findings about human nature and behavior that one would see in any introductory psychology text (biological bases of behavior, human development, sensation and perception, and so forth.) Each of the chapters contains some material connecting the psychological content to a point of connection with Christian thought.

David Myers is well known for making psychology accessible to many audiences. He is the author of the most-used introductory psychology textbook,[65] as well as the author of a social psychology textbook[66] and numerous books that address psychological research for popular

---

61. Jeeves, *Human nature*, 237.

62. Myers, A levels-of-explanation view, 60 (italics added).

63. It is claimed that science is a self-correcting discipline because it relies on empirical testing of hypotheses and replication. Critics contend that science is bound to ideology and to the reigning paradigms within a discipline to a far greater degree than modernist conceptions of science acknowledge.

---

64. Myers & Jeeves, *Psychology through the eyes of faith*, xi.

65. Myers, *Psychology*.

66. Myers, *Social psychology*.

audiences. He is also a productive social science researcher, with publications in over two dozen journals. Malcolm Jeeves has hundreds of professional and popular publications; his area of expertise is neuropsychology, especially neuroplasticity. Myers and Jeeves caution us to be wary of the reductionism in psychology that often threatens to "explain away" religious belief. They further highlight the fact that science may cause us to reconsider long-held theological beliefs. In fostering dialogue between psychology and theology, though, they see the disciplines as autonomous approaches that shed light from different directions that never completely meet. In one analogy, Myers describes how we can assess how well "insights into human nature gleaned from psychological research *correspond* to biblical and theological understanding" as being like boring a tunnel from two directions and "discovering how close the two approaches are to connecting."[67] He describes this association with words such as "echoes," "parallels,"[68] "two-sided truth,"[69] and "complementarity."[70] In another analogy, he describes psychology and theology as being like two ends of a rope found by a person in a deep well. Although the person cannot see how the ropes connect, wound around a pulley far above, "we grab both ropes, perhaps without fully grasping how they come together."[71]

Fraser Watts, an ordained Church of England minister who served as a President of the British Psychological Association, also argues that

> there can be fruitful dialogue between" psychology and theology.[72] Like Myers and Jeeves, he highlights the importance of disciplinary independence. "In relating psychological and theological aspects of a topic such as forgiveness, the integrity of both disciplines should be respected. Neither discipline should be subordinated or assimilated into the other, nor be allowed to dictate what propositions are permissible in the other discipline. The coming-together of the two disciplines should be on the basis of the two disciplines respecting the autonomy and contribution of the other."[73]

In the views of Myers, Jeeves, and Watts, human nature can be "mapped from two directions," the results can be "correlated," the disciplines can "engage in fruitful dialogue," and we can note the "complementarity" of their findings.

There is much to admire in this approach. Myers, Jeeves, and Watts have been incredibly productive—both as scholars and as people who attempt to foster dialogue between psychology and theology. Their approach recognizes that

---

67. Myers, A levels-of-explanation view, 59 (italics mine).

68. Ibid., 62.

69. Ibid., 64.

70. Ibid., 65.

71. Ibid.

72. Watts, *Relating*, 4.

73. Ibid.

the distinct methodologies and scope of each discipline need to be respected. A criticism of their approach is that they exert much more effort on identifying parallel findings than in searching for unifying concepts. While useful and interesting parallels may be discovered using this model, it does not tend to result in the extension of sufficient energies toward recognizing the ultimate underlying unity of our common subject, or a conceptual unity that transcends both disciplines.

Perhaps more importantly, the correlational approach is based on modernist assumptions about the ability to find truth apart from authority by leaning on rigorous observation and rationality alone. In this vein, adherents of the *Neutral Parties* model view the various academic disciplines merely as distinct perspectives without seriously confronting the degree to which assumptions shape those perspectives. While Myers and Jeeves acknowledge the degree to which our perspectives are themselves shaped by worldviews,[74] they nonetheless argue that we should not "replace science that aims to be value-free with a science that expresses one's values and assumptions."[75] Quoting Donald MacKay, they insist that, "our goal is objective, value-free knowledge."[76] The practical effect of this approach is that it tends to suppress the assumptions of one's worldview in an attempt to be "objective," but such objectivity is ultimately impossible. In contrast, Christian philosopher C. Stephen Evans contends that, "we ought to allow our Christian assumptions to interpenetrate our actual work as scientists" so we can do our scientific work "within a consciously Christian frame of reference."[77]

People who embrace the *Neutral Parties* model sometimes outline a few Christian claims that they admit will shape the way they approach psychology, but these are limited to a few, very broad claims. Myers and Scanzoni make the claim that "Christianity starts with two simple axioms: 1. There is a God. 2. It's not you (and it's not us)."[78] As much as we might agree with these two propositions, Christian theology makes a great many claims beyond this. By itself, these propositions are insufficient to define a thoroughly Christian worldview. Furthermore, Myers explicitly cautions against "absolutizing any of our theological or scientific ideas"[79] because of the "ever reforming" nature of Reformed theology. While we would be wise to heed his caution to hold our beliefs humbly, his approach severely constricts the impact of Christian theology on our understanding of human nature.

Christian theology makes some very specific claims about human nature

---

74. See Myers & Jeeves, *Psychology through the eyes of faith*. See especially chap. 3, Should there be a Christian psychology? 12–18.

75. Ibid., 15.

76. Ibid.

---

77. Evans, Healing old wounds, 85.

78. Myers & Scanzoni, *What God has joined together*, 7.

79. Ibid., 16.

that are foundational to a Christian worldview, and these claims make fundamental differences in how one understands what it means to be human. "What is really needed," claims Evans, "is a demonstration that basic biblical beliefs make a difference to the way Christians think of their disciplines, propose and evaluate explanations, and design and carry out research."[80] This is especially true regarding Christian understandings of personhood, the purpose of human life, our need for God, and the ethical teachings of Christian faith. These considerations are integral to psychology, not merely parallel to it.

Finally, some critics contend that by acknowledging the impact of worldviews and then attempting to transcend this impact by being "objective," people who follow a *Neutral Parties* perspective have embraced an inconsistent position. As Van Leeuwen observed, "they disavow reductionism in principle while preserving it in practice."[81] These critiques necessitate that we evaluate the modernist assumptions that undergird this view.

Christian philosopher Nicholas Wolterstorff provided the following summary of the modernist conception of science: "The classic theory of theorizing in the Western world is foundationalism. Simply put, the goal of scientific endeavor, according to the foundationalist, is to form a body of theories from which all

prejudice, bias, and unjustifiable conjecture have been eliminated."[82]

Wolterstorff traced this theory of science to six propositions endorsed by René Descartes. Although all of the propositions are in need of critique, the sixth proposition is particularly problematic. It first asserts that there are completely independent means of gaining knowledge—so theology and science are autonomous methodologies. This leads to the following conclusion: "To insert one's faith into the process of building up a science is to pollute that process with the very diversity and lack of consensus that we are struggling to eliminate [therefore] we must practice methodological atheism."[83] However, as we have already seen, our worldviews inevitably affect our observations.

The *Neutral Parties* view requires an optimistic view of human objectivity that could support a foundationalist approach purged of "all prejudice, bias, and unjustifiable conjecture."[84] The belief in such objectivity has been soundly critiqued by contemporary philosophy of science. As Wolterstorff proclaimed, "foundationalism has suffered a series of deadly blows."[85] Furthermore, science and its findings are not static. "Science is an ever-changing endeavor, a wholly human

---

80. Evans, Healing old wounds, 86.

81. Van Leeuwen, Psychology's "two cultures," 406–24.

82. Wolterstorff, *Reason within the bounds of religion*, 24.

83. Wolterstorff, Integration of faith and science, 12–19.

84. Wolterstorff, *Reason within the bounds of religion*, 24.

85. Ibid., 29.

artifact, and for that reason [it is] a good servant but a bad master."[86] The modernist assumptions that the *Neutral Parties* model embraces requires that science be a master, that we play by its rules in leaving faith out of the calculus of doing science. The result is that the only place for interaction between psychology and theology is in looking for points of overlap between psychological and theological findings while carefully segregating psychology and theology to their separate spheres, never allowing for deeper dialogue that would allow for genuine interaction or for the development of psychological theories that reflect Christian presuppositions.

Mary Stewart Van Leeuwen, citing postmodern critiques of modernist approaches to psychology, proposed that the objectivity sought by modernism is a barrier to progress. In her words:

> What does all this mean for the Christian student or the Christian observer of psychology? It means, in a sense, that the tables have been turned . . . If metaphysical world views affect the scientific practice of even professed atheists, then surely it is an advantage to have a world view that is articulated, recorded, and subject to ongoing discussion rather than one that remains unacknowledged. Not only is this more honest; it is also potentially more beneficial as a scientific catalyst, for it enables psychological

thinking and theological thinking to openly cross-fertilize each other . . .[87]

Van Leeuwen's critique should give us pause about the *Neutral Parties* model. Not only does this model require an unwarranted faith in human objectivity, but it sacrifices the role that one's worldview can play in forming theories and hypotheses that can be a source of scientific inquiry. Ultimately, this model fails to foster deep interaction between theology and psychology.

Is it possible to be completely objective and neutral? What are the advantages and disadvantages of trying to keep one's faith and worldview separate from one's psychological theorizing and practice?

One advantage of the *Neutral Parties* model is the recognition that psychology and theology are two distinct disciplines with their own histories and methodologies, yielding different but complementary perspectives. The difficulty, however, is that the *Neutral Parties* model tends to present a fragmented view of persons. Alan Tjeltveit, who is sympathetic to this view, nevertheless points out this significant problem.

> . . . I am partly convinced that psychology and theology address different topics (or different levels of

---

86. Livingstone, Reflections on the encounter between science and faith, 253.

87. Van Leeuwen, *The person in psychology*, 14.

explanation), with each field of study limited in scope and restricted to the logic of its disciplinary methods. However, this approach has significant weaknesses: It fails to capture the unity of persons. . . . Advocates of this levels-of-explanation approach almost never seem to get around to explaining how the psychological and the theological fit together to create comprehensive psychological understandings of persons.[88]

Despite these drawbacks, the correlational approach has been widely adopted and productive. Myers and Jeeves's book *Psychology through the Eyes of Faith* provides insightful discussions of basic areas of psychology such as biological bases of behavior, human development, and sensation and perception, as well as topics such as forgiveness, happiness, and the Fruit of the Spirit. Fraser Watts has helped us look at topics such as forgiveness from the divergent perspectives of psychology and theology,[89] and has helped us explore ways that psychology can aid Christian ministry.[90] David Myers has shared his wit and wisdom through his textbooks on psychology[91] and social psychology,[92] as well as books on happiness,[93] intuition,[94] hearing loss,[95] spiritual hunger and materialism,[96] and even a work of apologetics.[97] Myers is a prolific author and a first-rate scholar, but what impresses me most is his kind, gentle, and generous spirit. Nonetheless, I am convinced that deeper connections exist between psychology and theology than comparing them as different levels of explanation.

The *Neutral Parties* model avoids the hostility and rejection characteristic of the *Enemies* model and it avoids the reductionism and disciplinary supremacy found in the *Spies* model, as well as the theological imperialism and methodological disengagement of the *Colonialist* model. However, if both psychology and theology have their origin in the writings of a common author, then one must consider the possibility that an appropriately defined alliance between the two disciplines is preferable to the hostility, supremacy, or neutrality engendered by the models we have thus far considered. It is to such a possibility—developing an appropriate alliance—that we will turn our attention in the next chapter.

Summary

Between the outermost categories of *Enemies* and *Allies* reside the models of *Spies*,

88. Tjeltveit, *Lost opportunities*, 19

89. Watts, Relating the psychology and theology of forgiveness.

90. Watts, Nye, & Savage, *Psychology for Christian ministry*.

91. Myers, *Psychology*.

92. Myers, *Social psychology*.

93. Myers, *The pursuit of happiness*.

94. Myers, *Intuition*.

95. Myers, *A quiet world*.

96. Myers, *The American paradox*.

97. Myers, *A friendly letter to skeptics*.

Colonialists, *Rebuilders*, and *Neutral Parties*. *Spies* largely avoid the hostilities of the *Enemies* model, but they tend to be psychologically reductionistic and to ignore or water down the theological content of religious systems. Their tactic is to abstract from religious systems those psychological factors that contribute to mental well-being. *Colonialists* staunchly declare their allegiance to their theological Sovereign, but typically engage psychology through theological dominance, a failure to distinguish theological interpretation from biblical fact, and abdication of the methods and breadth of psychology as a discipline.

Rebuilders are critical of the secular foundations of contemporary psychology, and of its neglect of theological and philosophical reflection on issue of what it means to be human. Christian psychology attempts to recover ideas and practices that existed within the pages of Scripture and the teachings of Christians over the past two-thousand years. Drawing on these resources, those who embrace the Christian psychology model contend that we need Christ to be recognized as the Lord of psychology, to discern what God calls each of us to be, and to use transformational processes recovered from Christian tradition to create helpful mechanisms of soul care. While focused on the past, *Rebuilders* do not reject the present, and they contend that Christian psychology should be an approach to psychology which acknowledges its assumptions and dialogues with other psychological viewpoints in the modern academy, including the use

of scientific research methods, but with a careful eye towards the values and assumptions that are brought to the table.

The *Neutral Parties* model manages to avoid theological imperialism and to engage in a conversation that has the potential to align theological and psychological conclusions, but it fails to provide a holistic understanding of human behavior. It also tends to reflect modernist assumptions about objectivity, neutrality, and independence.

Each of these models has strengths and weaknesses. As we attempt to construct a model that builds on those strengths and avoids those weaknesses, we would be well advised to heed the wisdom of Gordon Allport's observation: "Although much of my writing is polemic in tone, I know in my bones that my opponents are partly right."[98]

Questions for Reflection and Discussion

1. What factors might encourage a secular psychologist to adopt the *Spies* model? Why would clinical pragmatism spur interest in religious beliefs and practices?

2. What is the difference between psychological espionage and religious espionage? Which one is more damaging to religious belief? Why?

3. In the liberal version, the domestic spy attempts to minister to tangible

---

98. Allport, *The person in psychology*, 405.

needs while rejecting Christian orthodoxy. In the conservative version, the domestic spy attempts to promote self-esteem and success while neglecting Christian orthodoxy. While they share a number of negative features, they are both attempting to be helpful. What do you see as the pros and cons of these two positions?

4. Abraham Maslow kept his disdain for religious beliefs sequestered in his private journals while publicly working with pastors to help them cultivate "the godlike within human nature" through preaching and teaching. Maslow's influence on these religious leaders suggests that we cannot always take someone's claims at face value. How might we exercise discernment about the hidden assumptions and values embedded within a theory?

5. The *Colonialist* model ostensibly recognizes the value of psychology, but it does not typically result in deep engagement with the findings or methods of psychology. How might this be applied to a topic such as eating disorders or depression? What would be some of the advantages and disadvantages of this approach?

6. The *Colonialist* model is intent on proclaiming the superiority of theology over psychology (nearly to the exclusion of psychology, in some cases), while the *Neutral Parties* model is intent on proclaiming the independence of psychology from any ideology including Christian theology. What concerns about the relationship of theology and psychology can you affirm in these two models, and what do you think is in need of critique?

7. In what ways is the *Rebuilders* model similar to the Colonialist model? How is it different?

8. The *Rebuilders* model contends that Christianity is fundamentally psychological, that it has an explicit view of who we are, who we should be, and how we should be transformed. What might be some of the advantages and disadvantages of using this model with a Christian client?

9. What might be some of the advantages and disadvantages of using the *Rebuilders* model with a non-Christian client?

10. How are the isolation and correlation versions of the *Neutral Parties* model (the *parallels* models) similar? How are the isolation and correlation versions of the *Neutral Parties* model (the *parallels* models) different? What factors might encourage a psychologist to adopt this approach? What are the advantages and disadvantages of this model?

11. The *Neutral Parties* approach of Myers, Jeeves, and Watts has produced a great deal of writing about parallel findings of psychology and theology. It has also sparked a significant amount of critique from people such as Evans, Van Leeuwen, and Wolterstorff about the influence of modernism in this

approach, and especially its quest for objectivity or neutrality. Summarize the arguments on both side of this issue (i.e., why do people who adopt a *Neutral Parties* model think that we should keep theology out of psychology, and why do their critics contend that it is dangerous to keep theology out of psychology?).

12. The author ended this chapter by quoting Gordon Allport: "Although much of my writing is polemic in tone, I know in my bones that my opponents are partly right." In the last chapter the author noted that "those with whom we disagree often have things to teach us" and issued a challenge to "ask ourselves what is to be learned and appreciated from" those with whom we disagree. Identify at least three things that you appreciate or can learn from each of the models reviewed in this chapter (the *Spies*, *Colonialists*, and *Neutral Parties* models).

11

Integrative Models of Disciplinary Relationship: Allies

Earth's crammed with heaven,
And every common bush afire with God;
But only he who sees, takes off his shoes,
The rest sit round it and pluck blackberries,
And daub their natural faces unaware.

—Elizabeth Barrett Browning[1]

Having moved many times in my adult life, one of the things I am all too well acquainted with is "church shopping." I dislike that phrase on many levels—American culture is infected with consumerism, and the last thing I would recommend is for anyone to pick a church based primarily on personal comfort. With this caution in mind, though, it is important to find a congregation in which one can worship and grow, and where one's theology and gifts fit the confessions and needs of the church. My father and I were talking about this phenomenon once, and he told me about his own experience looking for a church home in the late 1950s. The pastor of one church, when he learned that my father was a surgeon, assured him that no one

would expect him to believe that the miraculous claims of the Bible were historical events. Surely, modern science had banished forever the belief that a virgin gave birth to the Son of God, let alone that He was resurrected from the dead! For my father, that "assurance" was ample reason to look for another church.

My father never professed to have witnessed a miracle, but he believed in a God who sometimes brings forth miracles, and who consistently upholds nature. In my father's eyes, his own profession involved working with God to bring healing through the natural realm.[2]

---

1. Browning, *Aurora Leigh*, chap. 7.

2. My father was always a bit irritated, though, when people came to him solely because he was a Christian doctor, neglecting the fact that their surgical outcomes were dependent more on his technical skills than on the depth of his faith. In psychotherapy, though, one can

246

One of his favorite quotations was from the seventeenth-century French surgeon, Ambroise Paré, "I dressed the wound, God healed him."[3] The line reveals Paré's humility and his sense of partnership with God in bringing relief and healing. Paré, a devout Catholic, credited his numerous advances in surgical treatment to the insights of "divine grace." Recognizing the limitations of the healing arts, Paré offered another piece of sage advice: "Cure occasionally, relieve often, console always."[4]

My father saw medicine as an ally of Christianity partly because he believed that God gave us the light of reason to understand how nature works, and partly because he saw the medical arts as a means to minister God's grace. The same beliefs undergird the integration of psychology and Christianity. The discipline of psychology studies humanity in the natural realm through the light of reason. Moreover, those areas of psychology that lie within the healing arts can be an extension of God's healing grace.

These connections between psychology and Christianity, however, need to be tempered by several other considerations. My father found that medical practice involves ethical issues that—for the Christian—must be framed by a

Christian worldview and beliefs. If this is true of medicine, it is even more applicable to psychology, for the very idea of what it means to be human lies at the core of psychology, and a Christian view of humanity is sometimes startlingly different from the philosophical anthropology offered by rival worldviews. In this chapter, we will explore a final model for relating psychology and Christianity that attempts to take the foregoing observations seriously. I will argue that this model, while imperfect, as all models are, corrects many of the shortcomings of the previous models. In this chapter we will explore psychology and theology as *Allies as Subjects of one Sovereign*.

Allies as Subjects of One Sovereign

Therefore the lands belong to none of
*   you,*
The borders will not hold, the Law will
*   never serve the lawless.*
To every people the land is given on
*   condition.*
Perceived or not, there is a Covenant,
beyond the constitution, beyond
*   sovereign guarantee,*
beyond the nation's sweetest dreams of
*   itself.*

—Leonard Cohen[5]

The *Allies* model is premised on the belief that God's truths are revealed in the book of God's Word (Scripture) and the book of God's Works (creation). This model

---

argue that personal values and worldviews are sometimes so central to therapeutic processes that a shared faith commitment between therapist and client can often be advantageous.

3. "Je le pansai, Dieu le guérit."

4. "Guérir quelquefois, soulager souvent, consoler toujours."

5. Cohen, *Book of mercy*, 59.

rejects the claim of the *Enemies* model that psychology and Christianity are mutually exclusive, although it recognizes that there have been tensions and misunderstandings that have fostered such antagonism. The *Allies* model agrees with the *Spies* model that good psychology can be found in religion, but it categorically rejects the claim that religion is only valuable as a vehicle to express psychological truths and to foster psychological benefits.

The *Colonialist, Rebuilders, Neutral Parties*, and *Allies* models all affirm that psychology and theology can shed light on human behavior and that we can find numerous points of overlap between them. Like the *Colonialist* and *Rebuilders* models, the *Allies* model values Christian orthodoxy, but the *Allies* model does not agree that psychology as a discipline should be subservient to theology as a discipline. While the *Allies* model agrees with the *Rebuilders* model that secular assumptions often taint psychological theories and findings, the *Allies* model does not see the entire field as in need of complete overhaul. Rather, the *Allies* model recognizes that psychology has established itself as a unique discipline and affirms that people working in this field—whether in theory, research, or praxis—have unique insights with which we must be fully conversant if we are to engage the discipline as it exists today. The *Allies* model does caution, however, that we must be vigilant about ways that secular assumptions often shape the discipline of psychology in ways that may require critique from a Christian perspective.

The *Neutral Parties* model and the *Allies* model both generally accept the "two book" analogy, and agree that the books require proficiency in different ways of reading, or different methodologies. However, the *Allies* model contends that the degree of neutrality and independence required by the *Neutral Parties* model fails to ground scholarship and intervention sufficiently on a Christian understanding of persons. This failure leads people who follow the *Neutral Parties* model to embrace (at least loosely) modernist assumptions about objectivity and neutrality, and it handicaps their ability to portray a holistic understanding of human behavior.

The models that we have explored differ in the questions they ask and the answers they provide because they make different assumptions and have different goals. Recall the words of Chesterton's character, Mr. Pond; "Once assume the wrong beginning, and you'll not only give the wrong answer, but ask the wrong question."[6] Having a different set of assumptions, each of the models asks different questions, supplies different answers, and proceeds towards different destinations.

A visit to my in-laws one summer highlighted the importance of knowing our direction. I had traveled to a nearby town to meet a friend for breakfast. After we said our goodbyes, I decided to follow a serendipitous route back to my in-laws' house, driving on roads I had never been on before. Following only my sense

---

6. Chesterton, Ring of lovers, 88.

of direction, I kept heading north and west, knowing that doing so would take me where I needed to go. The roads wandered through cornfields filled with vigilant white-tailed deer, and along small wooded groves, frequently changing direction. With no map to follow, and few roads to choose from, I kept going more west than north, and I finally had to admit that I was lost. Entering a small town, I saw a police car driving down the road, so I pulled alongside and asked for help. I discovered that I had missed my mark by a few miles, and with the police officer's help, I quickly found a northerly route that put me back on track. When I asked for directions, I had to make some assumptions about the reliability of the police officer. Did he know where we were? Did he know how to get to where I wanted to go? Could I trust his directions?

Every scholar, regardless of discipline, essentially asks the same three questions: Where am I? Where am I trying to go? How can I get there? The first two questions are framed by one's worldview. The third question is a methodological and epistemological question. The *Allies* model begins with a biblical anthropology that makes certain assumptions about what it means to be human (e.g., created, fallen) and the purpose of human life (e.g., love of God and love of neighbor). These answers are unapologetically Christian—that is our starting point. Other people would certainly provide different answers to these questions. In both cases, however, we must begin with our assumptions about where we are and where we want to go. For those of us who intend to be intentionally Christian, some basic assumptions about God and human beings are the starting point from which our reasoning begins. All of us—whether Christian or not—need to be honest in declaring our allegiances at the outset. By doing so, we explicitly acknowledge the beliefs that shape how we understand the world. Furthermore, once acknowledged, our beliefs are available for debate and discussion. What we cannot do, however, is to pretend that we approach psychological scholarship or psychotherapy with complete neutrality and objectivity. Postmodern critiques of modernist epistemologies have certainly underscored this point.

In contrast to postmodernism, however, our answer to our third question ("How can I get where I want to go?") allows us to use various epistemic strategies once we have acknowledged that our beginning points are not beyond dispute. In essence, then, the integration of Christian faith and psychology requires us to begin by articulating the basic contours of the Christian faith and to engage the discipline of psychology informed by those beliefs.

To pursue this course of action, though, we must ask what the basic assumptions are that should frame our answer to the questions "Where are we?" and "Where am I trying to go?" In contrast to the previous models, the *Allies* model begins with the assertion that God's sovereignty reigns over all of life. Theology, psychology, and all other areas of inquiry are *subjects of One Sovereign*. First, they are His subjects in the sense that God created and sustains all truth. Thus, every academic subject that we study is God's subject. Second, because God is Sovereign, we need to be mindful of subjecting ourselves to His rule, which in part means employing theology, psychology, and every discipline toward godly ends. Because God has granted us these subjects, they can work together as *allies*. All of us who are scholars—theologians and psychologists included—are tenants of His realms, each using the unique methods of our respective disciplines to discern truth as best we can.[7] As we explore His Word and His Works, we seek to "think God's thoughts after Him."[8]

> Theological reflection typically focuses on *God's workings in the world*; psychological reflection typically focuses on *the workings of God's world*.

Given their diverse methods, source materials, and goals, theology and psychology emphasize different things. Theological reflection typically focuses on *God's workings in the world*. It tells

us the story of God's involvement with the world in creation and redemption. Psychological reflection typically focuses more on *the workings of God's world*. It helps us understand the mechanisms through which much of human behavior is mediated. When we move into the realm of psychotherapy, though, we enact our beliefs about how things should be. For instance, implicit in the treatment of anxiety disorders, depression, and psychosis are the assumptions that anxiety should be relieved, happiness is preferable to profound sadness, and impaired reality testing is problematic. A Christian worldview is directly relevant when we ask what values and goals we should embrace and pursue. In all circumstances, a Christian worldview frames the backdrop through which we view reality.

We should expect to find parallels between psychology and theology because they have a common Author and describe a single reality, but integration is about far more than simply identifying parallels between psychology and theology. While psychology and theology require some degree of independence, the two cannot be completely severed from one another. A Christian scholar, to be honest and intentionally Christian, must acknowledge the Christian assumptions that shape how he or she conceptualizes human nature, the methods that can be used to study human behavior, the ethics that guide the application of the discipline, the ends that we hope to achieve, and the research questions that we pose.

As we pursue an integrative understanding, we will sometimes find that

---

7. The tenant may or may not recognize God's sovereignty. To the degree that individuals fail to recognize God's sovereignty, the central precept of their work is missing and misleading; yet they may still discover truths. We are also free to critique the methodologies of our disciplines because our allegiance is not to the status quo, but to serving God, ministering to the needs of others, and seeking truth.

8. The phrase is attributed to Johannes Kepler (1571–1630).

our psychological and theological understandings do not match up perfectly. Sometimes we will read one book or the other incorrectly, and we will never fully grasp the nuances written in their pages, but we are given the task of reading from both books by the One who is the Author of the book of His Word written to us. It is also important to underscore that we are, ourselves, characters inscribed in the book of God's Works.[9] As Mary Stewart Van Leeuwen said, "all persons are 'characters in search of an author,'—that is, fundamentally worshiping beings who, if not committed to the one true God, will inevitably end up revering some substitute within God's creation."[10]

The way we read God's books will either lead us to revere our Author or to worship one of His creatures. Thus, one aim of integration should be simply and profoundly to stand in awe of, and to worship, our Creator.

Core Convictions

Every model has limitations, and the *Allies* model is no exception. One of our first obstacles is defining exactly what assumptions are constitutive of a uniquely Christian approach to psychology. How do we identify the core convictions of Christianity, and how can we leave room

for a divergence of different Christian approaches? The church has grappled with this question throughout its history, going back as far as its Jewish roots.

The most basic formulation of Jewish theology was the *Shema*: *Shemaʿ yiśraʾel ʾadonai ʾeloheynu ʾadonai ʾeḥad*, "Hear, O Israel: The LORD our God, the LORD is One" (Deut 6:4, NIV). "The Shema is not a prayer . . . but a confession of faith."[11] As this theology developed in Judaism, it emphasized "God's oneness," the call for Israel "to love him and obey his commandments." It also recounted the rewards for obedience and the consequences for disobedience, and the means for reminding one of the commandments (for example, through the garments still worn today by Orthodox Jews).[12] While Judaism affirmed the *Shema* as a creed, and while observant Jews attempt to follow Jewish laws, the primary concern of Judaism is relational. "In Hebrew thought the essence of true godliness is tied primarily to a relationship, not to a creed . . . For the Hebrews, personal or individual relationship has always been far more expressive of the heart of religious faith than mere intellectual assent to abstract statements or religious ideas."[13]

Interestingly, when asked about the most important commandment, Jesus affirmed the Shema and immediately proceeded to focus on the duty to love God and others (Matt 22:36–40). Thus Jesus affirmed the importance of correct

---

9. That we are characters does not imply that all of our actions are determined, for written into the fabric of creation is some degree of freedom.

10. Van Leeuwen, Five uneasy questions, 152.

---

11. Wilson, *Our father Abraham*, 123.

12. Ibid., 123–34.

13. Ibid., 138.

doctrine *and* the actions that should be impelled by belief (Mark 12:29–31).

Shortly after Jesus's death, the apostles became the living authorities who provided guidance on doctrinal matters. As the apostles died, the gospels and the epistles became important guides for faith and practice. Yet there remained the task of determining which writings were authoritative, and hence the councils of the church determined which writings should be in the canon of Scripture. As various debates emerged about what formed the core of Christian belief, councils convened to formulate the basis of the Christian confession.

Today, most Christians share a common canon of Scripture (although the Roman Catholic, Eastern Orthodox, and Oriental Orthodox include apocryphal collections in the Old Testament). Most Christians today embrace the Apostles' Creed and the Nicene Creed, although, here too, there are several Protestant denominations that are noncreedal or which affirm distinctive creeds.[14] Furthermore, denominations sometimes subtly alter the basic creeds to emphasize particular theological distinctions. The Nicene Creed summarizes

the most basic doctrines of the Christian faith that are held by Catholic, Orthodox, and the founders of the Protestant Reformation.[15] Beyond a few basic confessions held in common by all orthodox Christians at all times and places, distinctions between Christian movements are clearly evident.

Thus, we find substantial areas of agreement across the history of Christianity about a few core doctrines, with much divergence concerning peripheral issues. I must hasten to add, though, that well articulated theology is worthless unless it makes a tangible difference in how one lives. As James said, "Do what God's teaching says; when you only listen and do nothing, you are fooling yourselves" (Jas 1:22, NCV), and "faith by itself, if it is not accompanied by action, is dead" (Jas 2:17, NIV). Al Dueck, who comes from a noncreedal Christian tradition, echoes this concern: "I have had clients who assented to the creeds of the church but violently abused a spouse. What is missing in these and other instances is faithful practice."[16]

Orthodoxy (right belief) must exist hand in hand with orthopraxy (right action). This does not mean, however, that doctrine is unimportant. Doctrine anchors belief and practice. The modern era, however, has evidenced a tumultuous rejection of many core doctrines that have been affirmed by Christian

---

14. Thomas Oden points out that the Nicene Creed was developed for catechesis before baptism so that those who entered the Christian faith new and affirmed the basic teachings of the universal church. In contrast to those who see the creed as archaic or outmoded, Oden asserts that, "The ancient confession still serves as the most fitting and durable framework for the postmodern rediscovery of classic Christian teaching" (in George, *Evangelicals and Nicene Faith*, 8).

---

15. See Beckwith, in George, *Evangelicals and Nicene Faith*, 61ff.

16. Dueck, Honoring my tradition, forthcoming.

orthodoxy for most of the past two millennia. Consider, for example, the following section of the Nicene Creed, taken from the version published by the Episcopal Church in the 1979 *Book of Common Prayer*.

> We believe in one Lord, Jesus Christ, the only Son of God, eternally begotten of the Father, God from God, Light from Light, true God from true God, begotten, not made, of one Being with the Father. Through him all things were made. For us and for our salvation he came down from heaven: by the power of the Holy Spirit he became incarnate from the Virgin Mary, and was made man. For our sake he was crucified under Pontius Pilate; he suffered death and was buried. On the third day he rose again in accordance with the Scriptures; he ascended into heaven and is seated at the right hand of the Father.[17]

Historically, it has always been patently clear that the Nicene Creed proclaimed the mystery of a literal incarnation of the Son of God in human flesh through the Virgin Mary, and the literal death and resurrection of Jesus Christ. However, the orthodox understanding of the Creed and the Scriptures has been disputed by adherents of ancient and modern heresies.[18]

One example of those who want to call themselves Christians but deny the orthodox teaching of the church is retired Episcopal bishop, John Shelby Spong. Arguing that the Apostles' Creed and the Nicene Creed are products of a premodern worldview, Spong asserted, "If the God I worship must be identified with these ancient creedal words in any literal sense, God would become for me not just unbelievable, but in fact no longer worthy of the subject of my devotion."[19]

Reconceptualizing Christianity without belief in a literal incarnation and resurrection, and without acknowledging God as the Creator of the universe would fundamentally alter the central tenets of the faith. According to Spong, Christianity can be expressed in "nontheistic images,"[20] and the creeds and Scriptures can be seen as metaphorical realities. Spong willingly admits that this revisioning of Christianity requires sacrificing traditional beliefs about God, leaving "an almost contentless concept, which must be allowed to find new meaning or it will die."[21]

Orthodoxy cannot accommodate such a radical revisioning of Christianity. Such revisionist impulses proposed by Spong and others reflect liberal accommodations to modernism. A more

---

17. Episcopal Church, *Book of Common Prayer*.

18. According to the *Oxford English Dictionary* (*OED*), *heresy* refers to "theological or religious opinion or doctrine maintained in opposition, or held to be contrary, to the

'catholic' or orthodox doctrine of the Christian Church . . ." *OED*, vol. 7:164, *heresy* definition 1-a.

19. Spong, *Why Christianity must change or die*, 4.

20. Ibid., 57.

21. Ibid., 41.

constructive, orthodox proposal was offered by the late Robert Webber, whose entire career can be captured in the phrase *ancient-future Christianity*. Webber claimed that the road to the future of the church lies in embracing its past as we address the unique challenges of the present. According to Webber, "One of the major reasons why the church has fallen prey to a cultural accommodation is that it has become disconnected from its roots in Scripture, in the ancient church and in its heritage through the centuries."[22]

> If the story of creation, incarnation, and redemption is our starting point, then we must also remember that our destination is to be faithful stewards of all the God has entrusted to us.

Webber, who has always argued passionately the need to recover the creeds and practices of the church, embraced the notion that God's narrative must be our starting point. "Neither the ancient church fathers nor the Reformers looked to reason as the foundations of the Christian faith. For them the narrative of God's activity in history stood on its own. Instead of bringing reason to the narrative as a way of shoring it up and making it acceptable, they asked us to live in the narrative and interpret philosophy

and all other disciplines from within the narrative."[23]

And what is this narrative? In Webber's words, "The heart of the story is how God became one of us to take our suffering into himself, to deal with sin, overcome death, and to be resurrected to new life—all in order that fallen creation could be restored to right relationship with God."[24] This narrative is the lens through which everything must be seen for anyone who takes the orthodox expression of the Christian faith seriously.

One of the problems that has plagued faith-learning integration is our collective failure to adequately define the core convictions of Christian faith, and to recognize the insights that can be found in the distinctive expressions of the faith expressed by diverse branches of Christianity. God's activity in creation, incarnation, and redemption is our starting point. This narrative is expressed in Scripture, reflected in the great creeds of the church, and lived out in various denominational expressions. This starting point frees us to study psychology and all other academic disciplines from a perspective that is informed and sanctified by the story of God's grace.

If the story of creation, incarnation, and redemption is our starting point, then we must also remember that our destination is to be faithful stewards of all that God has entrusted to us. Christ calls us to serve and praise Him with all of our being. As His servants, we must seek to

---

22. Webber, *Who gets to narrate the world?*, 16.

23. Ibid., 128.

24. Ibid., 136.

be agents of reconciliation as we strive to love our neighbor. Thus the relational element that was central to Judaism, and that was affirmed by Jesus in His teaching on the greatest commandments, is integrally tied to the creeds of Christianity. Orthodoxy cannot be "right belief" without orthopraxy, "right action."

Developing an integrative perspective thus proceeds from a Christocentric framework, with particular ends in mind, but it is cultivated by hard work. It is a challenge, but not an impossibility. In the words of the Jesuit priest and psychoanalyst, William Meissner: "The great challenge to the Christian psychologists . . . is to shape a theory of man's psychological functioning which incorporates the data and insights of modern psychological understanding, and which is also fully consonant with the penetrating insights of the Christian tradition."[25]

Those who pursue an integrative viewpoint are not content to reject either of God's books, and they desire to read both of them competently. Those who embrace the *Allies* model are convinced that we will read more accurately when our reading is informed by a biblical worldview.

Procedures and Parallels

The *procedures* used in each of the four previous models have their place within an integrative model, but they are guided by different goals. While the *Allies* model

requires us to frame our understanding of the human condition within a biblical worldview, it does not limit us to investigating human nature through theological sources alone. It recognizes that disciplinary *segregation* is necessary for methodological purposes; psychology will always rely on the philosophical and historical underpinnings and empirical and non-empirical research methods unique to the discipline; Christian theology will utilize hermeneutics, history, critical reflection, and so forth in studying God's Word. However, we must also recall that even at the disciplinary level, we cannot claim to be agnostic—we take our basic beliefs with us and they inform the questions that we ask, the methods that we use, and the ends that we seek.

The *Allies* model, like several other models, allows us to observe the *psychological effects* of religious belief and practice. However, it is not simply concerned with whether or not a given religious practice is psychologically beneficial or harmful. It is equally interested in asking whether a given religious practice is theologically warranted. For example, imagine that we were to study levels of depression among people who sing contemporary Christian worship songs compared to those who sing traditional hymns in their worship services. Suppose that we were to find that those who sing contemporary worship songs had lower average levels of depression compared to the people who sing hymns. Would this mean that we should recommend the singing of contemporary Christian worship songs? An examination of the

---

25. Meissner, Problem and problematic, 4.

content of contemporary worship songs might well show that many of them reflect American individualism, a narcissistic focus on self, relatively little genuine worship, and poorly conceived theology. We need to ask what kind of "self" we should promote, whether in psychotherapy or in the lyrics and message of the typical church service. A narcissistic chorus might well reduce depression, but that would not necessarily make it genuinely Christian or psychologically healthy. This hypothetical scenario is not meant to denigrate all contemporary worship choruses or to espouse the superiority of hymns. The point is that our telos—whether in worship choruses, hymns, or psychotherapy—needs to be theologically sound. So, just as we would want to examine contemporary worship songs and hymns to assess their content as well as their effects, we need to explore whether psychological models and techniques are consonant with Christian beliefs and lead toward godly ends.

As we explore human nature, guided by basic Christian presuppositions and utilizing the methods of psychology and theology, we will encounter times when the two disciplines appear to give contradictory accounts. There are psychological and theological interpretations that will need to be *rejected* and *modified* as the clarity of one book helps us to identify our misinterpretations of the other book, or to flesh out details that one book or the other does not supply. For instance, psychological awareness of the multiple determinants of behavior (genes, social environment, reinforcement history, and

so forth) might help us understand why one individual struggles with certain sins while the same sins are not tempting for other individuals. Likewise, Christian theology could help us understand the pervasiveness of human sin that causes each of us to struggle with sin in some form or another.

The *observation of parallels* between psychology and Christian theology can be a first step toward integration, and an integrative view can lead to the search for such parallels. Integrationists will observe areas of overlapping interest between psychology and Christian theology, but integrationists are additionally concerned to bring the findings of the two disciplines into a consonant relationship.[26] For instance, the Bible offers instructions to discipline our children (Prov 19:18), to love our children (Titus 2:4), and not to exasperate them (Eph 6:4). Similarly, psychological research has demonstrated that the parenting style associated with the best outcomes involve moderate levels of control, ample expression of warmth and love, and open lines of communication.[27] Rather than

---

26. Their similarity and divergence can be seen in Bube's description of *complementarity*: "Science and theology tell us different kinds of things about the same things. Each, when true to its own authentic capabilities, provides us with valid insights into the nature of reality from different perspectives. *It is the task of individuals and communities of individuals to integrate these two types of insights to obtain an adequate and coherent view of reality*" (Bube, *Putting it all together*, 167; italics added).

27. See, for example, Baumrind, Child care practices; and Baumrind, Effective parenting.

simply noting such parallels, however, integrationists want to know how those findings help us to understand human behavior more fully, and to consider the practical psychological and theological consequences of a more accurate and complete understanding of human nature and functioning. Integrationists progress beyond dualistically examining separate facets of reality (psychological and theological), by trying to come to an understanding of reality that is informed by both perspectives.

Integration in Historical Context

The desire to pursue integration is not new. As we saw in chapter 1, the roots of the questions underlying integration go back at least to Tertullian, if not before. Within the American experience, it can be traced through the establishment of colleges such as Harvard and Yale by people who "believed in the unity and coherence of knowledge as reflective of the Creator."[28] Indeed, the founders of Harvard established it for the purpose "that students might be free to know truth and life in relation to Jesus Christ" in the belief that "the first step in learning about the world was to learn about the world's Creator" and that "a relationship with Christ could be celebrated in every area of life and study."[29] Integration is nothing new, yet every Christian who seeks to bring his or her faith into

contact with his or her activities in more than a superficial manner must approach it anew in every age.

We must contextualize the specific kind of integration with which this book is concerned within the larger efforts of scholars and students of the Christian liberal arts to integrate faith and learning. Coe made the following suggestion: "I propose . . . [that we should] maximize the dialogue between . . . theology and the natural disciplines. According to this model, the natural disciplines and theology by definition *depend upon one another for completing their respective tasks of exploring God and His world in order to provide the fullest possible picture of them.*"[30]

Hasker, also writing from this more comprehensive approach to Christian liberal arts, put forward the following description: "Faith-learning integration may be briefly described as *a scholarly project whose goal is to ascertain and to develop integral relationships which exist between the Christian faith and human knowledge, particularly as expressed in the various academic disciplines.*"[31]

Coe and Hasker's definitions of integration emphasize the exploration of God and His world, informed by the perspectives of various academic disciplines. Integration involves dialogue, but it goes beyond mere exchange of ideas in an attempt to discern integral relationships

---

28. Buss, Educating toward a Christian worldview, 63.

29. Monroe, *Finding God at Harvard*, 14–15.

30. Coe, *An interdependent model*, 111 (italics original).

31. Hasker, Faith-learning integration, 234 (italics original).

and develop a more complete picture of God and His world. Integration cannot be reduced to adding a devotional element to scholarly work, nor does reading Scripture or praying at the beginning of class result in a Christian lecture. Integration does not occur when we merely sandwich disciplinary content between prayer and a handful of Bible verses. Integration must involve genuine *interaction between* different perspectives on a topic of common interest.

While helpful, the views of Coe and Hasker are primarily concerned with scholarship. As important as this aspect of integration is, it cannot be isolated from that integration which has as its purpose the whole person, not just his or her mind. The mind is a crucial focus of integration because a Christian understanding of the world affects how we think about and understand the world. As Holmes asserted, "We see nature, persons, society, and the arts and sciences in proper relationship to their divine Creator and Lord."[32] In the end, though, integration is a never-ending quest to be transformed by "the integration of faith into every dimension of a person's life and character."[33]

Integration of What?

One of the immediate problems of integration is that we do not have uniformity of opinion on what is to be integrated.

When we move from the broad view of the Christian liberal arts to the more narrow view that is the specific subject of this book, we immediately run into a problem: what is to be integrated? Psychology and Theology? Psychology and Christianity? Psychotherapy and principles of biblical counseling? Some people reject the term "integration," seeing it as unnecessarily dualistic[34] and reflective of an unwarranted modernist reliance on positivism.[35] Regardless of the merits of these critiques, the name has stuck, and it is the framework that we have.[36]

In their introduction to a special issue of the *Journal of Psychology and Christianity* on the current state of integration, Kauffmann and Hill began with a dictionary definition of "integrate" and simply proceeded to note that "'Integration' has been the dominant term over the past few decades to describe the relationship

---

32. Holmes, *The idea of a Christian college*, 17.

33. Ibid., 46–47.

34. Van Leeuwen, Five uneasy questions, 150–60. Van Leeuwen prefers the idea of "unity of faith and learning" to avoid the perceived red flag of dualism. See also Van Leeuwen, *The sorcerer's apprentice*.

35. See Vande Kemp, *Psychology and Christian spirituality*. See also Van Leeuwen, *The person in psychology*.

36. The corrective of seeing knowledge as ultimately unified is valuable. Yet in a fractured world in which knowledge is fragmented, it seems to me that we do need to reintegrate or recognize the fundamental unity that we often fail to experience. Likewise the modernist and positivist notion that we will have all the answers by the by is not defensible. Nonetheless, the dominant paradigm within psychology continues to be the empirical one, yet room is increasingly being made by and for nonempirical approaches.

between psychology and the Christian faith" and dedicated the special issue to "what it means to be both a Christian and a psychologist and how our efforts in scholarship and practice should reflect an integrated unity."[37] This rather circular and nebulous definition demonstrates the problem. In the same issue Eck argued that "there is a need to develop a consistent definition of what integration means" because, short of agreeing on "the proposition that all truth is God's truth," authors espouse different types of integration and mean different things by the word.[38]

Steven Bouma-Prediger noted the difficulties caused by the lack of a shared definition of integration: "The literature is often unclear on what exactly integration is, and in personal conversations, all too often the parties involved in a dialogue regarding integration proceed without clarifying just what it is they are talking about."[39]

Bouma-Prediger proposed four different ways of talking about integration: *interdisciplinary*, *intradisciplinary*, *faith-praxis*, and *experiential*. *Interdisciplinary integration* involves a project of exploring the foundational philosophical assumptions of two or more disciplines that share a common subject. *Intradisciplinary integration* occurs within a discipline as one seeks to ensure that disciplinary theory and disciplinary practice are consistent.

In *faith-praxis integration* we are concerned with how our faith commitments are related to how we live our lives; it is thus personal rather than academic or theoretical. *Experiential integration* refers to striving for personal wholeness, including reconciliation with others and with God. As with the previous models, Bouma-Prediger helped to clarify what integration involves, but we are still left without a good working definition.

Toward a Definition of Integration

Since no single definition of *integration* has emerged, it may help to look at how the word is applied in conventional usage.[40] It is often noted that integration means to put things together into a whole; for instance, two companies may merge and integrate their work forces, releasing some workers, reassigning others, and altering the corporate structure in the hopes of making a single, smooth operation—"a well-oiled machine" by analogy. In some sense, this is what is done in interdisciplinary integration—the two disciplines adjust as some parts fit together nicely and others do not. But the analogy is imperfect; when we integrate psychology and Christianity, we do not necessarily end up with a hybrid

---

37. Kauffman & Hill, Guest editor's page, 99.

38. Eck, Integrating the integrators, 101.

39. Bouma-Prediger, The task of integration, 21.

40. For a different argument from analogy, see Robert Roberts's discussion of integration as *grafting*, *introducing*, and *adopting*; the discussion can be found in his response to Gary Collins in Johnson & Jones, *Psychology and Christianity*, 135–40.

"Christian psychology." A cleaner definition is thus called for than this analogy alone provides.

The word *integration* comes from the same root word from which we derive the mathematical term *integer*, that is, a whole number as opposed to a fractional one. Thus the word integration emphasizes an essential unity that is opposed to fractionalization. It is at this point that the problem seems to emerge. We live in a fractured world, and academia is particularly fragmented. We have specialists in diverse areas of medicine, science, literature, and theology, but very few people who intentionally draw our attention to the underlying connections and unity of the disparate parts, even though this is the ideal of a liberal arts education.

> The integration of psychology and Christianity is a multi-faceted attempt to discern the underlying truths about the nature and functioning of human beings from the unique vantage points of psychology (in its various sub-disciplines, utilizing diverse methodologies) and Christianity (in theology, faith, and practice).

Another definition of the word *integration*, according to the *Oxford English Dictionary*, is: "The combining of diverse parts into a complex whole; a complex state the parts of which are distinguishable."[41] Given this definition, it is not necessary to combine elements in a blender, as it were, in which the various parts are no longer distinguishable from one another. Rather, the origins and uniqueness of the parts may be recognized, but they are brought together in such a way that they function harmoniously—much as the various instruments in an orchestra can be brought together in a unity that provides something grander than any of its parts alone.

Yet another definition has its origins in the civil rights movement: "The bringing into equal membership of a common society those groups or persons previously discriminated against on racial or cultural grounds."[42] Once again, by analogy, this seems to have some applicability to the discussion, given the historical animosity of some psychologists toward religion, and some Christians toward psychology.

Given the foregoing etymological discussion, ideas garnered earlier in this book, and the insights brought by our forbearers in the Christian liberal arts and of those interested in integrating faith and learning within the field of psychology, let us propose an initial working definition of integration. *The integration of psychology and Christianity is a multi-faceted attempt to discern the underlying truths about the nature and functioning of human beings from the unique vantage points of psychology (in its various*

---

41. *The Oxford English dictionary*, vol. 7, *integration*, definition 1-b, 1065.

42. Ibid., definition 1-c, 1065.

subdisciplines, utilizing diverse methodologies) and Christianity (in theology, faith, and practice). Integration begins with basic Christian assumptions (creation, incarnation, reconciliation), and embraces a telos of faithful stewardship to God. Christian scholarship must be cognizant of our beginning points and our goals, recognizing the advantages, limitations, histories, assumptions, sources of data, methodologies, areas of overlap, and areas of uniqueness of psychological and theological perspectives on human nature and functioning.

Integration will take place in various ways. It will necessitate the ongoing development of a Christian *worldview* from which to evaluate our assumptions. It will involve explicating the *foundational* presuppositions and histories of our disciplines. It will be a *disciplinary and scholarly* exercise when one attempts to integrate the findings of the disciplines of psychology and Christian theology. It will be an *applied* integration when we ask how the findings of psychology can be used to assuage personal distress and cultural injustice. Finally, it will be *public and personal*; it will be a *shared responsibility* and a *personal quest* for wholeness by individuals within their communities and in relation to God. We might summarize the types and tasks of integration as follows.

Worldview Integration—developing a coherent worldview based on a Christian understanding of human beings in the context of our origin, purpose, and history as revealed in God's Word. Such a perspective will take into account an understanding of human beings as made in the image of God; created with finite capacities and a divinely appointed place within the created realm that was declared to be "very good"; fallen in sin and subsequently living in a broken world; and the focus of God's redemptive plan in history.

Foundational Integration—developing an understanding of the historical and philosophical foundations of psychology and Christian theology. For psychology this will include philosophy of science in general, as well as the diverse assumptions and histories of the various subfields of psychology. For theology this will include systematic theology, biblical theology, epistemology (including hermeneutics), and the historical and philosophical contexts from which various theological perspectives emerged. In comparing the disciplines at the foundational level we should expect to find that some of their assumptions overlap while others will differ based on the unique perspective and aims of the discipline. For example, some forms of psychology will make use of methodological naturalism while some theologies will focus on existential meaning.

Disciplinary and Scholarly Integration—developing a more complete picture of a common subject by exploring psychological and theological perspectives. At this level, there will always be disciplinary independence, but there will be an interaction in which the two are capable of informing and critiquing each other. For instance, theology can and should critique attempts at biological reductionism and strict determinism. Theology can also be one of the sources from which we create hypotheses that we can test empirically. On the other hand, psychology can and should critique theological attempts to see human beings in terms of spiritual reductionism that fails to appreciate the biological, psychological, and social dimensions. Typically, then, we are concerned with *interdisciplinary integration* at this level. However, this level also allows for *intradisciplinary integration*, that is, for examining whether praxis and theory are consistent within each discipline. To follow up on our previous examples, if a psychologist accepts the theological insight that humans are spiritual beings, yet completely neglects spiritual concerns in his or her practice, there is a problem at this level. Conversely, if a pastoral counselor admits that human beings are biological beings, yet persists in advocating only religious interventions in a case where there is need for biological intervention, there has been a failure of intradisciplinary integration.

Applied Integration—psychology and theology can be abstract or theoretical disciplines, but both of them have a keen interest in application. Applied integration asks how Christianity and psychology ought to be applied to concrete situations such as Alzheimer's disease, marital conflict, despair, and racism. At this level, we explore how psychology and Christian theology can aid us in confronting personal and social issues that are within the scope of their mutual concern. In the words of Stan Jones, "Christianity is not just a system of thought, but also of practice. This system of practice lays claim on every facet of our lives. In becoming one of Christ's followers, we become obliged to strive to bring glory to God by all our actions, to be God's agent of reconciliation and healing in the world, and to seek the immediate and ultimate good for those about us."[43] Integrative efforts that fail to result in praise of God, to bring a message of hope and reconciliation, and to minister grace and healing to the world can hardly be considered to be "Christian" in any true sense of the word.

"Grace must find expression in life, otherwise it is not grace."

—Karl Barth

Public and Personal Integration—integration is done by people, and importantly, by people who live and work in community. We must cultivate a culture in which integration is encouraged as a social enterprise in which dialogue, critique, and support are found. The integrative task is too large for any individual to accomplish effectively; it must be a shared responsibility.

Integration is also intensely *personal*. By this, I do not mean that it is subjective, or far less that it is relativistic. I want to emphasize, instead, that integration is a quest for personal wholeness. Several writers, notably Tan[44] and Bufford,[45] have highlighted the importance of personal

---

43. Jones, Reflections, 138.

44. Tan, Integration and beyond.

45. Bufford, Consecrated counseling.

integration. Tan convincingly argued that personal integration "is the most foundational area of integration."[46] Personal commitments and character are central to everything that we do. This applies to research and scholarship just as much as it does to counseling. Without personal "appropriation of faith and integration of psychological and spiritual experience" at the personal level, genuine integration at other levels is impossible.[47] Personal integration must be lived out as it is variously reflected in one's scholarly and vocational pursuits, one's relationship to others, one's relationship to God, and one's sense of purpose, wholeness, and fulfillment as an individual.

Personal integration is crucially involved in motivation. Why should we invest our time and energy in the difficult tasks of integration? Doing so only makes sense if we are motivated by the desire to know and serve God with all of our God-given abilities. This, in turn, requires personal dispositions such as humility and diligence. The result of our effort is not just knowledge--as important as that is. Ultimately, we are trying to love God with all of our being and to express love and compassion for our fellow human beings in a principled and humane fashion.

It should be evident that you have already encountered many of the issues discussed above in earlier chapters of this book, so you are already well on your way to putting the various pieces together. It should be apparent that these types of integration are not completely independent. Worldview assumptions affect foundational assumptions. Personal efforts take place in relationship with communities and ideas. And so forth.

The words of Pope John Paul II delivered to the World Psychiatric Association seem a fitting end to the concerns of this chapter, both for the academic and the clinical psychologist: "By its very nature, your work often brings you to the threshold of the human mystery. It involves a sensitivity to the often tangled workings of the human mind and heart, and an openness to the ultimate concerns which give meaning to people's lives. These are areas of utmost importance to the Church, and they call to mind the urgent need for a constructive dialogue between science and religion for the sake of shedding greater light on the mystery of man in its fullness."[48]

If we are to grasp even an inkling of the mystery of human beings, we need the light of God's Word and the light of His Works. And if we are to study this mystery as Christian scholars, then we must unapologetically admit that a Christian worldview informs our understanding of persons and our approach to the discipline of psychology.

---

46. Tan, Integration and beyond, 24.

47. Ibid.

48. John Paul II, quoted in Gillespie, *Psychology and American Catholicism*, 179.

Looking back: Take a moment to recall the unique foci of each of the types and tasks of integration: worldview integration, foundational integration, disciplinary and scholarly integration, applied integration, and public and personal integration.

Summary

The introduction of this book used the analogy that integration is like *taking the fork in the road*; that is, that psychology and Christian theology are both concerned with human nature and functioning—but utilizing different methods and source materials. We approach this fork in the road not as completely objective, neutral, disinterested parties, but as people who embrace the central message of the historic, orthodox Christian faith. God's activity in creation, incarnation, and redemption is our starting point, and our goal is to be His faithful servants, acknowledging His sovereignty over all of life. Wisely used, psychology and Christian theology can jointly give us a more complete and accurate picture than either could alone, because both of them are concerned with truths revealed by God in nature and in His Word. He is sovereign over the contents of both disciplines, and as we discover the wonders of His creation and His character we are left with awe and gratitude.

As we read the book of God's Word and the book of His Works, we must always remember that our perspective is limited and our opinions prone to error. In our humble efforts, though, the integrative model implies that there is no valid distinction between the "sacred" and the "secular." For the Christian, all that we do is an exercise of priestly stewardship of what God has given to us, and of the service that we owe Him in return. The words of Johannes Kepler are worth our contemplation:

> Then I think, since in relation to the book of nature, we astronomers are priests of Almighty God, we should not consider the glory of our intellects, but the glory of God . . . I am content with the honour of standing guard with my discovery at the door of the shrine at whose high altar Copernicus performs divine service.[49]

We who explore the book of God's Word and the book of God's Works likewise perform a divine service of worship as we explore the glory of God as it is arrayed before us.

Questions for Reflection and Discussion

1. How can the two quotations from Ambroise Paré, ("I dressed the

---

49. From a letter of Johannes Kepler to Herwart von Hohenburg, 26 March 1598; reprinted in Brocker, *Johannes Kepler*, 42.

wound, God healed him," and "Cure occasionally, relieve often, console always"), be applied to your own area of study?

2. Look at the two extended quotations from Elizabeth Barrett Browning and Leonard Cohen. How do these two quotations reflect the focus of the *Allies as Subjects of One Sovereign* model?

3. The author framed the chapter around three questions: "Where am I?" "Where am I trying to go?" and "How can I get there?" How do your answers to these questions frame the way you approach your intended profession?

4. The author claimed that one of the difficulties of integration is defining exactly what assumptions are constitutive of a uniquely Christian approach to psychology, and how we can leave room for a divergence of different Christian approaches. What do you see as nonnegotiable core convictions that guide your understanding of the world?

5. Spong and Webber take diametrically opposed approaches to faith in the modern world. Spong asserted that faith must be purged of its mythic elements to make it acceptable to the modern mind. Webber claimed that we must interpret reality from within the Christian narrative. Which approach do you affirm and why?

6. The author noted that "theological reflection typically focuses more on *God's workings in the world*, while psychological reflection typically focuses more on *the workings of God's world*." What implications does this statement have for integration?

7. American colleges, like Harvard and Yale, which were founded on Christian assumptions, gradually drifted away from their historical roots to the point where some of them embody anti-Christian sentiments. Is this drift inevitable? How can one keep a Christian worldview while exploring a diversity of "secular" disciplines and theories?

8. Hasker's view of integration is primarily one that takes place at the scholarly and disciplinary level. Other definitions (e.g., those of Bouma-Prediger, and Entwistle) add other levels of integration. Do you think integration should be viewed solely as a disciplinary matter? What are the advantages and disadvantages of limiting integration to a disciplinary level? What are the additional challenges of broadening integration to include other levels (e.g., worldview, personal, etc.)? What are the advantages and disadvantages of this broader conceptualization of integration?

9. The author provided the following definition: *the integration of psychology and Christianity is a multifaceted attempt to discern the underlying truths about the nature and functioning of human beings from the unique vantage points of psychology (in its*

various subdisciplines utilizing diverse methodologies) and Christianity (in theology, faith, and practice). Given this definition, what would integration look like for you in your current situation (e.g., as a student, professor, pastor, psychologist, etc.)?

10. The author noted that the quest for integration takes place at many levels: *worldview*; *foundational*; *disciplinary and scholarly*; *applied*; and *public and personal*. What does integration look like at these various levels? Give an example for each.

11. Kepler saw astronomers as "priests of Almighty God" who have "the honour of standing guard . . . at the door of the shrine at whose high altar Copernicus performs divine service." How might this sentiment apply to all of us who study the book of God's Works? How can we heed Kepler's warning to "not consider the glory of our intellects, but the glory of God" in our academic and disciplinary pursuits?

12

Integration in Research and Practice

Rarely do we find men who willingly engage in hard, solid thinking. There is an almost universal quest for easy answers and half-baked solutions. Nothing pains some people more than having to think.

—Martin Luther King Jr., *The strength to love*, 14

Thinking is easy, acting is difficult, and to put one's thoughts into action is the most difficult thing in the world.

—Johann Wolfgang von Goethe

Consider two scenes, one clinical, one academic.

Leslie sat in my office during an intake session. She was clearly distraught, and in her mind, her distress was caused by spiritual rebellion. When her son had been born eighteen months earlier, she and her husband decided to name him John. A few days later, she became convinced that God was telling her to name him Charlie. She and her husband discussed the situation, and he said that it was okay to change their son's name. But Leslie hated the name Charlie. And other people told her that they were not convinced that God had actually told her to change John's name. As I talked to Leslie, it was quite obvious that she had symptoms of depression and obsessive compulsive disorder. The burning question for Leslie, though, was whether or not she should change her son's name.

I am teaching a class, and we are discussing the work of John Chrysostom, a fourth-century priest and bishop known for his oratorical skills. John was unsparing in his criticism of how the needs of the poor were neglected. "Do you pay such honor to your excrements as to receive them into a silver chamber-pot when another man made in the image of God is perishing in the cold?" said the provocative bishop. Or yet again, "Slander is worse than cannibalism!" Chrysostom provokes us to think about our character and about what Christ requires of us. But as we delve into his history, we discover that Chrysostom sometimes

268 Integrative Approaches to Psychology and Christianity

took things to an extreme with dire consequences. For instance, he spent two years in a standing position—even while eating and sleeping—because he could not see how one could take the command of Jesus to "watch and pray" literally unless one remained upright. Doing so, however, left him with lifelong digestive problems.

Both Leslie and John Chrysostom clearly have some unusual—even unhealthy and distorted—religious beliefs. Both of them also have positive religious values and experiences that shape their idea of how they should live and of the coping resources available to them. Both stories clearly relate to psychological concerns. And both stories are complex. How do we interact with such complexities? As we move from somewhat abstract ideas about integration to more practical ones of how to do integration, we need to think about how integration is expressed through how we think about human nature and well-being, how we do research, and how we do clinical work.

Beyond the Foundations

In the previous chapter, I suggested that the Allies model requires that we specify the core convictions from which integration ensues. I argued that these core convictions should minimally involve the affirmation of God's activity in creation, incarnation, and redemption as our starting point. I also argued that the guiding ends that we strive for should include love of God and love of neighbor. Nicholas Wolterstorff offered a simple but crucial observation in this regard: "Anyone who is fundamentally committed to being a Christ-follower will in consequence do and believe certain things."[1] As important as these foundational beliefs are, though, they don't tell us much about how to build on them, which is our current concern. If we are to integrate psychology and Christianity, we must develop some guidelines about how we should proceed. In the next several sections, we will explore what integration might look like as we think about personality theories, as we do research, and as we do counseling or therapy.

Integration and Theory

In some ways, integration is easiest at the theoretical level. Unfortunately, integration has not focused on creating new, testable theories nearly as much as it has focused on critiquing the assumptions underlying secular theories. A few major exceptions to this trend exist, however. Christians have devoted significant efforts in developing theories and conducting research on God representations, attachment to God, forgiveness, gratitude, shame, and a handful of other topics that are clearly integral theological concerns.

Most critiques of secular theories loosely follow Farnsworth's description of the process of integration. Farnsworth

---

1. Wolterstorff, *Reason within the bounds*, 68.

suggested that the process of integration is one of "discovering God's truths through theology and psychology, verifying the accuracy of the findings, relating them, and applying them in one's life."[2] Although this framework lends itself well to analyzing secular theories, Farnsworth's proposal highlights the fact that integration is not just about believing the right things (orthodoxy); it also involves living the right way (orthopraxy). Integration should lead us not only to a more complete intellectual picture of the world, but additionally to a more faithful way of living in the world. Farnsworth proposed that disciplinary integration takes place in three stages: discovery, verification, and relation.

Discovery involves the rigorous application of the methods appropriate to our disciplines. For psychology, this means creating testable theories about human phenomena. Remember, however, that discovery is not a purely objective enterprise. What we choose to study, how we form our initial theories and hypotheses, what methodologies we use, and how we analyze and interpret our findings all involve subjective elements. This is true for both psychology and theology. It is important, therefore, that we engage in verification of initial findings. At this stage we evaluate the conclusions brought from either discipline by discerning if our psychological and theological beliefs "are based on sound as well as appropriate research methods: 'Good'

psychology and 'good' theology."[3] Only when the steps of discovery and verification have been carried out can we proceed to the level of relating psychological and theological conclusions. In the following section, we will consider how integrative scholarship can involve theological critique. We will examine the merits of the optimistic view of human nature provided by Abraham Maslow and Carl Rogers, followed by a consideration of Tal Ben-Shahar's positive psychology proposals about happiness.

Maslow and Rogers both subscribed to an optimistic view of human nature.[4] Maslow is best known for his hierarchy of human needs (physiological needs, safety needs, belongingness and love needs, esteem needs, self-actualization needs). Maslow believed that everyone naturally engages in a process of becoming "more and more what . . . one is capable of becoming."[5] Thus, as lower-level needs are satiated, higher-level needs tend to emerge. Rogers' theories also focused on self-actualization, a movement "toward completion or fulfillment of potentials" based on internal drives toward "psychological growth and maturity."[6] This nat-

---

2. Farnsworth, *Conduct of integration*, 310.

3. Ibid., 313.

4. Neither Maslow nor Rogers denied the reality of human evil. Maslow explained it based on "instinct remnants" and need frustration. However, both of them believed in a general unfolding toward self-actualization so long as basic needs were met and the cultural and social environment fostered growth.

5. Maslow, *Psychology of being*, 46.

6. Feist & Feist, *Theories of personality*, 459–60.

ural drive, he believed, was thwarted by the external demands and values of other people, causing the individual to doubt his or her own internal values. Rogers hypothesized that all human beings possess an "organismic valuing process," and that:

> when the human being is inwardly free to choose whatever he deeply values, he tends to value those objects, experiences, and goals which make for his own survival, growth, and development, and for the survival and development of others . . . when he is exposed to a growth promoting climate."[7] The individual, thus unshackled from external dictates, learns to "go by his own experiencing, which does not always coincide with social norms.[8]

We have thus far discovered an introductory understanding of the optimistic view of human nature posed by Maslow and Rogers.

Next, we must discover a biblical understanding of human nature. The Bible is replete with positive images of humanity. We might first observe that Scripture describes us as created in the image of God (Gen 1:27). Further, consider the following examples.

> When I consider your heavens, the work of your fingers, the moon and the stars, which you have set in place, what is man that you are mindful of him, the son of man that you care for him? You made him a little lower than the heavenly beings and crowned him with glory and honor. You made him ruler over the works of your hands; you put everything under his feet: all flocks and herds, and the beasts of the field, the birds of the air, and the fish of the sea, all that swim the paths of the seas. (Ps 8:3–8, NIV)

> For you created my inmost being; you knit me together in my mother's womb. I am fearfully and wonderfully made; your works are wonderful, I know that full well. (Ps 139:13–14, NIV)

An individualistic framework that emphasizes self-determination, and an optimistic outlook for human potential are widely held in some portions of American culture. Why might these views be so readily accepted in middle class, suburban America? Why might these views be more suspect to other Americans or to people in other parts of the world?

While these verses clearly indicate a high view of human beings, they provide only part of the picture. Consider the following verses:

> This is the verdict: Light has come into the world, but men loved dark-

---

7. Rogers, *Toward a modern approach to values*, 166.

8. Ibid., 163.

ness instead of light because their deeds were evil. (John 3:19, NIV)

There is no one righteous, not even one; there is no one who understands, no one who seeks God. All have turned away, they have together become worthless; there is no one who does good, not even one. (Rom 3:10b–12, NIV)

For out of the heart come evil thoughts, murder, adultery, sexual immorality, theft, false testimony, slander. (Matt 15:19, NIV)

Based on a small sampling of verses, the biblical view seems to be one that celebrates a high view of human beings as created in God's image, but it also paints a dark picture of a universally warped, twisted, and evil nature.

For anyone who is remotely familiar with the Psychology of Personality, the obvious fact is that Maslow and Rogers represent only two of many voices. Theirs are perhaps the most optimistic views of human personality, with more pessimistic views offered by Sigmund Freud and others, and most theorists falling between the extremes. It is also notable that both Maslow and Rogers derived their theories primarily from their own experiences. As Maslow admitted of his own theory, "It derives most directly, however, from clinical experience."[9] In many respects, their theories reflect philosophical positions rather than scientific findings. Nevertheless, both theories have led

to significant bodies of research, and the research evidence provides mixed results.

Some research supports the idea that lower-level needs (e.g., physical and safety needs) are more motivating than higher-level needs (e.g., self-actualization) when those needs are frustrated.[10] Reported levels of personal happiness, however, appear to have no relationship to the currently extant need-level at which a person is operating.[11] The conditions that Rogers believed to foster therapeutic success have been well researched and largely supported, and have led to significant research on empathy.[12] However, the assumption that people will invariably strive toward their own betterment and the well-being of others is not well supported. A host of research has explored discrimination,[13] failure to help others,[14] obedience to authority in carrying out aggressive behaviors,[15] and powerful forces that impel adoption of aggressive roles,[16] to name just a few of the many lines of research that cast doubt on optimism about human nature.

9. Maslow, *Motivation and personality*, 35.

10. Wicker, Brown, Weihe, Hagen, & Reed, *On reconsidering Maslow.*

11. Diener, Horwitz, & Emmons, *Happiness of the very wealthy.*

12. E.g., Truax & Carkhuff, *Toward effective counseling;* Cramer, *Toward assessing.*

13. Shariffe, *Intergroup conflict and cooperation.*

14. Darley & Batson, CD, From Jerusalem to Jericho.

15. Milgram, *Behavioral study of obedience.*

16. Zimbardo, Maslach, & Haney, *Reflections on the Stanford Prison Experiment.*

Whether or not the research offers support for various parts of their theories, it is notable that Maslow and Rogers formed their ideas, at least in part, in conscious opposition to religious teachings. Maslow, for instance, wrote the following entries in his personal journal:

> I think we can save everything worth saving in religion, everything real & true, without swallowing any of the crap. A new, true religion would certainly change things. Something really good to harness all the good impulses now wasted on nunneries & churches & Bibles.[17]

> I have a powerful instrument . . . which should take religion back from the priests & the idiots . . . It is clear that "faith" in something which has no empirical support (in a God, a church, etc.) . . . really rests upon lack of faith in the human being! Why else look away from human nature for the source of values?[18]

The optimistic view of human nature that Rogers espoused appears to be rooted in a rejection of the Christian concept of original sin,[19] as well as a negative reaction against his mother's judgmental attitudes and fundamentalism.[20] Regard-

less of the source and validity of their assumptions, however, *Rogers and Maslow created theories that have received mixed empirical support.*

Taken together, the evidence suggests that an optimistic view of human nature is a half-truth; it tells half of the story, and that imperfectly. Maslow and Rogers help us to understand that human beings have various levels of needs and that people do not thrive well when they are exposed to conditional acceptance. While they highlight the capacity of human beings to do good, this capacity is only one facet of human behavior and human nature. At best we must recognize that this tendency is neither innate nor inevitable. At worst, we must admit that there are powerful psychological forces that impel us toward conformity, selfishness, aggression, and other negative behaviors that are not adequately accounted for by Maslow and Rogers.

The verification of the psychological data above is much abbreviated, but it is sufficient to demonstrate the process. Similarly, the verification of the theological view of human nature would require an in-depth study of the passages noted, an exhaustive study of other relevant passages, consideration of the flow of redemptive history, analysis of exegetical

---

17. Lowry, *Journals of A. H. Maslow*, 6, entry of March 12, 1959 (italics original).

18. Ibid., 146–47, entry of March 24, 1962.

19. Thorn, *Rogers and the doctrine of original sin*.

20. One of Rogers' siblings reportedly described their mother as "a person that you didn't tell things to." In an autobiographical reflection, Rogers wrote that he was raised "in a narrowly

fundamentalist religious home, [and] I introjected the value attitudes toward others that were held by my parents." Rogers categorized these values as judgmentalism that resulted in "arrogant separateness" and lack of personal affirmation that led him to hide his true feelings and adopt a legalistic façade. The quotations are from Rogers, *A way of being*, 28–29.

accuracy, and so forth. What would result from such a study would be a biblical view of the complexity of human nature, with both its created goodness and its fallen depravity.

Once the steps of discovery and verification are complete, we can begin the task of relating. It is clear from the verification step that the optimistic view of human nature offered by Maslow and Rogers cannot be accepted without caveat or modification. While their theories have much to teach us about various types of needs, the value of empathy, and so forth, their view of human goodness is Pollyannaish; it is neither philosophically compelling nor consonant with numerous research findings. It is also evident that their views come into conflict with scriptural teachings about the depravity of human nature. Yet this does not mean that their theories are entirely false. We may reject the portions of their theories that are not supported by a fair reading of God's Works (through the available empirical evidence) and of God's Word. Further evaluation would likely lead us to conclude that portions of their theories are consonant with both of God's books (for example, empirical research and biblical teachings may be found to support the idea that harsh discipline and conditional acceptance foster animosity).

Personality theories inevitably overlap considerably with theology because both of them are concerned with the nature of the human condition. Counseling and psychotherapy share a similar overlapping interest with theology because they are concerned with the way things ought to be, the goals that we should strive toward. This issue can also be illustrated in Tal Ben-Shahar's writing. Ben-Shahar obtained a doctorate in Organizational Behavior from Harvard, where he once taught the most popular course (on positive psychology) as well as the third most popular course ("The Psychology of Leadership") with over 1,400 students per semester enrolled in his courses. Today, Ben-Shahar is a popular consultant and lecturer. His books have been translated into more than twenty-five languages. His purpose in life, he says, "is to bring happiness to life—in individuals, groups, and organizations."[21]

To understand Ben-Shahar's position, we must first look at the history of positive psychology. When Martin Seligman was elected as the president of the American Psychological Association in 1997, he hoped to refocus the energies of APA on prevention in addition to its standard focus on treatment. As he began to do so, however, he found himself dissatisfied with applying the medical model to preventive efforts in mental health. Over time, Seligman came to believe that "prevention was not about repairing damage," and that it should focus on building "hope, optimism, courage" and other strengths as a buffer against psychological illness.[22] His ideal, however, was handicapped by what he saw as psychology's weakness. In his words, "because psychology has been a profession

---

21. Online: www.talbenshahar.com.

22. Seligman, *Foreword: The past and future*, xvi.

and a science focused on what was wrong and what was weak, we know almost nothing about the strengths and virtues" that we need to build an adequate prevention program.[23]

To this point, there is much that Christians should affirm. The field of psychology in general, and clinical psychology in particular, has historically focused on the things that go wrong in human behavior and functioning, while understanding and optimizing the conditions of human well-being has lagged behind. Similarly, conservative Protestant theology has traditionally highlighted the problem of sin and its pervasive effects while it has not explored the implications of the *imago Dei* nearly as thoroughly as it could. Not surprisingly, this state of affairs has led to integrative efforts that concentrate on the darker side of human nature and give only passing mention to what is admirable and noble in human nature.[24]

While we should explore positive aspects of human behavior and strive to enhance human well-being, we need to be very careful about the telos that guides these endeavors. Seligman was interested in understanding and fostering "the strengths and virtues that enable individuals and communities to thrive."[25] The three pillars of positive psychology are "positive subjective experiences,"

"positive individual traits," and "positive institutions."[26] Note, however, that the question of what makes something "positive" is philosophical in nature. Positive psychology is "prescriptive in that it says that certain topics should be studied" and that certain ends are desirable.[27] Once these assumptions are granted, "the routes to the good life are an empirical matter."[28] While the mechanisms that lead to "the good life" may well be a matter of empirical interest, the definition of "the good life" is rooted in worldview considerations. Thus, while empirical research on this topic is warranted and possible, we would do well not to jump over the definitional issue of what constitutes "the good life" too quickly, and it is here that Ben-Shahar's proposals may give us pause.

"Happier" is a short, easy-to-read book authored by Ben-Shahar that served as the text for his Harvard course on positive psychology. As you read the following section from the book, try to identify the philosophical assumptions that Ben-Shahar makes.

> If we wanted to assess the worth of a business, we would use money as our means of measurement. We would calculate the dollar value of its assets and liabilities, profits and losses . . . In this case—in measuring a company's net worth—money is the ultimate currency. A human being, like a

23. Ibid., 16.

24. Entwistle & Moroney, Integrative perspectives on human flourishing.

25. University of Pennsylvania Positive Psychology Center, ¶1.

26. Peterson, *Primer in positive psychology*, 20.

27. Ibid., 15.

28. Ibid.

business, makes profits and suffers losses. For a human being, however, the ultimate currency is not money, nor is it any external measure, such as fame, fortune, or power. The ultimate currency for a human being is happiness.[29]

At a minimum, Ben-Shahar assumes that happiness is not only a measure of well-being, but that it is "the ultimate currency" of human life. But is it? And even if it is, how should we define happiness?

Theological reflection on this question is richly textured. The word "happiness" occurs only six times in the New International Version, and the word "happy" only twenty-one times.[30] Many of these occasions instruct us to be grateful for the gifts of God that bring us

happiness. Other times we are instructed to be aware of how fleeting happiness can be. Several times we see pictures of happiness being rooted in temporal affairs, such as Jonah being happy that God had caused a vine to give him shelter while he waited in anticipation for God to destroy the Ninevites. In Deuteronomy 24:5, we read that a recently married man is to be exempted from military service so he may bring happiness to his wife. In Esther 8:16, the Jewish people celebrate their deliverance as a time of joy, happiness, gladness, and honor. Job cries out in his suffering, "Remember, O God, that my life is but a breath; my eyes will never see happiness again" (Job 7:7, NIV). The author of Ecclesiastes proclaims that running after pleasure is meaningless, yet he sees wisdom, knowledge, and happiness as gifts that God gives to those that please Him (Eccl 2:26).

The last two passages that use the word "happiness" are from the parable of talents, in which the master commends the faithful servants and welcomes them to "come and share in your master's happiness" (Matt 25:21, 23, NIV)! While we need to guard against scattered proof texting, even a cursory glance at a few Scripture verses suggests that happiness is not an end in itself; happiness is a byproduct of other things (e.g., bringing happiness to others, health, serving God faithfully). Moreover, Scripture warns of the fleeting nature of pleasure and happiness and of the possibility of finding happiness in evil attitudes and actions, while

---

29. Ben-Shahar, *Happier*, 53.

30. However, one must keep in mind that the linguistic and cultural milieu of the Old and New Testaments makes direct comparisons difficult. For instance, the terms that are often translated as *joy* or *happiness* in English versions might better be translated *honorable* in some cases. Honor and shame were crucial concerns in Israelite and Judean culture, and the giving and receiving of honor and shame were means of influencing behavior. Because "honor is not simple self-esteem or pride" but "is a status-claim which is affirmed by the community," we cannot equate modern views of happiness with ancient middle-eastern views of joy/happiness/honor without keeping this context in mind (see Hanson, "How honorable!" "How shameful"). However, the ancient constellation of these factors (joy, happiness, and honor) suggests that our modern Western conceptualization of happiness tends to be too narrowly focused on personal pleasure and satisfaction, and too little focused on personal virtue and honor.

positively calling us to love of God and neighbor as our ultimate telos.

There is, however, a beautiful paradox here. Recall the first question of the Westminster Shorter Catechism: "What is the chief end of man?" to which the reply is, "Man's chief end is to love God and enjoy Him forever." When we strive to be faithful servants of God and to love others, it seems that we reside within conditions that usually foster our own temporal happiness. Then again, being faithful can lead to suffering—think of Jeremiah stuck in the mud when he was abandoned in an empty well for prophesying as God told him to! Jeremiah was not aiming for temporal happiness, and, in fact, experienced much suffering. Yet the Bible often weighs our temporal suffering against eternal happiness (Rom 8:18).

Compare the two quotations that follow. What values undergird these ways of thinking? How might these views reflect the culture and experiences of the theorists? In what ways is each viewpoint consonant or dissonant with biblical views?

"Experience is, for me, the highest authority. The touchstone of validity is my own experience. . . . It is to experience that I must return again and again, to discover a closer approximation to truth as it is in the process of becoming in me. Neither the Bible nor the prophets – neither Freud nor research – neither the revelations of God nor man – can take precedence over my own direct experience."

—Carl Rogers, *A Way of Being*

"The more one forgets himself—by giving himself to a cause to serve or another person to love—the more human he is and the more he actualizes himself. What is called self-actualization is not an attainable aim at all, for the simple reason that the more one would strive for it, the more he would miss it. In other words, self-actualization is possible only as a side-effect of self-transcendence."

—Victor Frankl, *Man's Search for Meaning*

None of this should be taken to say that Ben-Shahar is completely off the mark. In fact, many of his reflections and exercises are deeply insightful. For instance, he offers compelling critiques of materialism, encourages us to find our calling, emphasizes the importance of fostering gratitude, and highlights the importance of meaningful relationships. However, we cannot uncritically accept the entire proposal to make happiness "the ultimate currency."

The theories that guide our therapies are not value-neutral. Thus, we must always ask of our personality theories and our psychotherapies, "What is the end that this proposal aims toward?" In many cases, we will discover that psychological theories and techniques have goals that we can affirm, such as the alleviation of unnecessary suffering. Often, however, we will need to be alert for subtle (or obvious) goals that need to be rejected or modified if they are to be consonant with Christian ends.

Before leaving this topic, we need to address a perennial issue that Christians have to think about when "secular thinking" appears to conflict with "Christian" thinking." Is theology always a superior means to discerning truth?

Who's on First?

"Who's on First?" was one of the classic vaudeville routines of the 1930s and '40s. Abbott played the role of the manager of the baseball team, trying to enlighten the head of the sports department (played by Costello) about the names of the players on the team. Who is on first, What is on second, I Don't Know is on third, Why is in leftfield, Because is in centerfield, Tomorrow is the pitcher, Today is the catcher, and I Don't Give a Darn is the shortstop. The routine is humorous precisely because the two conversants keep misunderstanding each other, but somehow, they manage to hold a conversation, even though only one of them really understood it.

Sometimes we end up playing our own version of "Who's on First?" among integrationists. In our version, the question involves whether theology ("Christian thinking") or psychology ("secular thinking") comes first. Is Scripture or science a more sure way to truth? Just like Abbott and Costello, sometimes our routine generates more misunderstanding and irritation than insight and direction.

At the outset, we should remember that Blamires warned us that both "secular thinking" and "Christian thinking" can be done well or done poorly. If it was obvious that our theological thinking on a given topic was sound and secular psychological thinking was severely deficient, we would obviously have good reason to prefer the one over the other— and vice versa. However, what do we do when "secular thinking" and "Christian thinking" appear to be of similar quality? What do we do if our interpretation of the Bible appears to conflict with our interpretation of psychology?

While many authors disagree about how to reconcile apparent conflicts between theology and psychology, integrationists generally recognize that there are certain fundamental truths that we can only gain from Scripture, and that these truths shape the way that we understand the world. Scripture proclaims that—left to themselves—human beings are prone to self-deceit. It also asserts a claim for its authority in matters of faith and practice (2 Tim 3:13–17). How ought we to understand the biblical claim to authority? Theologian Millard Erickson put it this way: "By the authority of the Bible we mean that the Bible, as the expression of God's will to us, possesses the right supremely to define what we are to believe and how we are to conduct ourselves."[31]

The Bible thus makes a limited claim to its own authority, focusing especially on matters of faith and practice. A Christian worldview must take into account God as the Creator of the world and the subsequent history of sin, the unfolding of God's redemptive acts in history, and the future promise of consummation. The Bible is the most clear and complete source that we have for understanding the fundamental issues of human purpose.

While we must hasten to add that our interpretation of God's Word may be erroneous, rightly understood, the Word of God helps us to frame the way we ought to understand the Works of God. As noted theologian Erickson remarked,

> Taking the biblical concepts as the tenets of one's view of reality restricts considerably the range of philosophical worldviews that are acceptable. For instance, a naturalistic worldview is excluded, both because it restricts reality to the system of observable nature, and because possible occurrences within this system are restricted to what is in conformity with fixed laws.[32]

Nevertheless, this does not mean that the Word of God has preeminence over the Works of God. In Erikson's words,

> Since both creation and the gospel are intelligible and coherent revelations of God, there is harmony between the two, and mutual reinforcement of one by the other. The biblical revelation is not totally distinct from what is known of the natural realm.[33]

There is a fundamental harmony between biblical revelation and that which can be known by studying the created realm.

We must acknowledge, though, that the creation itself has been marred by sin (Gen 3:17–19; Rom 8:19–21). Moreover, sin distorts our perception. While sin distorts human thinking in general, it exerts more of an effect on our understanding of ourselves and of God than it does upon our understanding of matters that are less central to our perceptions of our place in the created realm. As Emil Bruner pointed out,

> The nearer anything lies to that center of existence where we are concerned with the whole, that is, with man's relation to God and the being of the person, the greater is the disturbance of rational knowledge by sin; the farther away anything lies from this center, the less is the disturbance

---

31. Erickson, *Christian theology*, 267.

32. Ibid., 57
33. Ibid., 199.

felt, and the less difference there is between knowing as a believer or an unbeliever.[34]

It is thus imperative that those areas that are more central to human existence (e.g., human nature) be examined in relation to both of God's books so that there is a system of checks and balances to help us see if we are reading the books correctly. As Erickson contended:

> We may understand more about the specially revealed truth by examining the general revelation . . . This should be considered a supplement to, not a substitute for, special revelation. Sin's distortion of human understanding of the general revelation is greater the closer one gets to the relationship between God and humans. Thus, sin produces relatively little obscuring effect upon the understanding of matters of physics, but a great deal with respect to matters of psychology and sociology. Yet it is at those places where the potential for distortion is greatest that the most complete understanding is possible.[35]

We must also acknowledge that individual and corporate sin can distort our reading of Scripture and our understanding of the created realm, although the cultivation of intellectual virtues, the careful use of reliable epistemic methods, and comparison of different sources can be useful in correcting our distortions.

Scripture is far more specific about things such as human sin and its cure than it is about many other matters. As such, it provides critical information without which the book of God's Works is easily misunderstood. The book of God's Word speaks with clarity about humans as created and fallen beings whom God loves and for whom Jesus Christ offered redemption through His death. We take these claims to be true based on God's authority.

Recognizing that authority rests ultimately in God the Author, we can affirm that "all truth is God's truth." Since our understanding will reflect theology and psychology rather than directly and perfectly reflecting Scripture or creation, we must look at the relationship of theology and psychology as interpretive disciplines.

Carter and Narramore provide a helpful way of understanding the scope of these two disciplines:

> The locus of explanation is different in theology and psychology. In theology, the locus of explanation is generally historical and sociocultural, while in psychology it is descriptive (clinical), developmental, and experimental. Finally, there is a difference of epistemology. Theology's epistemology is revelational while psychology's epistemology is empirical.[36]

They further note that the epistemic and metaphysical differences between the two disciplines shape their relationship.

---

34. Bruner, *Revelation and reason*, 383.

35. Erickson, Christian theology, 198–99.

36. Carter & Narramore, *The integration of psychology and theology*, 52–53.

In theology, the level of explanation is metaphysical. In psychology, the level of explanation is empirical or scientific . . . Since Scripture is metaphysical and revelational in character, theology tends to be more comprehensive than psychology in locus of explanation, level of explanation, and epistemology."[37]

This being the case, Christian theology always provides a context from which our psychological understanding will proceed, even though psychology sometimes supplies details that are not conveyed by theology.

So, who's on first? In a sense, one could say that theology is on first, to the degree that it shapes one's worldview and provides a context for all other disciplines. But one could also say that neither theology nor psychology is on first because both owe their allegiance to a common source of truth; God invests truth in both of them through His acts of revelation and creation. We are still left, then, with the question of how to reconcile apparent conflicts between theology and psychology, and it is to this question that we now turn our attention.

What's on Second?

It makes sense to acknowledge the primacy of theology to the degree that a Christian worldview is a necessary foundation from which integration ensues. Beyond this, is it necessary to posit that theological interpretation trumps psychological interpretation wherever the two appear to conflict? This issue involves the disciplinary level of integration. Integrationists believe that the two books of God cannot conflict, but our interpretations of the books will sometimes lead us to inconsistent conclusions. How do we reconcile apparent discrepancies between the findings of psychology and theology?

Three solutions to this problem have been offered, which can be described as: 1) integration as *levels of explanation*; 2) integration as *prima scriptura*; and 3) integration as *a quest for faithful reading*.

Disciplinary Integration as Levels of Explanation

Myers and Jeeves are commonly classified as representatives of the parallels model, or what I have called the Neutral Parties model. Myers and Jeeves stress parallelism and correlation between the findings of psychology and the findings of theology. Their dual emphasis on disciplinary independence and the quest for a more integrated understanding can be seen in the following quotation:

> The variety of possible perspectives— or levels of analysis, as they are also called, requires that we choose which level we wish to operate from. Each level entails its own questions and its own methods. Each provides a valu-

---

37. Ibid.

able way of looking at behavior, yet each by itself is incomplete. Thus each level complements the others; with all the perspectives we have a more complete view of our subject than provided by any one perspective.[38]

Myers and Jeeves desire to avoid injecting a Christian "ideology . . . into psychology."[39] They stress the importance of preserving the disciplinary integrity of psychology and avoiding theological propositions from being errantly foisted upon other levels of analysis. In Myers's words, "As much as anything, [our approach] contrasts with what else I read . . . as a science-friendly perspective."[40]

Myers and Jeeves offer a compelling case that integrative efforts must respect the methods and disciplinary autonomy of psychology. They point out that integration must incorporate all of psychology's subdisciplines, rather than narrowly focusing on clinical psychology. In emphasizing disciplinary independence they avoid psychological or theological reductionism, "while remaining open to the insights from either nature or Scripture . . ."[41] On the other hand, claiming complete neutrality between psychology and theology fails to sufficiently deal with "the very serious problems inherent in positing the autonomy of reason from faith.[42]

In the *levels of explanation* approach, apparent conflicts between theology and psychology can sometimes be resolved by seeing them as different perspectives of a common phenomenon; psychology and theology say different things about diverse elements of a single subject. In order to preserve disciplinary integrity, these different perspectives are construed as relatively non-overlapping spheres. Sometimes this approach results in discovering theological and psychological findings that support each other. However, there are times when such relegating fails to resolve a tension between a psychological and a theological position, and either one or the other explanation must be revised.

A modern example of a harmonious meeting of faith and science from a *levels of explanation* perspective can be seen in David Myers's handling of "family values" issues. On the one hand, Myers sees the scientific evidence as supporting Christian teachings about family values:

> I see myself as a family values guy. In my psychology textbooks, I document the corrosive effects of pornography, teen sexual activity, and family decline. I am on the advisory board of The National Marriage Project, whose recent cohabitation report concludes that trial marriages undermine marriage . . . I've always been pretty conservative on these family concerns, partly because the data are so persuasive.[43]

---

38. Myers & Jeeves, *Psychology through the eyes of faith*, 7.

39. Ibid., 15.

40. Personal communication.

41. Eck, Integrating the integrators, 108.

42. Narramore, Psychology and theology, 7.

---

43. Myers, The levels-of-explanation view, 76.

But what happens when theories based on scientific data appear to conflict with teaching based on Scripture? Myers uses his own advocacy for gay marriage as an example of how the *levels of explanation* view caused him to revise his previously held theological view.

Myers has been at the forefront of Christians who have noted that the scientific evidence suggests that sexual orientation is more determined than chosen. Such may well be the case, and this would not, in and of itself, contradict traditional scriptural interpretation.[44] Several of Myers's suggestions, however, go beyond this conclusion:

> . . . the Bible has little to say about homosexuality. Many of us have been surprised to learn how mute (or at least murky) the Bible is regarding a committed union between mature homosexual adults. Biblical scholars are debating the half dozen or so Scriptural passages referring to same sex activity, passages that sometimes also involve pagan idolatry, temple prostitution, or child exploitation. To be sure, Jesus affirmed marriage, and so should we. But he spoke no recorded words about homosexual behavior. Although he had much to say about the poor and powerless, homosexual-

ity was not one of the social issues on his radar screen.[45]

To suggest that sexual orientation may be disposed rather than chosen leaves one free to regard homosexuality, like left-handedness, a natural part of human diversity or as a lamentable aberration such as dyslexia.[46]

Can we accept gays who, not given what Catholics call the gift of celibacy, elect the functional equivalent of marriage (which society denies them) over promiscuity?[47]

I respect Myers for being willing to put the research on the table, and for encouraging the church to carefully consider its reaction to homosexuality.[48] The weight of scientific evidence suggests that sexual orientation is typically not a matter of personal choice and is resistant to change. But there are troubling aspects of how Myers has approached this issue.

---

44. Of course, the issue ultimately turns on truth, not interpretation. My point here is not that traditional interpretation is above challenge. Rather, the starting point is a conflict of interpretation, after which one works backwards to evaluate the validity of the theological and scientific interpretations.

45. Myers, Accepting what cannot be changed.

46. Myers, A levels-of-explanation view, 79 (italics added).

47. Myers, Accepting what cannot be changed, 5–7; also online.

48. While many ecclesiastical groups believe that homosexual behavior is condemned in Scripture, there are portions of the church that seem to overreact to homosexual sin while being relatively silent about heterosexual sin. The moral righteousness of the church is compromised when it tolerates (or worse, encourages) the violence, hatred, or discrimination that is directed toward homosexual individuals. Whatever one may think of homosexuality, we still have the duty to love our neighbor.

"A person once asked me, in a provocative manner, if I approved of homosexuality. I replied with another question: 'Tell me: when God looks at a gay person, does he endorse the existence of this person with love, or reject and condemn this person?' We must always consider the person."

—Pope Francis

While maintaining traditional Roman Catholic teachings about sexuality, Pope Francis also emphasizes traditional church teachings about the value of all people.

What are some common perceptions about how different segments of the Church think about sexual orientation?

In his earlier works, rather than engaging the biblical texts, Myers simply asserted that theologians are reconsidering the meaning of certain texts about homosexuality. In his most recent and extensive book on this topic, Myers and his coauthor, Letha Scanzoni, spend the first six chapters of the book reviewing psychosocial research and sociological phenomena before broaching the biblical texts in the seventh chapter.[49] The danger of doing so is that, by the time we get to the biblical texts, our thinking may already be conditioned by the current sociocultural climate. On the other hand, in their defense, Myers and Scanzoni could say something like this. "*Galileo didn't challenge the prevailing view of the world by beginning with Scripture. He observed the world, and discovered things that didn't make sense if the Bible were taken literally. His observations required a change in biblical interpretation. We're simply doing the same thing with a different issue.*"

To their credit, Myers and Scanzoni tackle the scriptural evidence in their recent work. In it, they address the majority of the scriptural passages that are commonly thought to refer to homosexual behavior, and they rightly point out that the context in several of these passages may involve violence or temple prostitution. They raise alternative interpretations, which they think fit better with the scientific data and the cultural framework of the Bible. It is, however, troubling that in his earlier work Myers invoked an *argument from silence* in discussing Jesus's stance on homosexuality; that Scripture does not record Jesus as having talked about homosexuality in no way says whether or not it was "on his radar screen"; clearly, not every word He spoke or issue He addressed is preserved for us (John 21:25).

---

49. Myers & Scanzoni, *What God has joined together.*

Myers claims that the scientific evidence which supports the contention that sexual orientation is largely determined by genetics or environment "leaves us free" to see it as a normal variant or a lamentable aberration. Critics of his view, though, would rightly point out that science is descriptive, not prescriptive. Science simply has no foundation from which to inform us if homosexual behavior—or a myriad of heterosexual behaviors, for that matter—are moral or not. Whenever we engage in moral reasoning, we leave the domain of science and enter the domains of philosophy, politics, and religion.

A further difficulty of the argument that Myers makes for gay marriage is that it sidesteps a host of other moral issues. What are we to think of sexual experimentation (for gay and heterosexual individuals)? What about the fact that many individuals—both heterosexual and homosexual—have serial monogamous relationships, and open relationships? How should we think about the difficulties faced by bisexual or gay individuals who become dissatisfied in a heterosexual marriage? Thus, even if we were to grant that Myers and Scanzoni made a compelling case for gay marriage, we would not have resolved many other ethical and practical issues that surround heterosexual and homosexual activity. Despite these shortcomings, Myers and Scanzoni have addressed an important and complex topic that is often poorly dealt with in the church. Religious conservatives, in particular, often oversimplify this issue and fail to

express grace, love, and compassion toward homosexual individuals.

Before leaving this issue, we must note that similar shortcomings may be found in the arguments of people who contend for a "traditional" understanding of scriptural teaching on homosexuality. Many people read the relatively few verses which might refer to homosexual activity with only a superficial reading of the text and without deep consideration of the cultural, linguistic, and theological context. Furthermore, efforts to change sexual orientation clearly have the potential to be coercive (especially for adolescents taken to therapists by their parents) or damaging. Additionally, it is troublesome that many conservative Christians focus on homosexuality while seemingly ignoring things such as child sexual abuse, sexual promiscuity, extramarital affairs, and so forth. Clearly, Christians will continue to struggle with how best to understand issues of sexual orientation and behavior and, just as importantly, how to extend the love of Christ to all of God's children.

Clinicians, though, must recognize that ecclesiastical views regarding sexual activity do not necessarily translate directly into clinical settings where the objective is to meet the needs of the client in ways that are ethical, professional, and hospitable. My point in raising this issue here is not so much to make a point about homosexuality as it is to illustrate the dynamics of the levels of explanation approach. For all of its merits, this approach can lead one to rely excessively on psychological interpretation, and it may cause us to neglect or prematurely alter theological positions. The assumption that science and theology occupy two relatively independent spheres is problematic because our assumptions influence our scientific and sociological reasoning; we do not approach any discipline as a blank slate. While Myers and Scanzoni's attempt to resolve this issue suffers from some deficiencies, it is important to note that they are sincere in their concerns for the church and for gay and lesbian people. Although many people who hold traditional scriptural interpretations disagree with their conclusions and proposals, all of us can learn from their reflections on psychosocial research, their theological deliberations, and their genuine concern for people who struggle with sexuality in the context of Christian faith.

Disciplinary Integration as Prima Scriptura[50]

In contrast to the view we have just considered, some people contend that the secular foundations of psychology necessitate a fundamental reorientation of the field. They insist that apparent conflicts between theology and psychology must be resolved by submitting to Scripture. Gary Collins is typical of the *prima scriptura* view of integration, as can be seen in his contention that biblical truth "is the only sure rock of stability amidst the shifting sands of the contemporary world. Scripture is the foundation from which we integrate Christianity into psychology."[51] Crabb echoed similar sentiments in claiming that the task of integration is to "carefully screen our concepts to determine their compatibility with Christian presuppositions."[52] Taken to an extreme, such a proposition could lend itself to theological reductionism. Yet these authors have an important point: Christianity must inform and critique all of our life, including our academic and vocational pursuits; there is no part of our life to which Christ does not lay claim. In the words of Abraham Kuyper,

> No single piece of our mental world is to be hermetically sealed off from the rest, and there is not a square inch in the whole domain of our human existence over which Christ, who is Sovereign over all, does not cry: "Mine!"[53]

---

50. The term *prima scriptura* is often used to describe a theological position that scripture is to be held above all other sources in determining Christian faith and practice. This view, in contrast to *sola scriptura*, implicitly acknowledges that extra-biblical sources (such as prophecy or church tradition) may shape faith and practice, but it holds that we should always defer to scripture if these sources are in conflict. Here, however, I am using the term *Integration as prima scriptura* not to describe primacy of scripture regarding doctrine, but the primacy of scripture as a way of knowing *in general*.

---

51. Collins, An integration view, 112.

52. Crabb, *Effective biblical counseling*, 48.

53. The quotation is taken from Kuyper's inaugural address of the Free University in Amsterdam. Reprinted in Bratt, *Abraham Kuyper*, 488.

God is sovereign over all, and faith must permeate all of our life. As Harvard Law professor Harold Berman said, "To be a scholar is to search for truth. And to search for truth is to be open to the possibility that some discovered truth will lay claim to one's allegiance."[54]

To be truly integrative, we must allow Scripture a primary role in determining a Christian worldview, we must allow our reasoning to be shaped by the biblical message, and we must recognize that God is sovereign over all of life. *Prima scriptura* integrationists, however, insist that it is necessary to see Scripture as more authoritative than other epistemic sources. For instance, Larry Crabb argued, "No psychology can claim to be Christian which directly or indirectly denies to the Scripture the role of final arbiter."[55] Crabb contended that those who adopt the "Two-Book View of Revelation" believe that "general revelation (nature) and special revelation (the Bible) provide Christians with equally clear, equally meaningful, and equally authoritative expressions of truth from God."[56] Many people would disagree with Crabb's characterization that holders of the "Two-Book View" believe that both books are "equally clear." All of what we perceive is, to some extent, filtered through our biases, experiences, and preconceptions; none of us has perfect epistemic vision.

Furthermore, the clarity found throughout each of God's books is not uniform.

Scripture is extremely explicit and clear on some matters, for example, "You shall not commit adultery" (Exod 20:14, NIV).[57] In other areas, Scripture offers indistinct accounts, making it difficult to generate clear interpretations.[58] Scripture is completely silent regarding many matters (e.g., how memories are stored and retrieved). Furthermore, it is often the case that the unfolding of archeological, historical, and grammatical studies eventually lead to greater clarity regarding the meaning of Scripture in one period of time than was possible in another.[59]

Similarly, the clarity that we find in studying psychology is varied. On some things, psychology provides clear and compelling ideas (such as Thorndike's law of effect). At other times, psychological investigation leads to contradictory accounts (such as the relative contributions of nature and nurture on personality

---

54. Berman, Judeo-Christian versus pagan scholarship, 291.

55. Crabb, Biblical authority and Christian psychology. 305.

56. Ibid., 307 (italics added).

57. Numerous other scriptural passages affirm this teaching, such as Matt 5:27ff.

58. For instance, the passage in 1 Cor 15:29 referring to baptism for the dead is extremely obscure and open to numerous interpretations, none of which are compelling because of the lack of context or any point of reference from which to understand Paul's point in mentioning this practice.

59. Conversely, the biases of a given epoch—whether ancient or modern—can cloud biblical interpretation or take it in errant directions. It is thus dangerous to assume that our theological or scientific conclusions are ever progressing toward truth; the thinking of each generation is clouded by the biases of its historical conditioning.

traits). On many matters, psychology is completely silent because its methods and scope do not apply to some areas of knowledge.[60] Nor is psychology static; new observations sometimes require us to reject formerly held positions.

The foregoing observations undermine Crabb's contention that the "Two-Book View" leads to a belief that each book is equally clear. In fact, it is more likely that this view helps us to recognize that each book is clear about some things, and unclear or even silent about many things. Crabb also claimed that holding the "Two-Book View" establishes two authorities, and that "wherever two authorities exist, there will eventually be an unsolvable impasse, an ascendance of one authority over the other, or the emergence of a superior third authority."[61]

Crabb committed a logical error by neglecting the primacy of the delegating authority; that is, whatever authority Scripture holds must be seen as derivative from God.[62] Scripture is true because God chose to reveal truth within its pages. There is only one ultimate authority—God, Who is the Author of both books—and truth, whatever its immediate source, comes from the Creator Himself.

Breshears and Larzelere highlighted a further problem with Crabb's position: Crabb perpetrated a confusion of categories by failing to distinguish Scripture from theological interpretation. In their words:

> Theological conclusions are the product of human reasoning from the data of Scripture. To the degree that such reasoning is involved, they are subject to mistake. Crabb's error comes from the attempt to invest the theological conclusions with the same authority as the Bible itself.[63]

While Brashears and Larzelere disagree with Crabb's desire to place

---

60. It is especially important to remember that most disciplines, including psychology, are more *descriptive* than *prescriptive*. Thus, if research revealed that adultery and premarital sexual intercourse are commonplace, it would tell us nothing about whether or not such behavior is morally acceptable. However, as an applied discipline, psychology does prescribe behavior (e.g., it is better for one not to be depressed), which does muddy the waters here. We should not be surprised, though, when biological, psychological, and sociological research demonstrates adverse consequences of such behaviors.

61. Crabb, Biblical authority and Christian psychology, 308.

62. Crabb's assertion of "authority" fails to adequately address the type and mechanisms of authority that he proposes. There are various theological understandings of the authority of scripture, ranging from the Roman Catholic emphasis on church tradition as the final arbiter of scriptural interpretation, to the neo-Orthodox view of direct revelation through Scripture (with no authority based in Scripture itself), to the charismatic view of prophetic interpretation, the rationalist view that reason alone can uncover the meaning of Scripture, the illumination of the Holy Spirit, etc. See Erickson's discussion of delegated authority and the major ways of conceptualizing the authority of Scripture. Erickson, *Christian theology*, 266–85.

63. Breshears & Larzelere, The authority of Scripture, 314.

Scripture as an epistemic source above all other sources, they have no desire to emasculate the derivative authority of Scripture.

> Scripture is authoritative for the social sciences in particular because it gives us God's Word on the origin, nature, and purpose of humanness, the source and nature of human sin, the majesty of God's redemption in Jesus Christ, and the Spirit-inspired instruction for our Christian life. The Bible's authority is particularly relevant to our world view, to the integrative framework, and to the hypotheses by which we integrate the data of revelation. The Bible gives us a Christian world view which acts as the proper spectacles to bring all of revelation into proper focus . . . Our world view according to which we interpret and categorize the data of experience comes primarily from the content of Scripture.[64]

Ellens, likewise responding to Crabb, wrote,

> The issue in relating faith and science is not a question of which to accord priority of authority. The question is how to insure equivalence of authority for truth wherever it shows up . . . Truth has equal warrant as truth, wherever it is found.[65]

Rather than concluding that Scripture is the final arbiter of truth, we need to recognize that all truth ultimately rests in God's sovereign rule over all of creation, whatever its more immediate source.

The *prima scriptura* model repeats one of the errors of the *Colonialist* model: the failure to adequately distinguish *Scripture* from *scriptural interpretation*. Jim Guy highlighted the problem of this confusion:

> Dr. Crabb [suggested] that the primary issue which must be resolved at the outset is to determine 'which source of data—the Bible or nature—has greater authority' in the task of integration. This would seem to erroneously imply the existence of a hierarchical structure wherein some truth is 'truer' than other truth. This also suggests a fallacious dichotomy, wherein one source of revealed truth, the Bible, is in conflict with another source of revealed truth, nature, with the implication that one must somehow choose between the two.[66]

If all truth is God's truth, then it would seem that the issue at hand is the accurate discernment of truth, not the hierarchical arrangement of sources of truth.

The failure to distinguish scriptural interpretation from Scripture itself may lead to an unwarranted and unconsidered acceptance of culturally constrained ecclesiastical positions and a failure to adequately examine the data and theories of the social and hard sciences. Steve Porter has developed an epistemological argument for scriptural primacy that is more nuanced and sophisticated than

---

64. Ibid., 315–16.

65. Ellens, Biblical authority, 323.

66. Guy, Affirming diversity in the task of integration, 36.

any other argument to date. Porter's argument is framed around the idea that theology is the queen of the sciences. In this view, well-grounded theological claims have more epistemic clout than equally well-grounded psychological claims because Scripture represents God's statement about reality, and God's position as the superior authority thus gives theological interpretation an epistemic edge. Hence, Porter contends that:

> as long as we have good reason to think that Scripture is God's word about the matters it addresses and that Scripture clearly supports a certain theological conclusion, then that theological position has a higher degree of authority than conclusions reached from any other source of knowledge.[67]

While there are aspects of Porter's argument that I think are flawed, his attempt to address this issue is an improvement over prior attempts to posit theological primacy.

First, Porter readily admits that his argument does not mean that theology always trumps psychology. In his words, "to say 'theology is queen' is not to say that the discipline in general has greater authority than the discipline of psychology or that theologians in general have greater authority than psychologists."[68] Consequently, Porter's argument applies only to those situations in which psychological and theological claims are equally

well-grounded, and such situations may be uncommon, or might only exist in theory. Thus, under normal circumstances, if a psychological claim is more well-grounded than a theological claim, the theological claim is at a disadvantage, and vice versa.

Porter's position is much more sophisticated than previous attempts to give more weight to theology in cases of conflict between it and other disciplines. However, I do not think he is ultimately successful in demonstrating that we have an epistemic duty to privilege theological reasoning when there appear to be conflicts of equally well-grounded claims. I think his argument supports the idea that one would be within his or her epistemic rights to prefer a theological understanding if two equally well-grounded claims were in conflict, if there was no discernible way of reconciling the conflict, and if one needed to chose between the two of them.[69] However, part of what concerns me is that those conditions will rarely be encountered, and I fear that some people will misuse Porter's argument to come to a foreclosed conclusion in real world situations.

While there are problems with the *prima scriptura* approach to integration, we must remember that Christian theology does provide a broader and more prescriptive perspective than other disciplines. Additionally, Christian theology spans several millennia over which it has been refined, while the social sciences are comparatively young. It should

---

67. Porter, Theology as queen, 5.

68. Ibid., 12.

---

69. Entwistle & Preston, Epistemic rights.

thus not be surprising if our psychologies may need the corrections offered by a broader theological framework more often than theology needs to be reformulated to take into account the recent findings of psychology. However, to assert as an *a priori* assumption that "Scripture is the final arbiter of truth" neglects both the reality of our own fallible interpretive frameworks and the rallying cry of integration that all truth is God's truth.

Disciplinary Integration as a Quest for Faithful Reading

The *levels of explanation* model can easily lead to compartmentalization or to neglecting the light of Scripture. The *prima scriptura* model, on the other hand, can too easily lead to a hierarchical arrangement of sources of truth and an attempt to confuse the authority of theological interpretation with the authority of Scripture. While one might disagree with the call for autonomous independence of the *levels of explanation* model and with the primacy of theological interpretation in the *prima scriptura* model, one must admit that there are dangers on both sides of this issue.

Neglecting the role of Scripture in creating a Christian worldview can lead to errant assumptions, and failing to attend adequately to theological analysis can lead to errant conclusions.[70] On the other hand, investing theological interpretation with a doctrine of theological inerrancy risks the state of affairs that led to Galileo's forced recantation. The situation is not unlike the danger faced by Odysseus on his homeward voyage, having to travel between the whirlpool of Charybdis and the man-eating Scylla.[71] Lean too far to one side, and one can founder on the rocks of secular assumptions and become lost in their vortex. Lean too far to the other side, and integration can be swallowed piecemeal by theological hegemony.[72] Steering a middle course requires that we begin with those things that are most central and clear.

Van Leeuwen offered the wise advice that, although the Bible is not a psychology textbook, it "provides us with certain background assumptions or

---

70. The reverse is also true. It was attending to evidence based on the book of God's Works that ultimately led to revised worldview conceptualizations that conform with the heliocentric theory, and failure to attend to scientific, philosophical, literary, and other analyses can lead to myopic scriptural interpretation. Likewise, the findings of psychology may challenge us to rethink our theological understanding of issues such as whether we wrongly equate sanctification with mere repression, whether motivation by guilt has biblical warrant, excessive individualism within American Christianity, and so forth.

71. The story occurs in Homer's *Odyssey*. I'm not sure if the analogy between the *Odyssey* and integration originated with me, or, if not, how much I altered it. If I borrowed this analogy from someone else, I trust that someone will let me know so that I can give credit where credit is due.

72. It is worth noting that Circe warned Odysseus that it was better to lose six men to Scylla than to lose his whole ship to Charybdis. Thus, while we might aim for a middle course, we might well ask at what point we risk six men for the safety of the whole ship.

'control beliefs' . . . by which Christians can both shape and judge psychological theories."[73] These background assumptions and control beliefs are contained in the worldview level of integration. The third model of disciplinary integration builds on the worldview level of integration and then proposes that we seek to integrate specific disciplinary content through a process of assessing the degree of confidence warranted by the quality of our data and reasoning. This model views disciplinary integration as a *quest for faithful reading*. It acknowledges that theological and psychological reasoning can be flawed, but it insists that apparent conflicts between them are solvable in principle. Much of the time, theological and psychological views will mesh naturally and harmoniously.

In cases where there are apparent contradictions between psychology and theology, rather than assuming that theological interpretation trumps psychological interpretation, it would be better to reexamine the assumptions, data, methodologies, and reasoning behind our theological and our psychological conclusions. At times, we will certainly find that our psychological conclusions are wrong, but there are also times when we will find that we invested more faith in our theological position than was warranted by the evidence.

The *quest for faithful reading* model argues that apparent conflicts should cause us to reconsider our data and reasoning as a first step in solving apparent conflicts. As a second step, we should consider whether one claim is better grounded than another is (i.e., is there stronger evidence on one side of the issue?). In many instances, we can discern whether psychology or theology speaks more clearly and fully on a given issue, and when this can be done, we place more weight on that side of the issue.[74] Whenever a well-grounded claim leads to greater certainty, that claim should be provisionally preferred. In the rare event that two well-grounded claims lead to identical levels of certainty, no preference should be accorded to either claim.

Figure 12.1 depicts the kinds of certainty that we might encounter when we attempt to integrate psychological and theological claims. The diagram depicts an area of overlapping claims where psychological and theological propositions are evidently compatible, and other areas where claims vary in whether or not they are more or less well-grounded, and more or less within the scope of one discipline or the other. In this proposal, theological propositions that are well-grounded should be preferred to alternative

---

73. Van Leeuwen, Five uneasy questions, 153.

---

74. For example, clear commandments regarding sexual purity are prescriptive and binding for the Christian. We cannot simply adopt humanistic values about loosening sexual constraints that are at odds with those teachings, however much they may be in vogue within a psychological theory or the broader culture. We should expect, however, that research on human behavior would find that there are adverse consequences of disregarding the sexual mores commended and commanded to us by Scripture.

psychological propositions that are less well grounded (C and C¹ in the diagram). This is, in fact, a very common situation.

For instance, humanistic psychology typically underestimates the degree to which human nature is prone to evil, which is a very well-grounded theological claim. On the other hand, psychological propositions that are well-grounded should be preferred to alternative theological propositions that are less well-grounded (D and D¹ in the diagram). If a well-grounded psychological finding were to conflict with a less-well-grounded theological finding, this should drive us to reexamine our theological sources and reasoning. For instance, in the well-known case of Galileo's proposal for a heliocentric system, the poorly grounded theological proposition gave way to the well-grounded scientific proposition

by recognizing the error inherent in the theological reasoning that produced the poorly-grounded proposition.

Obviously, where one discipline makes well-grounded claims that are not within the scope of the other discipline, then the well-grounded claim stands alone (F and G in the diagram). Less well-grounded claims made by one discipline that are not within the scope of the other discipline must be held provisionally (E and H in the diagram). This leaves only competing claims that are of equal grounding: two less-well-grounded claims (A and A¹) and two equally well-grounded claims (B and B¹). In both of these cases, unless there is a compelling reason to have to choose one proposition or the other, they are simply held tentatively as we revisit our interpretations of Scripture and of the psychological data. If

FIGURE 12.1: Proportional Confidence in Psychological and Theological Propositions

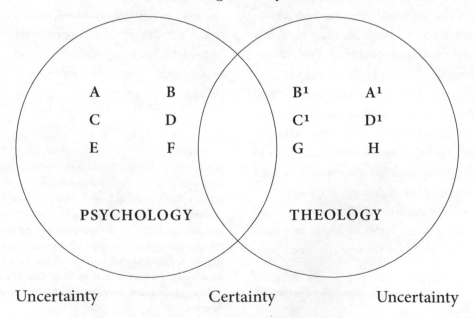

further investigation does not lead to further clarity, we should not force ourselves to make an arbitrary choice between the two propositions.

At times, we may need to suspend judgment and recognize that our current conclusions are in tension with one another. Nevertheless, much of the time, we can disentangle apparent contradictions by carefully examining our assumptions and sources of data. When faced with apparent conflicts, we need to affirm that there is but one truth, even though we will not be able to fully disentangle every conflict.

Uncertainty will sometimes remain despite our best efforts; multiple theological interpretations may be possible, the scientific data may be unclear, or our current interpretations and theories may simply conflict. While we must be willing to live with some level of ambiguity and uncertainty, we nevertheless continue the process of revisiting the data, reexamining our conclusions, and pursuing new lines of theological and scientific research that might clarify the situation.

It is the ideas that all truth comes from God and that we must humbly recognize the difference between facts and interpretation that underlie the integrative enterprise. Carter and Narramore affirmed this when they quoted the late theologian, Frank Gaebelein:

> we have fallen into the error of failing to see as clearly as we should that there are areas of truth not fully explicated in Scripture and that these,

too, are a part of God's truth. Thus we have made the misleading distinction between sacred and secular, forgetting that, as Cervantes said in one of those flashes of wisdom that punctuate the strange doings of Don Quixote, "Where the truth is, in so far as it is truth, there God is."[75]

Thus the truths found in God's Works may be of benefit as we seek to understand His Word, and the truths of His Word may help us better understand the truths found in His Works.

Looking Back: *Imagine that someone perceives a conflict between a theological view and a psychological view. How would a person try to resolve the conflict by employing each of the following approaches: levels of explanation, prima scriptura, quest for faithful reading?*

Integration and Research

Having extensively considered how we can competently engage theoretical issues from both theological and psychological perspectives, we know turn our

---

75. Gaebelein, quoted in Carter & Narramore, *The integration of psychology and theology*, 14. While Gaebelein may not have agreed that the two books were of equal authority, he clearly affirmed that both contain truth and that God stands behind both as the author of truth.

attention briefly to how Christian reflection might affect one's research agenda. First of all, Christianity may stimulate specific research interests because it calls us to care deeply about certain topics—such as forgiveness, reconciliation, or social justice. Secondly, Christianity clearly requires us to consider the means and the ends of our research—will it be carried out in ways that are ethical, and towards goals that are compatible with Christianity? Thirdly, we recognize that God has created each of us with unique interests and abilities that we can bring to bear on nearly any topic. In some cases, our interests may only indirectly relate to faith. For instance, there may be fewer obvious points of contact between Christianity and visual perception than between Christianity and reconciliation.

Many topics that are integral to Christianity have sparked theories and research among Christian psychologists. Forgiveness and gratitude, for instance, are central to the Christian message, and they are rich topics for psychological investigation. Christian theology and contemporary psychology share overlapping concerns with many phenomena such as marital and family success, childrearing, sexuality, poverty, reconciliation, and justice. Many of these topics are major foci of clinical and ecclesiastical concern, and the insights of theology and psychology together can help us to explore their complexity.

Many other topics do not share such obvious connections. At the very least, however, a Christian worldview always provides a context for psychological investigation. Sometimes, however, there are more connections than we might expect. We can see this in the work of one of my colleagues, Dr. Matthew Phelps. One of Matt's research interests is human limitations. On the surface it might seem as if the normal limitations of human memory have very little to do with theology, but then we must ask why we have these limitations and if we are morally culpable for them. Although Phelps addresses the limitations of memory, his framework can apply to other cognitive limitations.

Imagine the following situation, which involves automaticity and reaction time. A man approaches a red traffic light where he intends to turn left. On every prior occasion he has entered this intersection, the traffic light has gone from red to a green left turn arrow. This time, however, he arrived a moment too late to trigger the left turn arrow. When the light turns green, automaticity kicks in and he steps on the gas. As he enters the intersection, a woman approaching from the other side is unable to react fast enough to stop and crashes into him. Is the man responsible for the mishap in the sense that he committed some sort of sin? Is the woman responsible for the limitations of her reaction time that prevented her from being able to avoid the accident? One might well argue that both of the drivers suffered from cognitive limitations and that neither of them was morally negligent. They were simply limited creatures. So does this make cognitive limitations sinful? No, for in fact, finitude is part of what it means to be a creature. Thus the man and woman in this case, rather than accusing each other of negligence, might be better served by exercising humility and acceptance of their own—and others—limitations.

Phelps uses this as a point to help students think about the humanity of Jesus. If Jesus was fully human—as proclaimed by Christian orthodoxy—then, as a human, Jesus experienced human limitations. He could only be in one place at a time. He became hungry and tired. He suffered pain and even death. Yet somehow, we have trouble imagining a Jesus who could walk around a corner and bump into someone because he didn't see them coming from the other direction. We have trouble seeing Jesus as a small child who had such limited verbal and cognitive abilities that he perhaps did not yet have the aptitude to know that He was God or what the Father's long range plan was. And yet Scripture does hint at His limitations when, as a twelve-year old leaving the Temple, we are told, "The child Jesus grew. He became strong and wise, and God blessed him" (Matt 2:40, CEV). He grew. He became. He developed. And yet we often think of the humanity of God as somehow disappearing between the incarnation and the crucifixion. "The Word became flesh" (John 1:14, NIV).

> He made himself nothing by taking the very nature of a servant, being made in human likeness. And being found in appearance as a man, he humbled himself by becoming obedi-

ent to death—even death on a cross! (Phil 2:7–8)

If Jesus experienced human limitations, then these limitations are somehow affirmed as part of the goodness of creation.

Phelps observes that we often see human limitations as the result of the Fall, as something that is bad or aberrant. He argues that we ought not to see limitations in this way.

> I view normal memory limitations as a part of the way things are supposed to be, rather than as Fall-induced perversions of the mind. If cognitive limitations are not sins, and if they are an original aspect of the created order, then they are more than merely not evil; they are in fact good. They are good because they were created by a good God. They are good because human beings are supposed to be limited.[76]

Limitations remind us, among other things, that we are not God; we are finite creatures. Limitations provide opportunities for humility, and they are part of our identity. As Phelps notes, normal cognitive limitations

> make the human mind what it is and not something else. Therefore, they are to be acknowledged, accepted, and even affirmed with gratitude. Furthermore, they reveal the power and majesty of God by contrast in much the same way that exceptional

---

76. Phelps, *Imago Dei and limited,* 362–63.

human capacities directly inspire awe for the Creator . . .[77]

While the connections between theology and psychology may not be as intuitively obvious with cognitive limitations as with some other topics, Phelps demonstrates that there are often fascinating insights that can be gained from theology and psychology on such a topic.

Research can help us to celebrate the wonders of creation, to be humble before and in awe of God, and to understand and minister to the needs of a broken world. Many people, of course, enter the helping professions out of a desire to alleviate suffering and to bring healing to others, and it is to this topic that we now turn our attention.

What are some psychological topics that interest you? How could theology implicitly or explicitly relate to this topic?

Integration and Psychotherapy

When we come to the area of counseling interventions from a Christian perspective, we encounter many different voices. Some people propose that we cannot perform effective counseling unless we do so from an explicitly Christian standpoint. On the other hand, Christians who are trained and licensed mental health professionals believe that a wide variety of psychological techniques are consonant

with Christian belief and practice.[78] Addressing the ways that a client's spiritual and religious framework may be relevant to the clinical process is also widely recognized.[79] Beyond this, however, three issues deserve to be discussed in more detail: the constraints of professional ethics and workplace environments; religiously based interventions; and the ultimate goals of psychological intervention.

Professional Ethics

By design, most of this text has been concerned with broad issues in integration—worldviews, ways of knowing, models of integration, and so forth—that are relevant to any area of psychology. Recognizing that most readers of this text are interested in counseling or psychotherapy, however, we need to address a few things that are uniquely relevant for this audience. One thing that many Christians struggle with as counselors or psychologists is what role Christianity should take in their day-to-day interactions with clients. A Christian worldview may provide some important and broad principles about the value of human beings, understanding of brokenness, being agents of reconciliation, and so forth. Beyond this, however, one

---

77. Ibid., 366.

78. See Jones & Butman, *Modern psychotherapies.*

79. Aten & McMinn, Spirituality and the therapeutic process; Aten, O'Grady, & Worthington, The psychology of religion and spirituality; Worthington et al, *Evidence-based Practices for Christian counseling.*

needs to think about how one's own understandings of Christian faith might interact with the worldview of clients, who might come from similar backgrounds, other branches of Christianity, other religious traditions, and so forth. Even among these diverse groups, one must recognize that clients might have positive or negative religious experiences, different levels of openness to seeing their struggles as in any way framed by religious viewpoints, and assorted degrees of comfort in in discussing such things. That a therapist's worldview will implicitly impact his or her interactions with a client is inevitable, but this leaves open the question of how much and in what ways a therapist should explicitly draw on his or her religious framework in the counseling setting.

The first thing that we must point out is that licensed professionals exist to meet the needs of the client. The APA ethics code, for instance, points out that psychologists respect the dignity of all people, their right to self-determination, and their culture and values. While our values as professionals are not irrelevant, they cannot normally supersede those of the client. This is easiest to see if you imagine reversing roles. If you had a phobia of driving following an automobile accident, and your therapist suggested that your anxiety was related to an imbalance of your vital energies, you would likely believe that the therapist was acting unethically.

Joshua Hook helpfully puts this issue within the framework of cultural diversity and humility. [80] In our work with clients, we must become aware of our own values and recognize that our experiences will often be different from those of our clients. Such differences will often reflect cultural differences; sometimes they will reflect differences in religious framework. Hook contends that therapists must become "aware of their own cultural worldviews, biases, and blindspots," for without self-awareness, we too easily denigrate others and their experiences or push our own beliefs and agendas on them. Second, Hook notes that we need to actively place ourselves "in situations that stretch them to engage with individuals who are different from them."[81] So, awareness of self and other is a first step.

A more difficult issue for many Christians, though, involves areas of conflict between one's closely held values and those of a client. Bill Hathaway points out that anyone who voluntarily chooses to join a profession commits to upholding the ethical tenets held by the profession.[82] By extension, as Joshua Hook emphasizes, "Professional practice dictates that when value conflicts exist, the beliefs, values, and goals that must take precedence are those of the client."[83]

Tamara Anderson, who teaches ethics in a faith-based doctoral program,

---

80. Hook, *Engaging clients with cultural humility*, 279.

81. Ibid.

82. Hathaway, in Moriarty.

83. Hook, *Engaging clients with cultural humility*, 280

very helpfully points out that "there are ethical and unethical ways to integrate Christian ideals . . . into the therapeutic relationship."[84] A significant key for ethical practice of any sort is providing clear disclosure about the nature of therapy and obtaining informed consent. "If the Christian psychologist will overtly bring his or her faith into the room," writes Anderson, "this self-disclosure should be made at the beginning of the treatment relationship."[85] If the therapist begins to think that an interaction with a client is warranted because it is based on religious considerations even though they would violate professional ethics, the therapist is likely guilty of rationalization. "If God called me to this profession," Anderson asks, "then why would he set me up to lose my license by acting in an unethical manner with my client?"[86] None of the foregoing is intended to suggest that faith can never be explicitly expressed within therapy in an ethical manner, but it does highlight the fact that we need to think carefully about if and when and how to do so ethically. For those of you who are going to be doing clinical work, you will need to think about these matters in depth. A few resources that may help you do so are referenced in the footnote below.[87]

Workplace Environment and Informed Consent

The degree of latitude that one has in how overtly one addresses faith issues in counseling or psychotherapy is governed in part by the ethics of one's profession and the environment in which one works. Professional ethics recognize that professional practice must be guided by expectations about one's role and the duties incumbent upon someone in such a role. In most states, the psychology-licensing agency defers to or incorporates the ethical guidelines of the various counseling professions. One of the key provisions of all ethical code is the need to obtain informed consent. If a therapist plans to make explicit use of techniques or goals that reflect the therapist's religious beliefs, the client must be informed of and agree to this course of action, or the therapist would be acting unethically. Some authors recommend the use of an advanced or expanded informed consent when explicitly religious interventions are used.[88] Additionally, some workplace environments may expressly prohibit the therapist from addressing issues from a religious perspective, and in such cases, a therapist must either abide by these prohibitions or have the integrity to decline

---

84. Anderson, *Teaching professional ethics*, 165

85. Ibid., 168.

86. Ibid., 169.

87. In addition to the articles listed above, make sure to read the ethical code of your chosen profession and standard ethics texts

such as those by Corey, and Pope & Vasquez, as well as explicitly religious treatments of these topics, such as those by Gonsiorek, Richards, Pargament, & McMinn; Richards & Bergin; Sanders; and Walker, Gorsuch, & Worthington.

88. See: Yarhouse & VanOrman, *Psychologists and religious clients*. See also Hunter and Yarhouse, *Considerations*.

such employment if he or she is unwilling to do so.

Lest this sound too restrictive, it is important to note that understanding a client's spiritual and religious life can be extremely important, and many professionals include a spiritual history as part of their basic assessment interview. Similarly, when working with patients who have serious medical illnesses, physicians are encouraged to take a brief "spiritual assessment" by asking four simple questions:

- "Is faith (religion, spirituality) important to you in this illness?"
- "Has faith been important to you at other times in your life?"
- "Do you have someone to talk to about religious matters?"
- "Would you like to explore religious matters with someone?"[89]

While these questions may open the door to talking about spiritual issues, it is important to recognize that clients usually come to us to address self-identified needs. As such, psychology and medicine exist to serve the client. Spiritual issues may well emerge in this context. For instance, a client may struggle with attitudes about a church upbringing linked to authoritarianism, with Christian teachings about forgiveness, with the need to come to terms with guilt and sin, or with their own spiritual longings and emptiness.

If done appropriately—with informed consent and respect for self-determination—spiritual issues can be a legitimate focus of therapy. How one addresses these issues, though, will vary depending on one's theoretical frame of reference, practice setting, and the degree to which the informed consent process incorporates spiritual matters. I would caution, however, that one must be extremely cognizant of the power differential that exists in therapy, and the potential damage that can be done by exploitation of client vulnerability.

One of the difficulties faced by any counselor or therapist—Christian or not—is that our clients often come from different backgrounds and hold different values and commitments than we do. Recognizing this, professional associations stipulate that the role of the therapist is not to impose his or her values on clients except in very rare cases, such as to protect victims of abuse or to prevent suicide. For Christian therapists, this may be a particularly difficult area when our own values conflict with those of our clients.

Discussing multicultural competence for Christian therapists, Eriksson and Abernethy note that it is important to "see the world not only from our own perspective, but from others as well."[90] Misunderstanding, prejudice, and stereotypes easily arise because we tend to associate with people who share our values and perspectives. Moreover, humility and openness are especially important

---

89. Lo, Quill, & Tulsky, *Discussing palliative care.*

90. Eriksson & Abernethy, *Integration in multicultural competence*, 174.

when we encounter people "who differ from us on topics central to our identity or about which we care deeply."[91]

What are some important things to keep in mind when a therapist's values might conflict with those of a client? In what ways can a "spiritual assessment" be useful clinically?

Religiously Based Interventions

Christianity has a long history of spiritual disciplines, rituals, and practices that may have psychological benefits. In recent decades, there has been considerable interest in developing religiously based interventions that can be used as psychotherapy or as adjuncts to psychotherapy.[92]

Religiously based interventions can be as generic as encouraging a client to pray or read the Psalms, or they may govern the entire therapeutic process. Generic religiously based interventions do not usually create significant ethical concerns so long as informed consent is obtained and client rights for self-determination are respected. Religiously based interventions that are more specific and global, though, pose several problems.[93]

Psychologists—and other mental health professionals—are licensed or certified to provide "recognized techniques and procedures" that they are competent to perform based on education and training. Any licensed professional who intends to consider the impact of the client's spirituality or to include religiously based intervention should not do so without adequate training. Furthermore, competent therapists need to consider the client's welfare, best practices, and empirical evidence for the therapeutic techniques that he or she uses. A few resources are listed in the footnote below.[94]

When using religiously based interventions *at a minimum* a therapist needs to obtain informed consent that details the proposed procedures, available alternatives, potential risks, and the fact that the procedure is experimental in nature and is not a recognized psychological technique. There are also legal issues that could occur. For instance, if someone used a system of guided imagery and prayer, could this be billed as psychotherapy? These are issues that are obviously of much import.[95]

---

91. Van Tongeren et al, Meaning-based approach to humility, 63.

92. Anderson, Zuehlke, & Zuehlke, *Christ-centered therapy*.

93. My concerns about one of these approaches, Theophostic Ministry, are detailed in Entwistle, Shedding Light 1, and Shedding Light 2.

94. Aten & McMinn, *Spirituality and the therapeutic process*; Aten, O'Grady, & Worthington, *The psychology of religion and spirituality*; Wothington et al., *Evidence-based practices for Christian counseling*. Jones & Butman, *Modern psychotherapies: A comprehensive Christian appraisal*.

95. See, for example, Hathaway, Clinical use of explicitly religious approaches. See also Hunter & Yarhouse, Considerations and

I have argued elsewhere that we need to be cautious in the use of explicit religious interventions because of the power differential inherent in the therapeutic situation.

> Imagine that an individual tends to defer to religious authorities and may hide religious misgivings out of fear of condemnation. If a psychologist were to promote the use of religiously based interventions in such a case, she might well miss the opportunity to explore the client's religious misgivings and interpersonal dynamics. This is not to say that such interventions are never appropriate, but it is intended to highlight the fact that religiously based interventions should not be undertaken lightly. Where a client and therapist do not share a common religious framework, religious interventions that proceed from the stance of the therapist's religious viewpoint are particularly problematic.[96]

My own concerns, though, also extend to the potential damage that these approaches can do to faith itself. Again, as I argued elsewhere:

> An often overlooked problem in the use of religiously based therapeutic techniques is the risk of reducing religious beliefs to their pragmatic value as a source of morality and comfort. Sociology of religion researcher Christian Smith (2005) referred to this type of religious pragmatism

as "moralistic therapeutic Deism."[97] However, Christianity (and most other major religions) are not primarily designed to bring about personal satisfaction and fulfillment. Rather, the focus of Christianity (and most other major religions) is on transforming people into the kinds of persons and communities that the religious system says they should be. This, in turn, may have significant personal and interpersonal benefit, but such benefit is not the overarching aim of the religious system . . . The risk of treating religious faith primarily as a means to happiness and satisfaction is very significant when spiritual beliefs and practices are used as therapeutic interventions: we need to be very cautious, or in the name of "integration" we may actually propagate moralistic therapeutic Deism.[98]

Christian therapists need to attend to the whole person, including their client's spiritual beliefs and needs, but they need to do so ethically and with great care.

Summary

Disciplinary integration may often proceed by exploring connections between particular psychological theories and specific theological traditions. Theology provides a set of core beliefs that provide context for human understanding. This fact leaves open the question of how to

---

recommendation.

96 Entwistle, Holistic psychology of persons, 145.

97. Smith, *Soul searching*.

98. Entwistle, Holistic psychology of persons, 146.

resolve apparent contradictions between theology and psychology. Some have argued for a *levels of explanation* view of disciplinary integration, which relegates psychology and theology to relatively distinct spheres. In practice, however, this model often leads to the primacy of psychological interpretation, an inadequate attention to theological interpretation, and a failure to bring about sufficient dialogue between psychological and theological perspectives.

A second solution is to conceptualize disciplinary integration as *prima scriptura*, that is, to see scriptural interpretation as trumping scientific (or psychological) interpretation. This model tends to confuse the authority of Scripture with the authority of scriptural interpretation, usually by a reticence to reconsider one's theological positions. This model implicitly or explicitly unfolds from an *a priori* assumption that apparent conflicts should be solved by subjugating psychological interpretation to theological interpretation, or by recasting psychology in the light of a particular theological mold. The *prima scriptura* model can easily lead to foreclosed conclusions in which neither scriptural nor psychological interpretations are carefully reconsidered.

Finally, those who see disciplinary integration as a *quest for faithful reading* believe that the origin of truth is in God's action in word and deed. Since our ultimate allegiance is to God, and since He is the author of both books, it is assumed that truth can be found through theological and psychological investigation.

While each book provides details that the other does not, and while some biblical truths are foundational to a Christian worldview, the two books themselves cannot contradict each other. Since truth cannot be self-contradictory, the matter is thus one of faithfully reading both books and allowing for a mutual interaction in which we humbly bring our theological and psychological interpretations into dialogue with each other. When faced with apparent contradictions, we reexamine the psychological and theological evidence, lending greater weight to whichever source provides greater clarity. We will sometimes have to live with ambiguity and uncertainty, but we affirm that God is the author of all truth.

Farnsworth proposed that disciplinary integration involves discovery, verification, and relation. The theories of Maslow, Rogers, and Ben-Shahar were examined using this framework. We noted that topics that are central to Christianity—such as forgiveness, gratitude, and marital success—could be a useful impetus to psychological research, but that there are also less obvious connections between areas such as cognitive limitations and the Christian view of humans as limited creatures. When we turn our attention to psychotherapy, we noted that integration must take into account ethical and professional issues, and we addressed some potential advantages and concerns about religiously based interventions.

Questions for Reflection and Discussion

1. Maslow and Rogers both rejected Christianity. From what you read in the text, or what you know from other sources, what might be the source of their animosity? Does their rejection of Christianity necessarily mean that all of their theories are so flawed that they should be completely rejected?

2. In his critique of Maslow and Rogers, the author used Scripture as a touchstone to analyze their views, but he also used other psychological findings in his discussion. Why is it important to use both theological and psychological critique rather than relying only on one or the other?

3. The author explored Tal Ben-Shahar's view of happiness as an example of how we need to attend to the telos of a theory. What do you think is the "ultimate currency" of human life, and how did you form this belief? How does your understanding of the purpose of human life relate to temporal happiness?

4. Jesus was fully human as well as fully God; "Christ Jesus . . . although He existed in the form of God . . . emptied Himself, taking the form of a bondservant, and being made in the likeness of men" (Phil 2:5–7, NASB). The doctrine of the incarnation suggests that Jesus willingly took on human limitations. Identify some specific cognitive limitations that Jesus might have experienced and discuss how you react to the idea that Jesus willingly emptied himself not only in the ability to experience physical abuse and death, but to experience cognitive limitations.

5. Larry Crabb stated that "No psychology can claim to be Christian which directly or indirectly denies to the Scripture the role of final arbiter." Do you agree or disagree with his assertion? Why or why not?

6. Why is it important to distinguish between the *authority of Scripture* and the *authority of theological interpretation*?

7. In what way can theological interpretation be seen as foundational to integration? What are the essential elements of a Christian worldview? How do these elements shape the way a Christian might approach psychology differently compared to someone who embraces another worldview perspective?

8. Compare and contrast the way that someone would try to resolve an apparent conflict between theology and psychology using a *levels of explanation*, *prima scriptura*, or *quest for faithful reading approach*. What are the advantages and disadvantages of each view?

9. How is the issue of being faithful to discern both God's Word and His Works similar to Odysseus's having to straddle the twin perils of Charybdis

and Scylla? In a footnote, the author noted that Odysseus risked losing six men to Scylla or his whole ship to Charybdis. Does leaning too heavily toward theological hegemony or psychological partiality involve a similarly disproportionate risk?

10. How would you go about trying to discern whether psychology or theology provided more clarity on a given issue? Why is it hard to live with ambiguity and uncertainty when a clear resolution is not obvious or readily apparent?

11. The author noted that, at times, "the data are equivocal, and clear conclusions are elusive." How do you handle the ambiguity of such situations? Why is humility an important virtue for dealing with ambiguity?

12. In his discussion of psychotherapy, the author noted some of the ethical issues involved in addressing spiritual issues in therapy. How do you reconcile professional ethics with the call to be "salt and light" in the world?

13. What do you see as the advantages and disadvantages of using religiously based interventions? How would someone address the ethical issues of using such interventions?

14. What was the author cautioning against when he said that we need to be wary of propagating moralistic therapeutic Deism?

13

Discerning Your Place in the Integration Story

But an innovation, to grow organically from within, has to be based on an intact tradition, so our idea is to bring together musicians who represent all these traditions, in workshops, festivals, and concerts, to see how we can connect with each other in music.

—Yo-Yo Ma

Many people mistake our work for our vocation. Our vocation is the love of Jesus.

—Mother Teresa

Debbie, my wife, was sharing the kitchen with Ania and her next-door neighbor while Don, Mirek, and I sat in the other room—Polish households often follow traditional gender roles. The last time I had been at Mirek and Ania's house, Ania had made a Polish dish called krokiety, and I was smitten. So, two years later, when I returned with my wife, we had decided to exchange recipes. Ania taught Debbie how to make krokiety, and Debbie taught Ania how to make apple pie. But Ania spoke only Polish, and Debbie spoke only English. The problem was solved by adding a third woman to the kitchen, a Polish neighbor who spoke English with a delightful British accent. As Debbie tried to tell the other women

how to roll out the dough, the British-speaking-Polish-woman kept saying, "This is how you make the cake?" Debbie and I laugh and smile whenever we reminisce about that wonderful day, the exchange of food and traditions, and the knowledge that we have become part of the stories that other people share.

A similar kind of thing happens when people begin to learn about integration. At first, it is somewhat like reading a travel book about a foreign place. In time, they become acquainted with the ideas that shape this new place. They meet new people, and, if they continue on this journey, they add their own voices and bring their own experiences and traditions into the conversation. They find their place at the table, enjoying the contributions of others, and adding their own unique gifts and insights.

In this final chapter, I want to invite you to the table. We will begin with a travel book, of sorts. In this part, we will begin to learn about some different Christian traditions that shape our understanding of integration. From there, we will get to know a few of the other people who sit at the table, and we will hear their stories of how their faith traditions and personal experiences shape how they think about integration. Despite their differences, a common refrain will be a sense of calling to love God and to care for others. It should be a rich conversation!

Setting the Table

There are a variety of Christian worldviews that reflect somewhat different social circumstances, geographical and historical settings, and diverse viewpoints about what it means to be a Christian. These views are passed on through daily practices of interaction, education, and ritual. While most Christians share large portions of a basic Christian worldview, there are clearly some differences across subgroups.

Consider, for example, how people worship in a variety of settings: a Roman Catholic cathedral, a Pentecostal church, and a Quaker silent meeting. In a Roman Catholic church, people—and their view of reality—are formed by recitation of the Nicene Creed and daily prayers, listening

to Scripture and homilies, and rituals such as genuflection and the passing of the peace. The Pentecostal church, by contrast, is an entirely different culture, where people are shaped by the expectation of God's activity through the Holy Spirit, signs and wonders, and an entirely different kind of preaching. The Quaker silent meeting, on the other hand, has no formal clergy, and the meeting house is devoid of religious symbols, and people sit silently as they wait for God to speak to the congregation through His Spirit. People in all three of these groups seek to love God and to love their neighbor, but they do so in very diverse ways. In fact, if you were to pluck someone out of any of these services and put them in one of the others, they would probably be somewhat mystified and even uncomfortable. They might, in fact, believe that people in the other congregations are wrong about any number of doctrinal or practical issues, even if they agreed on the basic shape of the gospel.

Our own situation is also somewhat like this. Most of this book has been influenced by one particular model of thinking about integration, which, despite its Dutch Reformed roots, has had an enormous influence on Christian higher education in general. As we sit down to the table, however, it becomes clear that although those gathered here love the same God and believe many of the same things, there are unmistakable differences. The diverse personal experiences and faith traditions of these individuals shape the ways that they think about and practice integration.

Tradition Saturated Integration

Different branches of the Christian faith conceptualize the world somewhat uniquely, emphasizing variations of doctrine and practice. We should not be surprised, then, that clients who come from different Christian traditions have religious resources and religious difficulties that reflect the uniqueness of how faith is expressed in their religious traditions. Similarly, Christians who engage psychology—whether as clinicians or researchers—will do so somewhat differently from one another based in part on the unique emphases and practices of their own faith traditions. This means that there will be a plurality of types of integration, even as we affirm the underlying unity shared by all Christians. As C. Stephen Evans noted,

> Obviously there are large differences between various forms of Christianity . . . What does this pluralism imply for the project of integration? I would say two things: (1) The project of integrating Christianity into psychology is itself pluralistic, and different Christians, who may be equally faithful to their Christian callings, may disagree about the implications of Christian faith for various issues in psychology. (2) Nonetheless, faithful Christians can hope to find enough common ground in "mere Christianity" to constitute a genuine community that can make progress.[1]

Evans also points out that doing psychology as a Christian may take on different shape depending on what kind of work we are doing. For instance, even people who come from the same Christian tradition will think about integration in varied and dissimilar ways depending on their vocational context, such as doing research on neurobiology, helping families make decisions about caring for a loved one with Alzheimer's disease, working at a Christian counseling center, or working at a community mental health agency.

We need to be aware that there are many valid and effective ways to exercise a psychological vocation as a Christian. As Evans observed,

> Christian psychology can be the work of people who do not think of themselves as doing Christian psychology, and indeed might even reject the label . . . What makes their work Christian is not the label but the fact that it is done as part of a Christian calling and that the work itself is partly shaped by Christian character, emotions, and convictions . . . On my view, the primary goal of a Christian psychologist is not to be different but to be faithful.[2]

Al Dueck, similarly, points out that, "in contrast to psychology of religion, a religious psychology privileges the religious tradition" and the "assumptions, beliefs, practices, and rituals" that combine to make up its "psychological and

---

1. Evans, Doing psychology as a Christian, 33.

2. Ibid., 34.

theological anthropology."[3] To understand how any particular person thinks about psychology and faith, we need to understand the tradition from which he or she approaches integration.

The ways in which our theological traditions shape our lives—including our vocations—are not entirely conscious. They often operate in the background, giving rise to assumptions, feelings, cognitions, and even physical ways of being. According to Strawn, Wright, and Jones, theological traditions shape us, forming habits and ways of thinking through their liturgies and rituals, "conditioning how persons make meaning in the world" and directing them towards particular goals.[4]

Most of the published literature on integration, though, has focused narrowly on the idea of how a Christian worldview shapes academic discourse. This is a particular strength of the Reformed tradition, but this narrow focus sometimes leaves Christians from other traditions feeling a bit bewildered or even left out as they consider what their own Christian traditions might uniquely offer to their engagement with psychology. The fact is, integration will look different based on one's tradition, and this diversity can be a very good thing. When we recognize that integrative approaches are saturated by our own Christian tradition, it allow us to better recognize our "own contributions to the task" and to "more hospitably recognize" the unique contributions of others.[5]

In what ways does your own religious experience and tradition (or lack of religious experience and tradition) shape the way you think about psychology and theology?

In the following pages, we will sample a few recent discourses on how a particular theological tradition may shape how its adherents think about integration. The resulting pictures should be seen as only snapshots of many perspectives. Even though different ecclesiastic traditions share some common core convictions, they emphasize distinct theological perspectives on ecclesiology, personhood, sanctification, worship, and so forth. The diversity of these perspectives can enrich integration. My hope is that we will see greater appreciation for, and development of, tradition saturated integration in the coming decades. A few of the benefits of several traditions are reviewed in the following paragraphs.[6] As you read these perspectives, think about how integration might be done by someone who comes from these various

---

3. Dueck, Anabaptism, 365.

4. Strawn, Wright, and Jones, Tradition-based integration, 306.

5. Ibid., 308.

6. Only a handful of traditions are included here. Interested persons might also look at Fayard et al., Seventh-day Adventist tradition; Beck, Church of Christ; Watson, A Canterbury tale; and others.

branches of Christianity, working in a variety of settings. Additionally, it is worthwhile to consider how clients who come from these branches might think differently about the therapeutic experience.

Integration from a Reformed Perspective

The dominant evangelical models of integration have reflected Reformed thinking during the past half-century, and this has been a significant influence on the approach taken in this book. The Reformed model emphasizes the development of Christian scholarship from the standpoint of a Christian worldview, and it continues to be a valuable and important model.

One of the strengths of the Reformed perspective on faith-learning integration is its emphasis on core commitments that anchor Christian scholarship. Nicholas Wolterstorff referred to these core commitments as *control beliefs.*

> The Christian scholar ought to allow the belief-content of his authentic Christian commitment to function as control [beliefs] within his devising and weighing of theories . . . Since his fundamental commitment to following Christ ought to be decisively ultimate in his life, the rest of his life ought to be brought into harmony with it . . . Negatively, the Christian scholar ought to reject certain theories on the ground that they conflict or do not comport well with the belief-content of his authentic commitment. And positively he ought to devise theories which comport as well as possible with, or are at least consistent with, the belief-content of his authentic commitment . . . Only when the belief-content of the Christian scholar's authentic Christian commitment enters into his or her devising and weighing of psychological theories in this way can it be said that he or she is fully serious both as scholar and as Christian.[7]

Reformed approaches to integration such as this will undoubtedly continue to spur intellectual and theoretical engagement between the content of Christian faith and the discipline of psychology.

The Reformed approach helps us to anchor integration to a worldview that is common to most branches of historic, orthodox Christianity. It also emphasizes the life of the mind and the need to bring everything under the sovereignty of God. Much of the Christian liberal arts tradition in education has been heavily influenced by the Reformed tradition, even in Christian universities that have other denominational ties.

Integration from a Wesleyan Perspective

Wesleyan theology, of course, emerged from the work of the eighteenth-century revivalists John and Charles Wesley. Several images emerge as one thinks of the Wesleys: open air revivals, small groups that fostered "spiritual maturity and

---

7. Wolterstorff, *Reason within the bounds,* 72–73.

accountability," and songs that make up a huge portion of the modern hymnal.[8] Wesleyan theology "emphasizes a concern for the whole person and how spiritual experiences can impact personality change, particularly as it relates to growing love for God, self, and others."[9]

In the Wesleyan tradition, salvation involves sanctification, the gradual alteration of our thoughts and actions in the pursuit of holiness. This involves "a reorientation of the saved person's internal motivating system, or his/her moral affections."[10] Wesleyan theology assumes that our passions are disordered and must be reoriented. Spiritual health, then, involves psychological health as we learn to love and pursue the right things. Sanctification means that we develop an "increasing capacity for aligning one's life more closely with the heart of God" so that we think about and relate rightly "to God, others, and self."[11]

Within the Wesleyan tradition, Scripture, reason, tradition, and experience make up the four sources of authority that compose the Wesleyan quadrilateral, of which, Scripture is "traditionally viewed as the highest authority."[12] For those who attempt to do integration of faith and psychology from a Wesleyan tradition, these four sources, while not completely independent from each other, are brought into dialogue with each other, "held together in an attempt to understand more completely."[13] While other integrative approaches may focus primarily on conceptual understanding, the Wesleyan approach also emphasizes action: "We are not only, or primarily, what we think; we are what we have experienced and what we do."[14]

Some Wesleyan professors warn against a tendency that they see among their students to become so enamored with psychology that they too easily embrace the narratives and assumptions of the discipline of psychology with only superficial engagement with their own tradition, or, indeed, with even a generic Christian tradition. Fittingly, the Wesleyan approach to integration calls us back to the roots of our Christian traditions.

Our call for integrative psychologists to engage in Tradition-Based Integration is a call for clinicians and researchers to return to their roots, to their liturgies, to their habitus that are so deeply engrained in them that they do not even notice their impact, yet which have a profound influence on how they see, work, and imagine the task of integration. A return to our Tradition not only clarifies what we are doing as integrators, it also protects, respects, and welcomes the unique others that we meet in our

---

8. Holeman and Headley, *Wesleyan theology,* 335.

9. Ibid.

10. Ibid., 339.

11. Ibid., 340.

12. Wright, Jones, and Strawn, *Tradition-based integration,* 48.

---

13. Ibid., 49.

14. Strawn, Wright, and Jones, Tradition-based integration, 308.

laboratories, classrooms, professional societies, and therapy rooms.[15]

The Wesleyan tradition focuses on personal holiness and service. "Because of its emphasis on the sanctified life, the Wesleyan/Holiness tradition stresses what the saved self can become rather than what the sinful self has been."[16]

While the Wesleyan tradition is concerned with personal salvation and sanctification, it is also concerned with social transformation. The Salvation Army, for instance, ministers to the spiritual and the temporal needs of people who seek help through its shelters, soup kitchens, and other ministries. This is, indeed, a rich tradition that will continue to inform integration.

Integration from a Charismatic or Pentecostal Perspective

The Pentecostal tradition is perhaps the second largest Christian group, next to Roman Catholicism, and one of the fastest growing Christian branches throughout the modern world. Stephen Parker points out that Pentecostalism is "lively, exuberant, and physically expressive."[17] In worship services, Pentecostals expect to encounter God, not merely in an abstract, cognitive, doctrinal way, but through His active presence. Parker points out that testimonies are a common part of Pentecostal worship, wherein people will "voice their victories, concerns, and laments" as they "acknowledge the joys and sadness that are the fabric of life."[18] There is a social context to these testimonies, wherein others may pray for and touch each other as they acknowledge their joys and struggles and wait expectantly for God to intervene.

Pentecostals focus more on the lived experience of faith, less on doctrine as systematic theology. Parker, drawing on Dayton,[19] identified four religious movements that converge in Pentecostalism.

- Revivalism

- Holiness

- End-time prophecy

- Divine healing

To this, Parker adds the "Pentecostal focus on the active, present intervention of the Holy Spirit."[20]

Pentecostals share many doctrinal beliefs with most Christians, such as the conceptualization of creation, fall, and redemption, and the "Christological images of incarnation, crucifixion, and resurrection," the latter of which can inform a Pentecostal understanding of "empathy, suffering, and growth."[21] Perhaps one the most unique elements of Pentecostalism, though, is its emphasis on God's imminent presence to convict, equip, and heal,

---

15. Ibid., 309.

16. Hughes and Adrian, *Models for Christian higher education, 313.*

17. Parker, *A Pentecostal perspective,* 311.

18. Ibid., 311.

19. Dayton, *Theological roots of Pentecostalism.*

20. Parker, *A Pentecostal perspective,* 312.

21. Ibid., 314.

and its emphasis on "spiritual warfare." Given this emphasis, it is not surprising that most people in the "Inner Healing" movement—in which one seeks God's active healing for memories or emotional conflicts—come from or have been influenced by the Pentecostal or charismatic traditions.

Biblical stories, likewise, are often seen by Pentecostals as powerful images that we partake in, not just as a source of doctrine. The Pentecostal focus on embodiment of spiritual experience means that "God is not only interested in the saving of souls; God is interested in the restoration of bodies" and "gives great weight to the affective dimension of humans and does not simply treat us as 'thinking machines.'"[22] Hurting and marginalized individuals may sometimes find a welcoming community in Pentecostalism because of its focus on testimonies, relationships, and healing.

Integration from a Roman Catholic Perspective

Roman Catholicism, more than any other tradition which we are considering here, uses liturgy and ritual as character formation. This is carried out in response to the baptismal call to holiness, understood in terms of knowing, loving, and serving God and neighbor in this world and the next. The liturgical calendar provides a three-year cycle of important biblical stories and themes and doctrines: Advent, Christmas, Lent, Easter, and Pentecost frame the life of the church. Sacraments and symbols mediate grace into daily life as the Catholic seeks to follow Christ. Around the world, Roman Catholics share in the same biblical readings every day, participate in the same prayers, and recite the same confessions. The structure of worship is carefully and thoughtfully mapped out for the faithful.

Catholic theology embodies perspectives on faith and morals that span two-thousand years of church tradition, which Roman Catholics understand to involve an apostolic succession in teaching and ministry. Roman Catholic models of doctrine and morals emphasize the concord of faith and reason,[23] "respect for the cumulative wisdom of past generations," the sacramental nature of reality, inclusiveness, social dimension of redemption,[24] and the moral implications of following Christ.[25] The richly textured practices of Roman Catholic spiritual direction share much in common with counseling and psychotherapy, albeit from a deliberately spiritual perspective. Numerous Catholic theologians, clergy, and lay persons have written penetratingly about the interface of spirituality and psychotherapy. In recent years several papal encyclicals have engaged psychology directly, as well as less directly when speaking to social issues.[26]

---

22. Ibid., 315.

23. John Paul II, *Fides et ratio.*

24. Hellwig, *Roman Catholic tradition*, 14.

25. John Paul II, *Veritatis splendor.*

26. Benedict XVI, *Deus caritas est*; Francis, *Lumen fidei*; and Francis, *Evangelii gaudium.*

There is, of course, diversity in how individual Catholics engage psychology. As we saw earlier in this book, the tenor of that engagement changed significantly since the Second Vatican Council. Of note, though, is the longstanding Catholic view that grace builds on nature.[27] In part, this means that God works through the natural world to bring about His ends. Church sacraments, instituted by Christ, become means of God's grace working in our lives. Therapy, too, can then be a means through which we participate in God's redemptive work and call to goodness and holiness, whether explicitly religious or not. One Catholic psychologist, reflecting on this theme, put it this way:

> It is in this transitional and transformational space that I experience most profoundly the opportunity to cooperate and collaborate with God's redemptive movements in the life of my patients. How God will move is often a mystery to me; that God will move is a certainty. My part is to be attuned to my patient and to God; to pray to perceive what God is about in the space we share, and as best I am able to cooperate through my words and actions with what God is doing.[28]

The sacramental view recognizes that God is moving in all of life, including therapy, supervision, research, teaching, and every other space which is sacred because God is present.

Many Roman Catholic perspectives complement those found in other Christian traditions, such as the importance of a Christian anthropology that affirms the image of God, human sin, and God's redemptive acts. Roman Catholicism, guided by a teaching Magisterium[29] and in dialogue with the sciences, is quite explicit about affirming that the human person retains a basic human dignity and goodness, while being influenced by sin. An example of this teaching is found when John Paul II, in his encyclical on the value and inviolability of human life, affirms that every human person has dignity and should be respected "from conception to natural death."[30] As a natural extension of this, Roman Catholic theology and practice has a strong interest in both holiness (or sanctification) and social justice. Pope Francis has embodied love and justice as hallmarks of his papacy, sometimes in ways that ruffle the feathers of Catholics and non-Catholics alike.

For most of the twentieth century, Roman Catholic universities maintained strict control of their theology departments but allowed a plurality of perspectives in other academic areas and maintained a welcoming attitude to students and non-theology faculty

---

27. McCarthy, A Roman Catholic perspective.

28. Tisdale, A Catholic perspective, 360.

29. The magisterium is the authoritative teachings of the Roman Catholic Church, expressed through pronouncements of popes and bishops. Thus, the pronouncements of papal encyclicals and councils are a rich source of church teaching.

30. Ibid., 357. John Paul II, *Evangelium vitae*, n. 93.

regardless of religious background. There are obviously advantages of this approach, particularly in being a welcoming community of academic inquiry. However, this approach has tended to neglect overt integration of Catholic faith and other disciplines. One recent development that runs counter to this trend is the establishment of the Institute for the Psychological Sciences, "a Catholic graduate school of psychology founded in 1999 dedicated to the scientific study of psychology with a Catholic understanding of the person, marriage and the family."[31] IPS now offers both masters and doctoral degrees in psychology rooted in a model of integration of the psychological sciences and Church teaching that is distinctively Catholic.

A similar transition can be seen in Catholic professional associations. In 1946, the American Catholic Psychological Association (ACPA) was formed with the bidirectional goals of making psychology available to Catholics and bringing distinctively Catholic perspectives to psychology. By 1970, the ACPA become more pluralistic and it refocused its efforts on psychology and religious issues more broadly. In 1976 the association morphed into Division 36 of the American Psychological Association, Psychologists Interested in Religious Issues. The overtly religious focus was never a good fit in the secular APA, and in 1993, Division 36 was renamed Psychology of

Religion.[32] In 2011 it was again renamed, Psychology of Religion and Spirituality. While Division 36 has a strong presence of overtly religious members, the original intent of ACPA has been diminished in these transitions. In response, the Catholic Psychotherapy Association was organized in 2007, completely independent of APA. Its mission—"to support mental health practitioners by promoting the development of psychological theory and mental health practice which encompasses a full understanding of the human person and society in communion with the Magisterium of the Catholic Church"—is clearly aimed at a distinctively Catholic vision of psychology.[33]

My first postdoctoral job was at a residential treatment program for Catholic clergy and religious. While there, I gained a deep appreciation for liturgy, spiritual direction, and the depth of service to which Catholic priests, brothers, and sisters dedicate themselves. I appreciated their respect for me and our open discussions about our theological commonalities and differences. I will always remember fondly an elderly priest with whom I shared a conversation about our theological perspectives. When we were done, he smiled and said, "David, I honestly think I'll see you in heaven." And I look forward to seeing him there as well.

---

31. http://www.ipsciences.edu/mission-and -vision/.

32. Reuder, A history of Division 36, p. 91.

33. http://www.catholicpsychotherapy.org/ index.php/about-the-cpa/our-mission.

Integration from an Anabaptist Perspective

Anabaptists are among the most radical reformers of the Reformation tradition. They encompass groups as varied as the Amish and Hutterites, Brethren in Christ, and Mennonites. Despite their vast differences, there are some similarities among these groups that give them a unique vantage point from which to view psychology. When I was a student at Taylor University, I had a Mennonite sociology professor, Dan Yutzy, who had been raised Amish. Dr. Yutzy's interest in sociology was clearly related to his formative experiences of culture and community. Many decades after leaving the Amish community and obtaining a doctorate, Dr. Yutzy kept an Amish beard and mannerisms, and created a hospitable community in his classes and in his home, where students gathered for weekly Bible studies.

The Anabaptist traditions are quite distinct from each other, as can be seen especially in the degrees and ways in which they separate themselves from the world. They do have common roots, however, which lead them to emphasize a number of things including community, adult baptism, peacemaking, and pacifism. Al Dueck, who is Mennonite, observed that Mennonites do not base their model of personhood on philosophical grounds, but on ethics. "The benchmark of being human," he writes, "is the degree to which our lives reflect who Jesus is."[34]

Mennonite contributions to faith learning integration in psychology often emphasize service. During World War II, many Mennonites in the United States refused to serve in the armed services because of their pacifist beliefs. As conscientious objectors, they were allowed to perform alternative civilian public service (CPS). Not wanting to divert funds from the war effort, the federal government did not fund day-to-day operations of alternative service, nor did it pay conscientious objectors, other than a small monthly stipend. The churches from which these men came had to provide for their material support, including their daily food. While soldiers could send paychecks home to their families, the CPS men had no way to support their wives and children. Obviously, the cost of following one's conscience was significant. Additionally, CPS men served longer than most soldiers, and many were not released from service until many months after the war was over.

Early on, many of the CPS camps were dedicated to forestry and agriculture, but countless conscientious objectors desired more meaningful work. State mental hospitals were severely understaffed, and the government agreed to repurpose some of the CPS men to serve in the hospitals.

Over 1,000 Mennonites performed their civilian public service (CPS)

---

34. Dueck, Anabaptism, 369.

work in mental hospitals. For many, often from farms or small towns—with only high school educations—the sights, sounds, and smells of the large public psychiatric hospitals that predominated in 1940s America were a sobering revelation.[35]

The CPS men quickly pointed out the deplorable conditions of the hospitals to the general public. As peace loving people, they refused to carry batons into the locked wards, which other guards used to "control" the inmates. Much like Pinel's experiment in France two centuries earlier, when the inmates were treated with dignity, violence decreased; compassion achieved what coercion could not.[36]

Realizing the immense need for humane and compassionate psychiatric care, Mennonites founded several mental health centers after the war. They provided compassionate mental health care that was not just humane, it was loving; one of the best histories of the reform movement is titled, *If We Can Love*. Mentally ill people were not to be abused, feared, pitied, or tolerated; they were to be loved. Perhaps only a marginalized people like the Mennonites could transcend the barriers that led to such misunderstanding as a marginalized group like the seriously mentally ill in the days before the revolution in psychiatric medicine.

While Mennonites cared about the mentally ill, few Mennonites in the 1940s were trained as psychiatrists, psychologists, or social workers. Many of the Mennonite mental health centers hired professional staff who were from other Christian traditions, while Mennonites served as aides. Over the next several decades, more of the staffing could be done by Mennonites, especially in nursing and social work departments, as their members saw these as godly vocations.

The Mennonite model emphasizes faith and living more than faith and learning. "The religious orientation is expressed in compassion, empathy, and collaboration with the community."[37] Moreover, rather than directly incorporating evangelism or religion into the therapeutic process, ministry is conceived as the embodiment of compassion. Theologically, Mennonite care is grounded in an incarnational theology in which Jesus is "the Word made flesh" and the Church is "the body of Christ."[38] The Mennonite emphasis on service, justice, peace, and community is a rich resource for the integration of psychology and Christianity.

I completed my doctoral internship at a hospital where conservative Mennonite women in white head coverings worked in support staff roles, providing compassion and comfort—not to mention incredible Mennonite cooking. I am convinced that their loving concern and hospitality were as important to the

---

35. Levin, Mennonite MH system, 18.

36. Ediger, Roots of Mennonite mental health, in Neufeld, *If we can love*.

37. Francis Sparrow, MD, medical director of Philhaven Hospital, quoted in ibid.

38. Dueck, *Between Jerusalem and Athens*, 224.

therapeutic milieu as was the psycho-therapy and psychiatric care provided by the professional staff.

Much more could be said of insights and practices that can be mined from other Christian traditions, but at present, it is encouraging to see other perspectives being added to that of the Reformed view. The Reformed perspective has been extremely valuable in stimulating Christian thinking based on a Christian worldview, but it has sometimes tended to focus on faith and learning with inadequate attention to faith and living. Encouraging more input from other segments of Christianity can strengthen and broaden integrative efforts. It is likely that tradition saturated integration will continue to have a significant impact on the ongoing discussion about the relationship of Christianity and psychology.

From Traditions to Personal Experience

We are shaped, of course, not just by our own traditions, but by our own experiences. It is through our experiences that our interests and abilities are molded. It is also at the experiential level that we need to think about how integration is lived out in our day-to-day interactions with others, in the way that we use our resources, and so forth. Farnsworth proposed that integration must be "embodied," that it is about "living God's truth in addition to knowing about God's truth."[39] At this level we must ask how faith is expressed in how we live and how we interact with our larger society. Thus integration must involve such things as maintaining appropriate boundaries, making fee arrangements clear and fair, treating people with respect and dignity, and so forth. It also means that integration requires balance in life, for example, that we do not neglect our health or our families because we are caught up in academic or clinical success or the pursuit of financial gain. Integration is not just something we do in the classroom, the clinic, or the lab—it is reflected in all of life.

We can touch others with tangible expressions of grace only to the degree that integration is embodied in how we live. Personally, I find this to be the most humbling part of integration because I see at least dimly the gap between who I am and who I am called to be; it reminds me of my failures and need for grace, forgiveness, and transformation. If I overreact towards someone in anger, I need to repent of my inappropriate reaction, and of the hypocrisy that reveals the distance between my beliefs and my behaviors. When I fail to be present and welcoming to my students because they have imposed on my research time, I need to take a hard look at my priorities. When I hurt others because I am hung up on my own agendas and issues, I must realize my persistent and ongoing need for grace, forgiveness, and transformation. Fortunately, it is just that kind of grace that

---

39. Farnsworth, *Conduct of integration*, 317.

God extends to us, not just as a solo en-counter between an individual and God, but through the community of believers.

Embodied integration is seen best when we minister God's redemptive grace to those around us and live in ways that please God. Making sure that our business practices and clinical work uphold the highest of ethical standards is not an incidental part of integration! Being charitable, loving, gracious, and forgiving are better expressions of integration than simply doing research on these topics. Caring for and reaching out to the marginalized and the poor—not just to those who have good insurance and deep pockets—is surely part of our calling. (After all, the economy of the gospel specifically calls us to minister to the poor, the widow, the orphan, and the prisoner.) The ultimate questions are not about models of integration, but about how to love God with all of our hearts, souls, and minds, and how to love our neighbors.

This will look different for each of us, for none of us have exactly the same calling, personal experiences, Christian traditions, skills, and resources. So, at this point, I thought it would be good to see how all of these things come together in creating a wide range of ways that people live out their calling based on their own experiences.

Sitting Down at the Table

I asked several people to share their stories, and I deliberately cast a wide net, wanting to focus broadly on how faith commitments shape the ways that one can relate psychology and faith. The perspectives offered here are diverse, with stories from people who come from many Christian backgrounds (Mennonite, Plymouth Brethren, Roman Catholic, Baptist, Evangelical, and Charismatic, among others). If we could gather all these people at one time around our table, I think we would be in for some lively discussion. We would find that they disagree on many things, both psychologically and theologically. Moreover, they would not subscribe to the same idea of what "integration" is (or even if they like that word or concept!) even though they all make connections between their faith tradition and their vocation within psychology. However, I am quite sure that their conversation would be flavored with grace and respect, and a genuine desire to learn from each other. I am not holding any of these people up as the perfect prototype for how to relate psychology and Christianity. In fact, part of what their stories illustrate is that there are many ways to think about the relationship of faith, learning, and living. Nonetheless, all of these people have made significant contributions to theory, research, or practice by intentionally attending to connections between faith and psychology, and it will be instructive to listen to their stories.

Ana-María Rizzuto

Ana-María Rizzuto is a psychiatrist, dedicated to classical Freudian psychoanalysis. Her 1979 groundbreaking work, *The Birth of the Living God: A Psychoanalytic Study*, became an impetus to research on God representations, that is, the way individuals form their private conceptualization of God through their personal experiences. Raised in Argentina in a culture saturated with the teachings and traditions of Roman Catholicism, Rizzuto's interest in spiritual things was fostered early in life. She eventually became a medical doctor and a psychoanalyst. Rizzuto appreciated some of Freud's insights about the dynamic functions of religious belief, but she disagreed with Freud's description of religion as an infantile and immature clinging to parental protection.

In 1963, Dr. Rizzuto was asked to teach a course on pastoral care and the psychological foundations of religious belief to the advanced seminarians of the local Roman Catholic Seminary in Cordoba, Argentina. She quickly found that there was very little helpful literature on the topic. In 1965 she immigrated to the United States, and shortly thereafter she began a research project in which she attempted to understand the developmental nature of people's understandings of God. Her description of how our God-images begin in childhood and are gradually reformulated through our encounter with God and our religious communities is worthy of our contemplation.

But the child brings his own God, the one he has himself put together, to this official encounter [of God through the religious rituals of his or her religious tradition]. Now the God of religion and the God of the child-hero face each other. Reshaping, rethinking, and endless rumination, fantasies and defensive maneuvers, will come to help the child in his difficult task. This second birth of God may decide the conscious religious future of the child . . . The representation of God, like any other, is reshaped, refined, and retouched throughout life.[40]

It is doubtful that Rizzuto would ever have seen God representations as worthy of study if not for her own religious upbringing.

In an article written in 2004, Rizzuto went further, noting that Catholicism itself spurred her interest in psychoanalysis.

In short, my Catholic background gave me a rich experience of the depth of meaning of words and their transformative power. Psychoanalytic training had only to enlarge that experience and extend it to teach me to listen for unconscious derivatives of words and to realize the great complexity and imaginative ways of human defenses, feelings, and understanding.

In what way does my experience relate to my later analytic training? It seems to me that I arrived at my institute's door with the conviction

---

40. Rizzuto, *Birth of the living God*, 8.

that human beings cannot hide their secrets. I learned later that most pathology originates from desperate efforts to hide from oneself and others that which we find unbearable. It is true that there is a great difference between conscious hiding and unconscious defense mechanisms. Yet in all of us is the desire to be found out and not to be alone with our painful secrets, conscious or unconscious . . .

At the end of treatment, analysands need to be seen by their analysts and by themselves just as they are, without hiding anything. Is this too different from accepting that one cannot hide from God if one wants to be oneself?[41]

Dr. Rizzuto's interest in the religious and spiritual lives of her patients and her own faith tradition allowed her to look beyond Freud's biases so that she could mine his insights without discrediting religious experience itself.

Rizzuto helps us to see how our conceptions of God change over time. Perhaps you can relate to this. Imagine having grown up believing that God would never allow anything really bad to happen to you, because God loves you and looks after you. Invariably, though, if you live long enough, you will suffer. And God doesn't always take away your suffering—but perhaps you will come to conceive of Him as being with you in your suffering. Then again, perhaps you will experience what some people call the dark night of the soul, where God

seems to be entirely absent. If you cling to a God-image in which God is a sort of cosmic Santa Claus, your faith can never deepen or mature. You come to the startling realization, "God is not who I thought He was!" Do you then reject God, or allow your conception of who He is to change? Obviously, this can be a painful process. Imagine a client who is abused who decides that God has abandoned her, that He either doesn't exist or doesn't care (a thought sometimes found in the psalms of lament!). Or perhaps, in time, she will develop a God-image of One who suffered himself and who suffers with her. We do not conceive of God in identical ways, nor in completely accurate ways. For us to mature spiritually, our God-image must become more like God, and less like own projections of what we hope or fear He is like.

Robert Emmons

Another example of faith being a source of motivation for research can be found in the life and work of Dr. Robert Emmons, Professor of Psychology at University of California, Davis. With over 100 publications to his credit, Dr. Emmons is among the foremost researchers on gratitude. In addition to numerous empirical studies of gratitude, his work includes the psychology of religion, forgiveness, motivation, the assessment of gratitude, and other topics. I asked Bob how his own faith tradition influences his research. "I am an evangelical Christian," replied Emmons.

---

41. Rizzuto, *Roman Catholic background*, 438.

Without being a Christian I doubt very much that I would have been interested in this topic—it just would not have been on my radar. When I look at my life, I see that I have been given much more than I deserve, and that makes me grateful. When I look at my God, I see an awesome God and I am grateful to Him for who He is and what He has done.

Emmons gravitated to research topics that were pregnant with theological significance because of his faith tradition and because of their importance in understanding human personality.

As Emmons formulated his academic research, he developed a rich empirical program that is supported and stimulated by his faith commitment, but it is examined and evaluated with solid empirical research. "The ethic of thankfulness and its cognates (thanks, thanksgiving) appears about 150 times in the Hebrew Bible and New Testament" according to Emmons. "I am fortunate to be able to put to the empirical test concepts that have a rich Biblical basis and to use the scientific method to augment Divine revelation.[42] While gratitude continues to be an important focus of his research, Emmons also explores other topics in personality psychology, positive psychology.

Emmons was a co-recipient of a nearly one-million dollar Templeton grant to investigate the effects of Young Life on developing fruits of the spirit such as kindness, generosity, and selflessness.

He has written books for psychology courses and popular audiences on gratitude, personality, and spirituality, among other topics. I can imagine a rich conversation if we were to sit down with Bob for a chat. "What are you grateful for?" "How do you cultivate gratitude?" "How can we use gratitude enhancing techniques to improve the coping abilities of people with medical or psychological problems?" While his faith led Emmons to research gratitude, another person at the table found his faith and his personal experiences leading him in a related direction.

Everett L. Worthington Jr.

Type Everett Worthington's name into the PsycINFO search engine, and you will find over two-hundred-fifty books, articles, and measurement tools to his credit. His story, of course, doesn't begin there. Like many people who enter helping professions, Ev's story includes some significant personal struggles. He recounts some of these difficulties in a brief autobiographical account of his approach to integration. He recalls his mother being sent to a State Hospital and his father turning to alcohol when he was very young.

With an often-depressed mother and alcoholic father, my childhood was often sad, but there were beautiful moments. I can still remember my

---

42. Personal communication.

mother washing dishes or making beds and singing Southern Baptist songs: "What a Friend We Have in Jesus," "I Come to the Garden Alone," "The Old Rugged Cross." Those songs got into my heart and created a longing for God. When I was about eight, I started walking (about three miles) to church with my younger brother. I was searching for the way home through some thick family underbrush.[43]

Ev's encounter with God occurred in several stages, over many years, becoming increasingly evangelical and charismatic. He switched careers along the way, from Nuclear Physics (he has a masters from M.I.T.) to psychology. While pursuing his doctorate in psychology at a secular school, Ev had few people with whom to discuss what Christianity had to do with his profession, but he was a voracious reader of thoughtful Christian books in general and of some of the emerging integration literature.

Eventually, Ev took a position as a professor at Virginia Commonwealth University, and after a brief time doing research on pain control, he turned his attention to research on marital and family issues, and thinking about the role of faith and counseling. The majority of his research has been on forgiveness, along with research on marital counseling, integration, and other topics.

I asked Ev how his faith has shaped his thinking on, and interest in, these topics, and this is what he said.

Forgiveness, of course, is arguably the central part of Christianity (some would say love ranks equally high or higher). Clearly, then, my faith predisposed me to consider forgiveness extremely important in life. I got interested in forgiveness through observing couples in marriage counseling. One almost couldn't observe a counseling session between troubled partners without seeing issues of unforgiveness. With Christian faith arguing for how important forgiveness was and practice also arguing that it is central, I had to take it seriously.

When my mother was murdered, my forgiveness was stretched, and when my brother committed suicide as a consequence of that murder, self-forgiveness began to enter my research agenda.

Couples were always my major clinical interest—not just couple therapy, but especially couple enrichment. Because VCU doesn't have a marital therapy clinic, I gravitated more toward marital enrichment than therapy. I think Scripture clearly teaches that the marriage relationship is the metaphor of our bond with Christ, and that marriage itself is actually very important. It became a focus of both practice and research even when I was in graduate school.

Ev's faith frames his personal and professional experiences in ways that are

43. Worthington, Surprised by grace, in Moriarty, *Integrating faith*, 29.

unique among the people who sit at our table.

The distinctiveness of Ev's background has afforded remarkable opportunities. He has been called upon to testify before legislatures, present lectures at conferences, teach, do research, work on issues of truth and reconciliation in South Africa, and serve as the Executive Director of a multi-million dollar non-profit agency to fund forgiveness research. As with others at our table, we see a similar trend, where Worthington's personal experiences and faith commitment shape the way he sees the world, the issues that he is drawn to, and the research that he pursues.

Once again, it is interesting to imagine the conversations we could have. What have our own experiences of forgiving others, of seeking forgiveness, or even forging ourselves been like? What was it like to see forgiveness in the context of a national conversation about intergroup violence and reconciliation? We could talk about things as far-ranging as research, cross-cultural counseling, and openness to prophetic words. Indeed, the potential conversations around this table are diverse, interesting, and thought-provoking!

Elizabeth Lewis Hall

Elizabeth Lewis Hall is a Professor of Psychology at Rosemead School of Psychology. Dr. Hall's research interests include women and work, mothering, missions and mental health, and embodiment. She teaches undergraduate courses in integration, co-leads a graduate research team on women's issues, and maintains a small clinical practice.

Liz describes her experience of integration as one of *tearing down walls*, of

> bringing together pieces of life that have always belonged together, but which have been artificially separated because of opposing worldviews, the development of distinct academic disciplines, with their own vocabularies and intellectual histories and, of course, sin.[44]

Her own formative experiences, though, were of a family without artificial walls. Her parents' faith was integrated into their lives. Their decisions, finances, jobs, relationships, and commitments—their lives—"all reflected their desire to live life well in God's eyes."[45]

Raised in Argentina for much of her childhood, Liz is the daughter of an American father, whose parents had gone to Argentina as missionaries, and an Argentine mother. The family was Plymouth Brethren, a religious minority in a predominantly Catholic country. The Plymouth Brethren tend to be conservative and literal in their biblical interpretation, so Liz grew up wearing a skirt and a head covering, an image that conjures

---

44. Hall, Confessions of a tortoise, in Moriarty, *Integrating faith*, 112.

45. Ibid.

up gender roles that would later be one of her research concerns.

Although she now worships in a Baptist congregation, Liz cherishes many of the influences of her Plymouth Brethren heritage. Plymouth Brethren have very high regard for Scripture and a strong commitment to knowing, interpreting, and following the Bible. Where Scripture seems to her to make a clear claim that is politically unpopular in contemporary culture, her strength to take a public stand for her belief is rooted partly in her religious heritage. Her cross-cultural experiences and Plymouth Brethren background also contributed to her interest in research on missions[46] and cross-cultural adaptation.[47] Her work as a professor at a graduate school that takes faith-learning integration seriously has also prompted her writing and research on integration.

Sometimes, however, religious cultures are in need of critique and correction, especially when they prescribe rules and roles that are not actually biblical. Liz ran into several such rules when she became a mother and experienced a clash of expectations. Many people from her Baptist church assumed that she would give up her career, that motherhood precluded her from ongoing professional involvement. On the other hand, she found that her work environment often failed to accommodate the needs of working mothers and fathers. This clash of expectations drove her to the research literature, and it led to the organization of a research group that investigates the experiences of mothers who work in Christian academic settings.[48] In addition to contributing to an important area of research, this helped Liz to explore the psychological literature to discern what "children actually need, and what God really expects from me with respect to my children."[49]

For Liz, integration is partly "a cross cultural . . . journey."[50] It requires self-reflection on why we see the world as we do, and it requires translation between the languages of two disciplines. Liz notes that integration is also sometimes cross cultural in the sense that one's convictions may run counter to those of one or the other cultures that you shuttle between. At core, though, she sees integration as "living life well," that it is both conceptual (how we think about things) and experiential (embodied in how we live). And, of course, these two are interwoven with each other.

Again, we see opportunities for more conversation. Parenting. Motherhood. Gender roles. Psychological needs of missionaries. The need for family-friendly workplace policies in Christian organizations. Cross-cultural issues. So many rich topics can be discussed by so

46. E.g., Hall & Barber, Therapists in missions; Hall and Duvall, Married women in missions.

47. Hall, et al., Object relations and cultural adjustment.

48. Thorstad, Anderson, Hall, Willingham, & Carruthers, Breaking the mold.

49. Hall, Confessions of a tortoise, in Moriarty, Integration journeys, 126.

50. Ibid., 116.

many interesting people at this table, and we still have several more to meet!

Alvin Dueck

Dr. Alvin Dueck is a professor in the Clinical Psychology and Marriage and Family department at Fuller Theological Seminary. He traveled a circuitous route to this position. Al grew up as a religious and ethnic minority in Canada; his parents were Mennonites and German Ukrainian immigrants. Al grew up in poverty and loss, his father having drowned when he was young. "My mother raised my brother and me in a house that was not much larger than eight hundred square feet, and we lived on welfare for the first few years after my father's death."[51]

His views on integration have been profoundly affected by his personal experiences and his church tradition. "These are my particular people, the Mennonites, and you would not know who I am without knowing who they are—nor would you know how I 'integrate' faith and practice."[52] Three things stick out to me in Al's story: his concern for the poor and the oppressed, his sensitivity to cultural and ethnic issues, and his desire to understand the stories of those with whom he comes in contact. All of these flow from his Mennonite tradition and from his own story.

Developing a finely tuned theological system is less important to Mennonites than is "the simple call to follow Jesus in showing compassion, loving mercy, and being reconciled with one's enemies."[53] This call has led Dueck to places that most academics avoid. After college in the late 1960s, he worked with African American Mennonite churches in North Carolina, where segregation and prejudice were ubiquitous. Al and his wife were invited into the African American community where he helped in pastoral and youth ministry. He reconfigured his graduate plans so he could stay in this community. "The impact of these experiences on my view of the discipline of psychology and the profession of psychotherapy has been considerable. Even then I studied therapy in the context of a marginal community."[54] The experience of marginalization motivates not only his awareness of the effects of discrimination, but it spurs his intentional decision to enter the lives of the marginalized. It also provides many opportunities to seek justice and reconciliation, two things that are important Mennonite distinctives.

Dueck's own experiences as a religious and ethnic minority have also made him sensitive to cultural and ethnic issues. "We export our theories, our research, and our manuals, with the naïve assumption that no harm is being done in the process—and yet, the evidence

---

51. Dueck, Honoring my tradition, in Moriarty, *Integration journey*, 169.

52. Ibid.

53. Ibid.

54. Dueck, *Between Jerusalem and Athens*, 224.

suggests otherwise."[55] This awareness has led him to affirm indigenous approaches to Christian counseling in China and Africa. Again, this relates to the story of the Mennonites, who were often oppressed by other Christians of their day for their failure to "fit in" with the expected theological practices and beliefs of the dominant culture. Additionally, the Mennonite experience is a deeply communal one, which I am sure fostered in him a respect for culture and cultural embeddedness that is absent among Christian traditions that foster a more privatized faith. Finally, Dr. Dueck, more than many in the integration community, has been open to the insights of postmodern approaches to psychology. Postmodernism embraces life's narratives rather than trying to codify everything in neat categories. Dueck's own story is contextualized within the stories of his family and his religious tradition. Clients bring us their stories. The Word of God is full of stories. Stories have a unique power that can be lost when we reduce them to systematic theologies or empirical statistics. And Christianity is a great story, one which intersects with our own stories in surprising and unique ways.

Al, among many that sit at our table, would probably offer some critique of the table itself. Why are most of the people at this table white, middle-class Americans? There are a few people who are American ethnic minorities and a few people from outside of North America, but the table is, quite honestly, too white and too American. A few other people at the table have echoed this sentiment:

> The vast majority of humankind and the majority of Christians now live outside the West . . . [The] psychology/theology integration literature has paid little attention to this important dimension. Integration has almost exclusively meant the integration of Western psychology with Western theology.[56]

How can we expand the diversity of people we find at the table? We need to develop more cultural sensitivity, spending more time listening to others and learning from them. Some of the conversations around this table should cause some deep self-reflection!

Julie Exline

Julie Juola Exline, PhD, is a Professor of Psychology and Director of Clinical Training at Case Western Reserve University. Her interest in psychology came about somewhat late in life. Julie earned an undergraduate degree in computer science. She eventually left her computer job behind and pursued a doctorate in Clinical Psychology (with research training in Social Psychology).

As her computer science degree and research acumen suggest, she is good at analytical tasks, but she also sees herself as an intuitive person who does not discount the reality of things beyond our

---

55. Dueck, Honoring my tradition, 177.

56. Gingrich and Smith, Culture and ethnicity, 139.

senses. In her words: "I see my faith as a means of knowledge that stands beside others. I don't see it as something that can be completely dissected or explained using scientific tools. At the same time, I think that doctrines and practices from my tradition (as with any tradition) can be a fruitful source of hypotheses for empirical research."[57] With over seventy publications to her credit, Dr. Exline has made substantial contributions to both theory and research.

Many of the topics that Dr. Exline studies are of interest to her because of her Christian beliefs and upbringing. Growing up in a fundamentalist church with a heavy emphasis on hell did not consistently foster a positive God image. While not doubting God's love for her or for humankind, she was nonetheless troubled by the possibility that a loving God could send people to hell on the grounds of having failed to discern and embrace the "right belief." Personally wrestling with these sorts of questions would later spur her interest in other people's struggle with this and other issues. For instance, Exline published a study on the clinical implications of differences in doctrinal views of hell among people from various Christian traditions.[58]

Exline developed an interest in studying spiritual struggles,[59] including research on anger toward God. Her research extends to topics such as forgiveness, altruistic love, and humility. While seeing all of these as positive Christian virtues, Exline is also interested in how these virtues might be twisted into vices. "For example, at what point does humility cross the line to become self-derogation?" she asks. "At what point does forgiveness become unassertiveness? When does self-sacrifice make good Christian sense, and when is it just pointless (or even self-righteous) martyrdom?"[60]

Julie's research interests are broad, including the psychology of religion and spirituality, and he virtues of humility and forgiveness, among others. Her Christian faith experience is also wide-ranging. Julie identifies herself within the charismatic Christian tradition although she does not align herself strongly with any specific denomination. She has spent time in spiritual direction and in becoming trained as a spiritual director. As a researcher, clinician, and spiritual director, Exline's charismatic perspective creates openness to religious experiences and beliefs associated with the spiritual realm, such as miracles, healings, evil forces, prophetic words, and the ability to hear from God. This openness, in turn, fostered an interest in studying religious experiences and beliefs.

By now, you have surely realized that the topics we engage around this table are so diverse, that you are bound to find someone with whom you share clinical or research interests, and, in my experience, if you hang out here for long, you will find yourself developing friendships and perhaps finding mentors and

---

57. Personal communication.

58. Exline, Belief in Heaven and Hell.

59. Exline, Religious and spiritual struggles.

---

60. Personal communication.

research partners, too. So, on that note, let me introduce you to another of my friends.

Jamie Aten

During the course of his childhood, Jamie Aten attended a United Methodist Church, an Independent Christian Church, a Church of Christ, and an Independent Missionary Baptist Church. Although his faith was important to him, in many ways it felt like it was the faith that he had inherited from his parents. Yet, it was having his faith challenged in college that led him to feel that he had found his own faith.

While he was a student at Indiana State University, a professor asked to talk to him after class about a paper he had written. When he walked into the office the professor asked, "Are you a Christian?" When he said that he was, the professor asked, "Why?" Jamie was caught off guard, but this would later frame an important insight. In his words,

> I realized how important it was for Christians to learn how to communicate with people from other belief systems so that we would be heard, and so that we could hear and learn from others. This experience stuck with me. In many ways, much of my research and writing has been with this lesson in mind, with the hope of introducing Christian ideas to mainstream secular researchers and therapists as well as to Christians.[61]

Jamie went on to obtain a doctorate in counseling psychology, after which he took a position in the Counseling Psychology program at the University of Southern Mississippi.

Dr. Aten and his research program collided just after his move to Mississippi, six days before Hurricane Katrina devastated the Gulf Coast in 2005. Jamie quickly realized the role that psychology could play in dealing with the trauma that ensued, as well as the unique opportunity that this tragedy provided to conduct research. But who do you collaborate with in a tragedy? Why not reach out to the religious communities that have been there before the disaster, who had been with each other through the tragedy, and who will support each other and rebuild their lives together? Within a few months, Jamie had organized a research team that worked with local churches to meet the needs of local people affected by the hurricane. Jamie's experiences in several different denominations allowed him to work successfully across denominational boundaries to organize a more integrated response to disaster needs.[62]

In 2010, Jamie left Mississippi to accept an appointment at Wheaton College where he founded the Humanitarian Disaster Institute, which equips congregations and faith-based organizations to prepare for, respond to, and recover from disasters.[63] Since his first experience with disaster response, Jamie has

61. Personal communication.

62. Aten et al, God images following Hurricane Katrina.

63. http://www.wheaton.edu/hdi.

taken what he learned and applied it to disasters around the world. Jamie's experiences reinforced his belief that local religious organizations are ideally situated to lend tangible and spiritual aid in the midst of disasters, but that their effectiveness is handicapped by the fact that they rarely engage in advance planning for such events. He and his collaborators have received numerous grants to help faith communities affected by disasters, and to train ministers to equip their congregations to be able to respond to local disasters.[64]

More recently, Jamie has begun to apply lessons learned from studying natural disasters to helping people with "personal disasters." While recently going through a personal battle with cancer, Jamie co-edited a book on addressing spirituality and trauma in psychotherapy.[65] According to Jamie, working on this book while going through his own health crisis gave him a new perspective. In his words,

> I had spent a decade studying how people make sense of, relate to God, and grow in the wake of natural disasters. But nothing could have prepared me for cancer, or what I call the 'disaster within.' I had the rare opportunity to 'study' the impact of a disaster internally rather than externally. I realized that I was going through what I had been studying in disaster survivors around the

globe. As I tried to apply what I had learned to my own life, I struggled to make sense of my previous research findings. For example, I had found after Hurricane Katrina that survivors who spiritually surrendered to God fared better emotionally and spiritually. That had always puzzled me, as it seemed like a passive response. Yet, during one of the worst periods of my cancer journey, I remember handing over my deepest worries and control to God. Then it hit me. Surrender was not a passive experience, but quite the opposite; it was a willful act of obedience.

> In other ways my research also bolstered my faith and helped me to choose healthy coping strategies. It is interesting to note that every one of the doctoral students who I have mentored over the years did dissertations on religion and disasters. That is, all except my first doctoral advisee. He did a dissertation on, of all things, posttraumatic spiritual growth among cancer survivors. Although I am now free of cancer, the treatments that led to my cure took a toll on almost every part of my life. I can remember looking back at this research many times and finding hope, that though the journey would be difficult, there were ways in which my suffering could be redeemed by God.[66]

Jamie's faith is clearly not just wedded to academic topics, but it is also lived out as he helps people touched by tragedy and as he processes his own experience.

---

64. Aten & Boan, *Disaster ministry handbook.*

65. Aten & Leach, *Spirituality and the therapeutic process.*

66. Personal communication.

Perhaps Jamie's story highlights one last thing. The people at this table love to talk about faith and psychology. They love God and they express their love of their neighbors through their research, their clinical work, and the ways that they minister in various ways around the world. But perhaps what most makes this table special is that it creates opportunities for us to share our lives. And that is a gift.

My Story

My family has a deep religious heritage, with a lineage that includes pastors, missionaries, and theology professors. My parents bore the marks of being PKs (preacher's kids), in both beneficial and detrimental ways. My own story, though, is influenced mostly by my own experiences. I was raised in an independent, fundamental Baptist church for the first ten years of my life. When I was in fifth grade, we left the church and found our way to an Evangelical Free Church. This was a breath of fresh air for me, and it became a place where my faith was nourished intellectually, relationally, and practically.

In college, I found my academic niche in psychology, and more importantly, I met Debbie, with whom I have shared life's journey for over three decades. After graduating from college, Debbie and I moved to the West Coast so I could attend Rosemead School of Psychology's doctoral program in clinical psychology. At the time, Rosemead was one of two APA approved doctoral programs in the country that incorporated theology and integration courses as part of a clinical psychology degree. Graduate school was followed by internship in Pennsylvania at Philhaven Hospital, the same Mennonite psychiatric hospital that I had worked at in college. My first postdoctoral job was in Massachusetts at The House of Affirmation, a residential treatment program for Roman Catholic sisters, brothers, and priests. Unfortunately, the treatment center closed in my second year, and I took a job at a Christian counseling center in Connecticut. These experiences helped me to appreciate the value of different expressions of the Christian faith, and they highlighted the importance of faith in the midst of suffering and mental illness.

Perhaps the biggest change in my career trajectory, though, was impelled by family life. Within a few weeks of the birth of our first child, Kristen, it was clear that something was wrong. After a lot of worrying and months of tests, we learned that she had cystic fibrosis (CF). Those agonizing months were followed by the most difficult year of my life, in which my in-laws had a serious automobile accident, my wife fell down the stairs and fractured several vertebrae, my employer closed the residential center that I worked at, and we endured a painful church split. Those experiences and the subsequent years shaped me in profound ways. I cried and prayed more than at any time before or since. I also decided that I would not become the workaholic that I was prone to be. I wanted to be involved and present as a father. My daughter's illness and those difficult times taught me to seek God's grace in the midst of raw human experience. The amount of stress that we endured in that year was nearly unbearable, but faith, hope, and love—the three most tangible human expressions of divine grace, helped us immensely.

Life became more stable, and Debbie and I were blessed with two more children, Lauren and Cameron, coming at three-year intervals. Trying to balance our concern for Kristen's health, and the significant amount of time that her treatment and medications entailed, with Lauren and Cameron's need for a "normal" life has always been a challenge. No matter how we tried to be fair, there was no avoiding the fact that Kristen's care created a somewhat unfair situation for our other children.

After several years of clinical work and teaching part-time, I decided that teaching fit my interests and abilities and the needs of my family better than full-time clinical work, and I began praying for and seeking a full-time teaching appointment. Amazingly (miraculously?) my prayers were answered when I sent a blind letter of inquiry to Malone College (now Malone University), which I had never heard of before. A week after I sent the letter, I was invited to campus to interview for an unexpected faculty opening, and I have been there ever since.

One of the first things I did at Malone was to propose an integration course. Dissatisfied with the available materials for the course, I wrote the first

edition of this book to fill a gap that other professors had also identified. My own research has focused on a variety of areas, including how students approach issues of faith-learning integration. I am also active in trying to understand how individuals and families cope with chronic illness and transition from child-centered to adult-centered care.

One of my greatest joys is sitting around the table, enjoying good food and good conversation. Many of these conversations take place at conferences hosted by the Christian Association for Psychological Studies. If you are ever there, please say hello. A lot of people at CAPS and at gatherings of similarly-minded people all over the world—would like to welcome you to the table.

Finding Your Place at the Table

Each of the models that we explored in this book has strengths and weaknesses. Even the models that are the most hostile towards integration have things that we can and should value and from which we can learn. And each of the stories that you just read represents a fascinating interplay of personal interests, experiences, and faith traditions. Wherever you end up in your own approach to integration, though, your contribution can be important. Let's briefly look at a few things that you may want to consider.

Integrative efforts will always be handicapped by an antiquated or unsophisticated understanding of one or both disciplines. The more you can do to develop your knowledge-base in these areas, the more fruitful your attempts at integration can be. Some of you may want to pursue advanced degrees in philosophy or theology, and to help those of us in psychology think more clearly about the ways that core issues in those disciplines are relevant to psychology. Many of you may want to pursue advanced degrees in counseling or psychology. Remember, though, that you will need to work to deepen your theological reflection, too. Reading integrative journals like the *Journal of Psychology and Theology* and the *Journal of Psychology and Christianity* can stimulate your thinking. Attending CAPS conferences can help you develop relationships with like-minded people with whom you can discuss personal, clinical, and research issues. Collaborating with others on research projects can also be enriching. Of course, most of you reading this book may see yourselves doing counseling or clinical work. In whatever setting you find yourself, God can use you as a redemptive agent to bring healing and reconciliation in a broken world, but just what your approach to integration will look like will also be part of your journey.

Julie Exline asserts that "there's room for all of us" as we discern our own place "in the integration movement."[67] Specifically, Julie points out that your own approach to integration should involve reflecting about things such things as:

- What kinds of evidence is most meaningful to you? Some of us are naturally more inclined to empirical inquiry, others to qualitative research, others to theological reflection, others to more philosophical inquiry. We are made differently, and these differences can be strengths that lead us in particular directions.

- How much do you want to draw on a specific Christian tradition in your approach to integration? Would working in a faith-based or a secular setting be best for you?

- What are the personal skills, strengths, and weaknesses you have that might guide you into (or away from) particular vocational tasks?

- What wounds ("hurts, disappointments, or offenses") from your past might be areas that need to be healed or forgiven so that they don't block your effectiveness and satisfaction?

- What are you passionate about? How can you use your passions and interests to motivate research or clinical work?

Additionally, it is helpful to realize that your passions and talents may change over time. As you move through different seasons of life, opportunities and interests will change over time, and you may find that God uses these to call you in new directions as you seek to be faithful to your calling.

---

67. Exline, There's room, 60.

There is a story, which may or may not be true, that Karl Menninger once asked a group of psychiatry residents who among them intended to become a leader in psychiatry. When none of them raised a hand, Menninger reportedly asked, "If not you, who?" We could ask the same question about integration: Who among you is willing to join the conversation? Who among you will become leaders in relating the Christian faith to the field of psychology? I hope that some of you will raise your hands, because the story of integration is still being written.

Questions for Reflection and Discussion

1. Look at the two quotations on the title page of this chapter. Discuss ways that the contents of the chapter illustrate these sentiments.

2. What do you see as some of the unique strengths and potential weaknesses of a Reformed approach to integration?

3. What do you see as some of the unique strengths and potential weaknesses of a Wesleyan approach to integration?

4. What do you see as some of the unique strengths and potential weaknesses of a Charismatic / Pentecostal approach to integration?

5. What do you see as some of the unique strengths and potential weaknesses of a Roman Catholic approach to integration?

6. What do you see as some of the unique strengths and potential weaknesses of an Anabaptist approach to integration?

7. The author said that the personal or "embodied" level of integration is humbling because it brings us into contact with our own failures and need for grace, forgiveness, and transformation. What are some areas in which you are aware of needing grace, forgiveness, and transformation?

8. This chapter included several stories about people who have impacted the conversation about the nature of integration. Which story resonated most with you? Why? Which one was most foreign from your own experience? What could you learn from this person and his or her experiences and perspectives?

9. Pick one of the topics highlighted by the different stories (God-representations, gratitude, forgiveness, gender roles, cross cultural issues, spiritual struggles, church disaster response, etc.). What intrigues you about this topic? In what way could you contribute to this topic or apply it to your own life?

10. Write your own story. How does your personal and religious background affect how you think about integration?

11. Reflect on the questions that Julie Exline posed about how to discern your place in the integration movement. Discuss how your answers to her

questions can help you think about God's calling in your life.

12. How has your understanding of integration changed over the course of reading this book?

References

Adams, J. E. (1970). *Competent to counsel.* Grand Rapids: Zondervan.

Adams, J. E. (1972). *The big umbrella.* Grand Rapids: Baker.

Adams, J. E. (1973). *The Christian counselor's manual.* Philadelphia: Presbyterian & Reformed Publishing.

Alexander, T. D., & Rosner, B. S. (Eds.). (2000). *New dictionary of biblical theology.* Downers Grove, IL: InterVarsity Press.

Allport, G. W. (1950). *The individual and his religion, a psychological interpretation.* New York: Macmillan.

Allport, G. W. (1961). *Pattern and growth in personality.* New York: Rinehart & Winston.

Allport, G. W. (1968). *The person in psychology: Selected essays.* Boston: Beacon.

AllSands. (n.d.). *Healthy marriage.* Retrieved from http://www.allsands.com/Lifestyles/healthymarriage_rjd_gn.htm.

American Psychological Association. (2002). *Ethical principles of psychologists and code of conduct, 2002.* Washington, DC: APA.

Anderson, N. T., Zuehlke, T. E., & Zuehlke, J. S. (2000). *Christ-centered therapy: The practical integration of theology and psychology.* Grand Rapids: Zondervan.

Anderson, T. L. (2014). Teaching professional ethics in a faith-based doctoral program: Pedagogical strategies. *Journal of Psychology and Theology, 42*(1), 164–173.

Aristotle (1980). *The Nicomachean ethics / Aristotle* (David Ross, Trans.; J. L. Ackrill & J. O. Urmson, Rev.). The World's Classics. Oxford: Oxford University Press.

Aten, J. D., & Boan, D. M. (2015). *Disaster ministry handbook.* Downers Grove, IL: InterVarsity Press.

Aten, J. D., & Leach, M. (2009). (Eds.). *Spirituality and the therapeutic process: A comprehensive resource from intake through termination.* Washington, DC: American Psychological Association Books.

Aten, J., Moore, M., Denney, R., Bayne, T., Stagg, A., Owens, S., Daniels, S., Boswell, S., Schenck, J., Adams, J., & Jones, C. (2008). God images following Hurricane Katrina in South Mississippi: An exploratory study. *Journal of Psychology and Theology, 36*, 249–257.

Aten, J. D., O'Grady, K. A., & Worthington, E. L. (2012). *The psychology of religion and spirituality for clinicians: Using research in your practice.* New York: Routledge.

Audi, R. (Ed.). (1995). *The Cambridge dictionary of philosophy.* Cambridge: Cambridge University Press.

Augsburger, David W. (1986). *Pastoral counseling across cultures*. Philadelphia: Westminster.

Axelrod, D. (Producer). Jones, P. (Director). (2002). *NOVA: Galileo's battle for the heavens*. Boston: WGBH / Public Broadcasting Service.

Bacon, F. (1958). *The advancement of learning* (G. W. Kitchin, Ed.). New York: Dutton.

Baskin, T. W., & Enright, R. D. (2004). Intervention studies on forgiveness: A meta-analysis. *Journal of Counseling Development, 82*, 79–90.

Baumrind, D. (1967). Child care practices anteceding three patterns of preschool behavior. *Genetic Psychology Monographs, 75*, 43–88.

Baumrind, D. (1991). Effective parenting during the early adolescent transition. In P. A. Cowan & E. M. Hetherington (Eds.), *Family transitions*. Hillsdale, NJ: Erlbaum.

Beck, R. (2014). The integration of theology and psychology within the Church of Christ Tradition: Psychotherapy and positive psychology as case studies. *Journal of Psychology and Christianity, 33*(4), 344–353.

Ben-Shahar, T. (2007). *Happier: Learn the secrets to daily joy and lasting fulfillment*. New York: McGraw-Hill.

Ben-Shahar, T. (n.d.). *The positive psychology homepage*. Retrieved from http://www.talbenshahar.com.

Benedict XVI, Pope. (2009). *Encyclical letter, Caritas in Veritate of the Supreme Pontiff Benedict XVI*. Washington, DC: United States Catholic Conference.

Benedict XVI, Pope. (2008). *Address of His Holiness Benedict XVI to members of the pontifical academy of sciences on the occasion of their plenary assembly*.

Benedict XVI, Pope. (2005). *Encyclical letter, Deus caritas est, of the supreme pontiff Benedict XVI*. Washington, DC: United States Catholic Conference.

Bergin, A. E. (1980). Psychotherapy and religious values. *Journal of Consulting and Clinical Psychology, 48*, 95–105.

Bergin, A. E., & Jensen, J. P. (1990). Religiosity of psychotherapists: A national survey. *Psychotherapy: Theory, Research, Practice, Training, 27*, 3–7.

Berman, H. J. (1996). Judeo-Christian versus pagan scholarship. In K. K. Monroe (Ed.), *Finding God at Harvard: Spiritual journeys of thinking Christians*. Grand Rapids: Zondervan.

Berra, Y. (1998). *The Yogi book*. New York: Workman.

Blamires, H. (1963). *The Christian mind: How should a Christian think?* Ann Arbor: Servant.

Bobgan, M. & Bobgan, D. (1987). *Psychoheresy: The psychological seduction of Christianity*. Santa Barbara, CA: Eastgate.

Bobgan, M., & Bobgan, D. (1991). *12 steps to destruction: Codependency / recovery heresies*. Santa Barbara, CA: Eastgate.

Bobgan, M., & Bobgan, D. (1998a). *James Dobson's gospel of self-esteem and psychology*. Santa Barbara, CA: Eastgate.

Bobgan, M., & Bobgan, D. (1998b). *Larry Crabb's gospel*. Santa Barbara, CA: Eastgate.

Bonhoeffer, D. (1997). *Creation and Fall & Temptation: Two biblical studies*. Touchstone. New York: Simon & Schuster.

Borrell-Carrió, F., Suchmann, A. L. & Epstein, R. M. (2004). The biophychosocial model, 25 years later: Principles, practice, and scientific inquiry. *Annals of Family Medicine, 2*(6), 576–582.

Boschma, G. (2003). *The rise of mental health nursing: A history of psychiatric care in Dutch asylums.* Amsterdam: Amsterdam University Press.

Bouma-Prediger, S. (1990). The task of integration: A modest proposal. *Journal of Psychology and Theology, 18*(1), 21–31.

Bratt, J. D. (Ed.). (1998). *Abraham Kuyper: A centennial reader.* Grand Rapids: Eerdmans.

Brueggemann, W. (1993). *Texts under negotiation: The Bible and postmodern imagination.* Minneapolis: Fortress.

Breshears, G., & Larzelere, R. E. (1981). The authority of scripture and the unity of revelation: A response to Crabb. *Journal of Psychology and Theology, 9,* 312–317.

Brocker, M. (1971). *Johannes Kepler, 1571/1971.* Bonn: Inter Nationes.

Browning, D. S. (1990). The Protestant response to psychiatry. In D. S. Browning, T. Jobe, & I. S. Evison (Eds.), *Religious and ethical factors in psychiatric practice.* Chicago: Nelson-Hall.

Browning, D. S. (1992). Psychology in service of the church. *Journal of Psychology and Theology, 20,* 129.

Browning, D. S., & Evison, I. S. (1990). Introduction. In D. S. Browning, T. Jobe, & I. S. Evison. (Eds.), *Religious and ethical factors in psychiatric practice.* Chicago: Nelson-Hall.

Browning, D. S., Jobe, T., & Evison, I. S. (Eds.). (1990). *Religious and ethical factors in psychiatric practice.* Chicago: Nelson-Hall.

Browning, E. B. (1864). *Aurora Leigh: A poem.* London: J. Miller.

Brunner, E. (1936). *God and man: Four essays on the nature of personality* (D. Cairns, Trans.). London: Student Christian Movement.

Brunner, E. (1946). *Revelation and reason: The Christian doctrine of faith and knowledge* (O. Wyon, Trans.). Philadelphia: Westminster.

Brusher, J. S. (1980). *Popes through the ages* (3rd ed.). San Rafael, CA: Neff-Kane.

Bube, R. H. (1995). *Putting it all together: Seven patterns for relating science to the Christian faith.* Lanham, MD: University Press of America.

Buck v. Bell, 274 U.S. 200 (United States Supreme Court, 1927).

Bucky, P. A. (1992). *The private Albert Einstein.* Kansas City: Andrews & McMeel.

Bufford, R. K. (1997). Consecrated counseling: Reflections on the distinctive of Christian counseling. *Journal of Psychology and Theology, 25,* 111–122.

Bullis, R. K., & Mazur, C. S. (1993). *Legal issues and religious counseling.* Louisville: Westminster John Knox.

Buss, D. G. (1994). Educating toward a Christian worldview: Some historical perspectives and prescriptions. *Faculty Dialogue, 21,* 63–89.

Butcher, J. N., Mineka, S., & Hooley, J. M. (2007). *Abnormal psychology* (13th ed.). Boston: Pearson Education.

Campbell, D. (1926). *Arabian medicine and its influence on the Middle Ages.* New York: Dutton.

Carter, J. D. (1975). Adam's theory of nouthetic counseling. *Journal of Psychology and Theology, 3,* 143–155.

Carter, J. D. (1977). Secular and sacred models of psychology and religion. *Journal of Psychology and Theology, 5*, 197–208.

Carter, J. D. (1996). Success without finality: The continuing dialogue of faith and psychology. *Journal of Psychology and Christianity, 15*(2), 117.

Carter, J. D., & Narramore, S. B. (1979). *The integration of psychology and theology: An introduction.* Grand Rapids: Zondervan.

Charmaz, K. (2000).Grounded theory: Objectivist and constructivist methods. In N. K. Denzin & Y. S. Lincoln, (Eds.), *The handbook of qualitative research.* (2nd ed.). Thousand Oaks, CA: Sage.

Chesterton, G. K. (1908, 1990). *Orthodoxy.* New York: Doubleday.

Chesterton, G. K. (1936, 1990). Ring of lovers, in *The paradoxes of Mr. Pond, with a new introduction by Martin Gardner.* New York: Dover.

Coe, J. H. (1994). An interdependent model of integration and the Christian university. *Faculty Dialogue, 21*, 111–138.

Cohen, L. (1984). *Book of mercy.* New York: Villard.

Cole, S. J. (2002). How John Calvin led me to repent of Christian psychology. *Journal of Biblical Counseling, 20*(2), 31–39.

Cole, S. O. (1996). Reflections on integration by a biopsychologist. *Journal of Psychology and Theology, 24*, 292–300.

Collins, F. S. (2007). *Why this scientist believes in God.* CNN Commentary. Retrieved from http://www.cnn.com/2007/US/04/03/Collins.commentary/index.html.

Collins, G. R. (1977). *The rebuilding of psychology: An integration of psychology and theology.* Wheaton, IL: Tyndale.

Collins, G. R. (2000). An integration view. In E. L. Johnson & S. L. Jones (Eds.), *Psychology and Christianity: Four views.* Downers Grove, IL: InterVarsity Press.

Coreth, E. (1968). *Metaphysics* (J. Donceel, Trans.). New York: Herder & Herder.

Corey, G. (2011). *Issues and ethics in the helping professions* (8th ed.). Belmont, CA: Brooks/ Cole.

Cortés, Á. de J. (1999). Antecedents to the conflict between psychology and religion in America. *Journal of Psychology and Theology, 27*, 20–32.

Couvalis, G. (1997). *The philosophy of science: Science and objectivity.* Thousand Oaks, CA: Sage.

Crabb, L. J., Jr. (1977). *Effective biblical counseling: A model of helping caring Christians become capable counselors.* Grand Rapids: Zondervan.

Crabb, L. J., Jr. (1981). Biblical authority and Christian psychology. *Journal of Psychology and Theology, 9*, 305–311.

Cramer, D. (1990). Toward assessing the therapeutic value of Rogers' core conditions. *Counselling Psychology Quarterly, 3*(1), 57–66.

Crouch, A. (2013). *Playing God: Redeeming the gift of power.* Downers Grove, IL: InterVarsity Press.

Currid, H. D. (1997). *Ancient Egypt and the Old Testament.* Grand Rapids, MI: Baker.

Darley, J. M., & Batson, C. D. (1973). From Jersualem to Jericho: A study of situational and dispositional variables in helping behavior. *Journal of Personality and Social Psychology, 27*, 100–108.

Davies, P., Reid, D., & Weatherburn, P. (2002). *Putting it about: Health promotion for gay men with higher numbers of sexual partners.* London: Sigma Research, Univ. of Pourtsmouth.

Davis, E. B. (1999). Christianity and early modern science. In D. N. Livingstone, D. G. Hart, & M. A. Noll (Eds.), *Evangelicals and science in historical perspective.* New York: Oxford University Press.

Dayton, D. W. (1987). *Theological roots of Pentecostalism.* Peabody, MA: Hendrickson.

de Oliveira, E. A., & Braun, J. L. (2009). "Jesus didn't need a shrink": A critique of anti-psychological biblical sufficiency. *Journal of Psychology and Christianity, 28*(1), 13–21.

Del Vecchio, T., & O'Leary K. D. (2004). Effectiveness of anger treatments for specific anger problems: A meta-analytic review. *Clinical Psychology Review, 24,* 15–34.

Dew, J. K., Jr., & Foreman, M. W. (2014). How do we know? An introduction to epistemology. Downers Grove, IL: InterVarsity Press.

Diener, E., Horwitz, J., & Emmons, R.A. (1985). Happiness of the very wealthy. *Social Indicators Research, 16,* 263–274.

Doriani, D. (1996). Sin. In W. A. Elwell (Ed.), *Baker Theological Dictionary of the Bible.* Grand Rapids: Baker.

Drees, W. B. (1996). *Religion, science, and naturalism.* Cambridge: Cambridge University Press.

Dueck, A. C. (1995). *Between Jerusalem and Athens: Ethical perspectives on culture, religion, and psychotherapy.* Grand Rapids: Baker.

Dueck, A. C. (2010). Honoring my tradition: Particularity, practice, and patience. In G. L. Moriarty (Ed.). *Integration journeys: 12 psychologists tell their stories.* Downers Grove, IL: InterVarsity Press.

Dueck, A. (2014). Tradition sensitive psychotherapy: Anabaptism. *Journal of Psychology and Christianity, 33*(4), 364–373.

Duffy, E. (1997). *Saints and sinners: A history of the popes.* New Haven: Yale University Press.

Durst, D. L. (2002). Evangelical engagement with eugenics: 1900–1940. *Ethics & Medicine: An International Journal of Bioethics, 18*(2), 45–54.

Eck, B. E. (1996). Integrating the integrators: An organizing framework for a multifaceted process of integration. *Journal of Psychology and Christianity, 15*(2), 101–115.

Ediger, E. M.(1983). Roots of the Mennonite mental health story (pp. 3–28). In V. H. Neufeld (Ed.), *If we can love: The Mennonite mental health story.* Newton, KS: Faith & Life Press.

Ellens, J. H. (1981). Biblical authority and Christian psychology II. *Journal of Psychology and Theology, 9,* 318–325.

Ellis, A. (1980a). *The case against religion: A psychotherapist's view and the case against religiosity.* Austin, TX: American Atheist Press.

Ellis, A. (1980b). Psychotherapy and atheistic values: A response to A. E. Bergin's "Psychotherapy and religious values." *Journal of Consulting and Clinical Psychology, 48,* 635–639.

Ellis, A. (2002). No: Dogmatic devotion doesn't help, it hurts. In B. Slife (Ed.), *Taking sides: Psychological issues* (12th ed.). Columbus, OH: McGraw-Hill/Dushkin.

Ellis, B. J., & Malamuth, N. M. (2000). Love and anger in romantic relationships: A discrete systems model. *Journal of Personality, 68*(3), 525–556.

Enright, R. D., & Fitzgibbons, R. P. (2000). *Empirical validation of the process model of forgiveness.* Washington, DC: APA.

Entwistle, D. N. (2004a). Shedding light on Theophostic Ministry I: Practice issues. *Journal of Psychology and Theology, 32*(1), 26–34.

Entwistle, D. N. (2004b). Shedding light on Theophostic Ministry II: Ethical and legal issues. *Journal of Psychology and Theology, 32*(1), 35–42.

Entwistle, D. N. (2009). A holistic psychology of persons: Implications for theory and practice. *Journal of Psychology and Christianity, 28*(2), 141–148.

Entwistle, D. N., Kraynack, N. C., & Gothard, D. (2008). Coping, compliance, and adjustment among adolescents with cystic fibrosis. Abstract published in *Pediatric Pulmonology, Supplement 21*, 448.

Entwistle, D. N., & Moroney, S. K. (2011). Integrative perspectives on human flourishing: The *imago Dei* and positive psychology. *Journal of Psychology and Theology, 39*(4), 295–303.

Entwistle, D. N., & Preston, A. P. (2010). Epistemic rights vs. epistemic duties: A Reply to Porter. *Journal of Psychology and Christianity, 29*(1), 27–32.

Episcopal Church. (1979). *Book of common prayer and administration of the sacraments and other rites and ceremonies of the Church together with the psalter or psalms of David, according to the use of the Episcopal Church.* New York: Church Hymnal Corporation.

Eriksson, C. B., and Abernethy, A. D. (2014). Integration in multicultural competence and diversity training: Engaging difference and grace. *Journal of Psychology and Theology, 42*(1), 174–187.

Erickson, M. J. (1998). *Christian theology* (2nd ed.). Grand Rapids: Baker.

Evans, C. S. (2012). Doing psychology as a Christian: A plea for wholeness. *Journal of Psychology and Theology, 40*(1), 32–36.

Evans, C. S. (1977). *Preserving the person: A look at the human sciences.* Grand Rapids: Baker.

Evans, C. S. (1988). Healing old wounds and recovering old insights: Towards a Christian view of the person for today. In M. Noll & D. Wells (Eds.), *Christian faith and practice in the modern world: Theology from an evangelical point of view.* Grand Rapids: Eerdmans.

Exline, J. J. (2002–2003). Belief in heaven and hell among Christians in the United States: Denominational differences and clinical implications. *Omega: Journal of Death and Dying, 47*(2),155–168.

Exline, J. J. (2012). There's room for all of us: Discerning your role in the integration movement. *Journal of Psychology and Theology, 40*(1), 60–65.

Exline, J. J., & Rose, E. (2005). Religious and spiritual struggles. In R. F. Paloutzian, & C. L. Park (Eds.), *Handbook of the psychology of religion and spirituality*. New York: Guilford.

Farnsworth, K. E. (1982). The conduct of integration. *Journal of Psychology and Theology, 10*, 308–319.

Farnsworth, K. E. (1985). *Whole-hearted integration: Harmonizing psychology and Christianity through word and deed*. Grand Rapids: Baker.

Faw, H. W. (1998). Wilderness wanderings and promised integration: The quest for clarity. *Journal of Psychology and Theology, 26*(2), 147–158.

Fayard, C., Harding, G., Murdoch, W., & Brunt, J. (2007). Clinical implications for psychotherapy from the Seventh-day Adventist tradition. *Journal of Psychology and Christianity, 26*(3), 207–217.

Fee, G. D., & Stuart, D. (1993). *How to read the Bible for all its worth* (2nd ed.). Grand Rapids: Zondervan.

Feist J., & Feist, G. J. (1998). *Theories of personality* (4th ed.). Boston: McGraw Hill.

Finocchiaro, M. A. (Ed. & Trans.). (1989). *The Galileo affair: A documentary history*. Berkeley: University of California Press.

Floyd, S. (2010). Education as soulcraft: Exemplary intellectual practice and the cardinal virtues. *Studies in Christian Ethics, 23*(3), 249–266.

Francis, Pope. (2013a). *Encyclical letter, Evangelii gaudium, of the supreme pontiff Francis*. Washington, DC: United States Catholic Conference.

Francis, Pope. (2013b). *Encyclical letter, Lumen fidei, of the supreme pontiff Francis*. Washington, DC: United States Catholic Conference.

Freud, S. (1900). *The interpretation of dreams* (3rd ed., 1911; A. Brill, Trans.). New York: Macmillan.

Freud, S. (1919, 1946). *Totem and taboo* (A. A. Brill, Trans.). New York: Random House.

Freud, S. (1927, 1964). *The future of an illusion* (W. D. Robson-Scott, Trans.; James Strachey, Ed.). Garden City, NY: Doubleday.

Freud S. (1939). *Moses and monotheism: Three essays*. In J. Strachey (Ed. and Trans.), *The standard edition of the complete psychological works of Sigmund Freud*, Vol. 23, 1–137.

Gaede, S. D. (1985). *Where gods may dwell: On understanding the human condition*. Grand Rapids: Zondervan.

Gaggi, S. (1989). *Modern/postmodern*. Philadelphia: University of Pennsylvania Press.

Gaukroger, S. (2006). *The emergence of a scientific culture: Science and the shaping of modernity, 1210–1685*. Oxford: Oxford University Press.

George, T. (Ed.). (2011). *Evangelicals and Nicene faith: Reclaiming the apostolic witness*. Grand Rapids: Baker.

Gergen, K. (1991). *The saturated self*. New York: Basic Books.

Gettier, E. (1966). Is justified true belief knowledge? *Analysis, 23*, 121–123. Retrieved from http://philosophyfaculty.ucsd.edu/faculty/rarneson/Courses/gettierphilreading.pdf.

Gillespie, C. K. (2001). *Psychology and American Catholicism*. New York: Crossroad.

Gingrich, F., and Smith, B. M. (2014). Culture and ethnicity in Christianity/psychology integration: Review and future directions. *Journal of Psychology and Christianity, 33*(2), 139–155.

Glaser, B. G., & Strauss, A. L. (1968). *The discovery of grounded theory: Strategies for qualitative research*. Chicago: Aldine.

Goldman, A. L. (1991). *The search for God at Harvard*. New York: Ballantine.

Gonsiorek, J. C, Richards, P. S., Pargament, K. I., and McMinn, M. R. (2009). Ethical challenges and opportunities at the edge: Incorporating spirituality and religion into psychotherapy. *Professional Psychology: Research and Practice, 40*(4), 385–395.

Gordon, C. H., and Rendsburg, G. A. (1997). *The Bible and the ancient Near East* (4th ed.). New York: Norton.

Grant, R. M., with Tracy, D. (1984). *A short history of the interpretation of the Bible* (2nd ed.). Philadelphia: Fortress.

Griffiths, P. J. (2006). *The vice of curiosity: An essay on intellectual appetite.* Winnipeg: CMU.

Grudem, W. A. (1999). *Bible doctrine: Essential teachings of the Christian faith.* Grand Rapids: Zondervan.

Guenther, R. K. (1998). *Human cognition.* Upper Saddle River, NJ: Prentice Hall.

Guy, J. D., Jr. (1980). The search for truth in the task of integration. *Journal of Psychology and Theology, 8,* 27–32.

Hagee, J. (2009, January 15). *John Hagee Today.* Trinity Broadcasting Network.

Hall, M. E. L. (2004). God as cause or error? Academic psychology as Christian vocation. *Journal of Psychology and Theology, 32*(3) 200–209.

Hall, M. E. L. (in preparation). Confessions of a tortoise: Slow steps on an integrative journey. In G. L. Moriarty (Ed.), *Integration journeys: 12 psychologists tell their stories.* Downers Grove, IL: InterVarsity Press.

Hall, M. E. L., & Barber, B. A. (1996). The therapist in a missions context: Avoiding dual role conflicts. *Journal of Psychology and Theology, 24*(3), 212–219.

Hall, M. E. L., Duvall, N. S., Edwards, K. J., & Pike, P. L. (1999). The relationship of object relations development to cultural adjustment in a missionary sample. *Journal of Psychology and Theology, 27*(2), 139–153.

Hall, M. E. L., & Duvall, N. S. (2003). Married women in missions: The effects of cross-cultural and self gender role expectations on well-being, stress, and self-esteem. *Journal of Psychology and Theology, 31*(4), 303–314.

Hannam, J. (2011). *The genesis of science: How the Christina middle ages launched the scientific revolution.* Washington, DC: Regnery.

Hanson, K. C. (1994[96]) "How honorable!" "How shameful!" A cultural analysis of Matthew's markarisms and reproaches. *Semeia, 68,* 81–111. Retrieved from http://www.kchanson.com/ARTICLES/mak.html/.

Hart, D. G. (1999). Evangelicals, biblical scholarship, and the politics of the American academy. In D. N. Livingstone, D. G. Hart, & M. A. Noll (Eds.), *Evangelicals and science in historical perspective.* New York: Oxford University Press.

Hasker, W. (1992). Faith-learning integration: An overview. *Christian Scholar's Review, 21,* 234–238.

Hathaway, W. L. (2009). Clinical use of explicitly religious approaches: Christian role integration issues. Journal *of Psychology and Christianity, 28*(2), 105–112.

Hellwig, M. K. (1997). What can the Roman Catholic tradition contribute to Christian higher education? In R. T. Hughes & W. B. Adrian (Eds.), *Models for Christian higher education: Strategies for success in the twenty-first century.* Grand Rapids: Eerdmans.

Hickson, F. C., Davies, P. M., Hunt, A. J., Weatherburn, P., et al. (1992). Maintenance of open gay relationships: Some strategies for protection against HIV. *AIDS Care, 4,* 409–419.

Hiebert, E. N. (1986). Modern physics and Christian faith. In D. C. Lindberg, & R. L. Numbers (Eds.), *God and nature: Historical essays on the encounter between Christianity and science.* Berkeley: University of California Press.

Hillegass, C. K. (1971). *Cliffs notes on Shakespeare's Hamlet.* Lincoln, NE: Cliffs Notes.

Hodge, C. (1872, 1975). *Systematic theology, Volume II.* Grand Rapids: Eerdmans.

Hodges, B. H. (1987). Perception is relative and veridical: Ecological and biblical perspectives on knowing and doing the truth. In H. Heie, & D. L. Wolfe (Eds.), *The reality of Christian learning.* Grand Rapids: Eerdmans.

Hodges, B. H. (1994). Faith-learning integration: Appreciating the integrity of a shop-worn phrase. *Faculty Dialogue, 22,* 106.

Holeman, V. T., & Headley, A. J. (2014). Integration based upon Wesleyan theology. *Journal of Psychology and Christianity, 33*(4), 335–343.

Holifield, E. B. (1983). *A history of pastoral care in America: From salvation to self-realization.* Nashville: Abingdon.

Holmes, A. F. (1987). *The idea of a Christian college* (Rev. ed.). Grand Rapids: Eerdmans.

Homer. (1937). *The odyssey: The story of Odysseus* (W. H. D. Rouse, Trans.). New York: New American Library.

Hook, J. N. (2014). Engaging clients with cultural humility. *Journal of psychology and Christianity, 33*(3), 277–280.

Hopkins, J., & Richardson, H. (trans.). (2000). *Complete philosophical and theological treatises of Anselm of Canterbury.* Minneapolis: Banning.

Hooykaas, R. (1972). *Religion and the rise of modern science.* Grand Rapids: Eerdmans.

Hughes, R. T. (2005). *The vocation of the Christian Scholar: How Christian faith can sustain the life of the mind* (rev. ed.). Grand Rapids: Eerdmans.

Hughes, R. T., & Adrian, W. B. (Eds.). (1997). *Models for Christian higher education: Strategies for success in the twenty-first century.* Grand Rapids: Eerdmans.

Hume, D. (n.d.). The case against miracles. Reprinted in R. D. Geivett & G. R. Habermas (1997). *In defense of miracles.* Downers Grove, IL: InterVarsity Press.

Hunt, M. M. (1993). *The story of psychology.* New York: Anchor.

Hunter, L. A., & Yarhouse, M. A. (2009). Considerations and recommendations for use of religiously based interventions in a licensed setting. *Journal of Psychology and Christianity, 28*(2), 159–166.

Irwin, T. H. (1999). *Nichomachean ethics / Aristotle* (T. Irwin, Trans. and Ed.). 2nd ed. Indianapolis: Hackett.

Jacobsen, D. G., & Jacobsen, R. H. (2004). *Scholarship and Christian faith: Enlarging the conversation.* New York: Oxford University Press.

Jaegwon, K., & Sosa, E. (Eds.). (1995). *A companion to metaphysics.* Cambridge: Blackwell.

Jamieson, R., Fausset, A. R., & Brown, D. (c. 1870). *A commentary: Critical, practical and explanatory, on the Old and New Testaments.* London: Revell.

James, W. (1902, 1999). *The varieties of religious experience.* New York: Modern Library.

Jeeves, M. A. (1994). *Mind fields: Reflections on the science of mind and brain.* Grand Rapids: Baker.

Jeeves, M. A. (1997). *Human nature at the millennium: Reflections on the integration of psychology and theology.* Grand Rapids: Baker.

John Paul II, Pope. (1998). *Encyclical letter, Fides et ratio, of the supreme pontiff John Paul II.* Washington, DC: United States Catholic Conference.

Johnson, A. F., & Webber, R. E. (1993). *What Christians believe: A biblical and historical summary.* Grand Rapids: Zondervan.

Johnson, E. L. (1997). Christ, the Lord of psychology. *Journal of Psychology and Theology, 25*(1), 11–27.

Johnson, E. L. (2007). *Foundations for soul care: A Christian psychology proposal.* Downers Grove, IL: InterVarsity Press.

Johnson, E. L. (Ed.). (2010). *Psychology and Christianity: Five views.* Downers Grove, IL: InterVarsity Press.

Jones, S. L., & Butman, R. E. (2012). *Modern psychotherapies: A comprehensive Christian appraisal* (2nd ed.). Downers Grove, IL: IVP.

Johnson, E. L., & Jones, S. L. (2000a). A history of Christians in psychology. In E. L Johnson, & S. L. Jones (Eds.), *Psychology and Christianity: Four views.* Downers Grove, IL: InterVarsity Press.

Johnson, E. L. & Jones, S. L. (Eds.). (2000b). *Psychology and Christianity: Four views.* Downers Grove, IL: InterVarsity Press.

Jones, E. (1957). *The life and work of Sigmund Freud, Vol. 3: The last phase, 1919–1939.* New York: Basic Books.

Jones, S. L. (Ed.). (1986). *Psychology and the Christian faith: An introductory reader.* Grand Rapids: Baker.

Jones, S. L. (1996). Reflections on the nature and future of the Christian psychologies. *Journal of Psychology and Christianity, 15*(2), 133–142.

Jones, S. L., & Butman, R. E. (1991). *Modern psychotherapies: A comprehensive Christian appraisal.* Downers Grove, IL: InterVarsity Press.

Jung, C. G. (1928, 1931) Civilization in transition. Reprinted in J. Campbell (Ed.), (1971). *The portable Jung* (R. F. C. Hull, Trans.). New York: Penguin.

Kaiser, W. C., & Silva, M. (1994). *An introduction to biblical hermeneutics: The search for meaning.* Grand Rapids: Zondervan.

Kauffman, D. R., & Hill, P. C. (1996). Guest editor's page. *Journal of Psychology and Christianity, 15*(2), 99.

Kee, H. C. (Ed.). (1993). *The Bible in the twenty-first century.* New York: American Bible Society.

Kepnes, S. (1990). The Jewish response to psychiatry. In D. S. Browning, T. Jobe, & I. S. Evison (Eds.), *Religious and ethical factors in psychiatric practice.* Chicago: Nelson-Hall.

King, M. L., Jr. (1963, 1982). *Strength to love.* New York: Harper & Row. Reprinted, Minneapolis: Fortress.

Klooster, F. H. (1984). The role of the Holy Spirit in the hermeneutic process. In E. D. Radmacher, & R. D. Preus (Eds.), *Hermeneutics, inerrancy, and the Bible.* Grand Rapids: Zondervan.

Koch, S. (1999). *Psychology in human context: Essays in dissidence and deconstruction.* D. Finkelman (Ed.). Chicago: University of Chicago Press.

Koenig, H. G. (2005). *Faith and mental health: Religious resources for healing.* Philadelphia: Templeton Foundation Press.

Konstam, V., Chernoff, M., & Deveney, S. (2001). Toward forgiveness: The role of shame, guilt, anger, and empathy. *Counseling and Values, 46*(1), 26–39.

Kuhn T. S. (1970) *The structure of scientific revolutions.* Chicago: Chicago University Press.

Küng, H. (1979, 1990). *Freud and the problem of God* (E. Quinn, Trans.). New Haven: Yale University Press.

LaHaye, T. (1962, 1996). *Spirit controlled temperament.* Wheaton, IL: Tyndale House.

Lake, F. (1966). *Clinical theology.* London: Darton, Longman, & Todd.

Lankester, E. R. (1890). Biology and the state. In *The advancement of science: Occasional essays and addresses.* London: MacMillan.

LaSala, M. C. (2001). Monogamous or not: Understanding and counseling gay male couples. *Families in Society, 82,* 605–611.

Lasik, A. (2003). Structure and character of the camp SS administration. In F. Piper & T. Świebocka (Eds.), *Auschwitz: Nazi death camp* (D. Selvage, Trans.) Oświęcim, Poland: The Auschwitz-Birkenau State Museum in Oświęcim.

Layzer, D. (1984). *Constructing the universe.* New York: Freeman.

Levicoff, S. (1991). *Christian counseling and the law.* Chicago: Moody Press.

Levin, A. (2006, May 19). Mennonite MH system: Practicing what they preach. *Psychiatric News, 41*(10), 18.

Lewis, C. S. (1952). *Mere Christianity.* New York: Macmillan.

Lewis, C. S. (1947, 1996). *Miracles: A preliminary study.* New York: Touchstone.

Lewis, C. S. (1962, 1996). *The problem of pain.* New York: Touchstone.

Liddle, A. (1999). *An introduction to modern cosmology.* New York: Wiley.

Livingstone, D. N. (1988). Reflections on the encounter between science and faith. In M. Noll & D. Wells (Eds.), *Christian faith and practice in the modern world: Theology from an evangelical point of view.* Grand Rapids: Eerdmans.

Livingstone, D. N. (1999). Situating evangelical responses to evolution. In D. N. Livingstone, D. G. Hart, & M. A. Noll, (Eds.), *Evangelicals and science in historical perspective.* New York: Oxford University Press.

Livingstone, D. N., Hart, D. G., & Noll, M. A. (Eds.). (1999). *Evangelicals and science in historical perspective.* New York: Oxford University Press.

Lo, B., Quill, T., & Tulsky, J. (1999). Discussing palliative care with patients. *Annals of Internal Medicine, 130,* 744–749.

Lombardo, P. A. (2001). Carrie Buck's pedigree. *Journal of Laboratory and Clinical Medicine, 138,* 278–282.

Lowry, R. J. (1979). *The journals of Abraham Maslow, Volume 1.* Belmont, CA: Wadsworth.

MacArthur, J. F., Jr. (1991). *Our sufficiency in Christ.* Dallas: Word.

MacArthur, J. F., Jr. (1994). Preaching in biblical counseling. In J. F. MacArthur, Jr., W. Mack, & the Master's College Faculty. *Introduction to biblical counseling.* Dallas: Word.

MacArthur, J. F., Jr., Mack, W., & the Master's College Faculty. (1994). *Introduction to biblical counseling.* Dallas: Word.

Machen, J. G. (1947). *The Christian view of man.* Grand Rapids: Eerdmans.

Machery, E., & Mallon, R. Evolution of morality. In J. M. Doris (Ed.), *The moral psychology handbook.* New York: Oxford.

Mack, W. A. (1994). Taking counselee inventory: Collecting data. In J. F. MacArthur, Jr., W. Mack & the Master's College Faculty. *Introduction to biblical counseling.* Dallas: Word.

Mack, W. A. (1997). What is biblical counseling? In E. Hindson & H. Eyrich (Eds.), *Totally sufficient: The Bible and Christian counseling.* Eugene, OR: Harvest House.

Marsden, G. M. (1980). *Fundamentalism and American culture.* Oxford: Oxford University Press.

Marsden, G. M. (Ed.). (1984). *Evangelicalism and modern America.* Grand Rapids: Eerdmans.

Maslow, A. H. (1968). *Toward a psychology of being* (2nd ed.). New York: Harper & Row.

Maslow, A. H. (1970, 1954). *Motivation and personality* (2nd ed.). New York: Harper & Row.

Master's College. (n.d.). *Biblical studies.* Retrieved from http://www.masters.edu/DeptPageNew.asp?PageID=7.

May, R. (1972). *Power and innocence: A search for the sources of violence.* New York: Norton.

McCarthy, M. A. (1990). Roman Catholic perspective on psychiatry and religion. In D. S. Browning, T. Jobe, & I. S. Evison (Eds.), *Religious and ethical factors in psychiatric practice.* Chicago: Nelson-Hall.

McGrath, A. E. (2001). *A scientific theology, Volume I: Nature.* Grand Rapids: Eerdmans.

McMinn, M. R. and Phillips, T. R. (2001). *Care for the soul: Exploring the intersection of psychology and theology.* Downers Grove, IL: InterVarsity Press.

McMinn, M. R. (1996). *Psychology theology and spirituality in Christian counseling.* Wheaton, IL: Tyndale.

McMinn, M. R. (2004). *Why sin matters.* Wheaton, IL: Tyndale.

Meissner, W. W. (1966). Problem and problematic. In W. W. Meisner (Ed.), *Foundations for a psychology of grace.* Glen Rock, NY: Paulist.

Meng, H. & Freud, E. L. (Eds.). (1963). *Psychoanalysis and faith: The letters of Sigmund Freud & Oskar Pfister* (E. Mosbacher, Trans.). New York: Basic Books.

Merriam Webster's collegiate dictionary, 10th ed. (1993). Springfield, MA: Merriam-Webster.

Middleton, J. R. (1994). The liberating image? Interpreting the imago Dei in context. *Christian Scholar's Review, 24,* 8–25.

Milgram, S. (1963). Behavioral study of obedience. *Journal of Abnormal and Social Psychology, 67,* 371–378.

Milgrom, J. (2004). *Leviticus: A book of ritual and ethics.* Continental Commentaries. Minneapolis: Fortress.

Misiak, H., & Staudt, V. M. (1954). *Catholics in psychology: A historical survey.* New York: McGraw-Hill.

Moberg, D. O. (1979). *The great reversal: Evangelism and social concern* (Rev. ed.). Philadelphia, PA: Lippincott.

Monchar, F. J., & Titus, C. S. (2009). Foundations for a psychotherapy of virtue: An integrated Catholic perspective. *Journal of Psychology & Christianity, 28*(1), 22–35.

Monroe, K. K. (Ed.). (1996). *Finding God at Harvard: Spiritual journeys of thinking Christians.* Grand Rapids: Zondervan.

Moore, T. (1972). *Care of the soul: A guide for cultivating depth and sacredness in everyday life.* New York: HarperCollins.

Moriarty, G. L. (Ed.). (2010). *Integrating faith and psychology: 12 psychologists tell their stories*. Downers Grove, IL: InterVarsity Press.

Moroney, S. K. (1999). How sin affects scholarship: A new model. *Christian Scholar's Review, 28*(3), 432–451.

Moroney, S. K. (2000). *The noetic effects of sin: A historical and contemporary exploration of how sin affects our thinking*. Lanham, MD: Lexington.

Moroney, S. K. (2001). Thinking of ourselves more highly than we ought: A psychological and theological analysis. In M. R. McMinn, & T. R. Phillips (Eds.), *Care for the soul: Exploring the intersection of psychology and theology*. Downers Grove, IL: InterVarsity Press.

Moule, H. C. G. (1943). *Ephesian studies: Expository readings on the epistle of Saint Paul to the Ephesians*. London: Pickering & Inglis.

Moulton, H. K. (1852, 1978). *The analytical Greek lexicon to the New Testament*. Grand Rapids: Zondervan.

Myers, D. G. (1978) *The human puzzle: Psychological research and Christian belief*. New York: Harper & Row.

Myers, D. G. (1986). Social psychology. In S. L. Jones (Ed.), *Psychology and the Christian faith: An introductory reader*. Grand Rapids: Baker.

Myers, D. G. (1992). *The pursuit of happiness: Who is happy—and why*. New York: Morrow.

Myers, D. G. (1999, June). Accepting what cannot be changed. *Perspectives*, 5–7. Also available at: http://www.davidmyers.org/Brix?pageID=90/.

Myers, D. G. (2000a). *The American paradox: Spiritual hunger in an age of plenty*. New Haven: Yale University Press.

Myers, D. G. (2000b). A levels-of-explanation view. In E. L. Johnson, & S. L. Jones (Eds.), *Psychology and Christianity: Four views*. Downers Grove, IL: InterVarsity Press.

Myers, D. G. (2000c). *A quiet world: Living with hearing loss*. New Haven: Yale University Press.

Myers, D. G. (2002). *Intuition: Its powers and perils*. New Haven: Yale University Press.

Myers, D. G. (2008a). *A friendly letter to skeptics and atheists: Musings on why God is good and faith isn't evil*. San Francisco: Jossey-Bass.

Myers, D. G. (2008b). *Social Psychology* (9th ed.). Boston: McGraw-Hill.

Myers, D. G. (2010). *Psychology* (9th ed.). New York: Worth.

Myers, D. G., & Jeeves, M. A. (2003*). Psychology through the eyes of faith* (Rev. ed.). San Francisco: HarperCollins.

Myers, D. G., & Scanzoni, L. E. (2005). *What God has joined together: The Christian case for gay marriage*. San Francisco: HarperCollins.

Narramore, S. B. (1992). Barriers to the integration of faith and learning in Christian graduate training programs in clinical psychology. *Journal of Psychology and Theology, 20*, 119–126.

Narramore, S. B. (1997). Psychology and theology: Twenty-five years of theoretical integration. *Journal of Psychology and Theology, 25*(1), 6–10.

NASA, (n.d.) *Apollo 8 Christmas Eve Broadcast*. Retrieved from http://www.nssdc.gsfc.nasa.gov/planetary/lunar/apollo8_xmas.html.

Neufeld, V. H. (Ed.). (1983). *If we can love: The Mennonite mental health story*. Newton, KS: Faith and Life Press.

Neugebauer, Otto. (1969). *The exact sciences in antiquity* (2nd ed.). New York: Dover.

Niebuhr, H. R. (1951, 2001). *Christ and culture.* New York: Harper & Row. Reprinted, San Francisco: HarperSanFrancisco.

Niebuhr, R. (1941, 1996). *The nature and destiny of man: A Christian interpretation.* New York: Scribner. Reprinted, Library of Theological Ethics. Louisville: Westminster John Knox.

Nielsen, S. L., Johnson, W. B., & Ellis, A. (2001). *Counseling and psychotherapy with religious persons: A rational emotive behavior therapy approach.* Mahwah, NJ: Erlbaum.

Niiniluoto, I. (1999). *Critical scientific realism.* Oxford: Oxford University Press.

Noll, M. A. (1994). *The scandal of the Evangelical mind.* Grand Rapids: Eerdmans.

Noll, M. A. (1999). Science, theology, and society. In D. N. Livingstone, D. G. Hart, & M. A. Noll (Eds.), *Evangelicals and science in historical perspective.* New York: Oxford University Press.

Novaco, R. W. (1976). The functions and regulation of the arousal of anger. *American Journal of Psychiatry, 133,* 1124–1128.

Numbers, R. L. (1999). Creating creationism. In D. N. Livingstone, D. G. Hart, & M. A. Noll (Eds.), *Evangelicals and science in historical perspective.* New York: Oxford University Press.

Oppenheim, A. L. (1977). *Ancient Mesopotamia: Portrait of a dead civilization.* Chicago: Chicago University Press.

The Oxford English dictionary (2nd ed.). J. A. Simpson and E. S. C. Weiner (Eds.). Oxford: Clarendon.

Osborne, G. R. (1991). *The hermeneutical spiral: A comprehensive introduction to biblical interpretation.* Downers Grove, IL: InterVarsity Press.

Osteen, J. (2004). *Your best life now: 7 steps to living at your full potential.* New York: Warner.

Padmanabhan, T. (1998). *After the first three minutes: The story of our universe.* Cambridge: Cambridge University Press.

Pargament, K. I., Ensing, D. S., Falgout, K., Olsen, H., et al. (1990). God help me: I. Religious coping efforts as predictors of the outcome to significant negative life events. *American Journal of Community Psychology, 18,* 793–824.

Pargament, K. I., Olsen, H., Reilly, B., Falgout, K., et al. (1992). God help me: II. The relationship of religious orientations to religious coping with negative life events. *Journal for the Scientific Study of Religion, 31,* 504–513.

Parker, S. (2014). Tradition-based integration: A Pentecostal perspective. *Journal of Psychology and Christianity, 33*(4), 311–321.

Paul VI, Pope. (1965). *Pastoral constitution on the church in the modern world, Gaudium et spes.* Vatican City: Holy See.

PBS: Religion and Ethics Newsweekly. (2005, May 20). *Christian counseling.* Retrieved from http://www.pbs.org/wnet/religionandethics/week838/cover.html.

Peale, N. V. (1952). *The power of positive thinking.* New York: Prentice-Hall.

Pearcy, N. R., & Thaxton, C. B. (1994). *The soul of science.* Wheaton, IL: Crossway.

Peck, M. S. (1987). *The road less traveled: A new psychology of love, traditional values, and spiritual growth.* New York: Touchstone.

Pennington, J. T. (2007). *Heaven and Earth in the Gospel of Matthew*. Supplements to Novum Testamentum 126. Leiden: Brill.

Petersen, G. R. (2002). Mysterium tremendum. *Zygon, 37*(2), 361–380.

Peterson, C. (2006). *A primer in positive psychology*. New York: Oxford University Press.

Pettigrew, T. F. (1999). Gordon Willard Allport: A tribute. *Journal of Social Issues, 55*(3), 1–5.

Phelps, M. P. (2004, Spring). Imago Dei and limited creature: High and low views of human beings in Christianity and cognitive psychology. *Christian Scholar's Review, 33*, 345–366.

Pius, XII, Pope. (1950). *Encyclical humani generis of the Holy Father Pius XII*. Washington, D. C.: United States Catholic Conference.

Plantinga, C. (1995*). Not the way it's supposed to be: A breviary of sin*. Grand Rapids: Eerdmans.

Pope, K. S., & Vasquez, M. J. (2011). *Ethics in psychotherapy and counseling* (4th ed.). Hoboken, NJ: Wiley.

Porter, S. L. (2010). Theology as queen and psychology as handmaid: The authority of theology in integrative endeavors. *Journal of Psychology and Christianity, 29*(1), 3–14.

Powlison, D. (2000). A biblical counseling view. In E. L. Johnson & S. L. Jones (Eds.), *Psychology and Christianity: Four views*. Downers Grove, IL: InterVarsity Press.

PsychoHeresy Newsletter. (n.d.). *Dr. John MacArthur, Jr. and biblical counseling*. Retrieved from http://www.psychoheresy-aware.org/macarthbc.html

Purves, A. (2001). *Pastoral theology in the classical tradition*. Louisville: Westminster John Knox.

Rahner, K. (1974). *Theological investigations, 11* (D. Bourke, Trans.). New York: Seabury Press.

Rauschenbusch, W. (1945, 1997). *A theology for the social gospel*. Louisville: Westminster.

Reuder, M. E. (1999). A history of Division 36 (Psychology of Religion). In D. A. Dewsbury (Ed.)., *Unification through division: Histories of the divisions of the American Psychological Association* (Vol. 4, pp. 91–98). Washington, DC: APA.

Richards, P. S., & Bergin, A. E. (2005). *A spiritual strategy for counseling and psychotherapy* (2nd ed.). Washington, DC: American Psychological Association.

Richards, P. S., & Bergin, A. E. (Eds.). (2014). *Handbook of psychotherapy and religious diversity*, (2nd ed.). Washington, DC: American Psychological Association.

Richardson, R. W. (1996). *Creating a healthier church: Family systems theory, leadership, and congregational life*. Minneapolis: Fortress.

Rizzuto, A. (1979). *The birth of the living God: A psychoanalytic study*. Chicago: University of Chicago Press.

Rizzuto, A. (2004). Roman Catholic background and psychoanalysis. *Psychoanalytic Psychology, 21*(3), 436–441.

Roberts, R. C. (2000). A Christian psychology view. In E. L. Johnson & S. L. Jones (Eds.), *Psychology and Christianity: Four views*. Downers Grove, IL: InterVarsity Press.

Roberts, R. C. (2001) Psychotherapy and Christian Ministry, *Word and World, 21*(1), 42–50.

Roberts, R. C. (2007). *Spiritual emotions: A psychology of Christian virtues*. Grand Rapids: Eerdmans.

Rogers, C. R. (1964). Toward a modern approach to values: The valuing process in the mature person. *Journal of Abnormal and Social Psychology, 68*, 160–167.

Rogers, C. R. (1980). *A way of being*. Boston: Houghton Mifflin, 28–29.

Rohr, J. (Ed.) (1988). *Science & religion—Opposing viewpoints*. St. Paul, MN: Greenhaven.

Sanders, R. K. (Ed.). (2013). *Christian counseling ethics: A handbook for therapists, pastors, and counselors* (2nd ed.). Downers Grove, IL: InterVarsity Press.

Santos, C. (2002, February 17). Historic test case: Wrong done to Carries Buck remembered. *Charlottesville Times-Dispatch*, p. B1.

Sarles, K. L., Jr. (1994). Frequently asked questions about biblical counseling: Why does biblical counseling hold to a dichotomous rather than a trichotomous view of mankind? In J. F. MacArthur, Jr., W. Mack, & the Master's College Faculty. *Introduction to biblical counseling*. Dallas: Word.

Schnackenburg, R. (1991). *Ephesians: A commentary* (H. Heron, Trans.). Edinburgh: T. & T. Clark.

Seligman, M. E. P. (2003). Foreword: The past and future of positive psychology. In C. L. M., Keyes & J. Haidt (Eds.). *Flourishing: Positive psychology and the life well-lived*. Washington, DC: American Psychological Association.

Shakespeare, W. (n.d.). *The tragedy of Hamlet, Prince of Denmark* (E. Hubler, Ed.). (1963). New York: Signet Classics.

Shakespeare, W. (n.d.). *The tragedy of Julius Caesar* (A. D. Innes, Ed.). (1893). London: Blackie & Son.

Shakespeare, W. (n.d.). *The tragedy of Romeo and Juliet* (R. A. Law, Ed.). (1913). Boston: Heath.

Shapin, S. (1998). *The scientific revolution*. Chicago: University of Chicago Press.

Shariffe, M. (1961). *Intergroup conflict and cooperation: The robber's cave experiment*. Norman IL: Institute of Group Relations.

Silk, J. (1994). *A short history of the universe*. New York: Freeman.

Simpson, E. K., & Bruce, F. F. (1957). *Commentary on the epistles to the Ephesians and the Colossians*. The new international commentary on the New Testament. Grand Rapids: Eerdmans.

Sire, J. W. (1997). *The universe next door: A basic worldview catalog* (3rd ed.). Downers Grove, IL: InterVarsity Press.

Slife, B. D., & Reber, J. S. (2009). Is there a pervasive implicit bias against theism in psychology? *Journal of Theoretical and Philosophical Psychology, 29*(2), 63–79.

Slipp, S. (1993). *The Freudian mystique: Freud, women, and feminism*. New York: New York University Press.

Smith, C. S., with Denton, M. L. (2005). *Soul searching: The religious and spiritual lives of American teenagers*. New York: Oxford University Press.

Smith, J. K., & Deemer, D. K. (2000). The problem of criteria in the age of relativism. In N. K. Denzin & Y. S. Lincoln (Eds.), *The handbook of qualitative research* (2nd ed.). Thousand Oaks, CA: Sage.

Society for Christian Psychology. (n.d.). http://www.christianpsych.org.

Sorenson, R. L. (1997). Janusian integration. *Journal of Psychology and Theology, 25,* 254–259.

Sorenson, R. L. (2004). How to anticipate predictions about integrations future trends. *Journal of Psychology and Theology, 32*(3), 181–189.

Sorenson, R. L. (2004). *Minding spirituality.* Hillsdale, NJ: Analytic Press.

Spilka, B. (1987). Religion and science in early American psychology. *Journal of Psychology and Theology, 15,* 3–9.

Spong, J. S. (1998). *Why Christianity must change or die: A bishop speaks to believers in exile.* San Francisco: HarperSanFrancisco.

Stanley, J. E., & Stanley, S. C. What can the Wesleyan/Holiness tradition contribute to Christian higher education? In R. T. Hughes & W. B. Adrian (Eds.), *Models for Christian higher education: Strategies for success in the twenty-first century.* Grand Rapids: Eerdmans.

Strawn, B. D., Wright, R. W., & Jones, P. (2014). Tradition-based integration: Illuminating the stories and practices that shape our integrative imagination. *Journal of Psychology and Christianity, 33*(4), 300–310.

Street, J. D. (1994). Why biblical counseling and not psychology? In J. MacArthur & R. Mayhue (Eds.), *Think biblically: Recovering a Christian worldview.* Wheaton, IL: Crossway.

Tan, S.-Y. (2001). Integration and beyond: Principled, professional, and personal. *Journal of Psychology and Christianity, 20,* 18–28.

Tertullian, Q. (1963). On prescriptions against heretics. In A. Roberts & J. Donaldson (Eds.), *The Ante-Nicene fathers: Translations of the writings of the fathers down to A.D. 325, Vol. 3.* Grand Rapids: Eerdmans.

Thomas Aquinas. (1920) *The summa theologica of St. Thomas Aquinas, Second and Revised Edition, Literally translated by Fathers of the English Dominican Province.* London: Burns, Oates & Washbourne. Also available at: www.newadvent.org/summa

Thorn, B. (1990). Carl Rogers and the doctrine of original sin. *Person-Centered Review, 5,* 394–405.

Thorstad, R. R., Anderson, T. L., Hall, M. E. L., Willingham, M., & Carruthers, L. (2006). Breaking the mold: A qualitative exploration of mothers in Christian academia and their experiences of spousal support. *Journal of Family Issus, 27*(2), 229–251.

Tillich, P. (1957). *Systematic theology, Volume II.* Chicago: University of Chicago Press.

Tisdale, T. C. (2014). Tradition-based integration: A Roman Catholic perspective. *Journal of Psychology and Christianity, 33*(4), 354–363.

Tjeltveit, A. C. (2012). Lost opportunities, partial successes, and key questions: Some historical lessons. Journal of Psychology and Theology, 40(1), 16–20.

Tomes, N. (1994). *The art of asylum-keeping: Thomas Story Kirkbride and the origins of American Psychiatry.* Philadelphia: University of Pennsylvania Press.

Tozer, A. W. (1968). *The pursuit of God.* Harrisburg, PA: Christian Publications.

Truax, C. B., & Carkhuff, R. R. (1967). *Toward effective counseling and psychotherapy.* Chicago: Aldine.

Tuckman, B. W. (1965). Developmental sequence in small groups. *Psychological Bulletin, 63*(6), 384–399.

Twain, Mark. (1906, 1996). *What is man?* (Charles Johnson, Introduction; Linda Wagner-Martin, Afterword). Oxford: Oxford University Press.

University of Pennnsylvania Positive Psychology Center. (n.d.). http://www.ppc.sas.upenn.edu/executivesummary.htm

Valdesolo, P., & Graham, J. (2014). Awe, uncertainty, and agency detection. *Psychological Science, 25* (1), 170–178.

Van Atta, K., Roby, D. S., & Roby, R. R. (1980). *An account of the events surrounding the origin of Friends Hospital & a brief description of the early years of Friends Asylum 1817–1820.* Philadelphia: Friends Hospital. Available online: http://www.friendshospitalonline.org/eventsaccount.htm

Van Inwagen, P. (2015). *Metaphysics* (4th ed.). Boulder, CO: Westview.

Van Leeuwen, M. S. (1982). *The sorcerer's apprentice.* Downers Grove, IL: InterVarsity Press.

Van Leeuwen, M. S. (1985). *The person in psychology: A contemporary Christian appraisal.* Grand Rapids: Eerdmans.

Van Leeuwen, M. S. (1988). Psychology's "two cultures": A Christian analysis. *Christian Scholar's Review, 17,* 406–424.

Van Leeuwen, M. S. (1996). Five uneasy questions, or: Will success spoil Christian psychologists? *Journal of Psychology and Christianity, 15*(2), 150–160.

Vande Kemp, H. (1982). The tension between psychology and theology: The etymological roots. *Journal of Psychology and Theology, 10,* 105–112.

Vande Kemp, H. (1987). The sorcerer was a straw man—apologetics gone awry: A reaction to Foster and Ledbetter. *Journal of Psychology and Theology, 15,* 19–26.

Vande Kemp, H. (1996). Psychology and Christian spirituality: Explorations of the inner world. *Journal of Psychology and Christianity, 15*(2), 161–174.

Vanhoozer, K. J. (Ed.). (2005). *Dictionary for theological interpretation of the Bible.* Grand Rapids: Baker.

Van Tongeren, D. R., Green, J. D., Hulsey, T. L., Legare, C. H., Bromley, D. G., and Houtman, A. M. (2014). A meaning-based approach to humility: Relationship affirmation reduces worldview defense. *Journal of Psychology and Theology, 42*(1), 62–69

Vassiliades, L., Kim, L., and Kwon, U. (2007). A report on 2007 conference of the society, Christianity or secularism: Whose soul care? Which Psychology? *Soul and spirit, 1*(1), 8.

Villasante, O., & Dening, T. (2003). The unfulfilled project of the model mental hospital in Spain: Fifty years of the Santa Isabel madhouse, Leganés (1851–1900). *Historical psychiatry, 14*(1), 3–23.

Vincent, M. R. (1887, 1975). *Word studies in the New Testament, Vol. III: The Epistles of Paul.* Grand Rapids: Eerdmans.

Walker, D. F.; Worthington, E. L., Gartner, A. L., Gorsuch, R. L., and Hanshew, E. R. (2011). Religious commitment and expectations about psychotherapy among Christian clients. *Psychology of Religion and Spirituality, 3*(2), 98–114.

Walsh, B. J., & Middleton, J. R. (1984). *The transforming vision: Shaping a Christian world view.* Downers Grove, IL: InterVarsity Press.

Walter J. Nally et al., v. Grace Community Church of the Valley et al. (1988). 47 Cal. 3d 278.

Walton, J. H., Matthews, V. H., and Chavales, M. W. (2000). *The IVP Bible background commentary*. Downers Grove, IL: InterVarsity Press.

Watson, R. A. (2014). A Canterbury tale: One psychologist's pilgrimage. *Journal of Psychology and Christianity, 33*(4), 322–334.

Watts, F. (2002). *Theology and psychology*. Ashgate science and religion series. Aldershot, UK: Ashgate.

Watts, F. (2004). Relating the psychology and theology of forgiveness. In F. Watts & L. Gulliford (Eds.), *Forgiveness in context: Theology and psychology in creative dialogue*. London: T. & T. Clark.

Watts, F., Nye, R. & Savage, S. (2002). *Psychology for Christian ministry*. London: Routledge.

Webb, W. J. (2001). *Slaves, women & homosexuals: Exploring the hermeneutics of cultural analysis*. Downers Grove, IL: InterVarsity Press.

Webber, R. E. (2002). *The younger evangelicals*. Grand Rapids: Baker.

Webber, R. E. (2008). *Who gets to narrate the world? Contending for the Christian story in an age of rivals*. Downers Grove, IL: InterVarsity Press.

Webster's third new international dictionary of the English language. (1993). Springfield, MA: Merriam-Webster, Inc.

Weitz, M. A. (2001). *Clergy malpractice in America: Nally v. Grace Community Church of the Valley*. Lawrence: University Press of Kansas.

Welch, E., & Powlison, D. (1997). "Every common bush afire with God": The scripture's constitutive role for counseling. *Journal of Psychology and Christianity, 16*, 303–322.

Whitehead, A. N. (1925, 1958). *Science and the modern world*. New York: Mentor.

Wicker, F. W., Brown, G., Weihe, J. A., Hagen, A. S., & Reed, J. L. (1993). On reconsidering Maslow: An examination of the deprivation/domination proposition. *Journal of Research in Personality, 27*, 118–133.

Wiley, T. (1989). *Original sin: Origins, developments, and contemporary meanings*. Mahwah, NJ: Paulist.

Wilson, M. R. (1989). *Our father Abraham: Jewish roots of the Christian faith*. Grand Rapids: Eerdmans.

Wind, J. P. (1990). Enemies or fellow travelers? Religion and psychiatry in the nineteenth century. In D. S. Browning, T. Jobe, & I. S. Evison (Eds.), *Religious and ethical factors in psychiatric practice*. Chicago: Nelson-Hall.

Wolters, A. M. (1985). *Creation regained: Biblical basics for a Reformational worldview*. Grand Rapids: Eerdmans.

Wolterstorff, N. (1976). *Reason within the bounds of religion*. Grand Rapids: Eerdmanns.

Wolterstorff, N. (1984). Integration of faith and science—The very idea. *Journal of Psychology and Christianity, 3*(2), 12–19.

Wolfe, D. L. (1982). *Epistemology: The justification of belief*. Downers Grove, IL: InterVarsity Press.

Wolfe, D. L. (1994). The line of demarcation between integration and pseudointegration. In H. Heie & D. L. Wolfe, *The reality of Christian learning*. Grand Rapids: Eerdmans.

Wood, W. J. (1998). *Epistemology: Becoming intellectually virtuous.* Downers Grove, IL: InterVarsity Press.

Wood, W. J. (2014). Faith's intellectual rewards. In L. F. Callahan and T. O'Connor (Eds.). *Religious faith and intellectual virtue.* New York: Oxford Univ. Press.

Worshipers overcome by fumes. (1999, Dec. 19). *The Canton Repository.* A-5.

Worthington, E. L. (1988). Understanding the values of religious clients: A model and its application to counseling. *Journal of Counseling Psychology, 35,* 166–174.

Worthington, E. L., Johnson, E. L., Hook, J. N., & Aten, J. D. (2013). *Evidenced-based practices for Christian counseling and psychotherapy.* Downers Grove, IL: InterVarsity Press.

Wright, N. T. (2008). *Surprised by hope: Rethinking Heaven, the resurrection, and the mission of the Church.* New York: HarperCollins.

Wright, R. W., Jones, P., & Strawn, B. D., (2014). Tradition-based integration. In E. D. Bland & B. D. Strawn (Eds.). *Christianity and psychoanalysis: A new conversation* (pp. 37–54). Downers Grove, IL: IVP.

Wundt, W. (1862). Contributions to the theory of sensory perception. Translated and reprinted in T. Shipley (Ed.), (1961). *Classics in psychology.* New York: Philosophical Library.

Wundt, W. (1877). Philosophy in Germany. *Mind, 2*(8), 493–518.

Yandell, K. E. (1986). Protestant theology and natural science in the twentieth century. In D. C. Lindberg & R. L. Numbers (Eds.), *God and nature: Historical essays on the encounter between Christianity and science.* Berkeley: University of California Press.

Yancey, P. (2001). *Soul survivor.* New York: Doubleday.

Yancey, P. (2003). *Rumors of another world.* Grand Rapids: Zondervan.

Yarhouse, M. A., & VanOrman, B. T. (1999). When psychologists work with religious clients: Applications of the general principles of ethical conduct. *Professional Psychology: Research and Practice, 30,* 557–562.

Zilboorg, G., & Henry, G. W. (1941). *A history of medical psychology.* New York: Norton.

Zimbardo, P. G., Maslach, C., & Haney, C. (2000). Reflections on the Stanford Prison Experiment: Genesis, transformations, consquences. In T. Blass (Ed.), *Obedience to authority: Current Perspectives on the Milgram paradigm.* Mahwah, NJ: Erlbaum.

The Bible in Basic English. (*BBE*). Cambridge: Cambridge University Press in association with Evans Brothers, 1965, © 1949.

The Holy Bible, New Century Version. (*NCV*). (Formerly, *The International Children's Bible.*) Copyright © 2005 by Thomas Nelson, Inc. Used by permission. All rights reserved.

The Holy Bible, New International Version®. (*NIV*)®. *Copyright © 1973, 1978, 1984 by International Bible Society. Used by permission of Zondervan. All rights reserved.*

The Holy Bible Translated from the Latin Vulgate, Douay-Rheims Version. (1899). Baltimore: John Murphy. (*Douay-Rheims, Challoner revision—DR*).

New American Standard Bible®. (*NASB*). Copyright © 1960, 1962, 1963, 1968, 1971, 1972, 1973, 1975, 1977, 1995 by The Lockman Foundation. Used by permission.

The Twentieth Century New Testament: A Translation into Modern English Made from the Original Greek (Westcott & Hort's Text). (*20th Cent.*). 1904. New York: Revell.

Name Index

Subject Index

Scripture Index

Old Testament

About the Author

David Entwistle earned a B.A. in Psychology from Taylor University, and Master's and Doctoral degrees in Clinical Psychology from Rosemead School of Psychology, Biola University. Dr. Entwistle is a licensed psychologist and spent the first decade of his professional life providing psychotherapy in residential and outpatient settings. Since 1996, Dr. Entwistle has been on the faculty of Malone University in Canton, Ohio, where he teaches undergraduate courses in Abnormal Psychology, Counseling and Guidance, Personality, and Integration. He has also been a visiting professor at Uniwersytet Kardynała Stefana Wyszyńskiego in Warsaw, Poland.

Dr. Entwistle has been involved in regional and national projects to improve transition from pediatric to adult care for individuals with genetic illnesses and their families. His research interests include how patients cope with chronic medical conditions, and issues in teaching integration.

He and his wife live in Canton, Ohio, and have three adult children. David loves to travel and has led service-learning trips to Albania, Austria, China, Hong Kong, and Poland, and has traveled extensively in Europe and Africa. In his spare time he enjoys reading, home renovations, and long bicycle rides.